STOCKHOLM SYNDROME
CHRISTIANITY

STOCKHOLM SYNDROME CHRISTIANITY

WHY AMERICA'S CHRISTIAN LEADERS ARE FAILING — AND WHAT WE CAN DO ABOUT IT

JOHN G. WEST

SEATTLE   DISCOVERY INSTITUTE PRESS   2025

Description

What if American culture isn't collapsing because of crusading secularists? What if it's failing because leading Christians identify more with secular elites than with their fellow believers? Those are the provocative questions posed by *Stockholm Syndrome Christianity*, which exposes how influential Christian leaders are siding with their anti-Christian cultural captors on everything from biblical authority and science to sex, race, and religious liberty. Going beyond critique, the book identifies root causes and—most crucially—offers practical tips and strategies you can use to help your family, church, and community stand for truth. Read this book to become part of the solution.

Library Cataloging Data

Stockholm Syndrome Christianity: Why America's Christian Leaders Are Failing — and What We Can Do About It

by John G. West

Cover design by Nathan Jacobson.

358 pages, 6 x 9 inches

Library of Congress Control Number: 2024947021

ISBN: 978-1-63712-070-5 (paperback), 978-1-63712-068-2 (hardback), 978-1-63712-069-9 (Kindle), 978-1-63712-067-5 (EPUB)

BISAC: REL012110 RELIGION / Christian Living / Social Issues

BISAC: REL108030 RELIGION / Christian Living / Leadership & Mentoring

BISAC: REL108020 RELIGION / Christian Church / History

Publisher Information

Discovery Institute Press, 208 Columbia Street, Seattle, WA 98104

Internet: discovery.press

Published in the United States of America on acid-free paper.

First Edition, February 2025

ADVANCE PRAISE

In *Stockholm Syndrome Christianity*, John West skillfully tackles the most important cultural dumpster fires threatening Christian institutions and offers detailed examples (and convincing explanations) of how these organizations succumbed to cultural capitulation. If the church is to have any impact on the culture, we need to first protect our own institutions, which are supposed to uphold the biblical worldview. This may mean dying to career advancement, academic prestige, or cultural prominence. But some hills are worth dying on, and West compellingly makes the case for why. Every pastor, elder, Christian board member, or influencer *needs* to read this book to understand how to stop the theological drift that is taking over our institutions.

—**Hillary Morgan Ferrer**, president of Mama Bear Apologetics, editor and author of *Mama Bear Apologetics: Empowering Your Kids to Challenge Cultural Lies* and *Mama Bear Apologetics Guide to Sexuality and Gender Identity*

Stockholm Syndrome Christianity is a monumental achievement. Like Megan Basham's *Shepherds for Sale*, it will infuriate precisely the right people. Every thinking Christian has an obligation to read it to see exactly how ravening wolves entered the fold of Christendom—with the blithe complicity of many shepherds. John West gives us their names and the gruesome details. Will those guilty repent? That is the question.

—**Eric Metaxas**, #1 New York Times bestselling author of *Bonhoeffer: Pastor, Martyr, Prophet, Spy* and *Is Atheism Dead?*, founder and host of Socrates in the City

Jesus condemned the religiously comfortable for their inability to "discern the signs of the times." Dr. John West's *Stockholm Syndrome Christianity* is a must read for every Christian seeking to heed Christ's warning. A tour de force of outstanding research and exceptional writing. Everyone should buy and read this book.

—**Everett Piper**, PhD, President Emeritus Oklahoma Wesleyan University

It is one thing to complain that evangelicals too easily capitulate to worldliness and embrace false ideologies. It is quite another to meticulously document this phenomenon, to give careful case studies making the point, to explain how and why it happens, and to offer correctives and advice on preserving biblical truth in evangelical hearts, minds, lives, and institutions. We are in John West's debt for this courageous, kind, and much needed book.

—**Douglas Groothuis**, PhD, Distinguished University Research Professor of Apologetics and Christian Worldview, Cornerstone University

In every generation God raises up Church watchmen to guard the faith from compromise and dissolution. In this courageous tradition, John West has come forth with an insider's sharp but gracious defense of biblical truth in a clashing evangelical environment. In a book with over 700 footnotes, West, a scholar with the Discovery Institute, confronts the sacred cows of the accommodationist wing of evangelicalism.

—**Robert Case**, founding director of World Journalism Institute

Stockholm Syndrome Christianity is a much-needed gift to the 21st-century American church from someone who has experienced its consequences firsthand in multiple spheres of life. With the mind of a scholar, the engagement of a public intellectual, and the heart of a local church elder, Dr. West ably identifies the problems and offers real solutions for the church as we move forward. Pastors and laymen alike will benefit greatly from this work.

—**Ryan Polk**, Associate Pastor, Trinity Baptist Church, Norman, Oklahoma

C. S. Lewis called it "passion for the Inner Ring" that results in "making a man who is not yet a very bad man do very bad things." Many of our evangelical leaders and institutions have betrayed us. *Stockholm Syndrome Christianity* chronicles the drift toward cultural acceptance, a current that has drawn some into identifying more with secular culture than biblical truth. What should Christians do? Begin by reading the book.

—**Rich Hamlin**, Founding and Senior Pastor, Evangelical Reformed Church, Tacoma, Washington

John West has written a searing, prophetic account of evangelical elites in America, especially in higher education. *Stockholm Syndrome Christianity* will undoubtedly drive many evangelical families to reconsider their support for some Christian colleges, given that so many evangelical administrators freely check their moral probity at the gates of their institutions to chase after the latest intellectual fads. Drawing from his own experience in evangelical higher education, West not only challenges current academic pieties but names names. A thoroughly engrossing read.

—**Reed Davis**, PhD, Professor Emeritus of Political Science, Seattle Pacific University; author of *A Politics of Understanding*

If you've wondered why so many Christians and Christian institutions have lost their way, you'll find the answer in *Stockholm Syndrome Christianity*. John West offers an incisive critique of Christian leaders—many personally orthodox—who have surrendered the scandal of the gospel for the approval of men. This is no simplistic jeremiad. His diagnosis is consistently fair and nuanced, even when recounting his own painful experiences in his religious and academic life. That alone makes the book worthwhile. But his detailed advice to Christian parents and leaders makes this a guidebook on how to stop and even reverse the spiritual decay in our churches. Every thoughtful Christian should read this book.

—**Jay Richards,** PhD, co-author *of Fight the Good Fight: How an Alliance of Faith and Reason Can Win the Culture War*; Director, Richard and Helen DeVos Center for Life, Religion, and Family and the William E. Simon Senior Research Fellow in American Principles and Public Policy, Heritage Foundation

Many faithful Christians find themselves looking around and asking, "What in God's name is going on?" They're not using God's name in vain; they're wondering about what Christian leaders and Christian institutions they've prayed for and supported are doing in God's name. They rightly feel betrayed. My friend John West has diagnosed the problem: It's Stockholm Syndrome Christianity. I couldn't agree more. Like John, I've watched with growing dismay as church leaders, Christian colleges, and other Christian institutions have betrayed the faith once entrusted to the saints and are now flirting with apostasy. The good news is John does more than point out the problems, he directs us to the solutions.

—**C. R. Wiley,** author of *In the House of Tom Bombadil*; Senior Pastor, Westminster Presbyterian Church, Battle Ground, WA

To Francis A. Schaeffer (1912-1984),
who spoke the truth in love to my own generation;
and to all today "whose knees have not bowed down
to Baal and whose mouths have not kissed him"
(1 Kings 19:18 NIV).

Contents

Introduction:
Stockholm Syndrome
Christians

Stockholm Syndrome:
"the psychological tendency of a hostage to bond with,
identify with, or sympathize with his or her captor."
—Merriam-Webster Dictionary[1]

Those of us who are Christians often regard atheists, agnostics, and secularists as the prime movers of America's cultural collapse. Without question, they have helped spur our country's descent into chaos, anger, loneliness, and despair.

But we need to face an uncomfortable truth: Christians who aid, abet, and even encourage the rejection of historic Christian teachings are also playing a key role in our disintegration.

Biblical teachings "work" because they're true. Even prominent atheists and agnostics have acknowledged that the Bible's principles encourage better behavior and thus better societies and nations.[2] But you can't expect to long enjoy the fruit of a tree if you're hacking away at its root, or running interference for those who are, and that's precisely what many are doing.

If more Christians—especially Christian leaders—had been faithful to biblical Christianity, we likely would not be in our current mess. And if we want things to improve, we need to look at ourselves and get our own house in order.

I do not level these charges lightly. Much of my life has been spent participating in Christian institutions and observing Christian leaders at various levels. In addition to serving as a professor at a Christian university, I was ordained as an elder in two different Presbyterian denominations. I have served on the elder boards of two congregations. And I have spent nearly two decades working full-time as an executive at a nonprofit organization that deals with science and faith issues, which has led me to consult with and observe the actions of Christian leaders at all levels.

Tragically, I have seen Christian belief and practice undermined time and again not by crusading atheists or secularists, but by Christian leaders. For anyone willing to look, the evidence has been all around us:

- The pastor of one of America's largest evangelical megachurches says the Bible is no longer defensible in the public square. "The trustworthiness of the Bible is… not defensible in culture where seconds count and emotions run high," he asserts. Accordingly, this pastor urges Christians to stop citing the Bible as an authority, even in their own churches. He further urges Christians to "unhitch" their faith from the Old Testament, which he thinks would be better described as "The Obsolete Testament." We will delve into the views of this popular pastor in Chapter 1.

- The nation's most prominent evangelical Christian scientist has spent his career advancing policies incompatible with historic Christian morality and theology. Under his leadership, a federal agency spent millions of tax dollars to harvest body parts from late-term aborted babies for use in medical research, and it has funded removing the breasts of girls as young as thirteen to facilitate gender transitions. This same scientist spearheaded efforts to denounce and marginalize Christian scientists who believe that living things show evidence of intelligent design. We will explore this scientist's views and his impact in Chapter 2.

- The nation's most notable "born again" Christian politician during the past century insisted that "Jesus would approve of gay marriage" and "I think Jesus would encourage any love affair if it was honest and sincere and was not damaging to anyone else." We will learn more about this politician and others who share his views in Chapter 3.

- With the admirable goal of fighting racism, many churches and their pastors are platforming speakers and spreading ideas that run counter to the gospel's message of salvation. Speaking at a church in New York City, a prominent antiracist scholar denounced what he called "savior theology," the idea that "the job of the Christian is to go out and save these individuals… who are doing all of these evil, sinful things." He tied this view to "racist ideas and racist theology." According to him, true salvation comes by recognizing that "Jesus was a revolutionary, and the job of the Christian is to revolutionize society." We will look at how some Christians are adopting anti-Christian views on race and poverty in Chapter 4.

- A widely beloved Presbyterian pastor and author blamed Christians for provoking their own persecution. Predicting that "ten years from now, if you have evangelical convictions about sex and gender, you may not be able to work for a major university or for the government or for a big corporation," he claimed that "we brought it on ourselves" because "the Christian right" was not loving and "vilified" gays and Democrats. We will learn more about this influential author in Chapter 5.

Stockholm Syndrome Christianity

Why are so many Christians—especially those in positions of leadership and influence—failing to uphold historic biblical teaching or defend their fellow Christians from persecution?

Part of the cause is undoubtedly fear. If you stand up for biblical Christianity in today's culture, the consequences are undeniable. You can lose friends or colleagues; you can lose your job; you can be targeted for discrimination or persecution. Many leaders stay silent out of self-preservation.

But the problem goes much deeper: Many Christian leaders and laypeople who fail to uphold the historic standards of their faith do not think they are motivated by fear. They do not believe they are compromising with the world in the views they adopt. They sincerely believe that what they are doing is right.

They are Stockholm Syndrome Christians.

The "Stockholm Syndrome" takes its name from a bank robbery in Stockholm, Sweden in August 1973. One morning an escaped convict entered the bank with a submachine gun. For the next 131 hours, the convict (later joined by an accomplice) held four bank employees hostage.[3]

Over the course of the crisis, something strange happened. The hostages began to bond with the criminals and view the police and government as their enemies. Even when the criminals threatened violence, the hostages expressed gratitude to them. At one point, the main bank robber planned to shoot a hostage in the leg to show authorities he was serious. The hostage later recalled: "All that comes back to me is how kind I thought he was for saying it was just my leg he would shoot."[4]

The term "Stockholm Syndrome" was later coined to describe situations where hostages end up identifying with their captors. Although it remains controversial as a diagnosis, the label has since been used to describe victims who end up adopting the point of view of their captors or abusers.

How is this relevant to today's Christian community? Most Christians in America grow up in cultural captivity. They are immersed in a culture hostile to genuine Christianity at home, school, college, and the workplace. This is especially true of those who go on to be pastors, professors, ministry leaders, journalists, politicians, or to work in the entertainment industry. After they have been immersed for years in an elite culture that rejects orthodox Christianity, they can easily start identifying more with those who hate Christianity than those who embrace it. They can become Stockholm Syndrome Christians.

I've seen this attitude again and again—among church leaders, among Christian scientists and academics, among Christians in government, and among Christians in the media. At the Christian university where I taught, it was common for my colleagues to express their disdain for ordinary Christians in the pews. They didn't know as much as the professors, after all. They were crude. They were gullible. They were unsophisticated. They were annoying embarrassments who put everyone in danger because they attracted the attention and wrath of the anti-Christian majority.

You can see why it might happen. You can see why Stockholm Syndrome Christians, identifying more with the anti-Christian majority culture than with their brothers and sisters in Christ, might end up jettisoning historic Christianity.

This hurts fellow believers and, eventually, the culture at large. But it also hurts Stockholm Syndrome Christians themselves. Later in these pages I'll give examples of people who turned their backs on biblical teaching in favor of what is fashionable, only to discover that they had been sold a handful of nothing.

How Christian Institutions Fail: A Case Study

The problem isn't, of course, confined to individuals. Institutions can become filled with employees or board members who embrace Stockholm Syndrome Christianity. And that's particularly consequential, because institutions are only as sound as those who run them.

I've seen firsthand how a Christian institution can gradually lose its central beliefs and decay from the inside. For more than a decade, I served as a professor at Seattle Pacific University (SPU). This historically evangelical Christian university will serve as a case study at various places in these pages, but let me be clear: It is far from the only example of its kind. It's simply the one whose fate I witnessed from the inside.

Founded by pious Free Methodists in the 1890s, Seattle Pacific had a long history of standing for both personal holiness and biblical truth. Consider this statement from the college's 1929 yearbook: "The Bible is the very word of God, the Book of books. In this day when modernists, skeptics, and faithless scientists and philosophers are doing their utmost to discredit the Bible as the Word of God and to prove it only a collection of the myths and folk-lore of a primitive and semi-civilized people, our Bible School is glad to take its place in the front ranks of those standing for the inspiration and integrity of Scriptures."[5]

In the 1940s, the college constructed an auditorium and emblazoned the front side of the building with an image of the Bible, under which the word "TRUTH" was affixed.[6] During that same decade, Jake DeShazer, a member of the famous "Doolittle's Raiders" unit during World War II, studied at Seattle Pacific. DeShazer eventually became a Free Methodist missionary to Japan. Sometimes he spoke together with Mitsuo Fuchida, the pilot who led the attack on Pearl Harbor and who had also become a Christian.[7]

In the 1960s, the college's seal bore the motto "Valiant for the Truth,"[8] and conservative evangelical thinker Francis Schaeffer spoke at chapel.[9] In the 1970s, an institute devoted to putting on lectures and conferences about the ideas of C. S. Lewis became prominent on campus.[10]

By the time I joined Seattle Pacific's faculty in the 1990s, the school's stance was more ambiguous. There was still a core of genuinely orthodox Christians among faculty, staff, and administrators. But many others had become embarrassed by the school's historic identity.

Today Seattle Pacific still identifies as a "Christian university"[11] that is both "historically orthodox" and "clearly evangelical."[12] It remains a member in good standing of the Christian College Consortium along with other self-identified evangelical Christian institutions such as Wheaton College.[13] Prospective students are told that "At SPU, everything we do is rooted in faith…. Faculty integrate their faith into how they teach and how they live."[14]

Alumni of the university, however, might be wondering precisely what faith SPU faculty are now integrating in their teaching and their lives, given that most of them have repudiated the Bible's teaching about marriage. In the spring of 2021, SPU made national headlines when over 70 percent of the faculty voted "no confidence" in the school's board of trustees because the board failed to repeal a policy requiring employees to abide by the university's Statement on Human Sexuality.[15] The offending statement affirmed that "sexual experience is intended between a man and a woman" and "the full expression of sexuality is to be experienced and celebrated" within "the covenant of marriage between a man and a woman."[16]

Faculty were deeply, not to say histrionically, upset that the board wouldn't yield. The chair of the faculty senate declared, "This is traumatic… This is personal, it goes to one's humanity, this goes to outsiders defining people, of who is in and who is out."[17]

A theology professor complained of her shock "that with such an overwhelming faculty sense of wanting to remove this, that they still didn't remove it."[18] A communications professor lashed out at the trustees for opposing "the will of the SPU community."[19]

The faculty's stance on marriage isn't the only thing that now conforms to secular culture at SPU, as will become clear as I refer to this case study later in these pages. This, by the way, is not something I take delight in. The collapse of Seattle Pacific as a Christian institution has been painful for me and my extended family. Not only did my wife and her five siblings graduate from the university, but their father was a long-time professor there. In fact, he introduced me to Sonja (my wife) when I was a young faculty member. I ultimately served as a professor at SPU for twelve years, teaching over a thousand students, earning tenure, and chairing the Department of Political Science and Geography before I left in 2006.

By that time I had watched years of cumulative decisions begin to undermine the beliefs upon which the school was founded.

Several years after I left, a former staff member anonymously posted a review of the university at the site Glassdoor.com.[20] I do not know who posted the review, so I cannot vouch for all of the specifics in it. But many of the person's observations dovetailed with my own experiences. The former staff member wrote:

> I worked here for many years and also attended [the] school as an undergrad. I can tell you with all certainty that anyone on campus who expresses belief in the inerrancy of the Bible is labelled a

"Fundamentalist"—considered to be narrow-minded…. If, however, your faith has a generous blend of Worldliness diluting it, you will feel right at home at SPU.

…. Very few students, staff, or faculty leave SPU with a deeply rooted faith (at least not in the Jesus of my Bible). I have seen countless students come to SPU as freshmen fired up for the Lord, then leave as seniors either as atheists or embracing a very Worldly stance typical of modern culture… it's the norm, from what I've seen.

Although personal holiness was a pillar on which SPU was founded, the reviewer alleged that behavior on campus was no more Christian than the beliefs: "I've witnessed the campus rife with students who drink, do drugs, have premarital relations, experiment with gender roles, etc. In this respect, it is no different than any other college campus."

Even the office environment was not always faith-friendly:

One of the supervisors in my unit is a self-proclaimed atheist. This person doesn't even try to hide it (at least they're honest). They use profanity constantly, drink regularly, and claim to be a habitual marijuana user as well (now legal in our state, but violates SPU's lifestyle expectations). When employees would ask to use the office to hold a Bible study in the mornings before the business day started, consistently this person denied all requests.

This former student and staff member indicted SPU for pursuing "compromise in biblical adherence in the name of academic prestige… Over time, and by attrition, we now have this strikingly Post-Modern, Liberal culture, compromising the God of the Bible for the god of Academia and 'engaging the broader Culture.'"

The review ended with a Bible verse: "No man can serve two masters: for either he will hate the one, and love the other; or else he will hold to the one, and despise the other. Ye cannot serve God and mammon" (Matthew 6:24 KJV).

And yet Seattle Pacific had once been a light for Christian love and truth in its home city—a city that desperately needs Christian love and truth, as riots, violence, all manner of crime, and rising homelessness clearly indicate. But love and truth have one ultimate source, and that source is not ever-shifting human understanding. Darkness runs unchecked when Christians stop holding up the light of universal truth.

Many universities, both Christian and secular, adopted as their motto, or engraved on their buildings, "You shall know the truth, and the truth shall set you free" (John 8:32).[21] Truth was assumed to be knowable, permanent, and universal. When I began teaching at SPU in the early 1990s, the university's motto was "Wholeness in Truth." I don't know when it adopted that motto, but its message was a link to the roots of the institution.

After I became a professor, a new president was appointed who wanted to rebrand the institution with a new motto. "Wholeness in Truth" was out. "Engaging the Culture, Changing the World" was in. At first, I liked the new motto. But as time wore on, I began to wonder: Engage the culture *how*? Change the world based on *what*?

It eventually dawned on me that for many of my colleagues, "engaging the culture" really meant being *accepted* by the culture. As an institution, we became preoccupied with respectability rather than truth. The new motto might have been more aptly phrased as "Embracing the Culture, Being Changed by the World."

The scrapping of the previous motto had been more consequential than I had imagined.

Shaking off the Stockholm Syndrome

If you have already embraced Stockholm Syndrome Christianity, I doubt this book will persuade you to abandon it. But if you are one of the growing number of Christians troubled by the shocking failures of Christian leaders at all levels—and you want to become part of the solution—this book is for you.

This book is also for Christian leaders who are wondering whether and when to speak up. Maybe you aren't a Stockholm Syndrome Christian, but you have been reluctant to challenge your fellow leaders who are. Perhaps you don't want to be divisive. Or perhaps you are disturbed by the anger and lack of love you observe in some who claim to be fighting for truth. Those concerns are legitimate. *But if you fail to provide a clear alternative to Stockholm Syndrome Christianity, you are part of the problem.*

When ordinary Christians can't find good examples of faithful leaders, they become cynical and desperate, vulnerable to being manipulated by demagogues on both extremes of the social and political spectrum. If you want to prevent this, you need to show them there is a better way. As you read this book, I challenge you to prayerfully consider what you are being called to do as a leader. I challenge you to not prioritize "getting along" over everything else in situations where biblical truth is needed. "Speaking the truth in love," as Paul urges in his letter to the Ephesians, means *speaking*. Silence can sound a lot like acceptance. It certainly creates space that dissenting voices will fill. And when Paul writes those words, it's in the context of moving towards unity and away from the discord that comes from being easily deceived by whatever fashionable wind of doctrine is blowing.

As you may have noticed, this book is going to be direct. There is a time for speaking in soothing tones. But matters have progressed to their current state in large part because too many Christian leaders have failed to live the truth clearly and consistently. If we are to rebuild our churches and communities, we need to be honest with each other about how we got to this point—even if that honesty makes us uncomfortable.

Of course, being honest does not mean we should be unloving or unfair. Let me say it again: Most Stockholm Syndrome Christians believe they are doing the right thing. So we should be careful about attributing to them bad motives, and we should remember to treat those we disagree with as fellow creatures created in God's image. We also need to resist the temptation to become consumed by anger or bitterness, even when dealing with what we consider wrongdoing (Ephesians 4:31).

Over forty years ago, as he was dying from cancer, Christian thinker Francis Schaeffer struggled to finish his final book. Titled *The Great Evangelical Disaster*, the volume offered a dire warning about how evangelical Christian leaders of his own day were accommodating the culture and compromising the truth. I was in college at the time, and Schaeffer's book convinced me of the critical importance of standing steadfastly for the truth.

But as I grew older, I appreciated something else from the book. As its final chapter, Schaeffer included a booklet he had written years earlier called *The Mark of the Christian*. Schaeffer's booklet emphasized the importance of treating genuine Christians with whom we disagree with love and respect. When I was a college professor, I assigned *The Mark of the Christian* as required reading in some of my classes. If you end up being convinced by what I write in this book, I'd encourage you to read *The Mark of the Christian* as you begin to think about how you can apply what you learn here. It may help you interact with Christian friends and family members who don't yet understand the situation we are facing.

In the pages that follow, we will examine the root causes of Stockholm Syndrome Christianity, and strategies to overcome it. Most importantly, if you want to become part of the solution, this book will prepare you to become an agent for change. The final section will point you to a companion website that contains practical tools to help you resist captivity and stand for truth in your family, your church, and your community.

An online assessment will help you diagnose whether you or your church or school exhibit symptoms of Stockholm Syndrome Christianity. Discussion/study questions will help you apply what you are learning and share your new knowledge in small groups and adult education classes. A recommended list of resources (books, articles, websites, videos, and key organizations) will enable you to equip yourself to deal with the challenges of Stockholm Syndrome Christianity before they become acute in your circles of influence.

But before we can repair the damage caused by Stockholm Syndrome Christianity, we first need to better understand its symptoms.

SYMPTOMS

1. Merely Human

Stockholm Syndrome Christians' Dismissive View of the Bible

ANDY STANLEY IS LEAD PASTOR OF NORTHPOINT COMMUNITY Church in the Atlanta area, one of the largest evangelical churches in the United States. As founder of Northpoint Ministries, he oversees a network of close to 150 churches around the globe.[1] In 2010, a survey of American pastors identified Stanley "as one of the ten most influential living pastors in America."[2]

The author of more than twenty books, Stanley is looked to by many church leaders as a mentor and guide. "Leadership is complicated," he says on his personal website. "You want to get it right. I can help."[3]

Although a Baptist, Stanley's influence extends well beyond Baptist circles. When I was an elder at a Presbyterian church, I and other elders were urged by our senior pastor to study one of Stanley's books for guidance on how our church should change.

Stanley has a habit of making controversial statements. In 2009, he disparaged pastors who preach through books of the Bible as cheats. "Guys that preach verse-by-verse through books of the Bible—that is just cheating," he wrote. "It's cheating because that would be easy, first of all. That isn't how you grow people. No one in the Scripture modeled that. There's not one example of that."[4]

Stanley later got in hot water for berating people who don't attend large churches. "When I hear adults say 'well I don't like a big church. I like about 200, I want to be able to know everybody' I say you are so stinking selfish," he declared. "You care nothing about the next generation. All you care about is you and your five friends. You don't care about your kids, anybody else's kids."[5] He eventually apologized.

Stanley's most disturbing comments, however, have dealt with the authority of the Bible. In recent years, he's been arguing that Christians are making the Bible *too* central to their faith, especially the Old Testament. In his book *Irresistible* (2018) and related sermons, Stanley has urged Christians to "unhitch" Christianity from the Old Testament,[6] which he thinks would be better described as "The Obsolete Testament."[7]

The devaluation of Scripture—both the Old Testament and the New—is foundational to all other elements of Stockholm Syndrome Christianity. It's both symptom and cause, and as such is our first topic of discussion.

Discarding the Old Testament

In Stanley's view, the Old Testament is basically irrelevant for Christians. Its promises are for Jews alone. And while Stanley concedes that certain Old Testament books contain commonsense moral "principles," he argues that Christians should *not* try to apply the teachings found in the Old Testament to their lives. In his words: "The Old Testament is great for inspiration, but not application."[8] Not even the Ten Commandments are appropriate to guide Christians according to Stanley: "The Ten Commandments have no authority over you. None. To be clear: Thou shalt not obey the Ten Commandments."[9]

At best the Old Testament provides a "backstory" for Christianity that might be of historical interest. It certainly isn't needed to understand or apply the Christian faith. "The Christian faith doesn't need to be propped up by the Jewish Scriptures," Stanley writes.[10] So, just as we put away old cassette tapes, "we should put away" the books of the Old Testament. "We can appreciate them without playing them," he says—whatever that nonsensical comparison means.[11]

It gets worse.

Stanley blames virtually all the evils committed by Christians since the time of Jesus on the Old Testament. He writes: "The most shameful and embarrassing chapters in church history were not the result of anything Jesus or the apostle Paul taught. Our most embarrassing, indefensible moments resulted from Christians leveraging" concepts from the Old Testament.[12]

According to Stanley, the Old Testament promotes a "ritualistic, day-of-the-week, festival-driven, don't-forget-your-goat worship of an invisible and somewhat distant God."[13] Reliance on the Old Testament by Christians led to "the violence-affirming God of the church" and "paved the way for church support of slavery, anti-Semitism, inquisitions, forced conversions, and a host of other unJesus-like enterprises."[14] From the Old Testament, "you get the prosperity gospel, judgmentalism, fourteenth-century Catholicism, don't touch God's annointedism, [and] God will get'emism."[15] The Old Testament was used to justify "crusade[s]" and "incite... pogrom[s] against Jews."[16]

Yes, Stanley actually tries to blame the "Jewish Scriptures" for inciting historical persecution against Jews.

Stanley also blames the Old Testament for keeping people away from Christianity. "When it comes to stumbling blocks to faith," he writes, "the Old Testament is right up there at the top of the list."[17] Again: "The Old Testament is used far more than the New Testament to create doubt in the minds of undergrad and graduate students."[18] What does he mean?

> The Bible *says* Israel migrated from Egypt to ancient Canaan. Historians claim they didn't. If there was... no migration to Egypt, the Bible isn't true. If the Bible isn't true, our faith, like the walls of Jericho, comes tumbling down. Except, archaeologists say the walls of Jericho didn't come tumbling down. At least not as described in the Old Testament book of Joshua. If we can't trust what the Bible says about those things, can we trust what it says about *anything?*[19]

After this shocking pronouncement, Stanley backtracks—sort of. He mentions perfunctorily that there *is* evidence for these events recorded in the Old Testament after all. But he neglects to present any of it to readers.

Why? Probably because in his view defending the Bible is pointless. "The trustworthiness of the Bible is defensible in a controlled environment," he says. "It's not defensible in culture where seconds count and emotions run high."[20] Stanley adds that it doesn't matter whether there is any evidence for the events recorded in the Old Testament or not. Even if there were no evidence for those events, "that would in no way undermine the reliability of the accounts of Jesus' life found in the documents that comprise the New Testament."[21]

So, he argues, Christians should not be afraid to let the Old Testament go. "The credibility of our faith is not contingent upon the credibility of the events recorded in the Jewish Scriptures," he says. And moreover, "The credibility of our faith is not contingent upon our text being infallible or inerrant."[22]

Because Stanley wants to distance Christianity and Jesus as far as possible from God's revelation of Himself and his teachings in the Old Testament, he recommends renaming the Old Testament "the Jewish Scriptures" or "the Hebrew Bible,"[23] moving those Jewish books to the back of Christian Bibles, and re-ordering the New Testament to start with Luke rather than Matthew (presumably because Matthew stresses the continuity between Judaism and Christianity, which is something Stanley wishes to deny).[24]

Stanley's effort to "unhitch" Christianity from the Old Testament has been tried various times before, and the results weren't pretty.

In the second century, the Gnostic heretic Marcion tried to convince Christians to jettison the Old Testament, arguing that Jesus was the son of the New Testament God, and the Old Testament God was someone else entirely—an evil Creator, who created an evil world.[25] In American history, Thomas Jefferson created his own stripped-down version of the Bible that included only the life and teachings of Jesus (with most of the miracles removed).[26] Depicting Jesus's teachings as a radical break from Judaism, Jefferson denounced the God of the Old Testament as "cruel, vindictive, capricious and unjust"[27] and attacked the ethics of the Jews as "repulsive and anti-social."[28] In the twentieth century, the Nazis in Germany drew on Marcion to present Jesus as Aryan rather than Jewish, and they published a Bible that left out the Old Testament and rewrote the New Testament to excise Judaism.[29]

Andy Stanley is not a Marcion, and he certainly is no Nazi. But his approach is wrongheaded just the same.

Stanley insists emphatically that "Jesus was sent by the Father to introduce something *entirely new*"[30] (emphasis Stanley's) and that Jesus set "himself against the temple and *all* it represented"[31] (emphasis mine).

Actually, no.

Jesus didn't offer "something *entirely new*." He offered the fulfillment of promises that God made in the Old Testament, which even Stanley acknowledges. And Jesus didn't set himself against "all" the temple represented. He set himself up as the fulfillment of the temple's sacrificial system, the perfect "lamb of God who takes away the sins of the world" in the words of John the Baptist (John 1:29).

True, the Old Testament does not apply to Christians in the way it applied to the nation of Israel. But the mainstream Christian tradition—starting with the writers of the New Testament—offers a much better understanding of this truth than Stanley does.

The sacrificial system in the Old Testament does not apply to Christians because it was fulfilled in Christ. He is the perfect and final sacrifice that the sacrificial system pointed to. The civil and judicial laws of the Old Testament (including specific criminal penalties) were given to the historic nation of Israel and so are not binding on other nations—as Christian thinkers as different as Thomas Aquinas and John Calvin both recognized.[32] Likewise, certain dietary rules were set in place to help set Israel apart from the nations around them, and those are not binding on Christians today—as the New Testament explicitly makes clear in the description and explanation of Peter's visions (Acts 10:9–35).

At the same time, much of the Old Testament *does* remain fully applicable to Christians:

- The Old Testament reveals timeless truths about God's character—His eternal nature, His sovereignty, His omniscience, His justice, and His love. Read the book of

Isaiah, especially the passages revealing God's character (e.g., Isaiah 40:9–31, 45:5–12, 18–25). Try claiming with a straight face that those passages aren't relevant or authoritative for Christians today.

- Prophesies in the Old Testament provide stunning confirmations of God's foreknowledge and providence, and they help authenticate the New Testament's claims about who Jesus is.[33] Jesus himself pointed this out (Luke 24:25–27).

- The moral imperatives expressed in the Ten Commandments about honoring one's parents and refraining from murder, adultery, theft, perjury, and coveting certainly still apply today. As many Christian thinkers have argued, the Ten Commandments embody the moral law originally written on our hearts by God.[34]

The New Testament clearly teaches that the Old Testament should continue to be revered by Christians. Paul wrote approvingly to his associate Timothy about "how from infancy" Timothy had "known the Holy Scriptures, which are able to make you wise for salvation through faith in Christ Jesus." Paul then declares: "All Scripture is God-breathed and is useful for teaching, rebuking, correcting and training in righteousness, so that the servant of God may be thoroughly equipped for every good work" (2 Timothy 3:16–17, NIV). *All* Scripture, not some. And the "Scripture" to which Paul referred was primarily the books of the Old Testament, since the New Testament had yet to be assembled. Stanley quotes part of this passage from 2 Timothy but essentially neuters it.

Are some parts of the Old Testament difficult for certain people to accept today? Yes. But so are plenty of sections of the New Testament. If you find the miracle of the Red Sea hard to believe, you will likely find the feeding of the five thousand, the virgin birth, and, yes, the resurrection, hard to accept. If you are offended by the condemnation of homosexual behavior in the Old Testament, you are likely to be offended by the similar condemnation in Romans 1:26–27. If the goal is to avoid tough topics, much of the New Testament is going to have to be scrapped as well.

There is a better approach: Instead of disowning large swaths of the Bible, help people understand what the Bible actually teaches and help open their eyes to attacks on the Bible that are unsubstantiated. At the same time, we should remember that a person's acceptance of Christ ultimately depends on the work of the Holy Spirit, not on our ability to repackage Christianity to make it better fit modern culture.

Andy Stanley prefers that we de-emphasize the Bible rather than try to defend it. Indeed, in addition to scorning the Old Testament, he urges Christians to stop teaching that "the Bible says" or "the Word of God states."[35] According to Stanley, we can cite specific authors or individuals, like Paul or Jesus, but not the "Bible" as if it were an authoritative collection of books. Stanley's guidance contradicts the practice of New Testament authors themselves, who regularly referred to biblical writings collectively as "Scriptures" or attributed various biblical passages directly to God.[36]

Unfortunately, Stanley is far from the only Christian leader who has been marketing a diminished view of the Bible in our current culture. But before documenting just how widespread the decay of biblical authority is, we first need to remind ourselves what faithful Christians almost universally believed about the Bible until recently—and with good reason.

Holy Bible, Book Divine

The historic Christian view of the Bible is not hard to grasp. Christians from all three major branches of Christianity—Protestant, Catholic, and Orthodox—regarded the Bible as a whole as God's authoritative word for humanity. Although each individual biblical book had a human author, Christians traditionally affirmed that those human authors were divinely inspired, so what they wrote ultimately came from God Himself—not from the authors' own wisdom.[37]

In the words of the Apostle Paul, "All Scripture is breathed out by God" (2 Timothy 3:16). The Apostle Peter emphasized the same point when he wrote that "no prophecy of Scripture comes from someone's own interpretation. For no prophecy was ever produced by the will of man, but men spoke from God as they were carried along by the Holy Spirit" (2 Peter 1:20–21).

Because the Bible came directly from God, its teachings remain true across time and culture. According to the Psalmist, God's law is "true" and "perfect" (Psalm 19:7, 9), and God's word is "truth" (Psalm 119:160) and "firmly fixed in the heavens" (Psalm 119:89). Indeed, "every one" of His "righteous rules endures forever" (Psalm 119:160). Jesus similarly taught that God's "word is truth" (John 17:17) and that no Scripture can be annulled or broken (John 10:35).

New Testament writers repeatedly appealed to Old Testament passages as God's word. But the Apostle Paul also indicated that his own teaching had the same status, telling the Thessalonians that "when you received the word of God, which you heard from us, you accepted it not as the word of men but as what it really is, the word of God" (1 Thessalonians 2:13). The Apostle Peter also referred to Paul's writings in this way, calling them Scripture (2 Peter 3:16).

The Jewish historian Josephus lived in first century Palestine. His writings provide a window into how Jewish people regarded their Scriptures shortly after the time of Christ. Josephus makes clear that the Hebrew Scriptures were regarded by Jews as "decrees of God," to which "no-one has dared to add, to take away, or to alter anything." Indeed, it was "innate in every Judean, right from birth... to remain faithful to them and, if necessary, gladly to die on their behalf."[38]

Early Christians held the same reverence for their Scriptures. Clement of Rome (AD 30–100) called them "the true utterances of the Holy Spirit" and said "nothing of an unjust or counterfeit character is written in them."[39] Irenaeus (AD c. 130–c. 202) wrote that "the Scriptures are indeed perfect, since they were spoken by the Word of God and His Spirit."[40] Augustine (AD 354–430) affirmed the absolute truth of the accepted books of the Bible: "of these alone do I most firmly believe that the authors were completely free from error. And if in these writings I am perplexed by anything which appears to me opposed to truth, I do not hesitate to suppose that either the manuscript is faulty, or the translator has not caught the meaning of what was said, or I myself have failed to understand it."[41]

The medieval Roman Catholic theologian and philosopher Thomas Aquinas (1225–1274) likewise argued that "it is unlawful to hold that any false assertion is contained either in the Gospel or in any canonical Scripture, or that the writers thereof have told untruths."[42]

The Protestant Reformers expressed similar views. When reading the Bible, "You are not reading the word of a human being but the Word of God, the Most High," declared Martin Luther (1483–1546), who cited with approval Augustine's statement that the Bible was inerrant.[43]

The Westminster Confession of Faith (1646) proclaimed the "full persuasion and assurance of the infallible truth, and divine authority" of the Bible,[44] while the Belgic Confession (1561) stated that "we believe without a doubt all things contained in" the Bible,[45] and "we reject with all our hearts everything that does not agree with this infallible rule."[46]

The broad consensus held by faithful Christians across history about the Bible's truth and authority is hard to miss. Within that consensus, of course, there have been a variety of differences and plenty of room for disagreements.

For example, believing the Bible is true is not the same as believing all of it must be interpreted "literally." The Bible includes metaphors, just like our ordinary speech does. When someone tells you "it's raining cats and dogs," that doesn't mean mammals are falling from the sky. Likewise, when the Psalmist promises that God "will cover you with his feathers, and under his wings you will find refuge" (Psalm 91:4 NIV), no one seriously interprets that passage as teaching that God has feathers.

Believing the Bible is true also doesn't mean that every statement in the Bible represents God's position. Job's wife tells him to "curse God and die" (Job 2:9), but the Bible isn't endorsing her advice. Neither does it endorse the opinion of Job's friends, who tell him repeatedly and at length that God is punishing him for sinfulness, until God shows up and tells them he's angry because they have not spoken the truth about God (Job 42:7).

Nor is the Bible necessarily endorsing behaviors just by reporting them. The fact that both David and Solomon had multiple wives was not something celebrated in the Bible; it was something that helped explain David and Solomon's moral failings (1 Kings 11:1-6).

Believing the Bible is true also doesn't mean we should regard it as a scientific textbook or that we ought to judge the Bible by modern standards of reporting. Quotation marks were not used in the original biblical manuscripts since those designators didn't exist in ancient Hebrew or ancient Greek. It is not an error for a biblical author to accurately convey someone's comments through use of paraphrase or summary statements that may condense what was said or eliminate some of the details of an event. It isn't an error for a biblical author to round up or down a number rather than giving the exact figure. And it isn't an error for different eyewitnesses to focus on different aspects of what they saw.

In addition, believing the Bible is true obviously doesn't mean that we necessarily *understand* everything in it or that there cannot be legitimate disagreements over the meaning of certain passages.

Finally, believing the Bible is true doesn't mean that the copied texts of manuscripts that we have today might not have been corrupted in some way—although the thousands of text fragments that exist from biblical manuscripts over the past couple of thousand years show amazing agreement. Most of the variations are inconsequential.[47]

Despite these caveats, we shouldn't blind ourselves to the massive historical agreement among Christians on the central point: The Bible was true and trustworthy on all the matters it addressed and reported. This included not only theology and morality, but also history. Judaism and Christianity were not merely philosophical or theological or even ethical belief systems. They were based on concrete claims about God's actions in history, including miraculous interventions such as Israel's deliverance from slavery in the Old Testament and the resurrection of Jesus in the New Testament.

Unfortunately, something happened to this Christian consensus about the Bible on the way to the twentieth and twenty-first centuries.

Deconstructing God's Word

During the so-called Enlightenment of the seventeenth century and afterward, scholars deconstructed the Bible into a purely human creation through what became known as "historical criticism." The label was a misnomer. "Historical criticism" was actually an effort to show that the Bible was *not* really history or historically accurate. These debunkers often claimed that their efforts were justified by "science."

German Lutheran theologian Rudolf Bultmann (1884–1976) was one of the most influential advocates of historical criticism during the twentieth century. According to Bultmann, *"Man's knowledge and mastery of the world* have advanced to such an extent through science and technology that it is no longer possible for anyone seriously to hold the New Testament view of the world—in fact, there is no one who does." Bultmann went on to add, "It is impossible to use electric light and the wireless and to avail ourselves of modern medical and surgical discoveries, and at the same time to believe in the New Testament world of spirits and miracles."[48]

"Bultmann… stood like a colossus over academic biblical studies for much of the twentieth century," writes theologian John Snyder. "The movement of radical criticism has taken several different directions since his era, but he is the inspiration behind many of today's most vocal critics of the Bible. Building upon the literary principles of Bultmann, they assume that the vast majority of the recorded sayings and deeds of Jesus, although well-intentioned stories, are in the final analysis merely elaborate inventions of the early church."[49]

These efforts to "demythologize" the Bible were largely based on an unproven assumption of materialism—the philosophical idea that everything can be reduced to blind matter in motion. According to the ideology of these scholars, the supernatural did not exist, and so the miracles and prophesies reported in the Bible could not exist either. Nor could the Bible actually be a real communication from God in the sense believed by prior generations.[50]

The consequences of this frontal assault on the Bible were not hard to discern. Theologian John S. Feinberg cuts to the chase: "In light

of the withering critique of Scripture via historical criticism, many...
rejected Scripture as inspired and inerrant, let alone authoritative."[51]

The critics' diminished view of the Bible eventually came to be
embraced by many elites in both America and Europe, especially in
academia.

If you want a popularized version of the post-nineteenth-century
secularist vision of the Bible, read atheist evolutionary biologist Richard Dawkins's book *The God Delusion*.[52] Dawkins is not a scholar of
religion, and his views about the Bible are often shallow and crude.
But Dawkins's book is a splendid compilation of the secular caricatures
and prejudices Dawkins likely imbibed going through the British
educational system.

Dawkins dismisses the Bible as "a chaotically cobbled-together
anthology of disjointed documents, composed, revised, translated, distorted and 'improved' by hundreds of anonymous authors, editors and
copyists, unknown to us and mostly unknown to each other, spanning
nine centuries."[53] He calls "the God of the Old Testament... arguably
the most unpleasant character in all fiction: jealous and proud of it;
a petty, unjust, unforgiving control-freak; a vindictive, bloodthirsty
ethnic cleanser; a misogynistic, homophobic, racist, infanticidal,
genocidal, filicidal, pestilential, megalomaniacal, sadomasochistic,
capriciously malevolent bully."[54]

For similar views espoused by a scholar actually specializing in
the field of religion, check out the books of Hector Avalos, a professor
of religious studies at Iowa State University until his death in 2021.
Avalos—a professor of *religion*, mind you—was an avowed atheist.[55] He
asserted that "any act of love based on religion is immoral"[56] and suggested we need "to eliminate religion from human life altogether."[57] He
particularly despised Mother Teresa, who spent her life helping lepers
and the poor in India. "Mother Teresa... advocated policies that helped
to generate the very pool of poor people she was attempting to help,"
claimed Avalos.[58] In one of his books, Avalos essentially blamed Jews
for the Holocaust, claiming that "the supreme tragic irony of the Holocaust is that the genocidal policies first systematically enunciated in the
Hebrew scriptures" were then turned against the Jews by the Nazis.[59]

Hector Avalos was not a fringe figure in the academic discipline of religion. He held a Master of Theological Studies from Harvard Divinity School and a PhD in the Hebrew Bible and Near Eastern Studies from Harvard University. He spent most of his academic career at a respected state research university in America's heartland.

My point here is not to highlight the many atheist and agnostic academics who reject the Bible. What I want to bring attention to is how these atheist and agnostic academics shape the way the Bible is studied in universities and graduate schools, *which ends up influencing the views of the self-identified Christians who study there.* After pursuing degrees at universities and seminaries where the Bible's credibility is torn to shreds, these Christians can all too easily adopt assumptions and conclusions indistinguishable from those held by the Bible's debunkers. They become Stockholm Syndrome Christians.

The Big Shift

Evangelical Christians started the twentieth century by defining themselves as standing against theological liberalism and robustly defending biblical authority in books like *Christianity and Liberalism* by Princeton theologian J. Gresham Machen.[60] But the evangelicals' unified stance in support of the Bible's trustworthiness had frayed by the 1970s and '80s.

A pivotal moment was a 1980s controversy over the views of evangelical New Testament scholar Robert Gundry. A professor at evangelical Westmont College in southern California, Gundry published a commentary on the book of Matthew in 1982. The commentary provoked a tempest among traditional evangelicals by suggesting that significant portions of Matthew's account of Jesus's birth and infancy were fictional.

According to Gundry, Matthew invented the Magi's visit to Jesus as a substitute for the shepherds in Luke's account of Jesus's birth.[61] He likewise invented the star as a replacement for the angel and the heavenly host in Luke.[62] Gundry further suggested that Matthew fabricated Herod's slaughter of the infants out of Luke's story that Jesus's parents offered a Temple sacrifice.[63]

More generally, Gundry asserted that the words "Jesus said" or "Jesus did" in Matthew's gospel "need not always mean that in history

Jesus said or did what follows, but sometimes may mean that in the account at least partly constructed by Matthew himself Jesus said or did what follows."[64]

Gundry was a member of the Evangelical Theological Society (ETS), which had a statement of faith affirming that the Bible as originally written was "inerrant."[65] When his commentary sparked concerns among some of his ETS colleagues, Gundry insisted that he still believed the Bible was inerrant. He simply believed that Matthew wasn't intending to offer a factual account. His reasoning for that conclusion was not grounded in the biblical text or the church's universal understanding of the passages under study throughout history. Gundry may well have convinced himself that Matthew was intending to write fiction, but that conviction betrayed a Stockholm Syndrome mentality: He had embraced the worldview of the debunkers of Christianity in the face of two millennia of Christian belief that Matthew was intending to write fact, not fiction.

Regardless of the sincerity of Gundry's views, it doesn't take a biblical scholar to see that Gundry's approach was not consistent with the original meaning of the ETS statement on inerrancy. Most ETS members agreed, and by a vote of 74 percent they eventually asked Gundry to resign from the organization, which, to his credit, he did.[66]

But in many ways, Gundry's resignation from ETS represented a hollow victory. Gundry was a professor at a prominent evangelical Christian college, and he stayed in that position. In fact, his college appointed him to its first endowed professorship and eventually named another professorship in his honor, the Robert H. Gundry Professor in Biblical Studies.[67] Gundry finally retired in 2000 after transmitting his view of the Bible to thousands of students.[68]

Gundry is a single professor, but he represents many more. I don't think most evangelicals in the pews, including parents who mortgage their futures to send their children to Christian colleges, realize how deeply the Enlightenment approach to the Bible has penetrated the theology faculties of many Christian colleges and universities.

I found this out firsthand during my years as a professor at Seattle Pacific.

When a Christian College Abandons the Bible

Seattle Pacific was connected to the Free Methodist Church, whose Articles of Religion declare that the Bible is "completely truthful in all it affirms."[69]

But I quickly learned that for a number of my colleagues, especially those in the school of theology, such statements were considered cringeworthy at best. These professors belittled those who believed in anything approaching the complete truthfulness or authority of the Bible.

I believe there are sincere Christians who adopt the view that the Bible is authoritative even if it contains errors at certain points. C. S. Lewis did not believe that the Bible was error-free.[70] Nevertheless, in his writing and speaking he adopted a high view of the authority of biblical teachings, and he spent his life trying to defend an orthodox view of historic Christianity.

In a similar vein, there are various Christian scholars today who believe the Bible was uniquely inspired by God and is overwhelmingly trustworthy in the things it affirms, including its accounts of history and its prophesies. But they are open to the possibility that the Bible contains minor errors in its reporting. Although I myself do not embrace this view, I respect those who sincerely argue for this position.

But this was not the approach I encountered at SPU. Despite occasional lip-service to biblical authority, many of the theologians and Bible teachers at Seattle Pacific had more in common with the Bible's debunkers than with someone like C. S. Lewis.

I will say this for the theologians at SPU: They were more candid about their rejection of traditional inerrancy than someone like Gundry. Gundry offered a tortured explanation as to why his heterodox view of the Matthew was compatible with the Bible's inerrancy. My colleagues weren't so coy. One colleague boasted that members of SPU's theology department had refused to join the Evangelical Theology Society precisely because they could not endorse the idea that the Bible was without error.

I soon began to see the damage these colleagues were inflicting on students, many of whom had come to Seattle Pacific seeking to deepen their faith. Several years into my career at the university, a former student published an article in the student newspaper. It was heartbreaking. The article described how he underwent "a great deal of internal suffering" while attending Seattle Pacific because "the foundations of my Christian faith began to crumble."[71]

"At a Christian university, I expected to have my faith strengthened," he wrote. "Instead, it was virtually destroyed." The former student explained that his shaken faith was directly connected to my colleagues' devaluation of the Bible:

> All the campus talk about following Jesus began to lose its force as I began to believe that it was based on documents that were fundamentally unreliable and which described events that probably never happened, or at least not how they are described with all their "supernatural embellishments" or "late editorial redactions (changes and additions to the text)."

This student wasn't alone in what he experienced. One day one of my advisees came into my office during office hours. I'll call him "Matt." Matt was distraught. One of his professors, he told me, had been trying to convince him of something called "open theism." Open theism is the idea that God does not have certain knowledge of the future. Open theists claim that God isn't omniscient in any traditional sense.

The Bible teaches, and Christians have believed from the earliest days, that God has absolute knowledge of the past, present, and yes, the future. The Bible is replete with predictive prophesies by God as well as general statements about God's foreknowledge. "Now I declare new things; before they spring forth I proclaim them to you," says God in Isaiah (Isaiah 42:9). Again, He says, "I declared the former things long ago... Before they took place I proclaimed them to you" (Isaiah 48:3, 5). According to the Psalmist, "Even before there is a word on my tongue, behold, O LORD, You know it all" (Psalm 139:4). Jesus says to his disciples: "So from now on I am telling you before it comes to pass, so that when it does occur, you may believe that I am He" (John 13:19).

Simply put, open theism is not compatible with historic Christianity. Period.

But this was what was increasingly taught at Seattle Pacific. Those who tried to advocate for the traditional position of God's exhaustive knowledge of the future were told that they didn't understand the Wesleyan tradition. This was an attempt to reframe the debate over open theism as part of the dispute between Wesleyans/Arminians and Calvinists over predestination for salvation. But that was a red herring. John Wesley, James Arminius, and traditional Wesleyans no less than Calvinists had always asserted that God had exhaustive knowledge of the future.[72] As renowned Methodist scholar Thomas Oden put it succinctly, open theism was simply "heresy."[73]

Matt was not my only student who was disturbed by open theism. "Mary" also expressed her growing unease at what she was being taught. What disturbed Mary was not that she was exposed to open theism in her classes. After all, college is a time to wrestle with new and contrary ideas, even ideas that may be wrong. The problem was that her professors only presented the side in favor of open theism. Students were not given the opportunity to hear the responses from orthodox Christian theologians and philosophers. In other words, Mary felt she was being propagandized.

"I searched long and hard to find a good school," Mary told me. "It took three years of hard research before I decided to attend SPU."[74] But now she was so demoralized, she was thinking of leaving.

Mary had originally come to Seattle Pacific to double major in theology and political science. "However, after taking a few theology classes, this is no longer even a consideration," she said. While most of her theology professors were content to propagandize without belittling their students, Mary told me about one professor who mocked her and other students who still held to traditional Christian views that they had been brought up with.

Mary also told me about the other heterodox claims she encountered in her theology classes. She said she was told that "Jesus did not know he was God. It was something he had to learn. That is why he told people not to tell others who he was." She was taught that "it is not in the character of God to send people to hell; therefore, hell does not exist, or one can be saved from hell after having been sent there." Another professor "basically stated that 'community' is a higher authority than God. He did not use those exact words, but it was very directly implied."

"These teachings were not just considered, they were taught as being correct," said Mary, who added:

> I don't just throw things out the window if I disagree. I want to know what others believe and I want to consider them. I am open to different teachings and learning new things, but these teachings were not Scriptural in any way. You ask the teachers to prove their points and they can't. They make statements such as it's not in the character of God. I feel like I'm wasting my time and money on these classes. I want to learn what the Bible says and means, not weird beliefs that cannot be supported by the Bible.

This was already the state of Seattle Pacific two decades ago, and things continued to devolve from there.

Lincoln Keller graduated from SPU in 2021. Afterward, he wrote a book about his disillusionment with what he encountered. According to Lincoln, his professors taught that the Bible is flawed, contradictory, factually wrong, and unclear. As a consequence, "for certain professors and students, the Word of God was not supreme authority. Instead, contemporary scholarship, science, or culture had the final say on what professors and students should believe."[75]

Keller adds:

> It's very possible that one's faith would be safer in the hands of... [a secular] philosophy professor than in the hands of the SPU theology professor. At least with the former, there is clarity: "I'm attending a secular university so I will be taught secular ideas." With the latter, confusion can abound: "What this professor is saying doesn't really sound like the Bible, but she is using theological language so I think I can trust her."[76]

The growing rejection of biblical authority is not confined to Seattle Pacific University, and it is not limited to self-identified theological progressives.

Losing Our Nerve and Our Faith

The Evangelical Theological Society is a good barometer of the views of historically conservative theologians and Bible scholars. In the 1980s, you will recall, it asked Robert Gundry to resign for his claims about fictional narratives in the gospel of Matthew.

Fast forward to the early 2000s, when open theism began to sweep through evangelical Christian seminaries and universities like Seattle Pacific. In 2001, 70 percent of ETS members at its annual meeting approved a resolution stating that "the Bible clearly teaches that God has complete, accurate and infallible knowledge of all events past, present and future including all future decisions and actions of free moral agents."[77]

Well and good. But the resolution was non-binding. Two years later, ETS members voted down a proposal to remove two prominent open theist scholars from its membership.[78]

More recently, ETS has given a pass to another member, New Testament scholar Michael Licona. A professor at Houston Christian University, Licona is an articulate defender of the resurrection of Jesus. But he has become increasingly vocal in raising questions about the historical accuracy of the gospels.

Licona points out (rightly) that the gospels do not supply blow-by-blow accounts of the events they cover, nor do they report the comments of Jesus with the precision of a verbatim transcript.[79] That does not make the gospels inaccurate or untruthful. I agree with Licona that we shouldn't impose modern standards of precision on the New Testament, and there was nothing wrong with gospel writers simplifying or summarizing specific stories, choosing to focus on some story elements rather than others, organizing some narratives thematically rather than chronologically, or engaging in normal paraphrasing when relating what Jesus said.

The problem is that Licona goes a lot further. He compares the gospels to Hollywood movies that are "based on true events" but use "artistic license" to change the facts to better present the story they want to tell.[80] He suggests that the gospels' authors felt similarly free

to alter facts, invent stories, change the location and context of historical events, and even dramatically refashion what Jesus said to make
their theological points.

For example, Licona claims that the "Sermon on the Mount"
didn't take place on a mount at all. Instead, the location was likely
invented by the writer of Matthew to draw "a parallel between God
revealing the law to Moses on Sinai and Jesus revealing the correct
interpretation of the law to others on the mountain."[81] More dramatically, Licona has argued that the account in Matthew 27:52–53 of
additional people being resurrected after Jesus's resurrection may be
"legend" rather than fact,[82] asserting that the "most plausible" reading of the text is that it was simply literary "special effects."[83] In other
words, the story was likely a pious fabrication. After considerable
criticism,[84] Licona pulled back—a bit. He still didn't affirm that the
event described was real; but he said he now believed it was just as
likely to be factual as fictional.[85]

It's not just locations and events in the gospels that may have been
fictionalized, according to Licona. The very words attributed to Jesus
himself may differ—dramatically—from what Jesus actually said.
For instance, Licona suggests that John took Matthew's and Mark's
account of Jesus saying on the cross "My God, my God, why have
you forsaken me?" and transformed it into the statement "I thirst!"
(John 19:28). Licona asserts that "John has redacted Jesus's words but
has retained their meaning."[86] Philosopher Lydia McGrew calls Licona's claim "patently false."[87] The two statements are radically different.

Licona similarly contends that Jesus's words "it is finished" in
John 19:30 are not historical. They are supposedly a creative adapta-
tion of Jesus's words "Father, into your hands I entrust my spirit" in
Luke 23:46.[88] Licona likewise suggests that when the writer of John
attributes the statement "Receive the Holy Spirit" (John 20:22) to
Jesus, he may have invented the statement in order to foreshadow the
coming of Pentecost.[89] More broadly, Licona has raised questions
about whether the "I am" statements by Jesus reported by John (e.g.,
"I am the bread of life," "I am the light of the world," "I am the way,
the truth, and the life") were John's reinterpretations of what Jesus

really said.[90] "So how far did John go when restating Jesus's words?," he asks. "It is impossible to know."[91] Let's be clear. What Licona is describing is far more than the gospel writers merely "paraphrasing" Jesus's words. Whether he admits it or not, he is claiming that they contrived statements Jesus never said, almost like a scriptwriter for a Hollywood film.

Licona justifies his views in the same way as Robert Gundry: He asserts that the gospel writers embraced literary genres where fictionalization was expected. In *The Mirror and the Mask* (2019), Lydia McGrew meticulously rebuts Licona's claims,[92] making a convincing case for what she calls the "reportage model of the gospels," which views the authors as "trying to tell us what really happened" and "record[ing] what was said in a way that was recognizably historical." According to McGrew, and contra Licona, the evidence shows that the authors of the gospels "were highly successful at conveying true factual information, even in details."[93]

Licona still says he believes in the Bible's inerrancy. But he is trying to redefine the term, urging evangelicals to scrap "traditional inerrancy" in favor of what he calls "flexible inerrancy."[94] Licona proposes that Christians regard only the "message" of the Bible as inerrant, not its "words."[95] That may sound reasonable—until one reflects for a moment. The message of the Bible ultimately depends on its words. If the words chosen to express the message are as malleable (and fallible) as Licona suggests, it is hard to see why the Bible's message should be considered exempt from error or even clearly knowable.

I know Licona has many friends among still-orthodox evangelicals who do not fully share his views. I trust that Licona, like Gundry, is perfectly sincere in his position. But the issue isn't Licona's sincerity. It's that his views are incompatible with the original meaning of ETS's doctrinal statement. The fact that Licona remains a member in good standing of ETS, whereas Gundry was asked to leave, shows how times have changed. Even many conservative evangelical scholars have lost their nerve in upholding the reliability and truth of the Bible.

Sicknesses that start in the seminaries and colleges soon end up infecting people in the pews. After all, pastors are taught by professors, and so it's natural for them to spread what they learned in college to their parishioners. That's exactly what has happened.

According to a national survey in 2022, more than 1 in 4 (26 percent) evangelical Christians now believe that "the Bible, like all sacred writings, contains helpful accounts of ancient myths but is not literally true."[96] More than 4 in 10 evangelicals (43 percent) believe that "Jesus was a great teacher, but he was not God."[97] According to another survey in 2023, only 44 percent of "Born-Again Christians" believe that "Jesus did not commit sins during His time on Earth," and less than half (48 percent) believe that you can't earn a place in heaven through good works.[98]

The Cult of Secular Expertise

In churches and Christian schools where the Bible's authority is still officially upheld, the impact of Stockholm Syndrome Christianity may manifest itself in more subtle ways.

As trust in biblical authority has eroded, all too many have embraced what I will call the cult of secular expertise. There always must be a locus of authority. If the Bible's authority is denied, that doesn't mean there will be no authority among Christians or society. It merely means that there will be some *other* authority. In our society, those who attack the Bible often put forward some version of the neutral and objective expert as the alternative, especially those with "scientific" or "technical" knowledge. After all, the Bible is a crude and simple book written by pre-modern and superstitious people. Why should we rely on such an outdated and naïve source for making our decisions?

I am not against experts. Still less am I against scientific and technical knowledge or training. If I needed a brain tumor removed, I would want the best brain surgeon there is to do it, not someone who had purchased a medical diploma from a website for $49.99.

Nevertheless, the Bible is supposed to be the ultimate repository of wisdom for Christians. *But do we truly treat it like that?*

I served as an elder in a church that held to the infallibility of the Bible. But in my last years there, I experienced a growing sense of unease about how we made our decisions. We *said* we believed in the

Bible as our authority. But neither the study of the Bible nor prayer seemed to be at the center of our church's decision-making.

Instead, in our leadership deliberations we looked increasingly to church-growth consultants, books on church growth techniques or the latest intellectual trends, and books by mega-church pastors to whom we looked to tell us what to do. Of course, church-growth experts and mega-church pastors can be used by the Holy Spirit. But as we replaced one church-growth expert or consultant for another, it became harder to feel that the Bible was really being relied upon in a personal way as the guidebook for the direction of our church.

I think we had unconsciously adopted the worldview of secularists who dismiss the Bible and champion the cult of secular expertise. Sadly, we had bought into Stockholm Syndrome Christianity.

The good news is that the message of the Bible—when we trust and apply it—is just as powerful as it has ever been. And those who don't think it matters whether people believe in the Bible or not need to study more the impact of biblical ideas on history.

How the Bible Transformed the World

Frank Capra's iconic film *It's a Wonderful Life* (1946) explores what life would look like if George Bailey had never been born. But what might our world look like had the Bible never been written or believed?

The biblical worldview brought forth hospitals. In the ancient world, people were largely left to fend for themselves and die. The first network of hospitals to care for ordinary people started as adjuncts to cathedrals.[99]

The biblical worldview inspired the movements to eradicate slavery.[100] We will discuss in a future chapter some of the ways Christians have not always lived up to biblical teachings in the area of human equality. But slavery has existed throughout human history, and still exists in some parts of the world today. The fact that it doesn't exist in many nations is largely a result of the working out of the biblical view that all humans are created in the image of God.

The biblical worldview inspired the elevation of women.[101] Women were demeaned in ancient pagan society. Even in the past couple of centuries, practices prevailed like the burning of widows in India and female foot-binding in China. Today some cultures still engage in female genital mutilation.[102] In Saudi Arabia, women weren't allowed to drive until 2018.[103] Yet women were active in the early church, and Jesus himself modeled treating women as equal human beings with men. Think of his encounter with the Samaritan woman at the well (John 4:1–42).

These things are just a sampling. The Bible also contributed to literacy, science, the arts, and philanthropy more generally.[104] And, most importantly, the Bible offers us the gospel: the good news that we can be forgiven and restored to a relationship with our Creator through Jesus Christ's death and resurrection. This transforms not only our souls but also our relationships, as we learn to love as Christ loves us, and forgive as he forgives us.

My point is that the message of the Bible is transformative for individuals, families, communities, and nations. By degrading its truth and its authority, Stockholm Syndrome Christians impede its power to change our lives.

2. Secularist Science

Stockholm Syndrome Christians' Diminished Role for God in Creation

F RANCIS COLLINS IS PROBABLY THE MOST CELEBRATED EVANGELICAL Christian scientist in America. He catapulted to fame—and the cover of *TIME*—as head of the Human Genome Project, which announced a "working draft of the sequence of the human genome" in June 2000.[1] He then became a hero to many Christians with the publication in 2006 of his book *The Language of God*, which recounted his inspiring personal journey from atheism to Christianity.[2]

From 2009–2021, Collins served as the head of the National Institutes of Health (NIH), making him one of the federal government's most important science officials. More recently, he served as acting White House science advisor for President Joe Biden.[3]

For many Christians, Collins has achieved a status equivalent to a rock star's. Evangelical political commentator David French calls Collins "a national treasure."[4] Baptist theologian Russell Moore of *Christianity Today* magazine lauds Collins for his "wisdom, expertise, and most of all… Christian humility and grace."[5] Collins is admired by Christian leaders and laypeople alike as an exemplary model of a faithful Christian in science.

Unfortunately, Collins's model for integrating faith and science is deeply flawed. It depends largely on Christians conceding ground whenever their faith comes into conflict with claims made by the scientific establishment or the dominant culture.

I do not question the sincerity of Collins's faith. But he is not a good guide for integrating faith and science. Consider the issue of abortion. The Bible teaches that life inside the womb is created and planned by God. In the words of Psalm 139, "you created my inmost being; you knit me together in my mother's womb… all the days ordained for me were written in your book before one of them came to be" (Psalm 139:13, 16). From the earliest of times, Christians have believed abortion and infanticide were wrong.[6] In more recent decades, Catholics and evangelical Christians alike have been strongly opposed to abortion. Most people would expect Francis Collins to be "pro-life" since he is an evangelical Christian.

They would be wrong.[7]

First of all, Collins doesn't seem to know when human life begins. In an appendix to his book *The Language of God*, he casts doubt on "the insistence that the spiritual nature of a person is uniquely defined at the very moment of conception."[8] According to one media profile, "He sees a human embryo as a *potential* life, though he thinks that it is *not possible scientifically to settle precisely when life begins*"[9] (emphasis added). According to another journalist, Collins is "dubious of the idea that life begins at the very moment of conception."[10]

Collins has justified eugenic abortions of infants with Down Syndrome, telling *Beliefnet* that "in our current society, people are in a circumstance of being able to take advantage of those technologies [i.e., abortions]. And we have decided as a society that that choice needs to be defended."[11]

Collins's muddled and unbiblical thinking on abortion has had stark real-world consequences. As NIH Director, Collins championed the unrestricted funding of embryonic stem-cell research, which involves the destruction of human embryos for medical research.[12] And in 2021, Collins implemented the repeal of Trump-administration restrictions on the use of aborted fetal tissue in NIH-funded research.[13]

These actions were only the tip of the proverbial iceberg. We now know that the NIH under Collins funded macabre experiments[14] utilizing body parts collected from aborted human fetuses to create "humanized mouse and rodent models with full-thickness human skin."[15] For the experiments, researchers at the University of Pittsburgh cut into tiny pieces "human fetal spleen, thymus, and liver organs" and "then transplanted the tissues and hematopoietic stem cells into irradiated... mice." Researchers also sliced off skin from the scalp of the aborted babies and then grafted the fetal skin onto the mice. In the words of the scientists: "Full-thickness human fetal skin was processed via removal of excess fat tissues attached to the subcutaneous layer of the skin, then engrafted over the rib cage, where the mouse skin was previously excised."

The body parts used for these experiments were harvested from aborted human fetuses with a gestational age of 18–20 weeks. By that age, an unborn baby has brain waves[16] and a beating heart.[17] He can hear sounds and move his limbs and eyes, and his digestive system has started to work.[18] In other words, the human fetuses whose organs were harvested for this NIH-funded research were well-developed tiny humans, not blobs of undifferentiated cells.

Thanks to documents obtained through a Freedom of Information Act lawsuit, we also know about the NIH's role in facilitating the use of baby parts in research on a nationwide level. The lawsuit was filed by Judicial Watch and the Center for Medical Progress after Collins's NIH dragged its feet in responding. According to Judicial Watch, the documents show that the NIH has provided nearly three million in tax dollars to support a fetal organ harvesting operation by the University of Pittsburgh in its "quest to become a 'Tissue Hub' for human fetal tissue ranging from 6 to 42 [!] weeks gestation."[19]

David Daleiden, president of The Center for Medical Progress, commented: "The NIH grant application for just one of Pitt's numerous experiments with aborted infants reads like an episode of American Horror Story. Infants in the womb, some old enough to be viable, are being aborted alive and killed for organ harvesting, in order to bring in millions of dollars in taxpayer funding."[20]

Daleiden further alleged that NIH funding was used to underwrite "labor induction abortions, where the baby is pushed out of the mother whole" and then killed to obtain the desired tissues. In other words, the NIH was facilitating a process where "babies, some of the age of viability, [are] to be delivered alive, and then killing them by cutting their kidneys out."[21]

Abortion isn't the only area where Collins has conformed to the reigning culture. As NIH Director, he threw his enthusiastic support behind the LGTBQI political and social movement, pledging in 2021 to be "an ally and advocate" although he is merely "a White cisgender and heterosexual man."[22] But he didn't just offer verbal support. As journalist Megan Basham has reported, under Collins's leadership

> the NIH launched a new initiative to specifically direct funding to "sexual and gender minorities." On the ground, this has translated to awarding millions in grants to experimental transgender research on minors, like giving opposite-sex hormones to children as young as eight and mastectomies to girls as young as 13.[23]

Although Collins has repeatedly failed to challenge the secular establishment in the areas of abortion and sexuality during his career, he has been quite willing to challenge one group publicly: his fellow Christians. In particular, Collins has engaged in a years-long quest to marginalize and attack Christian scientists, scholars, and laypeople who are skeptical of Darwinian evolution or who think biology shows evidence of intelligent design.

Collins's views on evolution are also symptomatic of Stockholm Syndrome Christianity. But to understand why, we need to delve into the backstory.

Creator of All Things, Visible and Invisible

Physicist Karl Giberson is one of Collins's longtime friends and associates. In 2008 Giberson published a book with a foreword by Collins titled *Saving Darwin: How to Be a Christian and Believe in Evolution*. In the book, Giberson wrote dismissively of the Christian doctrine of creation, insisting that it is "a *secondary* doctrine for Christians. The central idea in Christianity concerns Jesus Christ and the claim that he was the Son of God."[24] Giberson's point seemed to be that so long as people accepted the divinity of Jesus, their view of God as Creator was unimportant.

Early Christian thinkers would have disagreed. For example, when Irenaeus (AD c. 130–200) began his refutation of Gnosticism in Book II of *Against Heresies*, he started not with the doctrine of Christ, but with what he called "the first and most important head," namely, the doctrine of "God the Creator, who made the heaven and the earth, and all things that are therein."[25]

Similarly, the Nicene Creed, which reaches back over 1600 years and is accepted by all major branches of Christianity as authoritative, begins by affirming "one God, the Father Almighty" who created "all things visible and invisible."[26] Many other affirmations of God as the Creator can be found in the early centuries of the church.[27] Far from regarding the doctrine of creation as secondary, early Christians took it as the indispensable starting point for their theology.

Why were early Christians so insistent about the doctrine of creation? One key reason is that without God as Creator, the rest of the Christian story makes very little sense. Church historian Philip Schaff rightly observed that "without a correct doctrine of creation there can be no true doctrine of redemption."[28] According to the traditional Christian narrative, redemption is understood in light of the fall, and the fall is understood in light of a prior good creation. Thus, efforts to disassociate the doctrine of creation from the doctrines of redemption and the fall are likely to result in theological incoherence.

A second reason why early Christians emphasized the doctrine of creation is that the Bible does too. According to the Bible, God "created all things" (Revelation 4:11). He is "the builder of all things" (Hebrews 3:4). He "made heaven and earth, the sea, and all that is in them" (Exodus 20:11). Not only did God create all things according to the Bible; He created them good: "And God saw everything that he had made, and behold, it was very good" (Genesis 1:31). He created things intentionally: "by your will they existed and were created" (Revelation 4:11). He created things intelligently: He "established the world by his wisdom, and by his understanding stretched out the heavens" (Jeremiah 10:12). According to the Bible, God's handiwork in nature is there for all to see: "The heavens declare the glory of God; the skies proclaim the work of his hands," declares the Psalmist in the Old Testament (Psalm 19:1 NIV). "For since the creation of the world His invisible attributes are clearly seen, being understood by the things that are made," proclaims the Apostle Paul in the New Testament (Romans 1:20 NKJV).

But there was a third key reason why early Christians emphasized the importance of God as Creator: They faced sharp opposition to the idea of God as Creator from the intellectual elites of their day.

Epicureans: Blind Material Processes Made the World

Opposition came from two distinct groups at the time of the early church. The first group, followers of the Greek atomists Democritus and Epicurus, explicitly denied that the wonders of nature were produced by a designing intelligence, asserting instead that everything ultimately arose through a blind and impersonal material process involving the chance collisions of atoms.[29]

Responding to the Epicureans' repudiation of design in nature, early Christians repeatedly argued that nature in fact provides compelling evidence that it was the product of a supreme intelligence. In their view, not only was design in nature real, it was plain and observable.

Writing in the second century, Bishop of Antioch Theophilus (AD c. 115–188) contended that "God cannot indeed be seen by human eyes, but is beheld and perceived through His providence and works."[30] What are these "works" through which we can see the intelligent activity of God? Theophilus went on to list the regularities of nature from astronomy, the plant world, the diverse species of animals, and the ecosystem. He concluded: Just "as any person, when he sees a ship on the sea rigged and in sail, and making for the harbor, will no doubt infer that there is a pilot in her who is steering her; so we must perceive that God is the governor [pilot] of the whole universe."[31]

Writing in the third century, the Bishop of Alexandria Dionysius (AD 200–265) offered similar arguments against those who claimed that the features of the universe were "only the works of common chance."[32] According to Dionysius, such persons fail to observe that "no object of any utility, fitted to be serviceable, is made without design or by mere chance, but is wrought by skill of hand, and is contrived so as to meet its proper use."[33]

Writing in the latter part of the third century and the early fourth century, Christian thinker Lactantius (AD c. 240–320) likewise declared that "it is more credible that matter was made by God, because He is all-powerful, than that the world was not made by God, because nothing can be made without mind, intelligence, and design."[34]

Such citations from the fathers of the early church could be multiplied.[35] Early Christians clearly and repeatedly taught that nature provides convincing evidence of God's design.

Gnostics: A Lesser God Made the World

Yet Epicurean materialists were not the only opponents of the idea of God as Creator in the early years of the church. Other opponents became known collectively as Gnostics. Unlike the materialists, the Gnostics considered themselves Christians. But that made matters worse in the eyes of the early leaders of the church, because it meant the Gnostics had a greater potential to confuse and mislead otherwise orthodox believers.

Most Gnostics shared two key beliefs about God and the natural world: First, they denied that nature was created good—in their view, matter was evil and the material world was flawed from the start. Second, because the material world was evil, the Gnostics denied that God created it. Instead, they claimed that the world was created by another entity, usually called the Demiurge. In creating the world, the Demiurge acted as if he were God, but in fact he operated blindly and ignorantly apart from God. According to Hippolytus, the Gnostics taught that "the Demiurge... knows nothing at all, but is, according to them, devoid of understanding, and silly, and is not conscious of what he is doing or working at... he himself imagines that he evolves the creation of the world out of himself."[36] The Gnostics' point was to disassociate God from any direct role in His creation, and thereby to deny that the world was the intentional and good result of God's specific design.

The leaders of the early church rejected the Gnostics' effort to distance God from His creation. Indeed, according to Irenaeus, the Gospel of John was written in part to counter these teachings of the Gnostics, especially those of an early Gnostic known as Cerinthus: "Cerinthus... taught that the world was not made by the primary God, but by a certain Power far separated from him, and at a distance from that Principality who is supreme over the universe, and ignorant of him who is above all."[37] John countered this claim, insisting in the opening lines of his gospel that "all things were made through" Christ who was God himself—not, by implication, through a secondary entity like the Demiurge.

This poses a problem for those today who intimate that Christians can dispense with the doctrine of God as Creator so long as they affirm Christ. In John 1:3, the Apostle John couldn't be any clearer: If one denies that God was the direct agent of creation, one is also denying Christ. The same teaching is articulated by the Apostle Paul in Colossians (Colossians 1:16) and by the writer of the Epistle to the Hebrews (Hebrews 1:2).

God as Creator

In the following centuries of the church, most Christian thinkers continued to embrace a robust view of nature showing evidence of God as Creator. Medieval theologian Thomas Aquinas argued that the rational operations of nature required "some intelligent being... by whom all natural things are directed to their end."[38] Reformation theologian John Calvin likewise argued that "both the heavens and the earth present us with innumerable proofs" of God's "wondrous wisdom."[39] This included the human body itself: "all men acknowledge that the human body bears on its face such proofs of ingenious contrivance as are sufficient to proclaim the admirable wisdom of its maker."[40]

None of this is to deny that faithful Christians have differed throughout history about how certain biblical passages should be interpreted in light of the human study of nature. For example, Christians have disagreed on the age of the earth and universe, and they have disagreed about how to understand the "days" in Genesis 1.

However, despite these disagreements about precisely how God created the world, there was an overwhelming consensus on two main points: (1) God intentionally and purposefully created the world as something good; and (2) God's intelligent design of creation can be plainly understood through our observation of nature. This consensus dominated Western thinking and culture for much of the past two millennia.

The consensus also encouraged the rise of modern science. Because early scientists thought nature was the product of intelligent design, they expected nature to be orderly, purposeful, governed by laws rather than chaos, and understandable through human reason. In the words of C. S. Lewis, "Men became scientific because they expected Law in Nature, and they expected Law in Nature because they believed in a Legislator."[41]

Sociologist Rodney Stark noted that "the leading scientific figures in the sixteenth and seventeenth centuries overwhelmingly were devout Christians who believed it their duty to comprehend God's handiwork."[42] He further claimed that "Christian theology was essential for the rise of science."[43] Even scholars who won't go that far acknowledge the positive relationship between the biblical worldview and the rise of science. In the words of historian Peter Harrison, "the Bible played a significant role in the development of modern science."[44]

Then something happened.

The Rise of "Scientific" Materialism

As previously discussed, the idea that nature is the product of blind material forces was part of the cultural debate in the early years of the church. Nevertheless, this kind of materialism was a hard sell for most of human history. After all, in our own actual experience, we don't see exquisitely functional and beautiful things being produced by unguided material processes. To use a famous example, we don't see jet airplanes being produced by tornadoes ripping through junkyards.

Why, then, should we expect to see molecular machines, working bodies, and finely tuned ecosystems produced by unguided processes? This seemed like simple common sense to most people.

After the rise of modern science, however, more thinkers began to argue that common sense was wrong. They claimed that science now proved that everything could be wholly explained by blind matter and energy. Thus, "scientific" materialism was born. By the end of the nineteenth century, it had begun to take over elite culture. English writer Hugh Elliot encapsulated the new view among elites when he wrote in 1919: "It may be said with truth that we are all materialists now."[45]

Charles Darwin: Unguided Processes

Charles Darwin played a pivotal role in the story of the hijacking of science on behalf of materialism. It's not because Darwin proposed that life had a long history. Lots of other people had proposed that. Nor is it primarily because he proposed the speculative idea that humans and other animals evolved from simpler organisms; other people had proposed that as well.

No, the truly radical part of Darwin's theory for culture was that Darwin thought he had discovered a mechanism that showed how life and morality and even religion developed as the product of a blind and unguided material process. That mechanism was natural selection (or survival of the fittest) acting on random variations found throughout nature.

The basic process is supposed to work like this: One or more organisms in a population might have a small accidental difference from other organisms in the population (let's call the difference "Trait A"). Organisms with Trait A survive and reproduce more than organisms without it. So over time, organisms with Trait A come to dominate the population. The population has "evolved" a new trait. This process repeats itself again and again with other traits. Over a long period of time, new traits accumulate in specific organisms, resulting in dramatically new kinds of organisms—all developed by trial and error without any preconceived plan or the guidance of a master planner.

It's critically important to understand that last point: Darwin thought this process of "natural" selection was unguided. You can have a type of guided evolution, but that's not what Darwin proposed, and that's not the mainstream theory of evolution today. In Darwin's words, "The old argument of design in nature... which formerly seemed to me so conclusive, fails, now that the law of natural selection has been discovered... There seems to be no more design in the variability of organic beings and in the action of natural selection, than in the course which the wind blows."[46]

Darwin's greatest contribution, according to materialist thinkers, was to kill the view that nature displays evidence of teleology (purpose). For example, Karl Marx wrote to a correspondent in 1861 that in Darwin's work "for the first time, 'teleology' in natural science is... dealt a mortal blow."[47]

The initial impact of Darwin's radical idea on Christians was muted. That's because Darwin was only partly successful in persuading his scientific peers of his claims. Although most scientists eventually accepted Darwin's idea that living things evolved over time, many remained skeptical on scientific grounds that his mechanism of natural selection was adequate.[48] They thought that unguided natural selection was insufficient to explain the development of all the dramatically different kinds of life forms we see on Earth.

Instead, according to historian Peter Bowler, there was widespread acceptance of the idea "that evolution was an essentially purposeful process... The human mind and moral values were seen as the intended outcome of a process that was built into the very fabric of nature and that could thus be interpreted as the Creator's plan."[49] Indeed, even the co-discoverer of the theory of evolution by natural selection, Alfred Russel Wallace, believed that the evidence from nature demonstrated that a cosmic mind was required to explain the development of many key features of life.[50]

Because so many scientists continued to reject unguided natural selection as an adequate explanation for living things, Christians in the nineteenth century who embraced evolution were able to argue for a kind of "theistic" evolution where God himself continued to direct the development of all life according to his preconceived plan, and where humans represented the intentional and unique culmination of God's creative activity.

However, the landscape of scientific and cultural opinion changed dramatically in the twentieth century. Darwin's theory received an infusion from the rising discipline of genetics, giving birth to what became known as "neo-Darwinism." Neo-Darwinism proposed that random mutations in genes provided the accidental variations natural selection needed to build new life forms. Like Darwin's original theory, neo-Darwinism emphasized the emergence and development of life as part of an impersonal and unintelligent process.

Neo-Darwinism's unguided version of evolution was soon adopted by the scientific establishment. It went on to provide inspiration for a new generation of "scientific" atheists.[51] Like the Epicurean materialists of old, these atheists repeatedly asserted that nature is the product of impersonal material forces rather than intelligent guidance. In the words of biologist Richard Dawkins, "the universe we observe has precisely the properties we should expect if there is, at bottom, no design, no purpose, no evil and no good, nothing but blind pitiless indifference."[52] While materialists in the ancient world drew from the atomic theories of Democritus and Leucippus for support, contemporary atheists are inspired largely by Charles Darwin and by the evolutionists who further developed his theory, because they supposedly showed how the apparent design observed throughout nature was produced by a blind and undirected process.

Can Christianity and Neo-Darwinism Be Reconciled?

Once neo-Darwinism was crowned king in science, Christians who hoped to reconcile their faith with evolution had dwindling options. One response was to challenge the scientific and philosophical shortcomings of Darwinian theory head on. As we shall see, there are plenty of problems with the theory, beginning with evolutionists' continued inability to demonstrate even the evolution of a fundamentally new bacterial or protein type from an earlier form, much less the evolution of all life from a single-celled organism. But taking on modern evolutionary theory invited snubs, persecution, and accusations of "creationism"— even if the focus was wholly on the scientific weaknesses of evolutionary theory, without reference to religious texts or tenets.

Another approach was to continue to champion a truly guided form of evolution, in which evolution unfolded according to a clear and specific plan that was conceived of and supervised by God. But this classic form of "theistic evolution" now invited cultural rejection, because the mainstream scientific view of evolution in the era of "neo-Darwinism" was clearly unguided and left little room for God or any kind of purposeful process planned by a creator.

A third option was to try to revise historic Christianity to make it fit within the straitjacket of neo-Darwinism. Instead of proposing that God intentionally planned the creation of new kinds of living things and specifically guided any evolutionary process to create them, efforts were made to downplay or even deny God's creative activity and foresight in bringing about new life forms, or at least to deny that we can see evidence of these in biology. For the sake of simplicity, I'll refer to this third option as "modern theistic evolution," although it's sometimes called other names like "evolutionary creation" or "biologos" (the term favored by Francis Collins). "Theistic" is also something of a misnomer, for that word implies an involved creator who is active in guiding the development of life.

Unfortunately, it's this third way that has been the preferred approach embraced by many Christian intellectuals over the past few decades. As we will see, the approach is like attempting to pound the proverbial square peg into a round hole. Something has to give way to make the effort work, and that something has been foundational biblical beliefs.

Darwin's Corrosive Idea

Secular philosopher Daniel Dennett has praised Darwinian theory as a "universal acid" because in his view it eats away traditional beliefs about religion, morality, and human responsibility.[53] Proponents of modern theistic evolution promise to neutralize Darwinism's universal acid by reconciling Christian theism with evolution. But they can't. The problem is that modern theistic evolution itself retains too much of Darwinism's acid. As a result, it has seriously corroded three foundational biblical beliefs for its proponents.

First, modern theistic evolution has corroded the biblical belief that God is the all-knowing Creator of everything. Traditional biblical theism claims that we and the rest of creation are wondrous products of a loving and all-wise God who intended us from eternity. But if evolution is a truly unguided process, God himself didn't control or necessarily even know what kinds of life forms evolution would produce. The late George Coyne, for example, asserted that "not even God could know... with certainty" that "human life would come to be."[54] Coyne was a Catholic priest and the Vatican's astronomer, yet clearly his views carried the implication that the biblical account of God's sovereignty, omniscience, and constant loving care must be abandoned.

Sadly, this view is not unique among Christian intellectuals who embrace theistic evolution. Like the Gnostics opposed by the early church, many of today's theistic evolutionists believe that God chose to "create" the world by setting up an undirected process over which he had no specific control and about which he did not even have foreknowledge of its particular outcomes. In a very real sense, God created a world that creates itself. Indeed, the late Anglican theistic evolutionist John Polkinghorne said exactly that: "An evolutionary universe is theologically understood as a creation allowed to make itself."[55]

A similar claim is made by Christian biologist Kenneth Miller of Brown University, author of the popular book *Finding Darwin's God*, which has been used in many Christian colleges. Miller insists that evolution is an undirected process, and flatly denies that God guided the evolutionary process to achieve any particular result—including the development of human beings. Indeed, he insists that "mankind's appearance on this planet was *not* preordained, that we are here... as an afterthought, a minor detail, a happenstance in a history that might just as well have left us out."[56]

Miller does say that God knew that the undirected process of evolution was so wonderful it would create something capable of praising Him eventually. But what that something would be was otherwise completely unpredictable. How unpredictable? At a conference where Miller and I appeared on a panel together, he said evolution could have produced "a big-brained dinosaur" or a "mollusk with exceptional mental capabilities" rather than human beings. God didn't know what it would be.[57]

Second, modern theistic evolution has corroded the biblical belief in our need for a savior. The Bible teaches that God created the world and human beings as "very good" (Genesis 1:31), and humans—made in God's image—started out moral, sinless, and in fellowship with God. Then things went awry because the first human couple freely chose to reject God. This is the reason we need a savior.

But leading proponents of theistic evolution today say that we have to jettison this view because it doesn't fit with the Darwinian story. Karl Giberson in his book *Saving Darwin* directly repudiates the idea that "sin originates in a free act of the first humans" and that "God gave humans free will and they used it to contaminate the entire creation."[58] Instead, Giberson basically argues that since we were created through Darwinian evolution, human beings were selfish and sinful to begin with. There was no Fall because there was nothing to fall from.

Like the Gnostics of old, Giberson essentially argues that the world—including the humans who inhabit it—was not created good. This makes hash of the Christian idea of salvation. If human beings were sinful to begin with, what is Christ saving us from? God's original botched job?

Prominent evolutionists who are former Christians understand this. Ron Numbers was a noted historian of science at the University of Wisconsin. By his own account, Numbers abandoned his belief in Christianity because of Darwinian evolution. According to Christianity, said Numbers, "We humans were perfect because we were created in the image of God. And then there was the fall. Death appears and the whole account [in the Bible] becomes one of deterioration and degeneration. So we then have Jesus in the New Testament, who promises redemption. Evolution completely flips that. With evolution, you don't start out with anything perfect…. There's no perfect state from which to fall. This makes the whole plan of salvation silly because there never was a fall."[59]

Third, *modern theistic evolution erodes the biblical teaching that God's activity can be clearly discerned through our observation of nature.* As discussed previously, the historic belief of both Jews and Christians is that nature supplies observable evidence of God's purposeful activity (Romans 1:20, Psalm 19).

Contrast this historic biblical belief to the views expressed by Francis Collins in his book *The Language of God.* Collins suggests that there may be evidence of design when it comes to physics and astronomy, but when it comes to biology, he thinks life looks like it developed through an unguided process.

How does Collins square this understanding of biology with his Christianity? He essentially argues that God misleads us. Perhaps God really did direct the evolution of life, says Collins. He just made the evolutionary process *look* like it was random and undirected. In Collins's words: "God *could* be completely and intimately involved in the creation of all species, while from our perspective... this would *appear* a random and undirected process."[60] (emphasis mine)

Collins's proposal that God may have made evolution *look* "random and undirected" is poor theology. It depicts God as misinforming His creatures through His creation by making it look like He didn't direct the development of life. Yet, in some ways, Collins's proposal is brilliant—at least for a Christian who wants to be accepted by secularist science. It provides a way someone could (sort of) believe in the intelligent design of life, but in a way that might not offend their secular colleagues. After all, if God truly made evolution look "random and undirected," you could fully affirm to materialist colleagues that you too believe the *scientific evidence* shows evolution is "random and undirected." Your private faith that God may have secretly directed the development of life need not be raised because it would make absolutely no difference.

Collins would no doubt contend that his embrace of evolution isn't just about secular acceptance. It's about being faithful to the scientific evidence, and in his view, the scientific evidence clearly supports evolution. Collins would likewise insist that he rejects intelligent design in the history of life because the biological evidence simply doesn't support intelligent design.

But what evidence does Collins marshal to support such a claim? There isn't space in this book to dig really deeply into this topic, but we can address some of the key pieces of evidence raised by Collins in his book *The Language of God*. That book was especially influential among Christians, convincing many that they had to embrace the idea of evolution and reject intelligent design in biology. But as it turns out, many of the scientific claims made by Collins in his book haven't aged well.

Following the Evidence

The title of Collins's book—*The Language of God*—refers to the DNA code. If you haven't read the book, you might assume from the title that Collins was arguing that DNA is intelligently designed by God. After all, it's a code, isn't it? And code requires a coder.

But that wasn't Collins's view. He asserted in the book that nearly half of the human genome is repetitive junk, or as he put it, "genetic flotsam and jetsam."[61] While conceding that "some might argue that these are actually functional elements placed there by the Creator for a good reason," Collins ended up dismissing that explanation. So in his view, DNA doesn't seem to be the language of God after all. Or at least it's a language God doesn't speak very well. "Junk" DNA nicely fits the evolutionary picture of an unguided process involving random mutations.

Unfortunately for Collins, his promotion of the idea of "junk DNA" as evidence for Darwinian evolution turned into one of the most embarrassing blunders of his career.[62]

Today the more scientists look at what they used to dismiss as "junk," the more exquisite functions they are discovering.[63] Since publication of the main results of the ENCODE project in 2012, genomics and bioinformatics research has established that the vast majority of the genome that Darwinists previously characterized as "junk" is actually biochemically functional.[64] Overall, the non-protein coding regions of the genome (previously called "junk"[65]) work much like an operating system in a computer controlling and regulating the timing and expression of other sections of code (in the biological case, the code for building proteins).[66] The scientific consensus has changed so much that a recent science journal article declared, "The days of 'junk DNA' are over!"[67] Even Collins seems to have abandoned the argument in recent years.[68]

Then there are Collins's attacks in *The Language of God* on Christian biochemist Michael Behe.[69] Behe has pointed out that many molecular systems are "irreducibly complex," meaning they require all of their parts to perform their function. Behe argues that such systems cannot be cobbled together by an unguided step-by-step process like Darwinian evolution because the individual parts don't have value for the system until they are all in place; hence, natural selection would never have selected them one at a time. Behe's most famous example of an "irreducibly complex" system is the bacterial flagellum, a sophisticated molecular propeller that enables bacteria to move through liquid.

Collins confidently assured his readers that producing the flagellum would pose no problem for Darwinian evolution because there is a less complex "type III secretory apparatus" that the flagellum could have evolved from.[70] However, scientists now think the flagellum originated *before* the type III secretory apparatus, and thus cannot have been its descendant.[71] Either the type III secretory apparatus devolved from the flagellum, or it originated independently of it. Either way, the flagellum existed first, and the secretory apparatus came later. Contra Collins, the secretory apparatus offers absolutely no explanation for how the flagellum might have come to be through a Darwinian process.[72]

Collins also offered up stickleback fish as evidence for how Darwinian evolution can build new species through many incremental steps. That example hasn't aged well either. It later turned out that the stickleback fish Collins cited represented another example of devolution, not evolution.[73] In other words, something broke. The original species of stickleback fish lost a biological feature, which led to another version of the same fish. Devolution is exactly the opposite of what

Darwinism needs. It shows that it's much easier to break something than to improve it.[74]

Many Christians were led to believe they had to embrace Darwinian theory by Collins's book. Most of them probably never bothered to read the people Collins was critiquing. They simply trusted Collins. After all, Collins was a famous scientist and a Christian, so why shouldn't they simply believe him?

Evangelizing for Darwin

Why has Collins been so insistent in trying to convince his fellow Christians to embrace Darwin? Why not simply accept the differences of opinion and focus more on reaching agnostics and atheists for Christ? Or why not simply focus on the positive role Christianity has played in the origin and development of science?

I think I understand why. For Christians who place a high value on cultural acceptance, the Darwin holdouts in their midst are a continuing embarrassment. Being confused for one of them can taint your reputation or derail your career. So it's far better to delegitimize them by never sharing a platform or engaging in debate with them, no matter what their credentials or how thoughtful their arguments. I know the mindset, and I've known a lot of fellow evangelical academics who think this way and see a fellow traveler in Collins.

Collins's interest in neutralizing Christians who raise scientific critiques of unguided evolution reaches back many years. Peter Wehner—a political appointee in the George W. Bush administration—reported that he and Bush speechwriter Michael Gerson had met Collins for lunch at the White House to strategize about "prominent Christians who were denying evolution, which we knew was anti-science and we believed was discrediting to the Christian witness."[75] Thus was born Collins's years-long crusade to delegitimize fellow Christian scientists, scholars, and laypeople skeptical of Darwinian evolution or supportive of intelligent design in biology.

In the foreword to one book, Collins characterized Christians who question Darwinian evolution as peddling "lies" and promoting "anti-scientific thinking."[76] In the endorsement of another book,

Collins gravely warned that intelligent design "is not only bad science but is potentially threatening in other deeper ways to America's future."[77]

As part of his efforts, Collins expressed a desire to bring together leading scientists, theologians, and pastors in order to "develop a new theology."[78] That led to his founding of the BioLogos Foundation with physicist Karl Giberson and biologist Darrel Falk.[79] The primary goal of the Foundation wasn't to witness to atheists or defend Christianity against scientific materialists. It was to change the minds of evangelical Christians who refused to get with the program and embrace Darwinian evolution like he did.

The creation of BioLogos was part of a multi-year initiative by the John Templeton Foundation, which spent more than twenty million dollars between 1996 and 2010 on projects that promoted theistic evolution as a major part of their mission.[80] Starting in 2009, BioLogos convened a series of closed-door gatherings of key evangelical Christian pastors, theologians, journalists, and other opinion-makers as part of its agenda of "promoting dialog,"[81] which had been one of Collins's stated goals: "I think it's critical that we have a meaningful dialogue between people of faith and people involved in science."[82]

But the range of scientific voices permitted at the meetings was sharply limited. Leading scientists and philosophers of science who were critical of neo-Darwinism or supportive of intelligent design in biology were excluded. Why? If Collins and other scientists had engaged in dialogue with scientists who held opposing viewpoints, wouldn't that have benefited the cause of truth, exposing lazy or poorly considered arguments and evidence on either side of the discussion? But instead of fostering open discussion of this kind, they went out of their way to quash any such opportunities.

Unfortunately, the effort to exclude critics of theistic evolution from the conversation was aided by many other leading evangelicals.

"Meaningful Dialogue" or Monologue?

Tim Keller was probably the most influential evangelical Presbyterian minister in the United States at the time. The founding pastor of

Redeemer Presbyterian Church in New York City, Keller was a beloved mentor to many evangelical leaders. By all accounts, he was gracious, kind, and gave generously of his time to others. In the late 1990s, my wife and I had the opportunity to visit his church in Manhattan. Joining more than a thousand people for worship on a Sunday morning in the heart of one of America's most important cities was inspiring.

Keller served as a minister in the theologically conservative Presbyterian Church in America. His denomination was on record as critical of Darwinian evolution.[83] Yet Keller was perhaps the person most responsible for giving Collins a one-sided platform to promote theistic evolution among evangelical leaders. The private meetings BioLogos put on to influence evangelical opinion-makers were hosted by Tim Keller, and Keller's glowing endorsement of BioLogos appeared prominently for many years on the BioLogos website.

Keller could have told Collins that he would only host the gatherings if Collins agreed to support real dialogue by including at least some Christian scientists who disagreed with his view. But he didn't.

Keller wasn't even willing to host a similar gathering that would bring evangelical opinion-makers together to hear credible scientists who disagreed with Darwinian evolution. In late 2010, I invited him to do just that. I had identified a Christian foundation willing to fund the event, and the Center for Science and Culture (which I help direct) would have handled all the logistics. I told him in my letter that "we are happy to schedule a meeting at a time and place that works for your schedule."

When Keller's assistant eventually responded, she indicated that "as much as Tim would like to do this, we have looked and don't see a way he could fit it in for at least the next couple of years." This was essentially a brush-off, despite the assistant adding that "the idea does appeal to him, so maybe at a later time something could work out." I had not limited the invitation to a specific time period. He could have named any time he liked, however far into the future.

Instead, Keller participated in another private gathering for BioLogos.

Keller wasn't the only prominent evangelical to assist Collins in his effort to silence debate over Darwinism among Christians.

Evangelical scholar Michael Cromartie was vice president of the influential Ethics and Public Policy Center in Washington DC. Starting in 1999, he organized a series of private gatherings for journalists to hear from leading voices in the faith community. The idea was to help journalists better understand people of faith so their reporting would be accurate and not filled with caricatures. When covering science and faith issues related to evolution, however, Cromartie only invited speakers who were proponents of theistic evolution.

I knew Cromartie personally, and we were on friendly terms for many years. After he invited the first theistic evolutionist to talk about evolution and intelligent design at one of his private meetings, I privately urged him to consider another event where proponents of intelligent design could speak for themselves. After all, if the goal was to disabuse journalists of their stereotypes, what better way than allow them to hear directly from people they otherwise wouldn't talk to?

At the time of our conversation, Mike told me that unfortunately they wouldn't be covering the issue of evolution again for the foreseeable future, because he had to do the topics that the journalists wanted, and they could only do the evolution issue so many times.

Imagine my surprise when a little over a year later, Mike held another one of his meetings with journalists, and the session largely focused on evolution again. This time the speaker was none other than Francis Collins himself.

A few years later, Cromartie went a step further and accepted funding from the BioLogos Foundation to bring a series of theistic evolution proponents to his private meetings with journalists. To my knowledge, Mike never tried to include a divergent point of view in any of the sessions.

Mike was a good and decent man who did fine work in many areas. Tragically, he later died of cancer. I think he shows how even otherwise fair-minded people can be roped into embracing Stockholm Syndrome Christianity.

But it wasn't just individual evangelicals who helped marginalize anyone who dissented from theistic evolution. It was also evangelical institutions.

The Council for Christian Colleges and Universities is the organization representing many evangelical colleges and universities. In 2010, they held the International Forum on Christian Higher Education in Atlanta, Georgia, attracting over a thousand attendees. They invited Francis Collins to address the forum to promote theistic evolution and attack intelligent design.[84] No one was invited to present a different view.

Christianity Today has long been considered the flagship magazine for evangelical Christians, in part because it was originally founded by iconic evangelist Billy Graham. The magazine used to regularly cover critical scientific voices in the Darwin debate. But post-Collins, it has largely embraced theistic evolution.

The same is true of InterVarsity Press (IVP), one of the top evangelical Christian book publishers. In the 1990s and early 2000s, it published many books critical of Darwin and supportive of intelligent design, most notably the bestseller *Darwin on Trial* (1991) by law professor Phillip Johnson[85] and *The Design Revolution* by mathematician William Dembski.[86] But once Collins and BioLogos came on the scene, IVP pretty much shut the door to anything other than theistic evolution.

This isn't mere supposition. In an unguarded moment, one IVP editor told a prospective author that the publishing house was no longer interested in works from scholars who questioned neo-Darwinism or favored intelligent design. Indeed, the editor baldly stated in an email, "To reject neo-Darwinism is to reject the modern synthesis, and I'm not interested in apologetic works that oppose this synthesis." Another staff person at IVP later assured me that this editor had misspoken. But no more books favorable to intelligent design were forthcoming.

The modern theistic evolutionists' rationale for excluding scientific views critical of Darwinism from faith-evolution discussions seems to be that Darwinian theory constitutes the consensus view of science, and questioning that consensus view supposedly demonstrates that one is "anti-science."

But this way of thinking betrays a strikingly unsophisticated understanding of science.

True Science Values Debate

The more one knows about the history of the scientific enterprise, the more skeptical he or she is likely to be about equating the current consensus view of science with science itself. Science is a wonderful human enterprise, but scientists can be just as blinded by their prejudices as anyone else.

In the last century, for example, the nation's leading evolutionary biologists at such institutions as Harvard, Princeton, Columbia, and Stanford enthusiastically promoted eugenics, the "science" of breeding better humans based on the principles of Darwinian biology. Eugenics was the "consensus" view of the scientific community for decades.[87] That did not make it good science. Eugenics provides a stark reminder about the susceptibility of even mainstream scientists to junk science.

Far from being anti-science, dissenting views in the scientific community help science thrive by counteracting groupthink and sparking debates that can lead to fresh discoveries. It is not too much to say that today's dissenting opinion in science may well turn into tomorrow's scientific consensus. So what is truly "anti-science" is to claim that the consensus view of evolutionary theory is all that matters, or that anyone who dissents from modern evolutionary orthodoxy is guilty of "opposing science."

A Growing Number of Scientists Are Questioning Darwinism

Skepticism toward modern Darwinism's all-encompassing claims regarding natural selection and random mutation is far more widespread among scientists than most people realize. In 2016 the Royal Society, arguably the most venerable and prestigious scientific group in the world, met to detail their dissatisfactions with modern evolutionary theory. The speakers described the many problems evolutionary theory has failed to solve, yet offered nothing in the way of credible solutions. One speaker, James Shapiro of the University of Chicago, even emphasized non-random processes and pre-programmed capacities that run directly counter to Darwinian theory.[88] The sad state of Darwinian theory is no secret among mainstream evolutionary biologists.

Growing numbers of scientists and philosophers are offering sophisticated critiques of the power of undirected natural selection and random variation from within science itself.[89] For example, research published by molecular biologist Douglas Axe in the *Journal of Molecular Biology* shows the astonishing rarity of certain working protein sequences, raising significant questions about how a blind process of natural selection acting on random mutations could generate them. In the words of Axe, the rarity of these working protein sequences among all the possible combinations is "less than one in a trillion trillion trillion trillion trillion trillion."[90] Before nature can build animals like mice, muskrats, or men, it first needs to build working protein sequences. If Darwinian evolution cannot account for the generation of such sequences, it can hardly account for the development of living organisms with even higher levels of complexity.

Similarly, multi-year experiments by University of Wisconsin-Superior biologist Ralph Seelke demonstrate the sharp limits of what natural selection can do to evolve new functions in bacteria. Seelke explained that he has tested "the ability of evolution to produce a new function when two changes are both needed at effectively the same time... in a population of trillions of bacteria and over thousands of generations."[91] The results? "A requirement for two changes effectively stops evolution."

Here's how bad the situation is for unguided evolutionary processes: Despite the high cost of publicly airing one's doubts about Darwin, more than one thousand doctoral scientists—from institutions such as Princeton, Ohio State, University of Michigan, and MIT—have signed a statement expressing their skepticism that the Darwinian mechanism is capable of explaining the complexity of life.[92]

One of the signers of the statement was National Academy of Sciences member Philip Skell, formerly the Evan Pugh Professor of Chemistry at Penn State University, one of America's major research universities. Skell stated: "Darwinian evolution has functioned more as a philosophical belief system than as a testable scientific hypothesis. This quasi-religious function of the theory is... why many scientists make public statements about the theory that they would not defend privately to other scientists."[93]

That's a problem. If scientists are clinging blindly to their personal worldview preferences, or remaining on the Darwinian bandwagon primarily to avoid blowback from their peers, then they're no longer prioritizing the pursuit of truth.

Happily, some top scientists, not to content to play it safe their entire careers, are now explicitly advancing the view that nature shows clear evidence of intelligent design. That was the message of the book *Foresight*, published in 2019 by Brazilian chemist Marcos Eberlin, a member of Brazil's National Academy of Sciences. Eberlin's book was endorsed by multiple Nobel-Prize winning scientists.[94] One of those Nobel laureates, physicist Brian Josephson of Cambridge University, later stated that "intelligent design is valid science."[95]

Making Concessions for No Good Reason

Before theologians and pastors decide to reinvent their theology in order to make it consistent with undirected Darwinism, they first ought to make sure that undirected Darwinism is true. But that cannot be done by listening only to the so-called consensus view of science. It also requires hearing the views of reasoned dissenters from the consensus.

When scientific dissenters aren't allowed to be heard, theologians and pastors may end up making embarrassing theological concessions that aren't required by the science. A good case in point: In its earliest years, BioLogos advanced the view that genetics had refuted the traditional Christian teaching that the human race began with an initial ancestral couple. BioLogos scientists asserted that to account for current genetic diversity, the earliest population of humans would have to number in the thousands, not just two people. So according to BioLogos, you could believe in an Adam and Eve—but only if you redefined them so they weren't the ancestors of the entire human race. In the words of Darrel Falk, BioLogos's president at the time, "there was never a time when there was a single first couple, two people who were the progenitors of the entire human race."[96] BioLogos's claim that modern genetics disproved the idea of an original ancestral couple was spread far and wide by its friends and supporters, including in a lengthy and largely uncritical article published by *Christianity Today*.[97]

Yet BioLogos's claim turned out to be wrong. My colleague biologist Ann Gauger was one of the first to refute it, followed by biologist Richard Buggs in England. Eventually even some scientists who advocate theistic evolution questioned the claim as well. In fact, current genetic diversity *can* be accounted for by an initial couple, and "science" does not rule out the existence of an original couple as the ancestors of the entire human race.[98]

BioLogos eventually quietly revised its original claim. But the damage had been done. Many Christians had been misled about what the science shows because many faith leaders were not interested in subjecting BioLogos's claim to robust scrutiny from scientists who disagreed.

Christian scientists like Collins who want to exclude scientific critics of undirected evolution from faith-and-science discussions betray an extraordinary level of insecurity. If the evidence for unguided Darwinism is really as overwhelming as they think, they should have nothing to fear from an open exchange of ideas.

Unfortunately, the intolerant and dismissive attitude displayed by Collins is not an outlier among evangelical Christian intellectuals. The same attitude is endemic at many evangelical Christian colleges and universities, as I discovered during my own academic career.

How to Get in Trouble at a Christian College

If you believed in intelligent design on my campus, you were definitely wise to keep it to yourself. And if you went beyond intelligent design and were, say, a biblical creationist—well, then, you might just as well leave.[99]

I recall being at lunch with some faculty colleagues, when a biology professor was bad-mouthing a young woman biology student because she was a "creationist." For this male professor that was tantamount to heresy. He basically boasted about trying to get this student to leave. Good riddance, in his view.

Needless to say, if you doubted Darwin, it's not something you'd want to let people know about in your job interviews on campus. I fortunately didn't become involved in the debate over Darwin until after

I had been hired. Otherwise I doubt I would have made it through the selection process. Even though I was in the Political Science Department, not Biology, certain litmus tests prevailed across campus.

When I did become involved in the Darwin debate, I got into plenty of trouble. I started organizing events on campus with speakers who challenged Darwinism. One was a campus screening of *Icons of Evolution*, a documentary for which I wrote the screenplay. Based on a book by biologist Jonathan Wells, the film tells the story of a high school science teacher who faces censorship and retaliation for trying to correct errors and overstatements about evolution that persist in school textbooks.

I tried to set up a panel with diverse voices for the post-screening discussion, inviting faculty from the biology department to participate. They didn't want to, which was certainly their right.

But the event sparked a faculty controversy about the limits of academic freedom. The very faculty who wanted carte blanche to argue that the Bible was riddled with errors now argued that holding a campus event that might offend the views of other colleagues was somehow a violation of Christian community. In other words, you had to get permission to speak from other faculty, which essentially made academic freedom a dead letter. The majority wanted a veto right to muzzle even the handful of dissenters on campus.

Of course, the people who suffered the most from faculty group-think about evolution on our campus were students. I recall the mother of one young woman telling me about how her daughter was reduced to tears after taking biology classes at SPU.

How did my faculty colleagues square their personal belief in God as Creator with a blind evolutionary process? At the time, Kenneth Miller's book *Finding Darwin's God* was the go-to source for many theistic evolutionists, and that was the book assigned to students on our campus. Miller, you might recall, is the one who argued that God himself doesn't know how evolution will turn out.

I soon learned that acceptance of Darwinism by a faculty member correlated with the holding of other less-than-orthodox views. For example, theology professors who embraced theistic evolution also tended to support open theism, which was discussed in the last chapter. It made sense: It's much easier to justify an evolutionary process not specifically guided by God if you believe that God can't actually know the future even if he wanted to.

Similarly, some of my same colleagues who supported theistic evolution also promoted the idea that humans are reducible to their physical bodies. We do not possess immaterial or immortal souls, they said. We go out of existence after death just like the scientific materialists claim.

What about the biblical promise of a resurrection and eternal life? According to them, apparently God eventually recreates us from scratch at some point in the future from his memory of us. In what sense God is resurrecting the same person if we have ceased to exist is unclear.

This is not historic Christian teaching, no matter what my colleagues tried to claim. And what was driving it was not the biblical text. The view was being offered as a necessary accommodation to modern neuroscience, which my colleagues sincerely believed had shown that our minds and selves could be reduced to our physical brains and bodies. (This is another idea, by the way, which is losing favor even among many mainstream scientists.[100])

You see, once you've made an idol of secularist science, it's the god that won't stop taking. You become captive to whatever claim happens to be made in the name of the current consensus—even if those claims aren't really based on science, and even if those claims repudiate historic Christian teachings.

As we will see in the next chapter, the impact of secularist science has had an especially devastating impact on Christians when it comes to ideas about sex and gender.

3. Sexual Suicide

Stockholm Syndrome Christians'
Damaged Understanding of Sex and Gender

ACCORDING TO GALLUP, 72 PERCENT OF AMERICANS NOW BELIEVE "sex between an unmarried man and woman" is "morally acceptable." Nearly 80 percent believe divorce is. And seven in ten Americans think "having a baby outside marriage" is moral.[1]

These views represent a sea change in American public opinion, not only over the past century, but over just the past couple of decades.

As recently as 2001, only 53 percent of Americans thought sex outside of marriage was moral, and less than five in ten Americans thought having babies out of wedlock was acceptable. Most Americans had already embraced the morality of divorce by the turn of the century, but even its approval rate in 2001 was still nineteen points less than in 2023.

Christians have not been immune to the sea change.

According to a nationwide survey in 2019, half of all self-identified Christians now agree that "casual sex between consenting adults who are not in a committed relationship" is sometimes or always acceptable. Even 36 percent of evangelical Christians say the same thing.[2]

The Christian community's failure to disciple the next generation with biblical standards of sexuality could be seen during the 2019 season of the popular television show *Bachelorette*.

Two of the show's stars that season, Hannah Brown and Luke Parker, were evangelical Christians. Both acknowledged previously having had sex outside of marriage. Luke said he was now trying to be abstinent until he married. Luke thought he and Hannah were on the same page. But as the season progressed, it became clear they weren't.[3] When Luke raised with Hannah the issue of not having sex before marriage, she became angry. She ended up boasting about having had sex four times in a one-night stand with one of the other contestants on the show.[4] She previously had gone bungee-jumping naked with a third contestant.[5]

Hannah—who, again, was outspoken in the media about being a Christian—gave the following responses when challenged about her behavior on the show:

- "It's my body."[6]
- "I'm a grown woman, and I can make my own decisions."[7]
- "I can do whatever, I sin daily, and Jesus still loves me... and if the Lord doesn't judge me, and it's all forgiven, then no other man, woman, animal, anything can judge me."[8]

Hannah was certainly right that we all sin daily—and that Jesus still loves us. This is an amazing truth. But it is *so* amazing, so gracious—so undeserved—that we shouldn't take it for granted or treat it like it means nothing. Hannah's public comments came tragically close to suggesting that God doesn't care whether we follow his standards or not, and that God forgives us even when we're unrepentant—indeed, even if we seem to boast about trashing his standards.

That is not what the Bible teaches about any kind of sin, sexual or otherwise.

I'm not trying to be hard on Ms. Brown. Her messed-up life—and her messed-up view of God—should be an occasion for sadness. Here is the point: Hannah Brown was not the product of Seattle or San Francisco or New York. Hannah Brown was raised in the heart of the Bible Belt in Alabama. If Christians in the Bible Belt are failing to disciple young believers like Hannah with solid teaching about sex, that should be a wake-up call.

Of course, the problem extends far beyond the Bible Belt.

Estimates vary, but large numbers of self-identified Christians today have sex outside of marriage, use pornography, and divorce each other. In his sobering book *After the Revolution*, Christian sociologist David Ayers carefully presents the data, and it's disturbing. "The overwhelming majority of evangelical singles engage in sex outside marriage," he writes. "Large percentages are extremely promiscuous."[9] Just how promiscuous? "Roughly six in ten [evangelical] men and more than four in ten [evangelical] women have had three or more sexual partners other than their spouse."[10]

Three or *more* sexual partners. This isn't just people cohabiting with the one person they choose to marry later, although that also is a growing issue among evangelical Christians.

The disconnect between evangelical Christians and historic Christian teachings on sex happens early. Among evangelicals 18–29 years old, already only 40 percent think that sex between unmarried adults is "always wrong" or "almost always wrong."[11]

And the fracturing of a Christian consensus about sex now extends to the definition of marriage itself.

Redefining Marriage

According to Gallup, an overwhelming majority of Americans now approve of same-sex marriages. This includes 70 percent of Americans who attend church up to a few times a month. Only weekly churchgoers are holdouts, and even their support for same-sex marriage has doubled from 20 percent in 2004 to 40 percent in 2022.[12]

This represents another massive shift in public opinion. In 1996, less than a third of Americans supported same-sex marriage.[13]

The new cultural consensus is the culmination of an aggressive multi-year push to normalize same-sex unions. Much of this push came from non-Christians, and many faithful Christians did try to counter it. At the same time, we need to face an uncomfortable truth: This change in public opinion was also made possible because of the inaction, cooperation, and even active support of many Christians.

Between 2005 and June 2015, when the United States Supreme Court declared a constitutional right to gay marriage, increasing numbers of self-identified Christian leaders and Christian denominations moved to support same-sex marriage in various ways.

In 2005, the United Church of Christ endorsed same-sex marriages.[14] In 2009, the Evangelical Lutheran Church of America effectively recognized the right of local congregations to conduct gay weddings.[15] In early 2015, the Presbyterian Church USA redefined marriage to include same-sex unions.[16]

Leading clergy and theologians added their voices of support to the movement.

Adam Hamilton is pastor of what Wikipedia describes as "one of the largest United Methodist congregations in the world" in Leawood, Kansas.[17] According to his own description, he used to consider himself a "traditionalist."[18] Hamilton is a gifted Bible teacher. When I was the elder in charge of adult Christian education at one of the churches where I served, I used some of his studies for Advent and Lent. They contained solid teaching.

Yet in 2014 Hamilton publicly renounced the Bible's traditional teaching on same-sex sexual relationships. He claimed that one could be a faithful Christian and support same-sex unions. In his words, "it is possible to be a faithful Christian who loves God and loves the Scriptures and at the same time to believe that the handful of verses on same-sex intimacy are like the hundreds of passages accepting and regulating slavery or other practices we today believe do not express the heart and character of God."[19]

During the same year, Seattle-area megachurch EastLake Community Church held its first gay wedding. It later publicly expressed a full affirmation of gay sexuality, leading *TIME* magazine to profile the church's pastor, Ryan Meeks, in early 2015. "I refuse to go to a church where my friends who are gay are excluded from Communion or a marriage covenant or the beauty of Christian community," Meeks told the writer for *TIME*. "It is a move of integrity for me—the message of Jesus was a message of wide inclusivity."[20]

To those who might regard his position as heresy, Meeks responded: "Every positive reforming movement in church history is first labeled heresy. Evangelicalism is way behind on this. We have a debt to pay."

Lobbying groups and activists added their well-funded voices to the fray. Matthew Vines, a twenty-something who identified as both gay and evangelical, founded the Reformation Project in 2013 to convince evangelicals to accept the legitimacy of same-sex sexual relationships.[21] Evangelicals for Marriage Equality likewise lobbied for the legitimacy of same-sex marriages.[22]

Keeping Their Heads Down

Some leading pastors who did not renounce traditional biblical teaching on homosexuality tried to avoid the topic as much as possible, and when they did speak, they were muddled.

Andy Stanley, so outspoken on many topics, found it hard to publicly affirm biblical teaching on same-sex relationships. In 2012, he spoke in a sermon about a couple where the man left his wife for another man. The man and his new partner moved to another campus of Stanley's church, but when Stanley found out he wouldn't let them volunteer at the new campus. Why? The man who left his wife hadn't divorced her yet, and so that was adultery. Stanley said nothing about the elephant in the room: the same-sex nature of the relationship. It was as if he did not think it was a problem.[23]

Biblical studies professor Dennis Burk found Stanley's sermon "troubling," commenting: "It was ambiguous at best. It was a total capitulation to the spirit of the age at worst."[24]

In 2015, to a conference of church leaders, Stanley stressed the importance of churches being welcoming to gays, but he was again unwilling to address whether same-sex relationships were acceptable. He merely stated that Christians disagreed: "There is not consensus in this room when it comes to same-sex attraction. There is not consensus in this room when it comes to gay marriage."[25]

A beacon of moral clarity, he was not.

Then there was the late Rev. Tim Keller, founding pastor of the megachurch Redeemer Presbyterian Church in New York City. Unlike Stanley, Keller was willing to publicly—if briefly—state that same-sex unions were inconsistent with biblical teaching. In 2009, Keller signed onto the "Manhattan Declaration," an ecumenical statement supporting the sanctity of life, traditional marriage, and religious liberty.[26] But as the biblical understanding of same-sex relationships became more controversial, Keller seemed to avoid talking about the topic as much as possible. When he did discuss the issue, the normally clear and articulate communicator could become halting, hesitant, and seemingly embarrassed by the biblical view.

Asked by a seminary student in 2010 about how to deal with the topic, Keller—clearly uncomfortable—stumbled through his answer. He indicated that while he might have to reference the biblical position in a sermon, he never wanted to preach a whole sermon on the topic. It would be too controversial for some of the people attending his church. Instead, he preferred to handle things behind the scenes, with non-public instruction to church staff.[27]

After reviewing a number of Keller's public statements on the topic, Presbyterian theologian Robert Gagnon expressed disappointment: "For a pastor who has no trouble talking about greed and social justice issues, Rev. Keller's refusal to discuss a Christian position on 'gay rights and gay marriage,' one of the central moral issues of our day, is both striking and disturbing."[28]

In 2013, Keller was asked to address gay marriage in a private meeting of journalists. To his credit, he made clear that the Bible did not support same-sex unions. But he then muddied the waters by stating that "you can believe homosexuality is a sin and still believe that same-sex marriage should be legal."[29]

Guess which statement of Keller about gay marriage made it into the press?[30]

After a backlash from some fellow Christians, Keller issued a clarification. He stated that he was merely describing one particular view some younger Christians held. "It *is* possible to hold that position," he stated, "though it isn't my position, nor was I promoting or endorsing the position."[31] He added that he did not "support the legalization of same-sex marriage."

True, Keller in his comments did not endorse the position that same-sex marriage should be legalized. But neither did he criticize the position, and by failing to criticize it or better articulate his own position, he made it easy for reporters to use his sound bite to advance support for gay marriage. At best, Keller tried to be a fence-sitter, not a leader.

How many others were encouraged into timidity by the examples of leaders like Keller and Stanley?

I was an elder at an historically evangelical urban Presbyterian church, where the staff and elders looked up to Keller and studied his books. Leadership from Keller on the gay marriage issue would have made an impact. Instead, we followed Keller's example in trying to downplay our beliefs as much as possible.

For some time, our church had included a brief statement in its weekly bulletin affirming three key truths: the truth of the Bible, the truth of Jesus as the one way of salvation, and the truth that marriage was a commitment between a man and a woman. But then the senior pastor convinced the majority of the Session (our board of elders) to remove these statements from the bulletin. The stated goal was to be more welcoming to those who visited. We wanted to de-emphasize truths they might find offensive in the hope that they would come back and develop a relationship with us.

The goal of being more welcoming to visitors was a good one, and I do not think that the pastor and elders who adopted the proposal were unfaithful to the Bible when they did so. But the action had consequences that many of them may not have anticipated.

At the time, it was promised that we would continue to emphasize these key truths in other ways. For example, the pastor would regularly preach about them, or at key times in the year we would insert something about our doctrinal commitments in our bulletin. That happened a handful of times, but then it was basically forgotten.

The result was that our church simply talked less and less about anything we feared might offend people.

When in Rome...

Christians are supposed to be salt and light in our culture. But if our salt is insipid and our light is dim and flickering, how can we expect the culture to turn out better than we are?

For that matter, if *church* leaders are muted or muddled in their declaration of biblical truth, how can we expect Christian politicians and policymakers to be any more consistent?

Former president Jimmy Carter was probably the best known "born again" Christian in American politics during the last several decades. A churchgoing Baptist, Carter was known for teaching Sunday School and helping build houses for the poor through Habitat for Humanity. A winner of the Nobel Peace Prize, Carter was admired for his sincere faith even by many who didn't share his liberal politics.

Carter's contribution to the gay marriage debate? In 2012, he opined, "I personally think it is very fine for gay people to be married in civil ceremonies."[32] By 2018, he went further, asserting that "Jesus would approve of gay marriage" and "I think Jesus would encourage any love affair if it was honest and sincere and was not damaging to anyone else and I don't see that gay marriage damages anyone else."[33] This is surely a warped view of Jesus, who said firmly that "in the beginning God made them male and female," and that as such they are able to join into one flesh.[34]

Moreover, gay marriage does hurt other people—not least children, for whom two mommies is not at all the same thing as one mother and one father. Indeed, many children of same-sex couples have spoken up to say gay marriage is yet another way children are being sacrificed on the altar of adult desires.[35]

Carter was a national figure, but there were plenty of local and regional Christian policymakers who acted similarly.

In my home state of Washington, the legislature enacted gay marriage in 2012. The legislation passed because a handful of Republican legislators joined with Democrats to support the new law. One of those deciding votes was cast by Republican state senator Cheryl Pflug.[36] Pflug was a longtime Sunday School teacher and church deacon, and the founder of a Christian preschool.[37]

In 2014, two federal district court judges declared a constitutional right to gay marriage. One judge, in Oregon, was an openly gay man appointed by Barack Obama. But the other judge, John E. Jones, was an active member of his local Lutheran church and appointed to the bench by evangelical Christian George W. Bush. Before ruling on gay marriage, Jones was best known for having declared the teaching of intelligent design in public schools unconstitutional.[38]

Just how consequential a single Christian's failure to uphold the truth can be was demonstrated on June 26, 2015. That was the date the Supreme Court of the United States finally weighed in on gay marriage.

It was the day when a majority of justices of the court invented a constitutional right to gay marriage in defiance of both history and the text of the Constitution itself. In the words of dissenting justice Antonin Scalia: "They have discovered in the Fourteenth Amendment a 'fundamental right' overlooked by every person alive at the time of ratification, and almost everyone else in the time since."[39]

The final decision in the case was rested on a 5–4 vote. Of the five justices who voted for gay marriage, four were appointed by Democratic presidents and known for politically and culturally "progressive" views. The fifth—the justice who cast the deciding vote—was not a Democrat, or an atheist or agnostic. Justice Anthony Kennedy was appointed to the court by Ronald Reagan and known as a "goody goody."[40] Kennedy was a lifelong Roman Catholic Christian, a former altar boy, and apparently attended Mass weekly.[41] And it was Kennedy who authored the majority opinion.

Let that sink in for a moment: Gay marriage was imposed on the entire United States not by an anti-Christian judge but by a self-identified, churchgoing Christian.

Again, if you think our only problem in America right now is with secularists and atheists, you are—sadly—mistaken.

By the way, June 2015 was the month Tim Keller finally chose to weigh in with an extended article rebutting claims that the Bible could be squared with homosexual unions. He wrote the article for his church newsletter. It was a very good piece.[42]

But some might have thought it was a little late.

And, following the Supreme Court decision, resistance continued to fall. By 2022, even many who had previously opposed same-sex marriage either passively or actively supported it. That year Congress passed the so-called "Respect for Marriage Act," which enshrined same-sex marriage protections in federal statutory law.[43]

The influential evangelical magazine *Christianity Today* previously opposed same-sex marriage. In 2022 it ran an article supporting the new law.[44] *Christianity Today's* current CEO is Timothy Dalrymple, who as early as 2012 had raised the suggestion of dropping opposition to legalizing gay marriage.[45] Shortly before he became CEO, he attended the gay wedding celebration of a colleague.[46]

Evangelical political commentator David French, meanwhile, had a similar conversion. Previously opposed to legalizing same-sex marriage, he now champions the new federal right to the institution. French insists he still *personally* opposes same-sex marriage. But he argues that "millions of Americans are living stable, joyful lives in LGBT families"[47] and "it would be profoundly disruptive and unjust to rip out the legal superstructure around which they've ordered their lives."[48]

Alistair Begg is senior pastor of Parkside Church in Ohio. He has his own radio show and is known for his biblical orthodoxy. Begg says he continues to uphold traditional Christian sexual standards. But he sparked controversy in 2024 after he advised a grandmother to attend the transgender wedding of her grandchild and to bring along a gift.[49] Many who respected Begg raised thoughtful objections to his advice. They agreed with Begg that Christians need to show love to LGBTQ individuals, but they argued that participating in someone's same-sex wedding would dishonor God. Just as most Christians wouldn't participate in a celebration of someone's abortion or a worship service for a pagan idol, they shouldn't participate in a same-sex wedding.

Clearly stung by the criticisms, Begg lashed out in a sermon at his church against those who criticized him.[50] In the sermon, Begg essentially branded those who criticized him as unloving and self-righteous Pharisees. Citing Jesus's parable of the prodigal son (Luke 15:11–32), Begg compared his critics to the unforgiving son who refuses to accept his wayward brother who has returned home. Of course, there was a critical difference: The prodigal son Jesus spoke about was *repentant*.

The other son was faulted for not accepting his brother's repentance. He wasn't faulted for not participating in or celebrating his brother's wayward lifestyle.

Begg was twisting Scripture, and his harsh sermon fairly reeked of self-righteousness. Originally from Scotland, he wanted to make sure no one mistook him for a backwards American fundamentalist: "I have never been a product of American fundamentalism," he declared. "I come from a world in which it is possible for people to actually grasp the fact that there are nuances in things." Sadly, his congregation broke into spontaneous applause at the end of the sermon.

Abandoning Biblical Standards

Growing acceptance of same-sex unions by many Christians shouldn't be seen in isolation. It is a symptom of what came before it. It followed decades of many Christians turning a blind eye to heterosexual promiscuity as well as rampant unbiblical divorces. Some faithful Christians and churches tried to stay faithful to biblical teaching in these areas. But too many acceded to the culture, creating conflicting messages and failing to disciple many Christians with solid teaching.

So how did we get here?

The increasing confusion among American Christians about sex isn't because the Bible doesn't offer clear and compelling guidance on the topic. The Apostle Paul urges Christians to "flee sexual immorality" (1 Corinthians 6:18). The Greek term Paul uses that is translated "sexual immorality" is *porneia*, which encompasses a wide range of behaviors, including any kind of sex between unmarried individuals. As theologian David Clyde Jones pointed out:

> *Porneia* is the general term for all illicit or immoral sexual intercourse. The specific form may sometimes be indicated by the context. If payment of wages is involved, it is *prostitution*. If it involves close relatives, it is *incest*. If it involves persons of the same sex, it is *homosexuality*. If it involves an unmarried couple, it is *unchastity*. If it involves a married person outside of marriage, it is *adultery*.[51]

The Bible's exhortation to avoid sexual immorality in general is backed up by plenty of specifics:

- According to Jesus, marriage is intended to be a life-long commitment between one man and one woman (Matthew 19:3–6). Although polygamous relationships were recorded in the Old Testament, those relationships typically showed how polygamy sowed family discord or drew people away from God. King David's multiple marriages led to civil war among warring factions of his sons. King Solomon's multiple wives led him away from worship of the true God.

- In the New Testament, Jesus presents divorce as a clear violation of God's intention for marriage and urges his followers to avoid it: "What therefore God has joined together, let not man separate" (Matthew 19:6). In the Old Testament, the prophet Malachi describes divorce as an act of faithlessness and violence (Malachi 2:13–16).

- The Ten Commandments explicitly forbid adultery (Exodus 20:14), and Christians are told to keep "the marriage bed… undefiled, for God will judge the sexually immoral and adulterous" (Hebrews 13:4).

- According to both the Old and New Testaments, same-sex sexual relationships are contrary to God's created order (Leviticus 18:22, Leviticus 20:13, Romans 1:26–27, 1 Corinthians 6:9, 1 Timothy 1:10). So are sexual relations with animals (Leviticus 18:23). So is confusing your gender identity by cross-dressing (Deuteronomy 22:5). God created human beings with only two genders: male and female (Genesis 1:27; Mark 10:6).

- Marrying people outside the faith is forbidden in the Old Testament (Deuteronomy. 7:1–4) and is likewise discouraged by applying the broader principle articulated by the Apostle Paul: "Do not be yoked together with unbelievers" (2 Corinthians 6:14).

The earliest Christians took these and other biblical commands relating to sex very seriously. Those who claim otherwise are attempting to rewrite history. As Barton Gingerich points out:

> Polycarp (student of St. John the Apostle) instructed women to be "loving all [others] equally in all chastity." Likewise, he urged young men to be "especially careful to preserve purity." Speaking of Valens (a man estranged from church discipline by his indiscretions), Polycarp taught, "I exhort you... that ye be chaste and truthful. 'Abstain from every form of evil.'" In the *Epistle of Mathetes to Diognetus*, the author famously describes Christians: "They marry, as do all [others]; they beget children; but they do not destroy their offspring. They have a common table, but not a common bed. They are in the flesh, but they do not live after the flesh." The Apostolic Fathers and their standards for the ancient church are clear. We must not form the past and its teaching to suit our wants.[52]

To be clear, there was no golden age when it comes to Christians and sex, and there has always been plenty of hypocrisy. Christians have also differed across history on the extent of the biblical justifications for divorce and remarriage. Nevertheless, we delude ourselves if we don't recognize the decisive shift that has occurred among many Christians and their leaders in recent decades.

Redefining Morality Because of "Science"

The rejection of biblical sexual morality is another cultural development that was largely justified in the name of "science." The revolution was part of a larger redefinition of morality by Charles Darwin and others. In his book *The Descent of Man*, Darwin argued that specific moral precepts develop because under certain environmental conditions they promote survival.[53] Once those conditions for survival change, however, so too do the dictates of morality. That's why we find in nature both the maternal instinct and infanticide, both honoring one's parents and killing them when they become feeble. Natural selection "chooses" whatever behavioral traits best promote survival under the existing circumstances.

A Darwinian understanding of morality makes it very difficult to condemn as evil any human behavior that has persisted, because every trait that continues to exist even among a subpopulation has an equal right to claim nature's sanction. Presumably even anti-social behaviors such as fraud, pedophilia, and rape must continue to exist among human beings because they were favored at some point by natural selection and therefore have some sort of biological basis.

Of course, one could still justly condemn such behaviors if there existed a permanent moral standard independent of natural selection. But the existence of such a standard is precisely what orthodox Darwinism denies.

For the most part, Darwin himself did not press his relativistic analysis of morality to its logical conclusion, but he laid the groundwork for others who came after him, and his ideas helped reshape how people today think about morality. In the United States, for example, 55 percent of adults now believe "evolution shows that moral beliefs evolve over time based on their survival value in various times and places."[54]

Nowhere has the Darwinian view of ethics had a harsher impact than in family life and human sexuality. Darwin himself supported monogamy as the preferred form of mating in nineteenth-century Victorian England. But in his opinion, there was nothing sacrosanct about monogamous marriage as the preferred form of human mating. It might be the preferred choice at the time he was living, but with a different environment in a different time, it might be the wrong choice; and it certainly wasn't the original model for human sexuality across time and culture. He wrote: "All those who have most closely studied the subject, and whose judgment is worth much more than mine, believe that communal marriage was the original and universal form throughout the world, including the intermarriage of brothers and sisters."[55]

Darwin's evolutionary account of human mating practices in *The Descent of Man* encouraged a relativistic understanding of sexual morality. Other thinkers soon pushed the envelope well beyond Darwin. Perhaps the figure most responsible for the breakdown of traditional sexual ethics in Western culture was a Harvard-trained evolutionary zoologist. His name? Alfred Kinsey.

In 1948, Kinsey released *Sexual Behavior in the Human Male*, a mammoth volume containing more than eight hundred pages of graphs, charts, and descriptions of nearly every conceivable sexual practice among white American males.[56] Unveiled with a publicity offensive that would have dazzled today's Madison Avenue, the book soon became the talk of the nation.[57] Kinsey claimed that, based on his interviews with thousands of Americans, America's sex taboos did not match social and biological reality.

Kinsey disparaged as childish those who believed bestiality was immoral,[58] and he suggested that taboos against bestiality originated in "superstition."[59] He claimed that male promiscuity[60] and sex behavior among pre-adolescent children were biologically natural.[61] Kinsey did not officially try to claim that adult-child sex was normal or acceptable. Nevertheless, he did downplay its seriousness and undercut the reasons for punishing it. Kinsey implied that the trauma of child-adult sexual contacts did not lie in the molestation itself but in the social disapproval that surrounded it.[62]

Kinsey made a similar argument regarding extramarital intercourse. While acknowledging that such activity could be disruptive to the marriage relationship, he implied that the disruption was caused more by intolerant morality than any inherent wrongfulness of the behavior.[63] Kinsey also purported to offer a biological justification for male adultery, suggesting that men, unlike women, were naturally programmed to seek a variety of sexual partners.[64]

Kinsey treated the "human animal" as merely another type of mammal whose mating behavior could be fully explicated in terms of biology and conditioning. Adopting a thoroughly Darwinian approach to sexual morality, Kinsey argued that any sexual practice that could be found somewhere among mammals could be regarded as normal mammalian behavior and, as such, was unobjectionable.[65]

Kinsey acknowledged that many Americans considered this view of sex "primitive, materialistic or animalistic, and beneath the dignity of a civilized and educated people,"[66] but he maintained that the materialistic view was simply the honest "acceptance of reality,"[67] whereas those who opposed it were simply "ignor[ing] the material origins of all behavior."[68]

Kinsey's studies of sex behavior in America were arguably the most influential social science research in American history. His findings were presented to the public as sound, objective scientific research conducted by a scholar motivated by nothing more than the impartial pursuit of scientific truth. Lawyers, judges, social scientists, policymakers, and educators soon used the findings to revolutionize how American society treated sexuality. Kinsey became a secular saint and a celebrated cultural icon.[69]

In reality, Kinsey's research was mostly junk science. Around half of those interviewed by Kinsey's team prior to publication of his book on male sexuality were sex offenders, pimps, prostitutes, psychopaths, prisoners, and other social or sexual deviants.[70] They were hardly a representative sample of the general male population of the United States.

Nor were the other half of his interviewees. Kinsey did not randomly select the people he interviewed. Instead, many of his subjects volunteered to tell their sexual histories after having heard him lecture.[71] Such self-selection bias is likely to produce data unrepresentative of the general population.

The highly skewed nature of Kinsey's results finally became apparent much later, when social scientists started to ask questions about sex practices in large, randomly sampled national surveys. These surveys demolished the accuracy of Kinsey's report.[72]

But the damage had been done. The largely uncritical acceptance of Kinsey by elite culture in America is a cautionary example of how dangerous it is to just uncritically accept anything marketed in the name of science.

Targeting Children

One of Kinsey's biggest impacts was on the field of sex education, where Kinsey's disciples sought to remold sex education to fit his philosophy. The main vehicle of transformation was the Sex Information and Education Council of the United States (SIECUS). Founded in 1964 and still the dominant sex ed lobbying group today, SIECUS supporters extolled moral relativism, disparaged biblical sexual morality as dogmatic and unrealistic, and even downplayed the seriousness of child molestation.[73]

The radical nature of SIECUS was on display in the 1971 book *The New Sexual Revolution*, edited by SIECUS co-founder and board member Lester Kirkendall. Its various chapters defended the benefits of incest,[74] justified men seducing women who had traditional sexual scruples in order to "depropagandize" them,[75] and urged "expanding the erotic community" during marriage to allow for extramarital affairs, mistresses, and even bigamy.[76]

In another SIECUS-inspired book, *Sex Education in the Eighties: The Challenge of Healthy Sexual Evolution* (1981),[77] child sexuality was one of the main themes. The essay dealing most directly with the topic was written by sociologist Floyd Martinson.[78]

Martinson suggested that incest could be a positive experience, quoting one scholar who affirmed the practice by observing that "childhood is the best time to learn."[79] Martinson defended child molestation by arguing that "In sex, as in most aspects of life, the older teach the younger."[80] He even lamented that words like "'Incest,' 'pedophilia,'... and 'child sex abuse' have become pejorative terms."[81]

Martinson wasn't a big bad atheist, and he didn't work at a secular university. Instead, he spent his career teaching at Gustavus Adolphus College, a church-related college whose trustees to this day are elected by congregations of the Evangelical Lutheran Church in America.[82] According to a fellow sociologist, Martinson "chose to be at a church-related school because he wanted to do research 'in the context of the church.'"[83] He was even active in various Lutheran groups.

In an autobiographical essay published in the late 1990s, Martinson indicated that far from receiving pushback from his college or his church, he received support. "I don't recall ever having any difficulty with the faculty," he wrote. "I also had no difficulty with the national church leadership."[84] In fact, he was elected to a committee to draft a denominational statement on marriage. Some local pastors did occasionally complain about him to his college president, but the president backed him up. Martinson ended his essay by lamenting "the hysteria over child sexual abuse."

There were laudable efforts by many Christians in the 1980s and 1990s to fight the ideas promoted by SIECUS, Martinson, and others. Starting in the 1980s, there was a reaction to SIECUS-inspired sex education curriculum, resulting in the renewal of teaching abstinence in many school districts.[85] In the 1990s, the "True Love Waits" movement reached hundreds of thousands of young people with a message of waiting until marriage for sexual relationships.[86] Whether these particular initiatives were successful is a complicated question, but at least large numbers of Christians and Christian groups were trying to grapple with the fallout of the rebellion against biblical standards of sexuality.

But by the current century, the energy to resist seems to have dissipated. SIECUS began pushing explicit sex education for children in kindergarten under the banner of "comprehensive sex education."[87] Among Christians, there was a backlash against so-called "purity culture."[88] Some of the criticisms may have been reasonable. For example, if some young women or men received the impression that their sexual sins made them "damaged goods," so they couldn't be fully forgiven or restored by Christ, then that falsehood needed to be corrected. At the same time, it is hard to avoid feeling that at least some of the push-back against "purity culture" was merely an effort to justify the de facto abandonment of biblical sexuality.

Certainly this was the agenda of some self-identified Christians who advocated "sex-positive" Christianity or spirituality. In their view, so long as sex is experienced "consensually" and "authentically" it is good. Any suggestion otherwise is likely branded "patriarchal, archaic, and puritanistic"—or worse.[89]

Hannah Brown's boasting about violating biblical teachings on sex was one of the fruits of this kind of false teaching. "I can be a woman of faith and also be sex-positive," she told *People* magazine. "And I am not going to stop talking about the things that I believe in."[90]

But even before the current collapse of resolve among many in the Christian community on issues relating to sex, the seeds of destruction had already been sown among many Christian institutions in America.

Christian Universities Shrug off Sexual Standards

When I joined the faculty of Seattle Pacific in the 1990s, the university's student code of conduct officially prohibited sex outside of marriage as well as homosexual relationships. But I discovered that the official code and what was actually practiced didn't always match up.

I still remember the evening in our home when a female student of mine shared with my wife and me the predicament she found herself in while living on campus. She said that her roommate insisted on bringing her boyfriend to their dorm room to have sex. But when my student raised this issue with campus authorities, they wouldn't do anything. They wouldn't even move her to another dorm room.

Another student of mine got someone pregnant. He was heartbroken because his girlfriend decided to have an abortion, which he didn't want. As he told things, he would go out each night and would come back to the dorm drunk. He said that although the residence life staff knew he was getting drunk, they did nothing to intervene—even though students weren't supposed to use alcohol. This student was an agnostic, and I tried to witness to him. But it struck me how our campus—which extolled fostering Christian community—had failed him. In letting standards slide, they failed to help him when he very much needed help.

In general, as far as I could tell while I was a professor, our university didn't do much to support biblical behavior in the realm of sex. Was this due to neglect? Cowardice? Or were campus leaders already buying into the rejection of historic Christian teachings? Perhaps it was all three. Whatever the specific reasons, I could see the institution heading further and further away from upholding orthodox Christianity the longer I was there.

Several years into my academic career, the university had to hire someone in the area of student mental health and counseling. There were two main candidates. While both self-identified as Christians, they definitely weren't the same. One attended a church in a progressive mainline Christian denomination. She had been active on her previous campus in promoting the affirmation of the LGBTQ community. The other candidate was a devout evangelical Christian who affirmed biblical standards of sexuality. She also happened to be a person of color. Guess who was appointed? It wasn't the devout evangelical. Indeed, as I recall it, that candidate's embrace of biblical sexual standards created pushback against her.

All of this occurred when our university was still officially upholding biblical standards of sexuality. But official standards are meaningless if you don't actually enforce them.

Years after I had left, my daughter attended Seattle Pacific. During her new student orientation, there was a session on student sexual conduct. The focus? The importance of consent. Nothing was said about biblical standards of chastity.

You see the implication. So long as both parties consented, their sexual behavior must be okay. Consent is obviously important, and coerced sex is unquestionably reprehensible. But it isn't the only sexual standard that Christians need to be concerned about.

The university did continue to maintain its official statement about marriage being between a man and a woman, but university officials and faculty increasingly flouted it. The university granted official recognition to a student group promoting the LGTBQ agenda. In a theology course, a professor assigned a book with the subtitle "Discovering the Queer Christ."[91] The School of Education hosted an official event with a speaker promoting transgenderism.[92] In short, faculty and administrators increasingly embraced the talking points of those opposed to Christianity.

Stockholm Syndrome Christianity was in full force. How did administrators and board members who were still personally orthodox justify welcoming to campus views opposed to historic Christian teaching? No doubt they convinced themselves they were staying silent out of Christian love. But since when does being loving mean providing a platform for those who want to subvert historic Christianity? If one truly believes that God's standards are intended for our good, just how loving is it to provide a platform for those standards to be undermined?

Others may have thought they were merely facilitating the discussion of different points of view on campus. But were they really even doing that? In 2021, a group of theologically orthodox students at the university sent a heartfelt letter to the board of trustees about the intolerant environment school administrators had created at the school. Was it intolerant of those who rejected biblical sexuality? No. It was intolerant of those who supported it. By laying out the welcome mat for those committed to trashing historic Christian teaching on sex, the university had enabled the bullying of any student who still upheld biblical sexuality.

"Students are routinely provided school-sponsored opportunities for LGBT activism, but the school sponsors no such opportunities for traditional viewpoints, even though it claims to offer an open dialogue," the students wrote.[93] They related how faculty members were allowed to provide time for LGBT advocacy in their classes, but not for advocacy of biblical standards. As a result, in such classes "no student would dare to openly admit that they supported a traditional stance on sexuality, for fear of public shaming, shunning, or even rebuke."

Seattle Pacific is far from the only evangelical Christian university where biblical standards on sexuality have been crowded out.

In 2015, Grand Canyon University authorized benefits for the same-sex spouses of employees.[94] In 2019, Azusa Pacific University removed from its student code of conduct a ban on "romanticized same-sex relationship[s]" and watered down its official statement on human sexuality.[95] In 2024, Fuller Theological Seminary was reported to be considering a change in its standards that would allow students in same-sex marriages to attend there. The same year, a prominent Fuller Seminary professor co-authored a book arguing for the full acceptance of same-sex sexuality by Christians. The book acknowledged that the Bible gives "unqualified disapproval" of "homoerotic activity." But it asserted that "God repeatedly changes his mind," and so should we—even if it means embracing a view that flatly contradicts the Bible's explicit teachings.[96]

Calvin University in Grand Rapids, Michigan is another prominent evangelical Christian educational institution. In 2022 its board voted to retain faculty who disagreed with the university's stated standards on sexuality. The board chair claimed at the time that the university was making room for "diverse viewpoints among its faculty while remaining committed to upholding... confessional standards."[97]

Perhaps Calvin's chairman of the board sincerely believed what he said. If so, he was deluding himself. The faculty at a Christian college are the primary vehicle for training and mentoring students. If faculty are retained who don't support the stated standards of the university, those stated standards won't be conveyed to students. So the claim that the university remains "committed to upholding... confessional standards" is pretty much a sham.

Churches Stay Silent on Sex

The same double-mindedness seen at Christian colleges can also be seen in evangelical churches.

During my service as an elder in an urban evangelical church, it became clear to me just how ambivalent even personally orthodox evangelical leaders can be when it comes to actually upholding or inculcating biblical sexuality. Our church said it embraced the Bible's teachings on sex, but I found myself wondering as time went on as to how we showed that commitment in practice.

One of the first warning signs for me was the reticence of our church to deal with biblical teaching on divorce. Our church had experienced a series of divorces among those who had been involved in various levels of leadership in the church. But there seemed to be a lack of enthusiasm in addressing the problem by teaching and discipling people about biblical marriage. I did eventually get approval for a task force on marriage, but as near as I could tell, its recommendations were largely left unimplemented. More disturbing still, I remember how our elders struggled over whether we should allow a celebration in our church of a remarriage that resulted from what we considered an unbiblical divorce. We ended up holding the line, but it struck me how much we agonized over what seemed to be a very clear-cut question.

Let me be very clear: I believe the Bible authorizes divorce in certain limited situations, and in our culture many divorced people are victims of their partner's unbiblical actions. I also think we cannot emphasize too much that forgiveness and restoration through Christ applies to all our actions, including divorce and other sins involving our sexual nature. It's also the case that lots of Christians are now divorced, and so it can be uncomfortable to address this issue.

At the same time, the failure of churches to disciple Christians in the area of marriage and divorce is a scandal. It not only dishonors God; it deprives people of the opportunity for genuine repentance and restoration. Instead, we enable fake repentance and fake healing.

While I was writing this chapter, a major news outlet ran a "human interest" feature story about Brad and Chelsea, a self-identified Christian couple in Tennessee who met while working at Walmart and fell deeply in love. They were married to other people, but that didn't stop them from cheating on their spouses. When they were discovered, they were mortified—though not so mortified as to change their behavior. "Despite the disapproval of the community," says the article, "Chelsea fell deeper in love with Brad."[98] Two years later they had a son. Three years after that they finally decided to get married.

In some sense, both Brad and Chelsea know they did something wrong. They say they have sought forgiveness from God and their ex-spouses. But Chelsea also says this: "It was an unconventional way to start a relationship and a family, but it worked. It sounds so cliche, but you should follow your heart, it knows exactly what you want… Don't be afraid to see where life takes you."

"Following our hearts" when our hearts contradict clear biblical teaching isn't sound Christianity. And you aren't repenting of something if you continue to defend it as having been right.

I don't know whether Brad and Chelsea are presently part of a Christian community, or whether a Christian pastor did their remarriage. If so, that demonstrates the lack of a clear line between the church's standards and the world's.

Such muddled thinking now pervades the Christian community when it comes to sex in all areas. Many sincere Christians, for instance, now justify attending and celebrating same-sex weddings. They even have led themselves to believe they are following what God wants, because God commands that we love others. But their concept of love is taken from the secular culture that rejects God's commands, not from the Bible or historic Christianity. Would God be honored if they attended and participated in worship for a pagan god? What about a divorce party by someone who proudly committed adultery? If you are truly celebrating something with others, you really don't think it is wrong. Whether you want to admit it to yourself or not, you've adopted the position of those who are celebrating.[99]

Politics... or Personal?

In my last year at the urban church where I had previously served on the elder board, a major controversy broke out in our state over a radical new sex education law. Promoted by Planned Parenthood, the law mandated "comprehensive sexual health education" starting in kindergarten, and it set up a system that effectively pressured school districts to adopt curricula from a list provided by the state. The curricular choices listed by the state were often extreme. One curriculum, for example, upheld "mutual masturbation" and "bathing together" for twelve-year-olds. The answer key informed teachers that "these behaviors are important because they can help people learn about their bodies and build connection between people without any risk of STDs (or pregnancy)."[100]

The law made it harder for local school districts to choose sex education curricula in line with the moral standards of their own communities. It also disempowered parents by not providing a right under the law for parents to monitor classes. The law was one result of years-long lobbying efforts by the Kinsey-inspired Sexuality Information and Education Council of the United States. For parents wanting to raise their kids according to Christian moral standards, the law was a terrible blow.

An effort was made to repeal the law, and some members of our church asked the current elders for permission to collect signatures in the church parking lot to get the referendum on the ballot. After some disagreement, the majority of elders agreed, and the referendum made the ballot. But then some members of the congregation asked the elders for our church to publicly support the repeal. After more discussion, the elders declined. It didn't help that certain members of the congregation who worked in public schools defended the new law.

Although I disagreed with the elders' decision to duck the debate, I thought their decision was defensible. The primary focus of churches should not be political action. It should be the gospel and discipleship. Those who wanted to stay out of the fray emphasized that they too were concerned about the abandonment of biblical sexuality by our culture. They just didn't think the church should involve itself in politics.

What came next, however, showed that the disagreement in our church went a lot deeper than people were willing to initially admit. Seeking common ground, some elders proposed our church should become more intentional and adopt a Christian sex education curriculum for its youth. This wasn't about politics. It was about classes taught in our congregation, about discipleship in an area where as a culture we were failing our kids.

But there was lots of hesitancy about the new proposal as well. Various new justifications were offered why we couldn't do anything for our youth. When those concerns were disposed of, things became a lot more frank. One church leader finally indicated that we couldn't teach biblical sexuality to our youth group because we might alienate many of the youth who attended.

I am sure that the person who said that was sincere. He likely believed that it was worth downplaying our beliefs so we could stay in relationship with the youth involved with our church, not all of whom were Christians. He likely thought that not giving offense now would give us the opportunity to disciple them later.

Again, I think this person believed what he was saying. But at some point, if you are no longer willing to provide biblical teaching either in public or private, you are probably deluding yourself into thinking you will ever get to the point of discipling someone in that area.

The fruit of such passive abandonment of biblical standards is all around us. Over the past century, too many Christians and churches turned a blind eye to no-fault divorce in their midst. Too many ignored heterosexual promiscuity. Too many didn't think it worthwhile to defend a biblical view of marriage. How well did that go?

The Road Ahead

It's not going to get easier in the coming decade. Churches composed of Stockholm Syndrome Christians will end up needing to trim more and more from biblical teaching the further away the culture moves from God.

Some Christians persuade themselves that if they only downplay "this one thing," everything will be okay. What they fail to acknowledge is that the downplaying never ends. Once you give up one thing as not important, the debate moves on. Then you have to give up something else. You eventually will find your views and actions indistinguishable from the rest of the culture.

The debates discussed earlier in this chapter are already moving on. If marriages can be redefined to include same-sex relationships, why can't they be redefined to involve more than two people as well? That's why there are increasingly mainstream discussions of the legitimacy of polygamy.[101] And why are we so sure that sexual relationships between adults and children are terrible? If children are sexual beings earlier than we thought, why shouldn't they be allowed to partner with an older person if they wish? That view is now being raised in a new push to mainstream pedophilia.[102]

Then there is the deconstruction of the very basis of all sexual relationships: biological sex. If our biological sex is merely an unplanned accident of evolutionary history, what is morally wrong about changing our sex through technology if we are able to do it? So we have "drag queen story hours" at libraries targeting children in an effort to confuse them about their gender and desensitize them to the costs of rejecting their biological sex.[103] Far worse, we are seeing a dramatic rise in surgeries to mutilate children and adults by removing their sex organs—a permanent change that they can never go back on.[104]

Christians who thought that muting ourselves from conversations about sex would have no serious consequences were wrong. When you fail to oppose something, you get more of it. The culture won't stay the same.

According to a Gallup survey in 2022, nearly 21 percent of "Generation Z" now identify as LGBT,[105] while another survey shows that nearly "40 percent of students identify as LGBTQ at liberal arts colleges."[106] Contrast this with two decades ago when only 3.5 percent of American adults identified as LGBT.[107]

If you truly believe that God's design for sexuality is monogamous heterosexual marriage, you should recognize that this revolution in people's self-identification is catastrophic. Note, too, that the change pretty much undermines previous "scientific" claims that sexual orientation is simply dictated by our biology. There is no credible *biological* reason for the stratospheric rise in LGBTQ identification. There are plenty of social and cultural reasons. It is interesting to note that nearly 6 in 10 LGBT people today identify as "bisexuals," suggesting that the majority of people who identify with this category can find fulfillment through heterosexual relationships.[108]

Unfortunately, Christian leaders who have failed to speak out in other areas are continuing down the same path as things further deteriorate. Take scientist Francis Collins. Collins is rarely pressed on any tough issues when interviewed by his friends in the faith community. But in one interview in 2021, leading Baptist Ed Stetzer tried to gently raise an issue touching on our culture's current gender wars. Assuring Collins "I'm on your team," Stetzer lamented that "it's becoming increasingly hard for me in the last few months, as one who wants to be your champion, when the apparatus that is under NIH and all the health stuff, seems to have been caught up in some of the currents of the day."[109] The example Stetzer offered is the Centers for Disease Control (CDC), which now describes mothers as "pregnant people," an Orwellian contortion of language presumably meant to avoid offending certain political activists.[110]

The idea that non-women can have babies not only flatly contradicts the historic Christian faith that Collins says he espouses, but also contradicts the basic facts of biology. Biological human males can't have babies. But in the topsy-turvy gender wars, you aren't supposed to say that, and so you can't reserve motherhood for women. Stetzer sensibly wanted to know how to answer his fellow church members who are skeptical of government scientists because they can see clear examples like this where ideology twists the scientists' supposed science.

Collins clearly didn't want to answer Stetzer's question, and he masterfully danced around the topic without saying anything substantive.

Or consider commentator David French, who has defended drag queen story hours in public libraries as "one of the blessings of liberty."[111] French no doubt thinks he is simply promoting free speech by this comment. After all, as he explained elsewhere, the same principle that allows drag story hours for children in public facilities also enables Christian groups to use public facilities.[112] There is a serious argument here, one to which I'm sympathetic. Nevertheless, French's argument isn't a slam-dunk: Messages targeting children for moral corruption have always been a special case when it comes to restrictions on speech, and so it's not clear that restrictions on drag queen story hours for kids would violate the principles of free speech.

But the real problem isn't French's principled view of free speech. It's the cavalier way he seems to be treating one of the symptoms of a cultural catastrophe that is destroying lives all around us. With all due respect to French, practices like drag queen hours aren't *blessings* of liberty. They are—at best—tragic *costs* of liberty. They are costs we bear because of the greater blessings of liberty we hope they will secure. But minimizing or denying these costs is neither helpful nor wise.

But Take Hope

Our current situation is undeniably bleak, but we shouldn't despair. For one thing, Christians have been here before. Early Christians lived in an empire plagued by forms of sexual anarchy that rival our own. Some succumbed to it. But many did not, and the Christian community became known for its honoring of marriage and sexual faithfulness.

We should obey God because He is our Creator and we are His creatures. But God loves us, and His design for sexuality is intended for our flourishing, not our frustration. One of our culture's biggest lies is that the biblical view is oppressive and anti-sex. In reality, God's plan for sex within marriage is good for us and has tremendous emotional, economic, and social benefits. It is associated with less depression, less risky behaviors, better mental and physical health, better economic outcomes, and more.[113]

This doesn't mean that everyone who is sexually faithful will have a good marriage or even a good sex life. It doesn't mean that everyone who wants marriage will be able to enter into one. We live in a broken world. This is not a gospel of health and wealth. Nevertheless, the ways of the LORD are righteous and good, and living in accord with how one was created leads to life.

Moreover, the good news of the gospel is that God is able and willing to redeem His people. No matter how far our culture descends into Hell, the pit is not too deep for God to rescue us. No matter how often we ourselves may fail to honor God's standards when it comes to sex, every day provides a new opportunity for us to repent and turn back to Him and His ways.

Biblical teachings are still true, and even if they are only followed by ourselves and our family members and Christian brothers and sisters, they can transform us. This was true in the past. It is true today.

Which brings me to my last point. The wholesale abandonment of sexual faithfulness by many Christians today is not inevitable. While we should grieve that large numbers of Christians are not living in line with the Bible's plans for sex, biblical faithfulness in this area is not merely "possible." A significant minority of Christians have stayed faithful.

In 2012, the National Association of Evangelicals commissioned a survey of millennial evangelicals and sex. The survey showed that 56 percent of "unmarried evangelicals ages 18–29 said they have never been sexually active."[114] That figure rose to 60–63 percent for evangelicals who frequently read the Bible or attend church once a week or more.[115] This data shocked many people at the time, who assumed that it was impossible to expect unmarried evangelicals to live in accord with biblical standards in our current culture.

Unfortunately, the best recent data shows much higher rates of sex outside of marriage among evangelicals. Among unmarried evangelicals 23–32 who attend church less than monthly, 94 percent now say they have had vaginal, oral, or anal intercourse, and 75 percent have had three or more sex partners.[116]

Nevertheless, those figures drop to 78 percent sexually active and 49 percent with three or more partners for unmarried evangelicals who attend church weekly or more.[117] And among unmarried evangelicals who believe that premarital sex is "always wrong," 40 percent report they have had no sex partners since age 18.[118] There is a strong connection between beliefs, religious commitment, and practice.

Analyzing the data, sociologist David Ayers argues that "it is not mainly becoming sexually active that reduces religious commitment, but the opposite."[119] In other words, it's not primarily that sexual activity outside of marriage causes Christians to fall away from historic beliefs and active engagement with their churches. It's that once they give up historic beliefs and active engagement, they are much more likely to act accordingly.

In sum, the more intentional Christian communities are about discipling people through example, practice, and teaching, the more likely their members will live according to biblical standards in the area of sex as well as elsewhere. This is good news, if we are willing to hear it and act on it.

There is also hope for those who struggle with gender identity and sexual orientation issues.

Perhaps the biggest lie told today by our culture and perpetuated by many Stockholm Syndrome Christians is that there is no possibility of healing when it comes to issues of orientation and gender identity.

Although sexual orientation may not be changeable for some young people (and it is probably difficult to change for many others), recent research has shown remarkable fluidity in sexual attraction, behavior, and identity among young people with same-sex attractions. Survey data from more than fourteen thousand teens tracked by the National Longitudinal Study of Adolescent Health show that "approximately 80% of adolescent boys and half of adolescent girls who expressed either partial or exclusive same-sex romantic attraction" eventually became heterosexual as young adults.[120] Refusing to accept this evidence, some researchers have speculated that the results must have been due to prank answers.[121] But other surveys have demonstrated similar fluidity in sexual identity among those with same-sex attractions.[122]

In fact, the evidence for changeability is becoming so pervasive that prominent sex researcher Lisa Diamond at the University of Utah, a self-identified lesbian, has urged the LGBT community to jettison their talking point that sexual orientation is immutable: "The queers have to stop saying 'Please help us, we're born this way and we can't change.'" She said that this argument "is going to bite us in the ass, because now we know there is enough data out there" showing it's not true.[123]

Similarly, there is growing recognition that confusion about gender identity among most children should not be treated as something permanent. A 2024 study from the Netherlands tracked the "gender non-contentedness" of nearly 2,800 adolescents from age 11 to age 26.[124] According to the researchers, "gender non-contentedness, while being relatively common during early adolescence, in general decreases with age and appears to be associated with a poorer self-concept and mental health throughout development."

At age 11, 11 percent of participants reported that they "wish[ed] to be of the opposite sex." By age 26, that number had dropped by nearly two-thirds to only 4 percent. In the words of the National Health Service in the UK, "in many cases gender variant behaviour or feelings disappear as children reach puberty."[125]

That is why there is now a growing push-back against gender-destructive treatments for non-adults.[126] The last thing we should be doing is validating a child's gender confusion or suggesting that it cannot be resolved.

And even in cases where gender dysphoria or same-sex attraction remains unresolved, there is hope. The same is true for Christian heterosexual singles who may never marry and thus be called to a life of chastity. Regardless of what the culture says, our "identity" does not rest on our sexual feelings. Our identity rests on Christ. And He can powerfully bless the faithful Christian even when a "thorn in the flesh" remains. Our job is to remain faithful. Our job is to turn away from all manner of temptations, take up our cross daily, and follow him—and know that he will make it all worthwhile.

The benefits of biblical Christianity are as vibrant and life-changing as ever—if we are willing to be faithful to our calling. But being a Stockholm Syndrome Christian will not lead to those benefits. It will lead us further down the path of destruction for ourselves and our families.

4. REBUILDING THE
WALLS OF HOSTILITY

STOCKHOLM CHRISTIANS'
DIVISIVE VIEW OF RACE AND CLASS

O N MAY 25, 2020, BLACK AMERICAN GEORGE FLOYD DIED WHILE in police custody in Minneapolis. Floyd's treatment by the police was captured in a horrifying video. Police officer Derek Chauvin kept his knee on Floyd's neck even while Floyd pled that he couldn't breathe. Chauvin was later convicted of Floyd's murder, and three assisting officers were convicted on other charges,[1] although questions remain about the actual cause of Floyd's death given his underlying health issues and drug use.[2]

In a nation already ravaged by the COVID-19 pandemic and a bitterly divisive presidential campaign, the death of George Floyd ignited an inferno.

In the resulting riots, an estimated $2 billion in damage was done, people died, and many minority-owned communities and businesses were destroyed. "The riots and arson that followed protests of George Floyd's death have devastated organizations and businesses that serve communities of color," writes journalist Maya Rao.[3]

The summer of 2020 was a wakeup call for many white evangelicals. Those who hadn't thought a lot about race now wanted to do something. Unfortunately, doing something and doing something constructive are not necessarily the same.

At the time, my wife and I were longtime members of an urban evangelical Presbyterian church. Our church's membership was almost all white and largely upper-class. At the suggestion of some of its members, the church appointed a Racism Task Force. Given the racial polarization in America, there was much to be commended in this action. But we began to hear reports of the kinds of books that were being discussed as resources. They included *White Fragility* by Robin DiAngelo, *Be the Bridge* by Latasha Morrison, and *The Color of Compromise* by Jemar Tisby.[4]

It seemed to me that our church was attracted to certain voices on racial issues largely because cultural elites and the secular media had identified them as the voices worth listening to. Our church members were not alone. As the year went on, it became evident that many evangelical leaders and churches were relying on secular cultural elites to decide who the legitimate authorities on racism were.

But if our cultural elites weren't wise guides when it came to sexuality or biblical authority, why should we rely on them when it comes to racial injustice and reconciliation?

As I began to read books and articles by those in what has become known as the "antiracist" movement, I became increasingly troubled. Although there were certainly differences between some of the authors, the general picture they painted was similar: Nearly everything bad in America ultimately derives from the sin of "whiteness" and "white supremacy." There is one oppressor group ("whites"), and everyone else is part of the oppressed. If you are white, you are guilty of racism no matter who you are, and racism permeates your life no matter what you say or think or do. In the words of Robin DiAngelo, "Racism cannot be avoided," and if you are white, you must acknowledge you are "unconsciously invested in racism," your bias "is implicit and unconscious," trying to be "good or bad is not relevant," and "nothing exempts [you]... from the forces of racism."[5] If you say you are color blind, you are a liar: "Because no one can actually be color blind in a racist society, the claim that you are color blind is not a truth; it is a false belief."[6]

Incredibly, even believing that Americans are less racist than in the past is a lie. "I am often asked if I think the younger generation is less racist," writes DiAngelo. "No, I don't. In some ways, racism's adaptations over time are more sinister than concrete rules such as Jim Crow."[7]

According to the new spokespersons for "antiracism," if you are white, you are responsible for everything bad any other white person ever did. You must take upon yourself the sins of all other whites from history, whether they actually were your ancestors or not.

According to some antiracists, believing that Jesus saves us from our own sins is simply more racism. Speaking at a church in New York City, prominent antiracist scholar Ibram X. Kendi denounced what he called "savior theology," the idea that "the job of the Christian is to go out and save these individuals… who are doing all of these evil, sinful things." He tied this view to "racist ideas and racist theology." According to him, true salvation comes by recognizing that "Jesus was a revolutionary, and the job of the Christian is to revolutionize society."[8]

Kendi was echoing here the views of black theologian James Cone (1938–2018), a champion of black liberation theology, who once wrote that "the black experience is the feeling one has when… throwing a Molotov cocktail into a white-owned building and watching it go up in flames."[9] Cone emphasized that he "read the Bible through the lens of a black tradition of struggle and not as the objective word of God."[10] He denied that the Bible is "infallible," and claimed that "whites who insist on verbal infallibility are often the most violent racists."[11] In his view, the Bible was "one witness to God's empowering presence" among many. "The other testimonies," he said, "include sacred documents of the African-American experience—such as the speeches of Malcolm X and Martin Luther King, Jr." Indeed, "Liberating stories, myths, and legends are also found among men and women of all races and cultures struggling to realize the divine intention for their lives."[12] Cone categorically rejected the belief "that the Bible is above criticism or that it serves as an absolute judge in faith and practice."[13] Similarly, he rejected Christ's atoning death on the cross "as reflecting the God of patriarchy, the values of the dominant group."[14]

According to this view, salvation is provided not by Christ's atoning death on the cross, but by our own work of liberation in the here and now. One of the people mentored by Cone was current US senator Raphael Warnock, also a black minister.[15] On Easter 2021, Warnock's Twitter account tweeted a message that could have come straight from Cone: "The meaning of Easter is more transcendent than the resurrection of Jesus Christ. Whether you are Christian or not, through a commitment to helping others we are able to save ourselves."[16]

For whites seeking absolution from the guilt of racism, the message is similar: The only way to save yourself is by earning your way out of racism. In the words of secular writer Robin DiAngelo, "the antidote to [white] guilt is action."[17]

Except it turns out that if you are white, your works won't really rescue you after all. "A positive white identity is an impossible goal," writes DiAngelo. "White identity is inherently racist; white people do not exist outside the system of white supremacy."[18] If you are white, you are forever tainted by the original sin of racism. You can't overcome it, no matter how good your actions. The best you can hope for is to "strive to be 'less white'" for the rest of your life.[19] No matter what you do, if you are white, you must accept your identity as irredeemably racist and engage in penance for the rest of your life.

If you disagree with any of this analysis, you are likely to be accused of "whitesplaining" and providing more evidence of your "white fragility." Instead, you should give up any thought of disagreeing or voicing your own opinions in discussions about race. That would be yet more racist behavior.

According to Latasha Morrison's ministry "Be the Bridge," white Christians need to "provide space" for persons of color [POCs] "to wail, cuss, or even yell at you. Jesus didn't hold back when he saw hypocrisy and oppression; POCs shouldn't have to either." When attacked, white Christians are advised: "Don't get defensive.... Don't try to explain yourself." Your duty is simply to "apologize and do better next time." Above all, if you are white, "Don't forget: racism is *our* problem. Our people created and sustained it, and now it's our job to dismantle it."[20]

So how should faithful Christians respond to these claims being made by "antiracist" writers? First, I think we should acknowledge some important truths they have raised.

America's Troubled History on Race

Christian antiracist writers like Jemar Tisby and Latasha Morrison are right to challenge the historical amnesia of many white Christians about the story of race relations in America. Tisby's *The Color of Compromise* offers a worthwhile account of how many white Christians compromised on the issue of human equality throughout American history. Morrison's *Be the Bridge* provides a poignant and insightful account of what it was like for the author to grow up as a black woman in America.

Like many white Christians, I learned some of our nation's history of racial injustices while growing up. I learned more while in graduate school when I studied the controversies over slavery and Jim Crow and civil rights. But a life-changing experience for me was writing and directing the documentary *Human Zoos* in (2018), which explored the history of scientific racism in America.[21] Producing that film helped me better understand just how deeply racism was baked into American culture, including science.

Scientific Racism

In 1904, nearly four decades after slavery's abolition, thousands of indigenous people were brought to the St. Louis World's Fair to be put on public display.[22] They were offered by scientists as examples of lower stages of human evolution. Some, notably "pygmies" from Africa, were presented to the public as "missing links" between humans and apes.[23]

Two years later Ota Benga, one of the Africans, was exhibited in a cage next to an orangutan in the Bronx Zoo primate house.[24] Benga's display caused a sensation in New York City, attracting hundreds of thousands of visitors.

Some Christian ministers objected. White minister Stuart MacArthur, pastor of the city's Calvary Baptist Church, declared: "The person responsible for this exhibition degrades himself as much as he does the African."[25] Black minister James Gordon attacked the presentation for propagandizing on behalf of Darwinian evolution, which he regarded as "absolutely opposed to Christianity."[26] In his words, "Neither the Negro nor the white man is related to the monkey, and such an exhibition only degrades a human being's manhood."

The city's secular elites, meanwhile, didn't see a problem. Evolutionary biologist Henry Fairfield Osborn of Columbia University praised Benga's exhibition at the zoo, and the *New York Times* complained it was "absurd to make moan over the imagined humiliation and degradation" of Benga.[27] The *Times* took special offense at Rev. Gordon's skepticism of evolution: "The reverend colored brother should be told that evolution, in one form or another, is now taught in the text books of all the schools, and that it is no more debatable than the multiplication table."[28]

As the statement by the *Times* attests, the racist presentation of Benga was largely approved by elites because they saw it as justified by the science of evolution. In his book *The Descent of Man*, Charles Darwin had claimed that the break between humans and apes fell "between the negro or Australian [aborigine] and the gorilla."[29] Thus, in Darwin's view, blacks were the closest humans to apes. Darwin also asserted that the differences in mental faculties "between the men of distinct races" were "greater" than the differences in "mental faculties in men of the same race," which fueled the idea that some races were naturally more intelligent than others.[30] As Nigerian scholar Olufemi Oluniyi has pointed out, "Darwin's... writings clearly demonstrate that by 'barbarous,' 'inferior,' or 'lower' peoples he usually meant dark-skinned people. The terms 'highly civilised' or 'superior' he applied to Caucasians."[31]

Darwinism's key contribution to racism was offering a seemingly plausible scientific rationale for racial inferiority. According to Darwin and his supporters, we should *expect* races to have unequal capacities because natural selection acting on different populations will evolve different traits for those populations based on their survival needs.

Darwin's view unquestionably helped solidify and spread scientific racism in America and around the world. As evolutionary biologist

Stephen Jay Gould observed, "Biological arguments for racism may have been common before 1859 [when Darwin published his book *On the Origin of Species*], but they increased by orders of magnitude following the acceptance of evolutionary theory."[32]

Only recently have many members of the scientific community begun to grapple with evolutionary biology's disturbing past. In 2022, a science journal published an article acknowledging that "the roots of evolutionary biology are steeped in histories of white supremacism, eugenics, and scientific racism."[33]

Christian Culpability

But it isn't just the scientific community that needs to deal with a troubled record on race. Prior to the Civil War, many white Christians in America approved of the enslavement of blacks. They supported a vile system where slave families were broken up and slave women and men were used to breed more slaves. They supported laws that banned slaves from learning to read, which included preventing slaves from reading the Bible. They embraced evolutionary views of Africans as either lesser evolved or separately evolved from whites. After the Civil War, many white Christians supported racial segregation and turned a blind eye to horrific injustices against blacks, including lynchings.

The same year Ota Benga was put on display in a cage at the Bronx Zoo, black American Luther Holbert and a black woman associated with him were murdered in a lynching in Mississippi. The crime involved such brutality that it is hard to write about it even today. Holbert was accused of the murder of a white planter, but he never received a trial. Instead, he and the woman were tortured and burned at the stake. An eyewitness account published in a newspaper at the time supplies the grisly details:

> The blacks were forced to hold out their hands while one finger at a time was chopped off. The fingers were distributed as souvenirs. The ears of the murderers were cut off. Holbert was severely beaten, his skull was fractured, and one of his eyes knocked out with a stick, hung by a shred from the socket.... The most excruciating form of

punishment consisted in the use of a large corkscrew in the hands of some of the mob. This instrument was bored into the flesh of the man and the woman, in the arms, legs and body, and then pulled out the spirals tearing out big places of raw, quivering flesh, every time it was withdrawn.[34]

This lynching was done on a Sunday, in view of a black church. As many as a thousand people attended. There weren't many atheists in Mississippi in 1904. How many of them in the mob were good churchgoing whites? And how many white ministers spoke out against the outrage? If local newspaper accounts are any indication, there were none.

Many white Christians persisted in their support for racist ideas and policies for a long time. Evangelist Bob Jones Sr. advocated racial segregation as a biblical imperative in the 1960s, and the university he founded banned blacks from admission until the early 1970s. It did not drop its ban on interracial dating until 2000.[35] Bob Jones University is based in South Carolina, but there were evangelical Christian institutions in the North that had similar policies.

In the late 1960s, a young black man named Sylvester Jacobs entered Moody Bible Institute in Chicago. He hoped to find genuine Christian community there. Instead, he found the same sort of racism he had encountered growing up. He was segregated in his own dorm room, initially not allowed to room with a white student.[36] He was warned that a white student had complained "about black students being allowed to talk to white girls."[37] He spoke with another white student who cavalierly used the "N" word in a conversation with him.[38] And he was told by university officials that he had to agree not to date any white women.[39]

"I... felt the way I'd never expected to feel in a Christian place," he wrote later. "Lonely."[40] The racism of fellow Christians caused him to doubt his own worth. "Maybe God really hates black people after all," he thought. "Maybe I should have seen it all along, as though it was something obvious that white folks knew. Maybe they are right and black people are really less. Not just less because of society, but less because God hates us and always has."[41]

It would be grossly inaccurate to say that times have not changed in America. They have. But you can't fully understand the current state of black-white relations in America without understanding the historical backdrop.

Alt-Right Resurrects Darwinian Racism

The initial version of my documentary *Human Zoos* focused on scientific racism in the distant past. But while I was finishing the film, a horrifying protest by white supremacists in Charlottesville, Virginia brought the topic much closer to home. In the ensuing violence, a white supremacist drove a car into counter-protestors, killing one woman and injuring dozens of others.

The Charlottesville violence prompted me to add another section to my documentary covering the so-called "alt-right" movement and how it has been resurrecting evolutionary arguments for racism in spreading racial hatred.

An article in one of the prominent alt-right journals argues: "Darwinism offers a compelling and rational justification for Whites to act on behalf of their ancestors and progeny, and feel a shared sense of destiny with their extended kin group."[42] In a 2017 study, more than four hundred self-identified members of the alt-right revealed that they view blacks, Mexicans, and other racial and ethnic groups as less evolved and closer to humans' ape-like ancestors than whites.[43]

Renewed evolutionary racism has fueled hatred and violence among some antisocial white males. In 2009, a white man drove to the Holocaust Museum in Washington DC, where he fatally shot an African-American security guard. The shooter had previously published a document arguing that "cross-breeding Whites with species lower on the evolutionary scale diminishes the White gene-pool while increasing the number of... mongrels."[44] In 2022, a teenage white male shooter murdered ten blacks at a supermarket in Buffalo, New York. In a manifesto he wrote before the shooting, the killer argued that blacks "are a different subspecies of human" because "Whites and Blacks are separated by tens of thousands of years of evolution, and our genetic material is obviously very different."[45]

Unfortunately, some white evangelicals have been drawn in by the evolutionary racism of the alt-right. Thomas Achord was headmaster of a Christian classical school in Louisiana, and co-host of a prominent Christian podcast. In 2021, Achord co-edited an anthology titled *Who Is My Neighbor?*[46] The titles assigned to the anthology's selections give the tenor of the volume: "Diversity Increases Psychosis," "Diversity Increases Student Suicide Risk," "Diversity Correlates With Violence," "Segregation Decreases Violence," and "Diversity = IQ Drop." Other selections negatively portray those who are "mixed-race": "Bi-Racial Depression," "Mixed-Race and Obesity," and "Mixed-Race Pregnancy Risks." Many of the passages draw on evolutionary theory to justify their claims.

Achord was exposed in 2022 for posting overtly racist messages under a pseudonym on social media.[47] "I want to provide formal help, tools, resources for white-advocates to take back the West for white peoples," read one post.[48] "Yes, racism is interwoven into every facet of society. It always has been and always will be… To act otherwise is to deny natural revelation and natural law. Best to keep it that way," read another post.[49]

White racists are fringe figures today. But their existence at all makes it harder to bridge racial divides, especially whenever racist views are espoused by someone who self-identifies as a Christian. And make no mistake, there are still serious racial divisions we need to heal as a society. This became clear to me when I began to screen my film *Human Zoos* for audiences across the country.

In inner city Chicago, I saw the despair and anger among students at a community college who saw the film. In New York City, I screened the film for a class of graduate students in journalism at New York University. During the rest of the class, students presented research about demeaning stereotypes of blacks that continue to appear in advertising, not only in America but in other parts of the world. At a historically segregated church in rural Texas, hundreds of blacks, whites, and Hispanics gathered together to watch the film and share their own pain and hurt from the legacy of racism. In Detroit, I heard from a grandmother about her experience at a state university in

Michigan in the late 1960s. She told how other students had followed her into the showers to see whether she had a tail like a monkey.

I began to understand that although American society has changed dramatically, we still have a long way to go to heal our racial divisions.

The Many Problems with Antiracism

But acknowledgment of this painful reality should not blind us to another important truth: There are serious problems with the so-called "antiracist" movement.

Whites Who Fought against Slavery

The first problem with the antiracist movement is its tendency to blame all "whites" or the entire "white" church for the sins of racism in America. Assigning blame based on someone's race or ethnicity is a perilous endeavor. Take the issue of slavery. There were many American Christian apologists for slavery, especially in the South. But there also were many white *opponents* of slavery. Jemar Tisby is justified in highlighting the contradiction of the American Revolution's proclamation that "all men are created equal" at the same time America was tolerating slavery.[50] But many white Americans during the founding of the nation also recognized the contradiction, and they worked to resolve it.

By the early 1800s, twelve of the original thirteen states had banned the importation of slaves, and eight states had acted to abolish slavery itself. There were also efforts to stop the spread of slavery to new states. In 1787, the Confederation Congress banned slavery in the Northwest Territory, the "massive tract of land that would eventually become the states of Illinois, Indiana, Michigan, Ohio, Wisconsin, and a section of Minnesota."[51]

Opposition to slavery among white Americans was overwhelmingly animated by Christian theology and fueled by many white churches. The Quakers were the earliest denomination in America to make the abolition of slavery a defining issue, with Quakers in Pennsylvania producing the first published condemnation of the practice in America in 1688.[52] In New England, Puritans Samuel Sewall and Cotton Mather produced early anti-slavery tracts.[53] By the time of the Revolution, the Quakers in Pennsylvania had decided to expel members who did not free their slaves;[54] and by the early 1800s, clergymen from a variety of denominations were calling for an end to the evil on the grounds that the Bible taught the doctrine of human equality.[55] Samuel Stanhope Smith, a Presbyterian minister and president of Princeton, advocated racial intermarriage between blacks and whites as a way of breaking down the social barriers between them.[56]

The 1830s saw the founding of the American Anti-Slavery Society, which soon became the focal point for much of the anti-slavery crusade.[57] Backers of the new society included brothers Lewis and Arthur Tappan, white evangelical businessmen who supported a variety of reform efforts in the antebellum era.[58]

Jemar Tisby recognizes that the Civil War was ultimately fought because of slavery.[59] But he seems to ignore the significance that it was fought at all. Slavery has existed throughout human history, and it still exists in various parts of the world today. If American whites (including white Christians) and their institutions were overwhelmingly supportive of slavery, why did the nation fight the bloodiest war in its history? It's precisely because so many white Americans became persuaded that slavery was an intolerable evil that the war came about. Many white Americans opposed slavery, and many lost their lives because they fought against the South. During the Civil War, over 359,000 predominantly white men were killed fighting against the Confederacy, and over 275,000 mostly white men were wounded.[60]

And it's because so many white Christians in America disagreed with slavery that national denominations of Methodists, Baptists, and Presbyterians ultimately split apart.[61]

Lumping together all whites as a class in order to assign blame may be convenient, but it is also inaccurate. The situation gets even more complicated once one realizes that millions of American whites never owned slaves, and millions more came to America well after slavery ended. Judging people simply based on their race or ethnicity is unjust, regardless of the race or ethnicity involved.

Causes of Inequalities

A second problem with the antiracists' narrative about race is the way it tries to affix blame for every existing social or economic problem on "white privilege" or "white supremacy." It is true that there are significant disparities between whites and blacks when it comes to income and many other factors. As we will discuss later, Christians ought to be concerned about those disparities. But recognizing the existence of group differences is not the same as identifying their causes. And there is plenty of data that raises questions about the narrative that "white privilege" is at the bottom of all of the differences we see.

Whites on average have higher incomes than blacks in America. But Asians have significantly higher incomes than both.[62] If "white privilege" is all-pervasive, how did Asian persons of color in America manage to become so much more economically successful than whites? For that matter, why do some sub-groups of blacks match or exceed white attainment in key areas?

The median household income of blacks of Nigerian ancestry in America is nearly the same as that of whites. And male-headed households of Nigerian ancestry actually have a higher median income than white male-headed households.[63]

Or consider educational attainment. While it is true that on average a higher percentage of whites in America have college degrees than blacks, blacks of Nigerian ancestry in America are far more educated than whites. In 2022, only 39 percent of whites had earned a bachelor's degree or higher, whereas 64 percent of persons of Nigerian ancestry had done so. Likewise, only 15 percent of whites had graduate or professional degrees, compared to 30 percent of those of Nigerian ancestry.[64] Clearly "white privilege" and "white racism" are insufficient categories to explain all of the social ills in America right now.

The Racism of Antiracism

A third problem with the antiracist movement is that it offers a patronizing view of black Americans that is itself racist. Antiracists depict black Americans as permanent victims who cannot succeed because of the dominant cultural standards imposed by "whiteness."

According to a graphic posted on the website of the Smithsonian's National Museum of African American History and Culture, these racist "white" standards include "self-reliance," "plan[ning] for the future," "the nuclear family" with a "father" and "mother," "delayed gratification," proper English, politeness, an "emphasis on the scientific method" (including "objective, rational linear thinking"), the idea that "hard work is the key to success"—and even acceptance of "Christianity... [as] the norm" in culture, including Christian holidays.[65]

The implicit—and offensive—assumption of the graphic was that blacks don't value self-reliance, science, reason, delayed gratification, and the like. Moreover, since these are only the values of "whiteness," blacks *need* not value these things. It would be hard to find a more demeaning—or untrue—depiction of the black experience in America.

Black economist Glenn Loury notes how the antiracists downplay the actual story of black success in America, which took place despite heart-breaking challenges. "Where did we start in 1865?" asks Loury. "You had four million people who had been enslaved persons, suddenly emancipated and made citizens. They were largely illiterate. They were largely landless. Some had skills because it was in the slave owner's interest to have his property with skills, but most did not."[66]

Yet despite the appalling injustices of slavery and Jim Crow, blacks in America after the Civil War represent an amazing success story. In 1870, 80 percent of blacks and other persons of color in America were illiterate. Fifty years later, illiteracy had plunged by nearly three-fourths to 23 percent.[67] Economic advancement was similarly dramatic, as black economist Thomas Sowell points out: "Despite the grand myth that black economic progress began or accelerated with the passage of the civil rights laws and 'war on poverty' programs of the 1960s, the cold fact is that the poverty rate among blacks fell from 87 percent in 1940 to 47 percent by 1960. This was before any of those programs began."[68]

The horrific injustices faced by blacks in American history were real—but so were the extraordinary successes of blacks in the face of those injustices. Consider the infamous Tulsa race massacre in 1921, which was sparked when a young black man was arrested. Black Tulsans feared he'd be lynched, so they gathered at the courthouse to support him. Opposing—and armed—whites gathered as well. The ensuing confrontation resulted in mass death and destruction in the city's thriving Greenwood neighborhood, known as "Black Wall Street."[69]

"Thanks to recent scholarship and pop culture depictions... more and more Americans are coming to know the story of the Tulsa Race Massacre that destroyed Black Wall Street," writes Carlos Moreno, author of *The Victory of Greenwood*.[70]

> But the common narrative—that the neighborhood never recovered after the massacre—is incorrect. In fact, Greenwood's resilient residents rebuilt their community almost immediately after the events—in defiance of hastily-enacted racist zoning codes—giving rise to the neighborhood's moniker of Black Wall Street *after*, not *before*, the massacre.

Moreno adds that "the scale of Greenwood's recovery" was nothing short of extraordinary, pointing out that "unlike other disasters like the 1889 Johnstown Flood in Pennsylvania or San Francisco's 1906 earthquake, Greenwood was left to rebuild entirely on its own."

Black Americans repeatedly have been persistent and resourceful in overcoming the obstacles placed in their path. The antiracists' depiction of blacks as almost completely dependent on white racists for their success or failure presents a distorted and unhelpful portrait of American history.

A Cure that Worsens the Disease

A fourth problem with many antiracist activists is that they assume that the only legitimate solutions to the country's social problems come from the left. According to Christian antiracist Jemar Tisby, there is no alternative if someone wants to deal with racism in America: "Addressing regressive racist stances *necessarily* implies adopting 'progressive' stances in order to make positive change"[71] (emphasis added). With a mindset like that, it is little wonder that prominent "antiracist" groups like Black Lives Matter reflexively advocate policies that are anti-capitalist, anti-nuclear family, anti-police, and anti-personal responsibility.[72]

Tisby himself frequently smears those he disagrees with as proponents of "white Christian nationalism," which he explicitly connects to the vilest forms of racism in America's past. "Now We Call It White Christian Nationalism," reads one of the headlines on his blog. "It Used to Just Be Called the KKK."[73] While there are some people on the fringe today who might be accurately described as "white Christian nationalists," Tisby seems to deploy the term as a catch-all to denounce anyone and anything politically or culturally conservative. According to Tisby, the Republican Speaker of the US House is a "White Christian Nationalist."[74] So is the Republican governor of Arkansas.[75] So is the Republican governor of Texas.[76] According to Tisby, indicators of whether you are a "white Christian nationalist" include a belief in "creationism," criticism of same-sex marriage, skepticism toward transgender rights, support for the police, and having "traditionalist gender attitudes."[77]

Ironically, by Tisby's standards, a majority of black Americans would need to be classified as "white Christian nationalists." Tisby actually cites a survey that identifies 38 percent of black Americans as either "adherents" or "sympathizers" of white Christian nationalism![78] How does Tisby explain this counterintuitive result? He invokes racial slurs and claims these blacks are traitors to their race: "There is always a small segment of the oppressed who cooperate with the oppressor," he writes. "This is how you get the 'Uncle Tom' or 'coon' trope. We have long known that members of oppressed groups may betray their own people to gain benefits from the dominant group."[79]

But are the blacks who disagree with Tisby and other professional antiracists really such a "small segment" of the black community?

Surveys suggest otherwise. For example, although a significant number of black Americans have concerns about mistreatment by police, only a small minority (21 percent) favor abolishing the police.[80] Not only that, but 81 percent of blacks want the police to "spend more" or "the same amount of time" in policing their communities. It also turns out that a majority of black Americans (56 percent) "have confidence in... [their] local police force," 60 percent are "satisfied... with the relationship between the police and [their]... local community,"

61 percent think "local police treat people like [themselves]… fairly," and 71 percent feel that if they "had an interaction with police in [their]… area" they would be treated "with courtesy and respect."[81]

Even when it comes to racial preferences in college admissions and employment, many black Americans are not in sync with the antiracist activists. According to a 2016 survey, 57 percent of blacks responded that "race or ethnicity… should not be a factor at all" in college admissions decisions.[82] According to a 2019 survey, a majority of black Americans believe that when employers hire people they should "only take a person's qualifications into account, even if it results in less diversity" rather than giving preferences to people based on their "race and ethnicity."[83] In 2023 the US Supreme Court ruled against using race as a factor in college admission decisions. According to a follow-up survey, 52 percent of all black adults thought the ruling was "mostly a good thing," as did 62 percent of black adults under 40.[84] In short, a majority of black Americans want to be treated based on their own capabilities and situations, not given preferences because of their race.

How many white evangelicals influenced by the antiracist movement have heard any of these things? Unfortunately, if my experience in a predominantly white urban evangelical church is any indication, not many. That is one of the problems with how discussions about race have played out in churches over the past several years. Perhaps the most insidious aspect of current discussions is the effort to marginalize or silence anyone who disagrees, whether white or a person of color.

In the name of "antiracism," too many Stockholm Syndrome Christians have participated in the effort to shut down legitimate debates over the claims of antiracist writers. And many of the people they're silencing are the very ones they purport to help.

Silencing Black Voices

During the summer of 2020, the church where my wife and I were members decided to participate in something called "Blackout Tuesday" on social media. "Blackout Tuesday" was supposed to be an effort to draw attention to racism and police brutality, and our church's

Facebook account posted something as part of the campaign, using its hash tag.

Coming in the midst of nationwide protests and riots, "Blackout Tuesday" had clear political overtones, and some in the community might have understood it to mean that the church was lending its support to various public policy proposals such as defunding the police. The actual date of Blackout Tuesday ended up being especially unfortunate, because early in the hours of the morning African-American policeman David Dorn was murdered trying to prevent the looting of a store.[85] Nevertheless, I thought our church's Facebook post (which included a Bible verse) appropriately focused on what the Bible teaches about injustice.

However, when a regular attendee of the church saw the Blackout Tuesday post, she posted a response on our Facebook page in response. The response was a meme which came from Ryan Bomberger, a biracial (half-African American) Christian who is pro-life.[86] The meme stated: "Planned Parenthood: The Leading Killer of Unarmed Black Lives." The meme offended certain members of the church's white staff and was quickly removed as divisive, despite the fact that it defended the worth of unborn black lives, which was in line with our church's stated position on abortion and which was consistent with at least the stated commitment of Blackout Tuesday to affirm black lives.

I understood the reasoning behind censoring the meme. It was in-your-face. But the fact remained that in the name of fighting racism, our white church was essentially deplatforming a pro-life person of color. Persons of color who did not fit the narrative were persona non grata.

I've seen this same attitude exhibited by many other white Christians. Those most eager to embrace antiracist writers like Jemar Tisby, Latasha Morrison, and Robin DiAngelo often show very little interest in hearing from black thinkers who dissent from current "antiracist" orthodoxy. Yet there are many such thinkers. They include evangelicals such as Voddie Baucham, author of *Fault Lines: The Social Justice Movement and Evangelicalism's Looming Catastrophe*;[87] Darrell Harrison and Virgil Walker, authors of *Just Thinking: About Ethnicity*;[88] Carol Swain, co-author of *Black Eye for America: How Critical Race*

Theory Is Burning Down the House;[89] online writers Delano Squires and Samuel Sey;[90] and Eric and Jennifer Wallace, founders of Freedom's Journal Institute in the greater Chicago area, which seeks to nurture "biblically-based, black conservatism."[91]

Outside the Christian community, dissenters from the "antiracist" movement include noted economist Thomas Sowell at Stanford's Hoover Institution,[92] linguist John McWhorter at Columbia University,[93] and writer/podcaster Coleman Hughes, author of *The End of Race Politics*.[94] Notably, all three of these men are atheists,[95] and they differ in their politics (Sowell is politically conservative, while McWhorter and Hughes are politically liberal). But each one agrees that the antiracist movement is badly flawed.

McWhorter authored a book titled *Woke Racism* where he compares antiracism to a religion.[96] "This is a religion where instead of it being about your faith in Jesus, it's about showing that you know that racism exists above all else," he says. Further, "the way we talk about white privilege is eerily consonant with the way one talks about original sin. You have it from the beginning, it's a stain that you'll never get rid of… white privilege becomes the original sin that you're supposed to live in a kind of atonement for."[97]

If you or members of your church have not heard of these black thinkers or at least similar views expressed by other blacks, then that is its own indictment. Conversations about race in many of America's churches right now are dominated by one side of the theological and political spectrum. This situation is not healthy, especially when a number of the voices being platformed are promoting ideas that are both factually disputed and theologically suspect.

Even theologically conservative Christian denominations have participated in trying to shut down different voices among faithful Christians on the topic of race. Consider debates in the Southern Baptist Convention (SBC) over the past few years regarding "critical race theory" and other ideas joined at the hip to the current antiracism movement.

In 2019, a Southern Baptist pastor proposed that the denomination at its annual meeting approve a resolution squarely condemning "critical race theory and intersectionality" as unbiblical. Instead of allowing a floor debate on the original resolution, the SBC Committee on Resolutions rewrote the resolution and then only allowed floor debate on their rewritten—and very different—version.[98] Tom Ascol, one of the "messengers" (delegates) to the annual meeting, accused the Committee on Resolutions of changing the original resolution so much that the revised resolution had "an almost opposite meaning from that which... [the original author] intended."[99] Instead of branding critical race theory and intersectionality as inherently unbiblical, the rewritten resolution merely condemned their "misuse," and it approved them as "analytical tools [that] can aid in evaluating a variety of human experiences," so long as they are "only... employed as... subordinate to Scripture."[100]

The revised version passed, but the attempt to stage-manage the process to prevent an open debate did not sit well with many people. So two years later, multiple resolutions were submitted to the Committee on Resolutions to give the 2021 annual meeting an opportunity to weigh in on whether critical race theory itself was unbiblical.

Again, the Committee tried to preempt an open debate. Refusing to send any of the pro or anti-critical race theory resolutions to the floor for discussion, it substituted a generic resolution that reaffirmed the importance of racial reconciliation and the sufficiency of the Bible, but sidestepped the question of critical race theory.

Floor debate on the generic resolution was sharply limited, despite the fact that there were many delegates who wanted to speak. One of them was black scholar Carol Swain, a representative of the Conservative Baptist Network. A former longtime professor of political science and law at Vanderbilt University, Swain is a prizewinning scholar who has written multiple books on issues dealing with race. Her law degree is from Yale, and her PhD is from the University of North Carolina at Chapel Hill.[101] But this distinguished scholar was not allowed to speak.

"Pretty much [the] proponents of critical theory, they are controlling the agenda of the Southern Baptist Convention," she said after the meeting. "And it's very top-down. A lot of elitism. And I think average people from the churches don't have influence because the leadership structure is controlled by people that are able because of that power to control what comes to the door, who gets to speak, and they can shut down debate." Swain continued:

> No minority got to speak on that issue. One white man spoke against that resolution and pointed out that it was discrimination. And he got blasted by someone from the stage by the chair of the resolutions committee. And then another person in the audience immediately called for the vote. And at that point, no one could speak against it. And so I was standing there. I've been there for a while, and no one on our side got to speak. No one from the Conservative Baptist Network was there to address the issue put forth by the resolution. We were not allowed to speak. And so I was very disheartened.[102]

There is something deeply disturbing about silencing one of the leading black Southern Baptist voices because her views don't fit the narrative preferred by white progressives.

The Southern Baptist Convention has plenty of baggage when it comes to race, having split from Baptists in the North over support for slavery in the nineteenth century. To their credit, today's Southern Baptists have apologized for their denomination's past involvement in racial discrimination and are seeking to promote racial reconciliation.[103] But given the denomination's painful history, I can understand why some of its leaders might be reluctant to allow what could become a heated public debate over critical race theory.

Nevertheless, attempts to suppress open criticism of the progressive agenda on race are misguided. The antiracist movement raises serious issues worthy of serious discussion. Attempts to stage-manage the conversation over these issues is patronizing and condescending and will likely only create more ill-will among those who feel they are being silenced.

Unfortunately, a culture of intimidation has already developed in many Christian circles designed to shut down any critical discussion of progressive views on race. Black Southern Baptist theologian Voddie Baucham reports hearing from dozens of ministry leaders, pastors, professors, and church staff who have been bullied into silence. "The environment within evangelicalism is so hostile [when it comes to racial issues] that is has a chilling effect," he says. "In this environment, dissent is not only unwelcome, but condemned. Consequently, many godly, thoughtful, well-meaning, justice-loving brethren are being silenced."[104]

I don't think that Christians who are enabling this intimidation truly understand the toxic spirit they are unleashing. If you want to see where this leads, look at how antiracist activists treat members of their own movement.

Vincent Lloyd is a black leftist professor at Villanova University outside Philadelphia. In 2022, he was asked to lead an exclusive summer seminar for high school students on "Race and the Limits of Law in America," sponsored by the elite Telluride Association.

As Lloyd tells it, the seminar devolved into a cult-like atmosphere where white and Asians students were expected to be silent and only blacks were supposed to speak. Two Asian students who continued to actively participate were expelled by a vote of the other students.

The remaining students eventually turned on Lloyd himself because of his supposed "countless microaggressions" and insufficient antiracist zeal, and the seminar was suspended before it was finished. One gets the impression Lloyd still doesn't fully comprehend how he could have received such treatment: "I am a black professor, I directed my university's black-studies program, I lead anti-racism and transformative-justice workshops, and I have published books on anti-black racism and prison abolition. I live in a predominantly black neighborhood of Philadelphia, my daughter went to an Afrocentric school."[105] But it wasn't enough to spare him from being canceled.

Racial prejudice and injustice are real problems that Christians ought to be concerned about. But to deal with the issues constructively, they would be better served in looking more to the Bible than to progressive "antiracism." Sadly, too many Christians are failing to do so.

The Bible as a Bulwark for Human Equality

In his book *Irresistible*, pastor Andy Stanley tells a revealing story from his pastoral ministry about a father and daughter who came to him for counseling. The father was upset his daughter was dating a black man, and he wanted to enlist Stanley's support. The father claimed that his objections were grounded in the Bible, especially the Old Testament. He cited Old Testament injunctions against marrying foreign wives and even claimed that "God did not allow Moses to enter the promised land" because "Moses had married a dark-skinned Midianite woman."[106]

The father was twisting the Bible. The prohibition against foreign wives in the Old Testament had nothing to do with race; it had to do with not marrying outside one's faith (Numbers 25:1–18; Deuteronomy 7:1–4). And nothing in the Bible suggests that God didn't let Moses enter the promised land because he "married a dark-skinned Midianite." In fact, God rebuked Moses's brother and sister for objecting to Moses's marriage to her (Numbers 12:1–16).

Despite the falsehoods being promoted by this father, Stanley says he didn't correct him, thinking it wouldn't be helpful. That is a pastoral judgment call, and I'm in no position to second-guess it. But what is appalling is the lesson Stanley drew from the experience: Christians shouldn't be relying on the Old Testament at all. "When you blend old with new, you'll get the worst of both," he comments.[107] Stanley uses the racist father as another example of why Christians should view the Old Testament as the "Obsolete Testament."

But isn't there a much more obvious lesson? The father's views provided an indictment of the preaching of white ministers in the South. Had Southern white ministers taught more about what the Old Testament really says when it comes to race and ethnicity, the father might have found it harder to twist the Old Testament to support his racism.

Yet Stanley's first inclination appeared to be to run away from the Bible's teaching rather than embrace and explain it. I think this reticence is shared by many Christians influenced by the antiracist movement. As I've read their comments, I am struck time and again by how little most of them ground their views in what the Bible says. To be sure, there are occasional citations of a few proof-texts. But as a rule, it is as if these Christians are embarrassed by the Bible when it comes to race, or as if they think it is largely irrelevant.

In truth, the Bible has served as the greatest bulwark against racism and for equality in human history.

Created in God's Image

First, the Bible plainly teaches that all human beings are members of one human race (Acts 17:26), which descended from a single ancestral couple created in God's own image (Genesis 1:26–27, 3:20). From this teaching comes the idea that all humans are made in God's image and share the same intrinsic worth. Far from promoting racism, biblical passages on the creation of humans formed a foundation for many Christians to argue for the equality of all.

Today we often miss just how radical the biblical account of the creation of humans truly is. But compare it to the Hindu creation story of humans in the Laws of Manu, and you will see the stark difference. In the Laws of Manu, humans are born into different castes reflecting the different body parts of the Creator Brahman from which they came.[108] Some are created to rule; others are created to serve. In other words, humans are born inherently unequal from the start. There is a reason why ideas of universal human equality and dignity arose in the Christian West.

Alike in Christ

Second, the New Testament teaches that ethnic, racial, and national distinctions pale in comparison to the unity we find in Christ. "Here there is not Greek and Jew, circumcised and uncircumcised, barbarian, Scythian, slave, free; but Christ is all, and in all" (Colossians 3:11; also see Galatians 3:28, Romans 10:12, and 1 Corinthians 12:13). The gospel knows no ethnic or national boundaries. Indeed, Christians are called to "go therefore and make disciples of *all* nations, baptizing them in the name of the Father and of the Son and of the Holy Spirit" (Matthew 28:19, emphasis added).

No Favoritism Based on Ethnicity

Third, both in the Old Testament and the New Testament, the Bible repeatedly teaches that it is wrong to show favoritism or partiality based on either ethnicity or class or other morally irrelevant characteristics. "For the Lord your God is God of gods and Lord of lords, the great, the mighty, and the awesome God, who is not partial and takes no bribe" (Deuteronomy 10:17). God himself "shows no partiality" to either Jews or Greeks when it comes to eternal salvation (Romans 2:11). Christians are called to show no favoritism to the rich over the poor (James 2:1–8). Old Testament Jews were required to treat aliens in their land fairly and with respect: "When a stranger sojourns with you in your land, you shall not do him wrong. You shall treat the stranger who sojourns with you as the native among you, and you shall love him as yourself, for you were strangers in the land of Egypt" (Leviticus 19:33–34).

Notably, many people of African ancestry played key roles in biblical history, from Ebed-Melech, who rescued the prophet Jeremiah in the Old Testament, to the Ethiopian official in the New Testament who was one of the earliest Christian converts from outside Judea and Samaria.[109]

Everyone Sins

Fourth, the Bible teaches that "all have sinned and fall short of the glory of God" (Romans 3:23). Consequently, there is not one human (apart from Christ) or one racial or ethnic group without sin or without a need for a savior. Or, to put this in contemporary terms, no group has a monopoly on oppressing or mistreating other people. Every one of us at times wrongs other people. And every one of us can be forgiven—and we likewise should forgive those who sin against us (Matthew 6:12–15, Matthew 18:21–35).

Accountable for Your Own Acts

Fifth, the Bible teaches the importance of individual accountability. Although there are passages about God's judgment on nations and groups, the general expectation for biblical justice is that people should be held accountable for their own acts, not the acts of others, including the wrongdoing of their ancestors or their ethnic group (Deuteronomy 24:16, Ezekiel 18:1–32, Romans 2:6).

Anti-Slavery

What about slavery? It is true that the Bible does not give an unqualified denunciation of every form of slavery. At the same time, many people today don't appreciate just how anti-slavery the Bible actually is.

In the Old Testament, the Mosaic law imposed the death penalty on anyone involved in kidnapping others and then selling them as slaves: "Whoever steals a man and sells him, and anyone found in possession of him, shall be put to death" (Exodus 21:16). In the New Testament, Paul reiterates that God's law condemns "enslavers" or "menstealers" (1 Timothy 1:10).

The African slave trade that supplied slaves for American plantations certainly violated these prohibitions. "Bands of slavers would roam the African country countryside, preying on villagers who let their guard down" to kidnap men and women for the transatlantic slave trade.[110]

Mosaic law also forbade the permanent enslavement of fellow Jews. Israelites could only hold their countrymen temporarily. Jewish slaves were more like indentured servants. They had to be released from bondage after six years (Exodus 21:2; Leviticus 25:39–43).

Punishments were imposed for the mistreatment of slaves. If a slave owner did permanent bodily damage to a slave, such as knocking out his tooth, the slave had to be freed (Exodus 21:26–27).

Finally, Mosaic law forbade the return of escaped slaves. "You shall not give up to his master a slave who has escaped from his master to you. He shall dwell with you, in your midst, in the place that he shall choose within one of your towns, wherever it suits him. You shall not wrong him" (Deuteronomy 23:15–16). Contrast this with the fugitive slave laws in antebellum American that required the forcible return of slaves to their masters and criminalized efforts by Christians and others to shelter them.

In the New Testament, various verses do encourage slaves and servants to obey their earthly masters (Titus 2:9–10, Ephesians 6:5, 1 Peter 2:18, 1 Timothy 6:1–2, Colossians 3:22)—but slaves are also encouraged to "try to gain your freedom if you can" (1 Corinthians 7:21). This seeming contradiction makes sense if we bear in mind that at this time the Jews were living under Roman rule. Some Jews and Christians (like Paul) were Roman citizens, but most were not. Some were slaves to Roman masters.[111] Much of the New Testament commentary about slavery, then, was not meant as an approval of it, but as advice on how Christian slaves could best cope with a bad situation.

The passages about behaving well as a slave are often embedded in passages that outline the mutual duties of all Christians to submit to each other. For instance, Paul in Ephesians 6 urges slaves to "obey your earthly masters with fear and trembling, with a sincere heart, as you would Christ." But he goes on to issue an equivalent command to their masters: "Masters, *do the same to them*, and stop your threatening, knowing that he who is both their Master and yours is in heaven, and that there is no partiality with him" (emphasis added, Ephesians 6:5–9; also see Colossians 4:1).

Paul demonstrated his own practical concern for the plight of slaves on at least two occasions. He intervened on behalf of runaway slave Onesimus with his master Philemon (who may have been Greek, based on his name, and who lived in what is now Turkey), urging Philemon to "welcome him as you would welcome me" and take him back "no longer as a slave, but better than a slave, as a dear brother" (Philemon 1:16–17). In Philippi (a city in Greece), Paul took the risky action of freeing a slave girl from a demon, depriving her owners of her economic value, since they sold her services as a fortune-teller. As a result he and his companion were severely beaten and imprisoned by the Roman authorities (Acts 16:16–24).

The Results of Following Biblical Principles

In sum, the Bible's emphasis on human equality and dignity, its obliteration of ethnic and other distinctions among Christians, and its call on Christians to love and serve others without partiality all struck blows against racial prejudice and discrimination. When Christians obeyed the Bible's teachings, positive results ensued.

Many early converts to Christianity freed their slaves.[112] Many other Christians were inspired to work for the abolition of slavery.[113]

Some faithful Christians stood against racial discrimination and prejudice even when it went against the social conventions of their time. For example, white American pastor and writer Francis

Schaeffer established a community known as L'Abri ("the shelter" in French) during the 1950s in Switzerland. The community was open to all seekers, regardless of race or religion.

Sylvester Jacobs, who as mentioned previously faced racism among white evangelicals at the Moody Bible Institute and elsewhere, eventually ended up at L'Abri in 1968. He met his future wife there, and he found validation for his calling as a photographer. But, most of all, he found love and acceptance, which opened the door to a deeper relationship with God. "If I, a black, matter to these people, could it be because I matter to God?" he asked himself.[114]

If Christians want to further genuine racial reconciliation, they would do well to base their efforts squarely on biblical principles rather than on the principles of secular antiracism. Demonizing one race over another, preaching either white or black superiority, and cultivating grievances based on the actions of people long dead are inconsistent with the biblical worldview. They are also dead ends for public policy. There are better ways to proceed.

We're All in This Together

The response to the errors of the modern antiracism movement should not be to do nothing. The antiracists are right about a key point: Many blacks and other ethnic minorities in America continue to face heart-wrenching challenges. Many are trapped in poverty. Many live in communities wracked by violent crime. Many minority children are forced to attend substandard schools. If white Christians love their neighbors as themselves, they will be concerned about addressing these problems.

But we need to make sure what we do is helpful.

A critically important principle is this: We must develop solutions that bring people together rather than tear them apart. If humans truly are created in the image of God regardless of race, if no race or ethnicity is inherently superior to any other, and if people of all races are sinners who need a redeemer, then our social programs ought to reflect those realities. That means, most of all, that our solutions should treat all people equally regardless of race. They should never be framed as entitlements or as punishments based on someone's race or ethnicity.

Not only does framing solutions in racial terms further divide people, it is also unjust. Black writer Samuel Sey lives in La Rue, a predominantly white city in rural Ohio. In a provocative essay titled "The Forgotten White People," Sey makes an important point: "The biggest issues in inner-city households are also the biggest issues in rural white towns like La Rue: bad or absentee fathers, the welfare system, drug addictions, and poor work ethic."[115]

It is true that American blacks as a group are disproportionately impacted by certain social ills. But it is equally true that those social problems typically impact many whites and people of other races as well. Half of all homeless people in America are white.[116] Nearly 45 percent of all Americans in poverty are white.[117] Over half of all suspects shot by police in America are white.[118] Social problems like poverty, crime, and dysfunctional schools do not just hurt people of one race. They hurt all of us.

My friends Eric and Jennifer Wallace made this point when they held a policy summit for blacks in Chicago in 2023. They subtitled the event "How to Fix Black America," but they crossed out the word "Black." Because yes, black America matters, but the social challenges confronting black Americans are also confronting whites and other races. If we want to escape an endless cycle of racial recriminations, Americans of all races need to recognize their common ground and join together in support of solutions that benefit everyone.

What Works?

Of course, this approach requires us to agree on what solutions will work. The Christian Church has two millennia of experience in helping to empower the poor, reform the criminal, save the sick, and rescue those in dire straits. Unfortunately, too many Christians today seem to have embraced secularism's operating assumption that the causes of poverty, crime, homelessness, and other forms of social distress are primarily material. This means that their solutions must be material as well: Simply transfer more material resources to those who suffer. If people are poor or engage in crime, government merely needs to give them more money and food and health care. If people are homeless, government merely needs to provide them with physical shelter.

Christian antiracist Jemar Tisby faults white Christians for their "over-spiritualizing of the Christian faith that ignores physical, material concerns like poverty, mass incarceration, voting rights, and other important issues."[119] We *are* physical beings, and providing material goods is definitely part of the Christian vocation to care for others. (James 2:15–17). That said, there is massive evidence that simply transferring material resources won't solve the problems Tisby is concerned about.

Poverty

In the fifty years since President Lyndon Johnson declared his "War on Poverty," "taxpayers have spent over $22 trillion on anti-poverty programs (in constant 2012 dollars)," point out Rachel Sheffield and Robert Rector. "Despite this mountain of spending," they say, "progress against poverty, at least as measured by the government, has been minimal."[120]

In the biblical view, this result is not hard to understand. The Bible teaches that human brokenness is not at its foundation caused by a lack of material goods. It is caused by humanity's spiritual rebellion against God, *which is a universal problem for all people, regardless of their race or class or sex.*

Human sinfulness can exhibit itself through the actions of the rich and powerful, when they oppress the poor by depriving them of material resources. But it can also manifest itself in the poor if people are enslaved by their own destructive passions. In a biblical worldview view, sin at its base inheres in *persons*. It involves sinful individuals who violate God's standards.

These sinful individuals can construct institutions, laws, and customs that oppress others. This means it can be appropriate in certain situations to talk about "structural sins" or "social sins." But such talk can also lead us astray.

Poverty in America and around the world has many causes. But long-term intergenerational poverty in America is largely tied to the breakdown of marriage and the two-parent family. This uncomfortable truth has been known for decades. Families headed by single women are dramatically more likely to fall below the poverty line than families headed by married couples.[121] *This holds true regardless of race.* So if you are truly concerned about reducing long-term intergenerational poverty in America, one of the best things you can do is support policies that encourage the embrace of traditional Christian standards of sexual behavior, including the creation of more families with both fathers and mothers.

Crime

What about crime? Do people commit crime in the United States primarily because of a lack of material resources? Once again, the disintegration of the traditional family is key. According to a 2023 research report from the Institute for Family Studies,

> the total crime rate in cities with high levels of single parenthood are [sic] 48% higher than those with low levels of single parenthood. When it comes to violent crime and homicide, cities with high levels of single parenthood have 118% higher rates of violence and 255% higher rates of homicide. And in Chicago, our analysis of census tract data from the city shows that tracts with high levels of single-parent-headed households face 137% higher total crime rates, 226% higher violent crime rates, and 436% higher homicide rates, compared to tracts with low levels of single parenthood.[122]

Our culture's abandonment of the two-parent family as its standard has doomed millions of Americans of all races to a hellish existence. None of this is intended to disparage the many heroic single parents who are doing their best to raise their children in challenging circumstances. Those parents need our support. At the same time, our goal should be to restore the norm of the two-parent family. At a societal level, the breakdown of the two-parent family breeds poverty, violence, and a range of social dysfunctions.

Stockholm Syndrome Christianity is partly to blame. When Christians abandon biblical sexual standards and instead embrace the secular culture's sexual ethics, the consequences don't just stay in the bedroom. They spread through the entire culture.

Family disintegration is a problem for people of all ethnicities in America. For example, nearly 28 percent of white children in America today are born to unmarried women, and over 28 percent of white households with children under 25 are headed by single men or women or unmarried couples.[123] Unquestionably, however, the disintegration of the two-parent family has hit the black community hardest. Today over 70 percent of black children in America are born to unmarried women, and over 60 percent of black households with children under 25 are headed by single men or women or unmarried couples.[124] (And unmarried cohabiting couples don't produce the same stability and other benefits that married couples do.)

The lopsided nature of these statistics by race is one reason many people avoid the topic. If you talk about the role of family breakdown in perpetuating poverty and cultivating crime, you are liable to be accused of racism.

As a result, Christians who should know better self-censor. When Pastor Tim Keller wrote his book on poverty, *Generous Justice*, he devoted plenty of space to the "structural" causes of poverty.[125] But his mentions of family breakdown were glancing and dismissive. Christians who let themselves be intimidated into silence on this topic are not being kind. They are being cruel. If the goal is wholeness and restoration, there is nothing kind or "antiracist" about suppressing the truth about broken families. Instead, what is truly racist is perpetuating the falsehood that the two-parent family is somehow an invention of "whites," or that single-parent families are natural or inevitable for non-whites.

There is nothing inevitable about broken families for either blacks or whites. While it is true that more than 70 percent of black children today are born to unmarried people, it is equally true that this was not always the case. As black economist Walter Williams pointed out, only 19 percent of black children were born out of wedlock in 1940, and blacks had a higher marriage rate than whites up to 1940.[126]

Civil rights activist Robert Woodson grew up in a black neighborhood in Philadelphia in the 1930s and 40s. Born in the midst of the Great Depression and the injustices of segregation, Woodson nevertheless experienced a different world:

> I never heard a gun fired in my life in the time I was there through high school... 98% of all the households had a man and a woman raising children. I never heard of an elderly person being mugged in my neighborhood. I never heard of a child being shot in their crib. All of these [things] occurred... between 1930 and 1940, when racism was enshrined in law. Black America had the highest marriage rate of any group in society and elderly people could walk safely there.[127]

The destruction of the nuclear family in America is not inevitable for either blacks or whites, and we shouldn't act as if it is.

Homelessness

Unfortunately, poverty and crime aren't the only social problems where some Christians have abandoned biblical truth in favor of solutions based on secular materialism. Consider America's related—and growing—epidemic of homelessness. People can become homeless for many reasons. Nevertheless, most chronic homelessness in modern America does not arise simply because of a lack of material resources. It is tied to substance abuse, addiction, mental illness, and trauma.[128]

Despite this reality, the federal government has pushed "Housing First" policies that prioritize physical shelter over dealing with the underlying reasons people become homeless. The result has not been a reduction in homelessness. Instead, homelessness has exploded.[129] If we want to solve the homelessness crisis, we need to address the whole person, not just a person's material needs. Yet even many Christians have been misled into thinking otherwise.

When I taught state and local politics as a college professor, I invited a man to speak who ran a program for the homeless in Seattle. When fundraising for his program at churches, this man would be sure to wear his clerical collar, which created the impression that his homeless outreach was a Christian ministry. But when he spoke to my class, it soon became clear that there was very little that was distinctly Christian in the program he ran. All the program did was to try to get people physical shelter.

There is nothing wrong with providing shelter. But shelter alone does little to address the root causes of homelessness for many people, which are primarily psychological, social, and spiritual.

A single program can't accomplish everything, but this minister's lack of interest about even trying to find out what led to a person's homelessness was striking. Even more stunning was that his program apparently offered no spiritual help for the people he was trying to shelter. He disparaged rescue missions that require recipients to attend a religious service to receive help, and while I agree that such a requirement isn't a great idea, his program didn't even seem to offer voluntary opportunities for those who might be hungering for a connection to God. This Christian minister belonged to a theologically conservative denomination that officially preached the need for everyone to embrace Jesus as their Lord and Savior to become whole. Yet for all practical purposes, he operated his "ministry" on the principles of secular materialism.

Education

Another area where some Christians embrace a fundamentally materialistic approach is education.

Many of America's students are failing. Once again, the problem extends beyond racial lines. Although many black children may be hardest hit, white children are experiencing the same challenges. Black education reformer Ian Rowe, writing prior to the COVID-19 pandemic, points out that "only 37% of all American kids are reading at grade level, and even white kids have never been higher than about 44% of white kids reading at grade level. So what's interesting about that, it's unlikely that systemic racism is the reason, right, that white kids are not reading at grade level. So the question is what are the factors beyond race that are driving low performance outcomes for kids of all races?"[130]

The progressives' standard solution is simply to advocate for more money for existing public schools. While money certainly is an important component of good schools, it is hard to argue that a lack of money is the fundamental cause of America's current failures in education. Since 1919, per pupil spending on education in America in constant dollars has risen nearly 1,900 percent.[131] The main problem with the educational system in America has not been a lack of money. It is what is done with that money. Effective education requires high standards and discipline. It also requires character training.

Fortunately, a growing number of Americans of all races are beginning to understand this. One of the most inspiring meetings I have ever was attended was a session on education at the Freedom's Journal Institute summit for black leaders and activists. There I listened to a black pastor tell about plans for character-based Christian schools sponsored by his church in Chicago, and I heard Ian Rowe discuss his new venture in New York City to create a "network of character-based, International Baccalaureate public charter high schools."[132] The curriculum of those schools not only sets high academic standards for students; it also seeks to train students in four "cardinal virtues": courage, justice, temperance, and wisdom.[133] Public charter schools in New York City offer a pathway to success for all students, but especially for minorities trapped in a regular district school that is dysfunctional. In 2023, black students enrolled in New York City charter schools achieved proficiency scores that were 45 percent higher in English and 78 percent higher in math than the scores of black students enrolled in their regular district school.[134]

Ironically, progressive antiracist activists often oppose school choice. This is another area where they clearly do not represent the majority of the black community. According to a 2023 national survey of registered voters, 73 percent of blacks favor public and private school choice, a higher percentage than whites.[135]

Antiracist Christians are correct that Christians should be concerned about curbing injustices and helping people who are hurting or oppressed. The gospel most certainly has social implications. But helping others will require an honest discussion of *all* of the options for solutions, not just those from the progressive end of the political spectrum, especially proposals premised on a materialistic conception of human nature.

5. We Must Obey Men Rather than God

Stockholm Christians' Abandonment of Religious Liberty

IN 2017, RUSSELL VOUGHT WAS UP FOR US SENATE CONFIRMATION for a post in the federal Office of Management and Budget. He ended up being shouted down by a sitting United States senator.[1]

His crime? In his capacity as a private citizen, Vought had defended the right of a Christian college, Wheaton, to hire faculty who embraced its statement of faith. He also expressed his view as a Christian that Jesus is the only way of salvation.

According to two sitting United States senators, Vought's personal view that salvation is only through Jesus meant he was disqualified from holding a job in the federal government.

If you think the freedom to practice your faith is alive and well in America, you haven't been paying attention.

In 2013, students in a class at Florida Atlantic University were instructed as part of a class exercise to write the word "Jesus" on a piece of paper and then step on it. A student who refused and complained to the administration was charged with violating the student code and ordered not to return to class. After a public outcry, the university ultimately apologized, rescinded the student's punishment, and promised the lesson wouldn't be taught again. Amazingly, the faculty union and a "free speech" group then suggested that forbidding the lesson without getting the faculty's permission violated academic freedom. What about the religious freedom rights of the students not to be pressured to desecrate the name of Jesus?[2]

In 2014, a community college in Maryland denied a Christian student entry to its radiation therapy program. His offense? An admissions committee asked him what the most important thing in his life was, and he answered, "My God."[3] Another Christian student was denied entrance to the same program after being asked what he based his morals on and answering "my faith."[4] College officials regarded those answers as inappropriate.

In 2016, the US Commission on Civil Rights issued a lengthy report basically repudiating religious liberty. Indeed, the chair of the Commission publicly claimed that the phrases "religious liberty" and "religious freedom" were actually "code words for discrimination, intolerance, racism, sexism, homophobia, Islamophobia, Christian supremacy."[5]

From May 2020 to mid-2024, there were more than 500 attacks on Catholic churches and pro-life centers across America, "including arson attacks which damaged or destroyed historic churches; spray-painting and graffiti of satanic messages; rocks and bricks thrown through windows; and statues destroyed (often with heads cut off)."[6]

Throughout the United States, doctors, nurses, pharmacists, and religious hospitals are facing pressure to participate in abortions, gender reassignment surgeries, and other medical services that violate their Christian convictions.[7] Florists, wedding photographers, and caterers have faced ruinous fines or litigation if they choose not to service same-sex weddings.[8]

With increasing frequency, biblically orthodox Christians are being fired simply for expressing unpopular Christian beliefs. Flight attendants Marli Brown and Lacey Smith were fired by Alaska Airlines because they criticized proposed federal gay rights legislation that would erode religious liberty protections. The airlines had endorsed the legislation, but it explicitly invited comments about its stance from its employees on a private company forum. When Brown and Smith offered their critical comments, they were investigated and ultimately discharged.[9]

In another case, Southwest Airlines terminated a flight attendant after she posted something on Facebook criticizing a flight union official for participating in a pro-abortion event in Washington, DC.[10]

Some private businesses, meanwhile, are now discriminating against Christian customers with impunity. In Richmond, Virginia, a restaurant canceled a private party for the Family Foundation after discovering its traditional views on marriage and its opposition to abortion. The organization was given less than two hours' notice of the cancellation.[11]

In Seattle, a group of pro-life Christians had been distributing leaflets against abortion and sharing the gospel on the streets of the city. Taking a break from their activities, they went into a Seattle coffee shop to have some coffee. They did not go into the coffee shop to distribute their leaflets or to argue their case. But the owner discovered who they were and found one of their leaflets outside the shop on public property. He read it and was enraged. He told them his restaurant wouldn't serve them and demanded that they leave. Not only that, he spewed vile insults, including talking about how he'd like to have anal sex with Jesus because he's "hot."[12]

These two situations are not the same, by the way, as that of a baker who is willing to serve gay customers but unwilling to create products specifically in support of gay marriage. More on this later.

Sam Brownback is a former US governor, former US senator, and former US Ambassador at Large for International Religious Freedom. He currently chairs the National Committee for Religious Freedom, a bipartisan political action committee that funds candidates who support religious liberty.[13] The committee's advisory board includes an array of Catholic, Protestant, Jewish, Muslim, and Hindu leaders, as well as former members of Congress and an emeritus professor at Harvard University. Yet in 2022, Chase Bank closed the committee's bank account without warning or explanation. After the committee challenged the action, Chase began demanding private donor and financial information not required by the IRS.[14] Let that sink in.

University of Virginia law professor Douglas Laycock is one of the nation's most respected authorities on religious liberty law. He now warns: "For the first time in nearly three hundred years, important forces in American society are questioning the free exercise of religion *in principle*—suggesting that free exercise of religion may be a bad idea, or at least, a right to be minimized."[15]

There is little question that the ability of Christians to freely practice and articulate their faith is under increasing attack in America. What might surprise you, however, is that many of these attacks have been enabled and even supported by self-identified Christians.

In Acts 5:29, when the Apostles are told by the Sanhedrin not to teach in the name of Jesus, "Peter and the apostles answered, 'We must obey God rather than men.'"

That's the biblical standard, and it's ultimately why Christians should support religious liberty. But Stockholm Syndrome Christians effectively turn this teaching on its head. Instead of "We must obey God rather than men," they skirt dangerously close to "We must obey *men* rather than God!" And when other Christians are facing persecution or hardship, they turn a blind eye—or even facilitate the persecution.

We should have seen it coming.

Trial Run: Deplatforming Churches in NYC

In 2011, churches in New York City became embroiled in a major battle over religious liberty. New York City schools allowed a wide array of community groups to rent school facilities outside of normal school hours. The city's board of education, however, wanted to ban churches from renting school facilities for worship. The proposed ban was blatantly discriminatory, because the district planned to continue to rent its facilities to everyone else.[16]

Unfortunately, a federal appeals court okayed the plan.

At risk was the very existence of more than sixty churches that had been renting school facilities throughout the city. Most of these churches served racial and ethnic minorities, and they could not easily afford to rent elsewhere.

This was a big deal. Yet many of New York City's most prominent and biggest churches stayed out of the fray. A steering committee of pastors impacted by the ban asked, "Where are these pastors who have these huge churches? They have been absolutely silent."[17]

One of the pastors most conspicuously absent from the public debate was Presbyterian megachurch pastor Tim Keller of Redeemer Presbyterian Church in the heart of Manhattan. The lack of leadership from Keller was particularly noticeable since several churches affiliated with Redeemer were meeting in public schools at the time.

New York pastor Bill Devlin, who helped lead protests against the new policy, said he had personally approached various megachurch pastors with appeals for help. One said he was working behind the scenes. Others offered prayers but not public support. One of the pastors he appealed to was Tim Keller, with whom he had a personal connection. "He signed my diploma. He was a professor of Practical Theology," said Devlin.[18] But to no avail.

The Christian Post made multiple requests for an interview with Keller or another church spokesperson but was rebuffed. Instead, the church issued the following written statement: "Redeemer has been actively engaged with the pastors who have been directly affected by the school decision. We have hosted daily prayer meetings for them and are providing support as we can."[19]

A city councilman who was also the pastor of a church complained: "I've been very disappointed with those who call themselves fathers in the city, who have megachurches and have not stepped up. They are happy they have a building. I have mine as well, what about the other people? Maybe some [megachurches] are working behind the scenes, but this is not the time for that. This is the time for a frontal attack."[20]

Pastor Devlin accused the megachurch pastors of lacking courage in their failure to publicly support fellow congregations about to lose their places of worship. "These are your brothers in Christ," he said. "These are not some activists from Occupy Wall Street. These are men that are in the same gospel ministry as you are. They happen to have more people of color, more poor people, more of the meek, the weak[,] more low-income. They don't have a building. These big dog pastors, they are lacking courage."[21]

The day after *The Christian Post* ran its story criticizing him, Keller finally issued a public statement of support for the embattled churches. In the statement, he criticized the federal appellate court ruling okaying the church ban—the ruling that had been issued eight months earlier.[22]

Because some Christians were willing to continue to fight, the discriminatory policy was eventually overturned by local officials.[23] But the controversy over equal access of religious groups to public facilities should have been a wake-up call. If prominent pastors aren't even willing to stand up for the right to worship, that does not bode well for the future.

More recent events have borne out those concerns.

Conscripting Christians to Support Same-Sex Marriage

In late 2022, the US Congress enshrined same-sex marriage into federal law through the so-called "Respect for Marriage Act." As discussed in Chapter 3, some Christians used the opportunity to recant their previous opposition to the legalization of same-sex marriage.

But the Respect of Marriage Act was about more than simple legalization. Many legal scholars and public policy analysts raised alarms about its lack of real protections for religious liberty.[24] True, the law contained some boilerplate language about how it didn't authorize violating the Constitution or other statutes. It made clear that the law couldn't be used to force churches and religious groups to hold gay weddings or wedding celebrations.

But churches and religious groups aren't the only ones whose rights are at stake. For individuals and businesses currently being persecuted for their views on gay marriage, the law made things worse, not better. It created a new statutory right to sue people. It also failed to provide any protection for small business owners from being compelled to service same-sex marriages against their Christian convictions. Finally, the law equated same-sex marriage with interracial marriage, effectively lumping together opponents of same-sex marriage with racists.

The Respect for Marriage Act could not have passed Congress without the active support of self-identified Christians in the US Senate. Key US senators who voted for the final bill included Missouri senator Roy Blunt, a devout Baptist who had at one point been the president of a Baptist university.[25] These self-identified Christians made the difference.

The Christians in Congress who supported the bill were given cover by an array of Christian groups. These included liberal Protestant denominations like the Presbyterian Church USA and the Evangelical Lutheran Church in the United States.[26] But supporters also included the National Association of Evangelicals, which offered the bill effusive praise even while stating that the NAE continued to affirm biblical marriage.[27]

Christianity Today likewise published an article endorsing the law.[28] Although the article carried a disclaimer that it didn't necessarily represent the views of the magazine, no article with a contrary view was published.

Evangelical Christians who supported the bill emphasized their concern and support for LGBTQ+ rights and needs. The National Association of Evangelicals argued that their support signaled they were "respecting our fellow citizens" who don't share Christian religious beliefs. Of course we should respect the rights of others to hold different religious beliefs. That does not mean we should codify into law positions that run counter to worldwide historical beliefs about the nature of men, women, and marriage—especially when these positions carry with them devastating cultural consequences like the breakdown of the mother/father family. As we saw in the last chapter, disrupting the family means exacerbating poverty, homelessness, and myriad other ills.

Nor should we codify into law views that undermine constitutional rights such as religious liberty. Those who supported the (misnamed)

Respect for Marriage Act seem uncaring or at least oblivious to the plight of the growing number of fellow believers suffering for their stand on biblical marriage. It's classic Stockholm Syndrome Christianity: Take the side of the secular culture and pat yourself on the back for enabling their further oppression of others. At the same time, ignore the suffering of those who are supposed to be your brothers and sisters in Christ.

And, make no mistake, our brothers and sisters have been suffering.

In Oregon, Melissa and Aaron Klein owned a bakery that created cakes for special occasions. Then a lesbian couple asked the Kleins to create a cake to celebrate their same-sex wedding. Melissa and Aaron gladly served clients of all orientations, but they didn't feel they could use their talents to celebrate a ceremony that went against their Christian beliefs. The State of Oregon ultimately fined the Kleins $135,000 and even ordered them not to talk about their Christian beliefs. The Kleins and their children received death threats. Their property was vandalized. Their home was broken into. Melissa was called vile names I won't repeat here, and they were sent messages such as "I hope all your children die" and "Enjoy living as the scum on society." The Kleins were ultimately driven out of business.[29]

In my own state of Washington, grandmother Barronelle Stutzman was driven out of business as a florist after she refused to use her creative talents to create special floral arrangements for same-sex weddings. "I am a Christian, and I believe the Bible to be the Word of God," Stutzman said. "That Word makes it clear that God loves all people so much that He sent His Son to die in their place. And it also teaches that He designed marriage to be only the union of one man and one woman. I could not take the artistic talents God Himself gave me and use them to contradict and dishonor His Word."[30]

Stutzman faced lawsuits from both the ACLU and the Washington State Attorney General. After nearly nine years of litigation where her rights were continually denied, she finally gave up her business in 2021.[31]

"At one point, those aligned against me suggested that I could keep my shop if I paid a fine and promised to create custom designs for same-sex ceremonies in the future," she said. "I refused because I could not betray my conscience."[32]

These efforts to compel Christians to violate their consciences aren't just being pushed by non-Christians or atheists. They are being facilitated and promoted by Christians.

In Washington state, the persecution of Barronelle Stutzman was made possible by self-identified Christian legislators who enacted gay marriage by statute. Civil libertarians warned them the law they were about to enact did not adequately protect religious liberty rights. But Christian legislators who voted for gay marriage did not heed the warnings and did nothing to secure the rights of Christians not to facilitate gay weddings.

Bob Ferguson, the state Attorney General who sued Barronelle Stutzman, is another self-identified Christian, highlighting in the official voter's pamphlet his active membership in a local Catholic church.[33] The Catholic Church upholds the same view of gay marriage as Stutzman, and the US Catholic Bishops, the Catholic Medical Association, the Catholic Bar Association, and other Catholic groups urged the United States Supreme Court to protect the conscience rights of people like Stutzman in a similar case.[34] Ferguson was persecuting Stutzman for exercising rights of conscience that his own church supported.

Nationally, some of the same prominent Christian pastors who either waffled on gay marriage or argued for its acceptance stoked the flames of intolerance against their fellow Christians who did not want to participate in putting on or celebrating same-sex weddings. In 2014, Methodist pastor Adam Hamilton in Kansas was outraged at a proposed state law that would have protected people who disagreed with the morality of gay marriage from being conscripted to facilitate same-sex marriages. Hamilton implied that helping put on a gay marriage had now become a Christian duty: "Jesus routinely healed, fed and ministered to people whose personal lifestyle he likely disagreed with."[35]

Andy Stanley expressed a similar view. He called it "offensive that Christians would leverage faith to support the Kansas law." He also suggested that Christians now had a moral imperative to help with gay weddings: "Serving people we don't see eye to eye with is the essence of Christianity. Jesus died for a world with which he didn't see eye to eye. If a bakery doesn't want to sell its products to a gay couple, it's their business. Literally. But leave Jesus out of it."[36]

Republican John Kasich, former governor of Ohio, is another self-identified Christian. He wrote a *New York Times* bestseller about his Bible study group and cited the Bible to defend Obamacare. "My faith is part of me," he affirmed publicly. "In terms of how it affects my public policy... on my best days, I sort of have an eternal perspective."[37]

While running for president in 2015 and 2016, Kasich claimed he supported "traditional marriage." At the same time, he boasted that he had attended a friend's gay wedding and urged Christian business owners who didn't want to facilitate gay weddings to "move on."[38]

"If you're a cupcake maker and somebody wants a cupcake, make them a cupcake," he said. "Let's not have a big lawsuit or argument over all this stuff—move on. The next thing, you know, they might be saying, if you're divorced you shouldn't get a cupcake."[39]

Bearing false witness is not a virtue, and Hamilton, Stanley, Kasich, and similar Christian leaders were bearing false witness against their fellow Christians by caricaturing their real concerns.

What Religious Liberty Means

To be absolutely clear, Christian bakers, florists, and videographers were *not* asking for a right to refuse any gay person a generic product or service. They were asking that they not be coerced into creating goods and services specifically designed to celebrate a gay wedding. For example, they didn't want to create a cake specifically for someone's same-sex wedding that had two women on it and inscribe it with the message, "God bless Melissa and Mary as they tie the knot." They didn't want to spend hours of their time and talent to create a wedding video celebrating someone's gay wedding. They didn't want to be coerced into partnering to put on a same-sex wedding.

The conscience issue here is pretty basic and shouldn't be hard to understand. Should a Jewish graphic designer be coerced into designing a poster for a Holocaust denial conference? Should a Muslim baker be compelled to inscribe a cake with message that attacks Muhammad? Should a gay videographer be forced to create a video celebrating a conference urging for the abolition of same-sex marriage? For that matter, should a pastor like Andy Stanley be compelled to officiate at a gay wedding?

If not, then why should Christian artists and bakers and more be compelled to facilitate gay weddings?

Some Christians who initially stood up for the rights of conscience regarding gay marriage retreated at the first sign of controversy. Evangelical Christian Mike Pence is a former vice president of the United States. When he served as governor of Indiana in 2015, Pence initially supported a religious liberty bill designed to protect Indianans from government actions that "substantially burdened" their "exercise of religion."[40] The bill's protections would have extended to bakers, florists, videographers, and the like who had religious objections to participating in same-sex weddings.

But within just a couple of days of passage of the bill, Pence could not stand the heat. Journalist Mark Hemingway wrote about what happened next: "Once it became clear that Pence was going to have to make a stand on religious freedom, he folded. Indiana's religious freedom law was gutted at Pence's direction within a week of it being passed."[41] The new language made clear that Christian bakers and others would no longer be protected from being conscripted to support and service gay weddings.

Fortunately, in 2023, a majority of justices of the US Supreme Court finally did what many Stockholm Syndrome Christians had refused to do: defend a person's right to not be compelled by the government to support ideas that violate their religious principles. In *303 Creative v. Elenis*, the court upheld the free speech rights of a web designer who didn't want to design custom websites to celebrate same-sex weddings or promote ideas that conflicted with her Christian convictions.[42]

While this court ruling should be welcomed, it remains to be seen whether state and local governments will faithfully comply with the ruling or try to evade it. Despite *Elenis*, Colorado baker Jack Phillips in Colorado was still defending himself in 2024 from a lawsuit designed to punish him for refusing to create custom wedding cakes that celebrate gay or transgender weddings. It was the third punitive lawsuit he had faced since 2012. The Colorado Supreme Court finally dismissed the case against Phillips on a technicality, but it left the door open to future lawsuits against both him and others.[43]

If Stockholm Syndrome Christians continue to refuse to stand for religious liberty, expect the persecution to continue.

And the unwillingness to defend Christian bakers and florists is far from the only problem.

Failing the COVID Test

In the years leading up to the COVID-19 pandemic, there was a trend among secular progressives and their religious allies to redefine religious liberty as merely "the right to worship." According to this new view, you could persecute Christians all you want for their conscience-inspired behaviors and beliefs. You could force Christian bakers, florists, and photographers to service gay weddings. You could compel Christian doctors and nurses to offer abortions and gender reassignment surgeries. You just couldn't restrict their worship at church on Sundays. Worship was the one thing that was still inviolable.

Or so the argument ran pre-COVID-19. In 2020, we learned that those who reduced religious liberty to "the right to worship" didn't really believe even in the right to worship. In many states, we saw churches shut down by governments for months on end, and some of the same Christians who wouldn't stand up for robust rights of conscience in other areas, now also failed to stand up when the right to worship itself was curtailed.

I want to be careful here. People of faith had sincere differences of opinion about what was safe in the era of COVID-19. As an evangelical Christian, I saw many fellow believers struggle to do their absolute best caring for their congregants and their local communities while navigating ever-changing government requirements, conflicting expert advice, and passionate disagreements among those in the pews.

We shouldn't fault anyone simply because they assessed risk differently than we did. It's admirable that Christians tried to protect the health and safety of both their fellow believers and their communities.

Still, it was disturbing to see so many church leaders stand by silently in certain states when big box stores and casinos were allowed to operate more freely than houses of worship. Whatever you think of the long-term shutdown of in-person worship, if it was so critical for churches, it ought to have been equally critical for everyone else. The double standard should have at least provoked Christian leaders to raise some tough questions. Many of them didn't, including many self-identified Christians in government.

In 2020 Nevada limited places of worship to just fifty worshippers, no matter the size of the church and no matter what social distancing rules were in place. By contrast, casinos were authorized to operate at 50 percent capacity, which at large casinos could mean thousands of customers. Bowling alleys, breweries, and fitness facilities were likewise allowed to operate at 50 percent capacity.[44]

These rules were blatantly discriminatory, but they weren't drafted by atheists. They were imposed by Nevada governor Steve Sisolak, previously described in the media as a "devout Catholic" who regularly attended Mass.[45] In July 2020, the US Supreme Court refused to issue an injunction against Nevada's discriminatory rules. The deciding vote was cast by another "devout Catholic," Chief Justice John Roberts, appointed to the court by evangelical Christian George W. Bush.[46]

But the failure of some Christian leaders to defend the right to worship was only the start. The debate among Christians over vaccine mandates was equally disheartening.

Dehumanizing the Unvaccinated

Reasonable people can differ about whether the COVID-19 vaccines are safe and effective. Some people have been wary of taking a poorly tested vaccine that was rushed into play. Others have conscientious objections because various brands of the vaccine were developed, tested, or produced using cell lines taken from aborted fetuses.

At the time the vaccines were rolled out, I thought it was reasonable for those most at risk from COVID-19 to take the vaccines. I also thought that those who supported the vaccines had the right to say so and even recommend that others get them.

But that is not all that happened. A number of Christian leaders—some of whom were enlisted by the government to sway public behavior—began to stridently condemn fellow Christians who didn't want to be vaccinated, calling them selfish, uncaring, or worse. They not only attacked their fellow Christians for what was a sincere and conscientious difference of opinion, they encouraged their dehumanization and persecution. All in the name of loving thy neighbor—a biblical injunction which they weaponized against other Christians.

Let's take the case of Francis Collins, the nation's top scientist at the time, and one of the government officials who led efforts to combat COVID-19.

In April of 2021, at an online townhall, Collins promised: "There's not going to be any mandating of vaccines from the US government, I can assure you."[47] But just a few months later, Collins himself was publicly advocating vaccine mandates, including ones imposed by the federal government. Indeed, his support for federal vaccine mandates became increasingly shrill and aggressive in following months.

Appearing on MSNBC in September 2021, Collins took aim at unvaccinated people, declaring that "this is really an occasion to think about loving your neighbor, not just yourself."[48] He dismissed concerns about vaccines and vaccine mandates as a "philosophical political argument" that was part of the "culture war." "And this culture war, in this case, is killing people," he said. "Including, I'm sad to say, some children."

Following up that grab-bag of emotionally manipulative arguments, Collins invoked Abraham Lincoln and accused leaders opposed to compulsory COVID-19 vaccinations as being on the wrong side of history. "I would like to say particularly to those leaders who are on the wrong side of this, what Lincoln said one time," he declared. "Citizens, we will not escape history. Do you want to be looked at in the lens of that backward look ten years from now and defend what you did when in fact, we are losing tens of thousands of lives that didn't have to die?"

That interview was typical of many others. Collins could have carefully and seriously addressed moral or medical concerns (which were being expressed not only by private citizens, but by medical professionals and epidemiologists). He could have taken up the—surely important—question of bodily autonomy. He could, in short, have treated concerned citizens and his fellow Christians with courtesy and respect. But it was far easier to accuse others of "tribalism."[49]

As one physician and professor of epidemiology put it, if Collins had "chosen dialogue instead of contributing to animosity and combativeness, we might have been in a better place today."[50] Unfortunately, various other Christian leaders followed Collins's lead and all but abandoned the principles of mutual respect and the rights of conscience when it came to COVID-19. These leaders came from different parts of the political spectrum.

Consider Robert Jeffress, the Pastor of First Baptist Church of Dallas, and David French, a prominent evangelical Christian pundit. Jeffress was a politically conservative pro-Trump partisan. French was a never-Trumper. Both scoffed at the idea that their fellow Christians could have sincere religious objections to taking a COVID-19 vaccine.

Jeffress boasted at one point that his church denied religious exemptions to every staff member who requested them: "Since there is no credible biblical argument against vaccines, we have refused to offer exemptions to the handful of people who have requested them," Jeffress told the Associated Press via email. "People may have strong medical or political objections to government-mandated vaccines, but just because those objections are strongly felt does not elevate them to a religious belief that should be accommodated."[51] Note that this came from a *Baptist* pastor, representing a tradition that historically has prized religious conscience rights above all.

As Jeffress knew, a number of Christians didn't want to receive a COVID-19 vaccination because the available vaccines used cell lines originally derived from abortion in their development, testing, or production in order to be brought to market.[52] His response? "Christians who are troubled by the use of a fetal cell line for the testing of the vaccines would also have to abstain from the use of Tylenol, Pepto Bismol,

Ibuprofen, and other products that used the same cell line if they are sincere in their objection."[53] Jeffress was spreading misinformation. None of the products he mentioned were developed for medical use by testing them with abortion-derived cell lines.[54] So there was no hypocrisy at all on the part of someone who used Tylenol or ibuprofen but had moral qualms about COVID-19 vaccines.[55]

Unfortunately, Jeffress was far from the only evangelical Christian leader who spread this falsehood. Also unfortunately, the falsehood had a cruel impact. One hospital even tried to force staff members who wouldn't take the vaccine for religious reasons to agree they would forgo the use of aspirin, TUMS, Sudafed, antibiotics, and many other drugs.[56]

Then there is the case of Christian attorney and pundit David French, who used to be a serious civil libertarian. In the summer of 2021, he flatly asserted in an article: "There is no religious liberty interest in refusing the COVID vaccine."[57] That's right, *none*. French went on to condemn those seeking vaccine exemptions as having "hardened heart[s]" that "reason and virtue have difficulty penetrating." They have a "moral framework that's broken." They are "dangerous," "extreme," and examples of "libertinism" that is a threat to liberty itself.

Both French and Jeffress seemed certain that their fellow believers' religious objections couldn't be sincere. This view certainly lacked humility and love. It also doesn't match my experience. I know many thoughtful people who hold sincere religious objections to the COVID-19 vaccines.

A neighbor of our family declined the vaccine after spending significant time seeking God's direct guidance through prayer. He was willing to lose his job and his retirement rather than be vaccinated.

A young couple we know were sincerely concerned about the vaccines' links to abortion, and also had concerns about how the vaccine might impact an unborn child should the wife become pregnant.

Still others were rightfully concerned about forcing their children to be vaccinated due to heart problems arising after vaccinations, especially in young males.[58] While French or Jeffress might dismiss this concern as simply a medical rather than religious objection, such a response would be misguided. If you are a Christian parent, your duty to care for your child isn't merely a secular obligation. It is a duty to God, who created the family as the primary authority when it comes to caring for children, not the state. If you think you are being asked to do something that will hurt your child by the government, it certainly is part of your religious duty to refuse.

Christian leaders who, like Collins, Jeffress, and French, demonized other Christians who held sincere and serious objections to COVID-19 vaccines failed to follow the teaching of the Apostle Paul in 1 Corinthians 8. There Paul discussed the sincere objections some Christians of his own day had to eating meat that had been previously offered to idols (as was common practice at the time). Paul wrote that eating such meat was fine (because there's only one God, so "idols" are actually nonentities). But he added an important caveat: It was important to treat with respect the scruples of Christians who were bothered by the association. In fact, Paul pledged not to eat food that had been offered to idols if eating such food would wound the consciences of other Christians.

Unfortunately, many Christians did not heed Paul's approach when it came to dealing with fellow Christians who in good conscience couldn't take a COVID-19 vaccine.

Again, I am not criticizing anyone who took a COVID-19 vaccine or Christian leaders who supported vaccination. I *am* criticizing those who demonized fellow Christians for following their consciences on an issue where Scripture allows differences of opinion. I am also faulting Christian leaders who stood by silently while the unvaccinated were increasingly dehumanized in 2021 and early 2022 as killers, "parasites," "leech[es]," "child abusers," or "unpatriotic," as well as being denied access to stores, medical care, grad schools, and more. They lost jobs. They were removed from military service. They were denied the right to travel.[59]

Standing silent in the face of this kind of dehumanization and discrimination most assuredly was *not* loving one's neighbor.

Certain Christian leaders need to take a hard look at their actions and repent for how they enabled persecution of their fellow

Christians in the COVID era. Unfortunately, such repentance has been hard to find.

Why Didn't You Stand Up for Religious Liberty?

In recent years many Christians in the US have faced hardships for sticking to their beliefs, whether those beliefs have to do with sex and gender, marriage, vaccines, church closures, abortion, or what have you. Often they have stood alone, with precious little support from Christian leaders.

What do the Christian leaders who have chosen not to stand up for their fellow believers have to say about their inaction? Many present classic Stockholm Syndrome responses.

Consider Tim Keller. In a 2021 podcast for church leaders he said, "Ten years from now, if you have evangelical convictions about sex and gender, you may not be able to work for a major university or for the government or for a big corporation."[60] But, he said, "we nurtured this... we brought it on ourselves."

What did he mean? Was he pointing the finger at himself for not to doing more to support and defend his fellow Christians under attack? Nope. He blamed evangelicals who joined the "Christian right." "They just said awful things and vilified people," argued Keller. "It's one of the reasons why so many gay activists now just don't want to forgive evangelicals." He accused "Christian right" evangelicals of embracing the power-mad philosophy of nineteenth-century German thinker Friedrich Nietzsche. They spent "a long time just keeping evangelicals frothing at the mouth about how everything is going so bad and making everybody so angry."

It is difficult to miss Keller's "blame the victim" mentality. I'm sure Keller sincerely believed everything he said, but his critique was largely based on the assumptions and views of those responsible for the persecution of his fellow Christians.

I've heard another pastor downplay concerns by Christians about persecution in America because he thinks God can use persecution to deepen our faith. Notably, the pastor who expressed this view was not himself facing any persecution.

Now, his underlying point is true. God can use affliction to refine us (Zechariah 13:9, Malachi 3:3), and "for those who love God, all things work together for good" (Romans 8:28). At the same time, God's providential ability to bring good out of evil offers us no excuse for ignoring other people's suffering or mistreatment. Imagine you see a woman on the sidewalk screaming for help because she is being brutally assaulted, and you think to yourself, "I don't need to do anything because God is using this experience to deepen her faith."

On the contrary, the prophet Isaiah tells us, "Learn to do good; seek justice, correct oppression" (Isaiah 1:17). Proverbs likewise urges us to "rescue those who are being taken away to death; hold back those who are stumbling to the slaughter" (Proverbs 24:11).

Many Christians refuse to stand up for their fellow believers because they themselves aren't in trouble. They don't want to rock the boat, and they think if they just keep their heads down, persecution in America will never reach them.

We need only look around the world to see the foolhardiness of such a view.

Religious Liberty under Assault throughout the West

In England, Christians are now being arrested and prosecuted merely for praying *silently* outside abortion clinics.[61]

In Finland, parliament member Päivi Räsänen has faced repeated criminal prosecutions after sharing a tweet in 2019 that "questioned her church's sponsorship of an LGBTQ Pride event, and linked to an Instagram post with a picture of Romans 1:24–27." In 2023, Räsänen was acquitted a second time, but the government appealed, and she had to defend herself again before the Finnish Supreme Court in 2024.[62] The years of investigations, prosecutions, and appeals were their own punishment.

Finnish prosecutors did not hide their anti-Christian animus in their campaign against Räsänen, at one point comparing the Bible to Hitler's *Mein Kampf.* One prosecutor indicated that while people in Finland were permitted to "cite the Bible," it was illegal for them to interpret the Bible differently from how the government does: "It is Räsänen's interpretation and opinion about the Bible verses that are criminal."[63]

In Germany, Christian homeschooling parents have faced ruinous fines, jail, and even lost custody of their children.[64] Because of such persecution, homeschooling parents Uwe and Hannelore Romeike fled from Germany to the United States in 2008, where they ultimately were denied asylum and spent years fighting deportation. After a public uproar, they were allowed to stay. But in 2023, the Biden administration tried to re-initiate their deportation.[65]

Astonishingly, some European Christians have defended Germany's criminalization of homeschooling, a policy which apparently dates back to the Nazis.[66]

In 2013, noted evangelical thinker Udo Middelman denounced the Romeikes when they appealed their denial of asylum in the United States. Middelman said "their appeal and the fact that it was reported by the Christian media" was "another nail in the coffin of the wisdom of Christians."[67] He thought the Romeikes should be deported back to Germany "for the better [sic] of their children and a more coherent and sane expression of Christianity."

Apparently classifying homeschooling as "parental indoctrination," Middelman further asserted: "There is no human right... or even possibility of parents to control what ideas a child is exposed to and needs to sort through, examine and evaluate." Moreover, homeschool parents are "arrogant in their belief in the finality of their own views and practices." Middelman essentially argued that it was good for the state to force children into state schools, where the views of the students and their parents could be challenged by government teachers. It is hard to see this view as anything more than Stockholm Syndrome Christianity.

"Parents do not own their children," Middelman insisted. True, but neither does the state. And it's parents who are called by God to "train up a child in the way he should go" (Proverbs 22:6). In fact, centralized government schooling is a relatively new phenomenon. Christian parents—or secular parents—wanting to direct the teaching of their children are following a time-honored practice in human civilization. Worldwide, for most of human history children were taught by their parents or by tutors.[68] This included Germany.[69] This does not, by the way, mean contemporary homeschooling is an anachronistic or outdated method of education. Academically, homeschooled students outperform students in other schools.[70]

Christians who love their children should want to nurture and protect them from pernicious influences until they become mature enough to grapple with them. Children are not mini-adults. Throwing them into a hostile secular environment before they have been well-grounded is like throwing your son into a lake before teaching him how to swim.

Of course secular society doesn't want parents to shape children; it wants to shape them. And it does. Stockholm Syndrome Christians think that's just fine.

To be sure, the Christians in many places outside the West face far greater persecution. Christianity is the most populous faith in Africa, but treatment of Christians there does not always reflect that fact.[71] In Nigeria, Christians are effectively second-class citizens, and are subjected to assaults, kidnappings, and mass murders.

Nigerian evangelist Oscar Amaechina recently published a sober warning for American Christians who think things here are unlikely to get appreciably worse for Christians. According to Amaechina, the persecution of Christians in Nigeria didn't start with violence. "It started from marginalization, social exclusion, and persecution in their workplaces before it turned to physical attacks and mass murders," he said, "which is now the order of the day."[72]

The persecution continued to rachet up because "there were no strong dissenting voices that opposed the abuse of the fundamental human rights of Christians," Amaechina says. Many Christians did not stand up for other Christians even when those Christians were murdered: "When they kill a Catholic priest, the Pentecostals will keep quiet. When they kill a Pentecostal pastor, other denominations keep quiet. This trend was allowed to continue until the present day; and now, it's everywhere."

Amaechina ends with an appeal that Stockholm Syndrome Christians in America would do well to consider: He urges Christians to fight for religious freedom. "Otherwise," he says, "it won't be long before those rights disappear completely."

6. Some Slopes
Really Are Slippery

In an earlier chapter, we met Ryan Meeks, Pastor of EastLake Community Church, a large, hip evangelical church in the greater Seattle area. Meeks was featured in *TIME* magazine as a new breed of evangelical who embraced gay marriage and the LGBTQ+ movement.

But if you search out Meeks today, you won't find him at EastLake Community Church—or any Christian church, for that matter.

And if you search for EastLake Community Church, you will discover it no longer exists. It officially shut down at the end of 2023; but it had stopped being a Christian church many years before that.

Ryan Meeks explains that his "worldview deconstructed" in 2010. As a result, his church "evolved into more of a quirky interfaith (and non-faith) spiritual community with a deep appreciation for all great teachers of Love and Self-Actualization. In short, we began a slow, five year exit from Christianity."[1]

If you went to EastLake's website before it shut down completely, you would have found that it occasionally posted videos, but it didn't hold worship services anymore. And there was no longer any mention of Jesus in their description of who they were. As they put it: "We don't have a need for everyone to agree on a bunch of abstract dogmatic theories."[2] They no longer focused "on escaping to a renewed, peaceful world in some heavenly afterlife." Their goal was simply to create a better world "here and now." Their motto came from Mr. Rogers, "Life is for service."[3]

They may not have been sure what they believed any longer, but they were committed to affirming each other as they explored new horizons: "We want this community to be a safe place... to take the next step in our further conversion, collective evolution, and personal salvation."

EastLake's final mission sounds traditional compared to the new beliefs of their former pastor and his wife. The Meekses now live in Bend, Oregon. Here is what their website says about their new callings: Ryan "helps people who identify as non-religious or those who have left their childhood faith to cultivate a sacred way of living beyond the boundaries of any one tradition."[4] But that's not all. A key part of their work involves tripping out on psychedelic drugs. As they explain: "In the realm of psychedelic work, we help people prepare for a high-dose medicine journey, set clear intentions, and get the most out of their psychedelic exploration—whether it's with us or on their own. We also sit for psychedelic journeys as compassionate guides."

Ryan Meeks and EastLake Community Church embody the key takeaway of this chapter: Things don't stay the same. Many Stockholm Syndrome Christians and their enablers downplay the compromises they are making to the Christian faith. Maybe they are stretching things a bit, but it's just a bit, and otherwise they insist they still can be faithful Christians.

But Stockholm Syndrome Christianity isn't a very solid place to try to plant yourself. It's like the proverbial slippery slope. Once you adopt the operating assumptions of those who oppose Christ, you are likely to continue to slide down the slope along with the culture. As the culture slides away from Christ and truth, so will you.

Christian thinker Francis Schaeffer made this point in his final book, *The Great Evangelical Disaster*, which I referenced in the Introduction. Published forty years ago, shortly before his death, the book delivered a prophetic warning that many evangelical pastors, teachers, and professors were sliding down the slippery slope. Schaeffer indicted evangelicals for seeking to accommodate their Christian faith to the thought forms and teachings of secular culture, warning that once people begin down that path, it is very hard to stop. As he put it, "Accommodation leads to accommodation—which leads to accommodation."[5]

Examples of what he warned about abound today.

Some Sliders Down the Slippery Slope

In earlier chapters, I discussed Pastor Andy Stanley because of his harsh attacks on the Old Testament, his dismissal of treating the Bible as authoritative, and his failure to stand up for religious liberty. After I started writing this book, Stanley got into more hot water for a talk he gave in 2022 at a conference for pastors and church leaders, where he praised gay Christians and denounced heterosexual Christians for not having their level of faith.[6]

The circulation of Stanley's 2022 public comments led Arizona pastor Ryan Visconti to disclose comments Stanley had made at a private dinner in 2019 with Visconti and fourteen other pastors. Visconti republished a text he had sent a fellow pastor the day after the dinner:

> So 15 of us having dinner and doing Q and A with Andy, and he basically said everything short of calling homosexuality NOT a sin… He said homosexuality is "really a disability" and used the analogy that telling gay people they have to stop being gay to follow Christ is like "taking a wheelchair away from a guy who can't walk." He said "I don't do gay weddings, but I can't say I would never do a gay wedding.… If my granddaughter asked me someday, maybe I would." He said "we need to make room for gay men who choose to be married to each other in our churches, because that's as close as they can get to a New Testament framework of marriage."… He said, "I know I shouldn't let experience dictate my theology, but I have. Maybe I'm wrong." These are quotes. If it was just one statement, I would have assumed I misunderstood what he meant to say. But we were pushing back and talking about this for an hour and half. I'm not even telling the half of it.[7]

Two other pastors who attended the dinner later corroborated Visconti's account.[8] I reached out to Pastor Stanley through his website so he could share his perspective about his reported comments, but I did not receive a response.

Once you start down the path of accepting the assumptions of those who reject Christianity, it's natural to continue down the path.

Consider Brian McLaren, who was honored by *TIME* magazine in 2015 as one of "The 25 Most Influential Evangelicals in America."[9] In the early 2000s he was one of the leaders of the so-called "emerging church movement" with his books *A New Kind of Christian* in 2001 and *A New Kind of Christianity* in 2010.[10] But now McLaren no longer identifies as an evangelical, and it is an open question as to whether he really identifies as a Christian.

McLaren certainly has left behind biblical teachings about sexuality and biblical authority. And this is how he describes his current view of the Bible: "Scripture faithfully reveals the evolution of our ancestors' best attempts to communicate their successive best understandings of God. As human capacity grows to conceive of a higher and wiser view of God, each new vision is faithfully preserved in Scripture like fossils in layers of sediment."[11] In the words of one critic, "This is nothing less than theological liberalism in twenty-first century, post-modern clothing."[12]

It's not just pastors and theologians who are sliding.

In the 1990s, physicist Howard Van Till at Calvin College was the pre-eminent example of a Christian scientist who claimed to hold evangelical beliefs (in this case Calvinist beliefs) while embracing a theistic version of evolution. Van Till was an early critic of fellow Christian scientists who were articulating the idea that nature displayed clear evidence of intelligent design. Many evangelicals have cited Van Till in this context, even in recent years.

But after retiring from Calvin, Van Till evolved away from Christianity altogether. By 2006, he was declaring himself a freethinker. By 2016, he indicated that he identified with what he called "a *comprehensively naturalistic worldview*," which he described as a belief "that the physical universe is the only reality… and that it is not dependent on a non-corporeal, person-like Agent (the Abrahamic God, for example) to give it being or to guide its evolution."[13]

One of the Christian scientists who liked to cite Van Till as a model for integrating orthodox Christianity with evolution was Karl Giberson, whom we met in Chapter 2. A physicist, Giberson has been a longtime associate of geneticist Francis Collins, with whom he coauthored a book. Giberson also helped Francis Collins start the BioLogos Foundation to promote theistic evolution. For many years, Giberson was a professor at Eastern Nazarene University, an explicitly evangelical Christian institution.

Giberson hasn't yet slid as far down the slope as Van Till. But, sadly, he appears to be on the same trajectory.

In his book *Saving Darwin*, Giberson denied a historical fall, arguing that humans were not created good. They were selfish and evil from the start, since evolution is driven by selfishness. Giberson nevertheless maintained that he was a committed Christian who believed in the Christian teaching about an eternal paradise where all the hurts of the present world are healed.

But his reasons for staying a Christian were rather shaky. He acknowledged poignantly that "my belief in God is tinged with doubts and, in my more reflective moments, I sometimes wonder if I am perhaps simply continuing along the trajectory of a childhood faith that should be abandoned."[14] So why did he stay a Christian? "As a purely practical matter, I have compelling reasons to believe in God. My parents are deeply committed Christians and would be devastated were I to reject my faith. My wife and children believe in God, and we attend church together regularly. Most of my friends are believers. I have a job I love at a Christian college that would be forced to dismiss me if I were to reject the faith that underpins the mission of the college. Abandoning belief in God would be disruptive, sending my life completely off the rails."[15] Note that Dr. Giberson's "compelling reasons" to believe in God were sociological. They weren't about whether Christianity is *true*.

Within a few years of writing *Saving Darwin*, Giberson resigned his post at the Christian university where he taught. In a book following his departure, he made fairly clear that he now regards the Bible as a mish-mash of divergent stories from one particular tribe rather than a divinely inspired text featuring God's authoritative message.

Indeed, Giberson intimated that Jesus himself was a fallible human being. He also thinks Jesus viewed himself as only having a message for the Jews. According to Giberson, "Virtually nothing suggests that Jesus had any significance beyond Judaism."[16] In making this claim Giberson ignores not only the Great Commission, where Jesus urged his disciples to carry the good news to all nations, but also many Old Testament Scriptures about all nations being invited to come to salvation.[17]

Instead of Jesus, Giberson says it was Paul who invented the key teachings of Christianity, "including the divinity of Christ and the universal availability of salvation."[18] Again, this ignores many Scriptures where Jesus clearly claims to be divine.[19] Giberson also reiterated that he believes "there is no original sin and there was no original sinner."[20] And he thinks if Christianity wants to survive it needs to evolve: "Christianity emerged in a different time and must be prepared to evolve like everything else."[21]

The book where Giberson made these claims was published by an arm of the Unitarian Universalist Association. I have sat on the same stage with Giberson and interacted with him in public. His candor is commendable, yet heartbreaking.

Perhaps one of the saddest cases of the results of Stockholm Syndrome Christianity is writer Frank "Franky" Schaeffer. He is the son of the late Francis and Edith Schaeffer. When Francis Schaeffer issued a prophetic warning before his death about the slide among evangelical elites, little did he know that what he warned about would be fulfilled in his own son.

For a while after his father's death Frank stayed a Christian, converting to Eastern Orthodoxy. Soon, however, he began to embrace the operating assumptions of secularist culture one by one. Many Christians did their best to give him the benefit of the doubt. In 2007, after he wrote an exposé of his parents, whom he accused of being "Crazy for God," the Christian magazine *WORLD* interviewed Frank and did its best to place him in the best possible light. The writer for *WORLD* observed that "underneath your disdain for what you believe is the artificiality of evangelicalism, you still hold many of the same beliefs. You're still a practicing Christian. You are still pro-life, though you're not politically active on that issue anymore. You've remained married to the same woman for almost 40 years now."[22] Schaeffer seemed to agree: "In many ways, theologically and philosophically, I still believe much of what I believed in those days, and what my dad believed. But I've thrown overboard the cultural baggage."

Yet Frank Schaeffer didn't stay where he was on the slope. Just a few years later, in 2012, he publicly stated that he only went to a Greek Orthodox church because he "happen[ed] to like Byzantine liturgies because it's mostly in Greek so I can't understand them." He just wanted a place to be quiet in. For Schaeffer now, "to be a Christian is not to believe in Jesus in terms of who he was, whether he is the Son of God, rose from the dead or not, it is to believe in that life as an example."[23] Although he no longer believed in Christianity, he still took communion each week.

By 2014, Schaeffer had fully embraced postmodern irrationality, publishing a book with the title *Why I Am an Atheist Who Believes in God.*[24] The next year, he explained his beliefs this way: "These days, I hold two ideas about God simultaneously. He, she, or it exists, and he, she, or it doesn't exist. I don't seesaw between these opposites, I embrace them."[25]

Schaeffer did continue to claim for a longer time that he was pro-life, although that commitment eventually withered as well. First, he claimed to be pro-life while simultaneously railing against those who wanted to restrict abortion. By 2020, he was "call[ing] himself pro-choice but [still] anti-*Roe v. Wade*."[26] By 2021, when the Supreme Court was preparing to hear the case where it would ultimately overrule *Roe v. Wade*, Schaeffer had evolved again. He now claimed that the pro-life movement provided "the toxic ideological incentive for millions of Christians in the evangelical subculture to turn into a xenophobic aggrieved and perpetually angry mob."[27] In May 2022, he tweeted: "Roe now, gay rights next, the evangelical led right-wing will not stop. THE USA is going to be the Christian version of Iran."[28] After *Roe v. Wade* was actually overturned, Schaeffer taped a video where he declared, "What we see today is not just a reversal of *Roe v Wade*. What we see today is the establishment of a theocracy."[29]

Once you start embracing the cultural assumptions of those who reject Christianity, you are on a path that doesn't have a logical stopping point. That's a key reason why faithful Christians cannot ignore or paper over when their leaders become Stockholm Syndrome Christians.

The examples of our fellow Christians sliding down the slippery slope are admittedly bleak. Nevertheless, we shouldn't despair. God remains sovereign, and He can push people back up the slippery slope if He chooses to. Here are a few instances where He has done just that.

The Road Upward

Günter Bechly is a friend and colleague of mine who lives in Austria. A distinguished scientist, Günter previously was a curator at one of Germany's leading natural history museums, the State Museum of Natural History in Stuttgart. Günter was not raised in a religious home. He wasn't baptized as a child. He didn't think much about spiritual matters. He became an avowed atheist, and his heroes were scientific atheists like evolutionary biologist Richard Dawkins. But that wasn't the end of the story. Here is what Günter says in recounting his eventual journey:

> When atheists hear conversion stories that begin with, "I was a staunch atheist and then...", they tend to roll their eyes and doubt the claim. However, this is exactly what happened to me. I had been a 150-percent atheist and materialist for almost forty years before I embarked on a spiritual journey that ultimately, after many twists and turns, led me to belief in God and Christianity. I had no life crisis, no epiphany, and no spiritual experiences at all. It was the result of purely rational, scientific, philosophical, and historical arguments that gradually changed my mind as a scientist.[30]

Günter first started to read books about modern physics and cosmology and realized that the picture of the world they painted did not fit the idea that the universe could be reduced to blind matter in motion. Next Günter was put in charge of developing a major exhibition at his museum in 2009 to celebrate the 200th anniversary of Darwin's birth and the 150th anniversary of the publication of Darwin's *On the*

Origin of Species. As part of the research around that exhibit, he started to read the critics of Darwin and intelligent design-supporting scientists like biochemist Michael Behe. He soon came to doubt Darwin himself. And he eventually became convinced that biology showed clear evidence of intelligent design.[31] Günter continued his journey by exploring what might explain that intelligent design. He ultimately came to Christ.

But it's not just scientists whom God can call back up the slope.

Eta Linnemann was a distinguished liberal biblical scholar from Germany.[32] In fact, she studied under Rudolf Bultmann himself, the massively influential liberal theologian we discussed in Chapter 1 who played a critical role in attempts to debunk the Bible in the name of science.

As a young woman, Eta had gone to a retreat where she heard for the first time the offer of the gospel. She accepted Christ. She then went to Marburg, Germany to study theology under Bultmann, who was regarded as one of the greatest theologians of his day. And she soon was persuaded out of her simplistic Christian beliefs. It happened in her very first term in lectures from Bultmann. She later recalled: "I learned as a young student in my very first term that we were not allowed to think of the resurrection of Christ as a historical fact. This great professor had said it, so it had to be. After all, how could I, as a young student, know more than my professors!"[33]

"Additionally, we were taught that we must study as if there were no God," she said. "Although it can happen that when you study the Bible like that, you might experience something of him, in general, you have not the slightest chance of finding God this way... If you decide to study as if there were no God, you will not meet him."

Eta was also taught to abandon the belief that the Bible gave a true account of history: "We were... taught that when we read something in the Bible, we must realize it could have never taken place... As students, we were supposed to believe what these professors said, and sadly, we did."

Eta eventually became a distinguished professor herself and started to spread the same dead teachings she herself had imbibed.

Then one week she was assigned to read a certain student's dissertation. The dissertation gave what seemed to her to be a credible account about a church in Africa where there were modern-day miracles and prophesies. Now I don't know whether that account was right.[34] But this dissertation made an impression on Eta. As she put it, "This was amazing to someone who did not even really believe in the prophesies of the Bible!" It piqued her interest, although not enough for her to do anything about it.

Several months later, however, she had to lecture to students on the miracles of the Bible and she was planning to tell the students that they "were not allowed to take for granted that the miracles in the New Testament actually happened." Yet that's not what she ended up saying.

"I don't know how far I got," she said, "but when I opened my mouth to speak, I heard myself saying, 'But so-and-so wrote about this in his doctor's thesis,' and I proceeded to tell my students about the miracles recorded in the doctor's thesis." It turned out that this term Eta was teaching a class that had some real Christians in it:

> Normally there might be one, or at most, two. But this class had six or seven, so when I spoke about this miracle, they thought, "Oh maybe even a professor is able to repent," and started to pray for me. These students prayed, their families prayed, and all their prayer circles prayed for me. It must have been really a big campaign. Later on, people would come up to me and say, "We remember praying for you."

Eta started to attend a prayer meeting where some of her students went. She was amazed that they prayed to God as if He were really there and could really answer their prayers. One day she heard the gospel message again. "Then I knew it was for me. I lifted my arm, the Lord saw my heart, and my life was changed."

Eta ultimately rejected the historical criticism of the Bible she had been taught and began to write books and articles and give lectures defending the truth of the Bible and critiquing the views of Bultmann and others.

As she said, "I found out you can trust your Bible. You cannot trust historical critical theology or higher criticism. It is not trustworthy. I praise God for bringing me out of it, and pray that he will use me to bring others from criticism to Christ."

By the time Eta died in 2009, she had spent more than three decades as an outspoken defender of the Bible against the biblical criticism that she had once championed.

CAUSES

7. Listening to the Wrong Voices

In the first part of this book, we looked at the symptoms of Stockholm Syndrome Christianity, meeting many Christians who have increasingly adopted the assumptions and worldviews of the secular world, rejecting Christian principles with regard to the authority of the Bible, science, sex, race, class, and religious liberty. In this section, we are going to look at some *root causes* of Stockholm Syndrome Christianity. What practices have helped bring about a situation where there are so many Stockholm Syndrome Christians?

Wrong Voices

In this chapter, we are going to focus on how listening to the wrong voices can lead us away from genuine Christianity.

Each of us tends to choose information sources we believe present an accurate picture of reality. What happens when those information sources say Christian beliefs contradict reality?

For example, what if your information sources tell you that it's impossible to live according to Christian sexual standards; or that same-sex orientation is absolutely unchangeable, and that everyone has a right to fulfill their sexual desires; or that science proves the human species is the product of an undirected evolutionary process? You are going to experience an increasing disconnect between biblical teachings and the real world and, in consequence, it is going to be increasingly difficult for you to hold to the Bible's teachings.

So the sources from which we get our information about the world are critically important. If we spend our time listening to unreliable sources whose motives, assumptions, and claims undermine biblical teachings, we are preparing ourselves and our loved ones to become Stockholm Syndrome Christians, no matter what we may start out thinking.

Many people who end up embracing the assumptions of the secular world start down that path when they are overly attracted to, or influenced by, information sources they think give insight into reality, but which in fact lead away from the truth.

In the pages that follow, we will examine seven key sources of information that can make Christians susceptible to Stockholm Syndrome Christianity.

1. Traditional News Media

The first sources of information are traditional news media such as newspapers, magazines, radio shows, and television news. Even in the era of social media and online sources such as Wikipedia and ChatGPT, traditional news media generate much of the underlying content and perspectives to be shared and circulated. News and information media have tremendous power to shape *what* we think about, what we think is *important*, and what claims are *credible*.

Surveys continue to show that most Americans want the news media to be fair in their news coverage, cover all sides equally, and let the viewers decide how to interpret the news. In fact 76 percent of Americans say journalists should try to cover all sides equally. By contrast, 55 percent of journalists believe they *shouldn't* cover all sides equally.[1]

Most journalists acknowledge that media outlets don't cover all sides equally. Indeed, 60 percent of journalists admit that "news organizations mostly... tend to favor one side" in presenting the news.[2]

More than 40 percent admit that "journalists are often unable to separate their views from what they report on," although 82 percent sheepishly admit that they should try to separate their views from what they report on.[3]

The goal of many journalists today is not to report on the world and let you decide. It's to reform the world and enlist you in its reformation. According to one survey, 65 percent of national reporters and 79 percent of local reporters believe for the journalists they know that "working to reform society" is a very or fairly important reason they are journalists.[4]

But if you are going to reform the world, you need to have an idea of exactly what you want to reshape the world into. That involves views of good and bad, moral and immoral, justice and injustice. So your underlying worldview becomes all-important.

Here is the problem: Most journalists in America don't hold the views and worldviews of the majority of Americans, especially Christians. In the last decade, scholars have shied away from trying to do detailed surveys of the personal beliefs of journalists. But from the 1960s through the first decade of the twenty-first century, we have all sorts of data that consistently showed that journalists are overwhelmingly more secular than most Americans. They are overwhelmingly more liberal on both social and economic issues. And they overwhelmingly favor candidates from one party over another. We could spend the entire chapter unpacking those five decades of studies about journalists, but let me present just a sampling.

According to a 2007 survey of national and local journalists, only 8 percent of national and 14 percent of local journalists went to church weekly.[5] During the same year, 39 percent of Americans as a whole attended church at least once a week, and another 33 percent attended a least a few times a year.[6] This is an extraordinary gap. National journalists attended church or a place of worship weekly at a rate five times lower than the population as a whole.

Similarly, only 8 percent of national journalists and 14 percent of local journalists in 2007 described themselves as "conservative" or "very conservative."[7] During the same year, 37 percent of Americans as a whole described themselves in this way.[8] Another stunning gap.

By 2020, according to yet another survey of journalists, 78 percent identified as liberal, and only 22 percent identified as conservative (among those willing to identify their leanings).[9] Among journalists on Twitter, 84 percent identified as liberal and only 16 percent as conservative.[10]

The percentage of Republicans among journalists has continued to drop, while the percentage of Democrats continues to rise. According to Gallup, Americans in 2022 were evenly split among Republicans and Democrats, with each party representing 28 percent of the total adult population.[11] The remaining Americans were independents. By contrast, 36 percent of journalists in 2022 were Democrats (29 percent more than the general population), and only 3.4 percent were Republicans (88 percent lower than the general population).[12]

Other surveys of journalists over the years have shown overwhelming support for abortion and gay rights.[13]

Defenders of the news media typically claim that just because journalists are overwhelmingly secular and progressive, this doesn't mean they can't write a fair story. They can keep their biases to themselves. This is a theoretical argument that might be true with certain reporters. In fact, I can think of some reporters I've known who did try to be fair despite their underlying beliefs. But I can think of many others who didn't. But more than that, there is plenty of empirical evidence that news reporting closely tracks with the secular and liberal outlook of most reporters. In fact, there are at least four key ways the overwhelmingly secular and progressive bias of most reporters shows up.

Agenda Setting

One of the most important ways journalists shape what we think is by setting the agenda for what we think about.

Every day a countless number of events occur. We can't possibly report them all. For example, perhaps you went shopping for groceries today. When you got home, you didn't tell your family or roommates every detail about your trip. Maybe you hit a few highlights—milk prices were up, the road to the store was under construction yet again. But hitting everything would have been tiresome. At the same time, you probably left out some details that would have proven interesting to your listeners. Why did you leave them out? Simply because they were uninteresting to you, so you hardly noticed them.

In the same way, reporters have to determine what is newsworthy. They have to make this choice every day. And if religion is not personally important or interesting to a reporter, it's quite natural for that reporter to leave it out of his reporting.

That's precisely what we see in how religion is covered by the traditional news media. Other than scandals, religion largely *isn't* covered, especially biblical Christianity. It's not considered important or even particularly relevant to daily life. And every time we ingest reporting that treats religion as unimportant or irrelevant, we are being shaped by that.

Someone might respond that the news media primarily focus on scandal and negative news, so their coverage of religion isn't any different than their coverage of anything else. It's not a secular bias. But I'd like to ask you to think a little more carefully about all of the things that the news and information media actually cover.

Professional and nonprofessional sports get an entire section in most newspapers. So do movies, entertainment, and the arts. So do health and lifestyle issues. So does business. All of these topics draw extensive coverage. Although this coverage can include scandals, scandals are far from the only thing covered. There are lots of "soft" news stories about sports, entertainment, business, and health.

Yet there isn't much soft news reporting about Christians. There are no daily sections in major media outlets focusing on religion at all. Maybe if you are lucky you have a once-a-week religion page or half-page.

At one time, some American newspapers carried reports on sermons given on Sundays. Why don't they do that now? The newspapers might argue it's because religion isn't considered important by most Americans anymore. People are more interested in sports, movies, or lifestyle advice.

It's certainly true we are a more secular culture than we were previously. But is it really true that we are so secular that most people aren't interested in articles about faith? Consider this: Close to 60 percent of Americans consider themselves sports fans.[14] That's why we have a sports section in newspapers each day. But as recently as

2023, 71 percent of Americans said religion was important to them personally, with 45 percent saying it was very important.[15] So why doesn't religion get as much coverage as sports or entertainment?

Is it because more people attend sporting events or movies than religious services?

According to government statistics from 2012, 21 percent of Americans visit an art museum or gallery in a year,[16] 30 percent attend at least one sporting event,[17] 37 percent attend at least one performing arts event,[18] and 59 percent go to a movie.[19] But pre-pandemic, do you know how many Americans attended a religious service at least a few times a year? Nearly two-thirds.[20] Even post-pandemic, 55 percent of Americans attend religious services at least once a year.[21]

Perhaps it's because religious services are more or less the same each week, whereas movies come and go, sporting events are different each time, and so forth. Maybe religion just isn't "news" in the sense these other activities are. Even this, I'd argue, is not true. There's a reason many churches have weekly newsletters or bulletins. In addition to "private" matters like prayer requests, these newsletters announce service projects to help the community, visiting speakers, conferences on marriage or parenting, blood drives, fundraisers for projects like digging wells in water-poor areas of Africa, new sermon series, and so forth. Often churches must resort to paying for advertising for these events in order to alert the public and let the public know they're welcome to attend. Events open to the public that help the community surely are newsworthy.

By any objective measure, the downplaying of religion as an aspect of American culture is not based on an objective or neutral standard of newsworthiness.

It's also not objective news coverage to ignore attacks on crisis pregnancy centers and churches. Nor is it objective to provide much less coverage of bestselling religious books than for secular books. Nor is it objective to ignore blatant human rights violations such as the imprisoning or killing of Christians worldwide. The category of religious liberty alone would keep news outlets amply supplied with dramatic religion-related news stories—if only they were of interest to journalists.

Whether they realize it or not, Christians who rely on the secular media for their information are having their views about what is important reshaped by journalists who do not share their views. These journalists channel the direction of our thoughts. They focus our attention on things that are important to them, and divert our attention away from many things that should be important to us.

But journalists don't just influence our views by setting the agenda. They also shape our views by how they *frame* the issues they cover.

Issue Framing

In March 2023, a woman who identified as a man massacred six people, including three children, at a Christian school in Nashville, Tennessee.[22] If you followed news coverage of this horrific mass murder, you will know that the story wasn't framed by major media outlets as an example of transgender violence or extremism, even though the mass shooting took place the very week that transgender activists had called for a "Trans Day of Vengeance" in the nation's capital.[23] Nor were most news stories framing the attack as an example of a hate crime or as the targeting of Christians, even though there had been a dramatic spike in attacks on churches over the previous year.

Instead, news stories largely focused on using the attack as a way of discussing how the transgender community is a victim of intolerance.[24] Framing coverage in that way is not a neutral decision. It's a value-laden decision flowing from the ideology of most reporters. It's a decision by journalists that shapes how the public views the world.

Similarly, consider how reporters might frame a job termination if someone were discharged from a religious school because of their sexual orientation and behavior. It would likely be framed as an issue of gay rights, not as an issue of religious liberty on the part of the school. Again, there is nothing neutral about such a choice; the framing is designed to shape your views.

News media coverage of debates over Darwinian evolution provide another example of how framing can manipulate the presentation of an issue. There are a growing number of sophisticated scientific challenges to traditional Darwinian theory—and, as mentioned earlier, these largely are acknowledged by the scientific community[25]—but most journalists uniformly portray any criticism of Darwinism as based on religion rather than science.

Where I work, we maintain a list of over a thousand doctoral scientists who are skeptical that random mutation and natural selection can explain the complexity of life.[26] The *New York Times* once did a major story on scientists who signed this "Dissent from Darwin" statement, but—guess what?—the story did not focus on the scientific credentials or views of those signing the statement. Instead, it focused on trying to uncover their religious views, seeking to portray the scientists as almost wholly motivated by religion rather than science.[27]

The framing of the *Times'* story wasn't just biased. It was false. Under questioning from one of my staff, the reporter for the story later admitted that of the twenty signers of the statement he interviewed, no more than five indicated that their doubts about Darwin began when they increased their involvement in Christian churches. In other words, 75 percent of the people he interviewed did not fit the stereotype the *New York Times* was trying to promote in the story.[28] Yet the actual facts didn't matter. The reporter and his editors apparently didn't want to let the facts get in the way of the message they wanted to convey.

Or consider how the news and information media frame religious holidays like Easter.

According to a study by the Culture and Media Institute, nearly two-thirds of stories about Easter in 2010 by the "big three" broadcast networks (ABC, NBC, CBS) were negative.[29] Of those negative stories, 91 percent focused on sex scandals in the Catholic Church. The abuse scandals definitely merited widespread coverage. But so did Easter itself, the holiest day on the Christian calendar. Hijacking the holiday to run stories focusing only on abuse in the Catholic church was not justified. After all, there are twice as many Protestants as Catholics in the United States, and so Easter's significance as a cultural celebration reaches far beyond the Catholic church.

Perhaps you think that the negativity in coverage of Easter is because the media always focus on the negative, even when it comes to holidays. But that is not true. In contrast to the negative coverage of Easter, 100 percent of broadcast news stories about Earth Day in 2010 were positive.[30]

Of the few positive stories about Easter, most had virtually nothing to do with explaining the Christian meaning of the holiday. Seven out of nine stories merely included fleeting references to the holiday. For example, CBS *Evening News* anchor Katie Couric told her viewers to have a "great weekend and happy Easter," and NBC News noted that President Obama "took time out for prayer and reflection" on Easter Sunday.

Or consider the disparity in media coverage of two blockbuster Hollywood feature films dealing with the Christian message. One film was *The Passion of the Christ* (2004), which told the story of Christ's trial and crucifixion. The other was *The Da Vinci Code* (2006), a thriller adapted from a novel that portrayed Christianity as a false religion, denied the central Christian doctrine that Christ is God, argued that Christianity was based on a fraud, and even claimed that Jesus was married to Mary Magdalene.

The first thing to note about the coverage of these two films is that *The Da Vinci Code* received 50 percent more coverage on network news shows before its release than *The Passion of the Christ*[31] (a clear instance of agenda setting). But even more pronounced was the kind of coverage—the framing—these two films received.

As one media analysis explained: "*The Passion of the Christ* was treated as a social problem—the biggest TV anti-Semitism story of that year—while *The Da Vinci Code* was presented more often as an 'intriguing' theory rather than threatening or offensive to Christians."[32] Did *The Passion of the Christ* ignore or minimize the role of the Romans in the crucifixion of Christ in order to play up the role of the Jewish leaders? Not at all. Nevertheless, virtually 100 percent of the network news stories about *The Passion of the Christ* dealt with complaints and objections to the upcoming film, but only 27 percent of the stories about *The Da Vinci Code* dealt with objections Christians were raising to that film.[33] In other words, the disparity in coverage was over 70 percent. Moreover, as a media analyst explains, "In their push to promote *The Da Vinci Code*, the networks routinely failed to address the aspect of the [original] book that most offended Christian sensitivities: the claim that Christianity itself is a lie."[34]

George Yancey is a professor of sociology at Baylor University in Texas, and Alicia Brunson is an associate professor of sociology at Georgia Southern University. In 2019, they published the results of a study that provides even more evidence as to how journalists engage in anti-Christian bias by how they frame stories.[35] Yancey and Brunson surveyed several hundred journalists about how they would cover certain hypothetical stories. But the two researchers changed key elements in the stories to surface how changing those elements might affect how journalists framed the stories.

In one scenario, a person murders people at either a mosque or a church. In the version dealing with a mosque, journalists "were more willing to see this event as an example of discrimination... and likely to see it as an example of a hate crime" than in the version where the place of attack was a Christian church. According to Yancey and Brunson, "the almost total lack of perception" of anti-Christian violence "when a church is shot up" suggested that the journalists surveyed "perceive[d] that religious prejudice against Christians is non-existent."[36]

The reactions to another hypothetical story were even more striking. In this scenario, a college professor is under fire for hateful comments. In one version, the professor calls "LGBT individuals... immoral, hateful people." In another version, the professor calls "conservative Christians... immoral, hateful people."[37] The journalists' reactions were instructive. Journalists were three times more likely to depict the professor attacking gays as a bigot than the professor attacking conservative Christians.[38] Similarly, journalists were three times more likely to view the controversy over the professor attacking Christians as a conflict over the free speech rights of the professor, than the controversy over the professor attacking gays.[39] This is bias, plain and simple, and it is shaping how even Christians think of what is happening in the world.

Finally, consider one specific form of framing: *labeling.* The labels and terms reporters use in news reports shape the messages they convey. Consider the term "gender affirming."

According to Newspapers.com, the term "gender affirming" only appears fourteen times in its database of newspaper stories up to 2010. In the earliest years, the term was typically used to speak of policies that affirmed women as being valuable members of society and culture. In other words, the term originally meant affirming one's biological gender, and it typically appeared in stories emphasizing the value and rights of women. Even so, the term didn't appear very widely in news reports.

From 2010 to 2019, the term appeared 259 times. In 2022, it appeared 2,321 times. In the process of this explosion of use, the term's meaning completely changed.[40] It no longer meant policies and beliefs that affirm your biological sex. It instead referred to what in fact are gender-*destroying* treatments like cutting off one's genitals or filling someone with hormones of the opposite sex. The choice of reporters to frame these gender-destructive treatments as "gender affirming" is not neutral. It is an ideological choice made by reporters seeking to push a particular narrative.

Media coverage of abortion shows similar slanted labeling. Journalists typically describe abortion proponents using their preferred labels ("pro-choice" or "abortion rights"). But they refuse to use the pro-life movement's label of choice, calling them anti-abortion or anti-abortion rights rather than "pro-life" or "right to life." This bias goes back decades. According to a study of news coverage at the major networks in 1989, 74 percent of stories referred to the pro-abortion side as "pro-choice," and 26 percent of the time as "abortion rights." By contrast, pro-lifers were described as "pro-life" or "right to life" only 6 percent of the time. Around 94 percent of the time they were referred to as anti-abortion.[41] Studies of news stories in the mid-1990s found similar results.[42] Journalists have continued to frame the abortion debate in terms used by those who favor abortion.

Agenda setting and issue framing together serve as potent means at journalists' disposal for reshaping our view of reality. These techniques are joined by a third: the selection of sources journalists choose to cite in their articles.

Lopsided Sources

Studies show that journalists overwhelmingly cite experts from the liberal or progressive or secular side of the ideological spectrum in their stories. When they do this, the message you're getting is that beliefs on the other side of the spectrum—the conservative side—must not be well grounded or substantiated, because they apparently aren't supported by any experts.

The selection of experts is also intertwined with framing. Even when a journalist does cite someone who may have a more biblical view of something, they are likely to be labeled in a pejorative way or in a way that marginalizes them, whereas the other experts will be given a neutral label. For example, an article might refer to "conservative scholar Robert P. George" rather than "Princeton legal scholar Robert P. George." Rarely if ever will you see anyone labeled as a "liberal scholar." The implication? Liberals are the norm. It's conservatives who are outliers.

And it's not just the selection of experts and the way they are described that is lopsided. The overall citation of sources of all kinds tends to be heavily skewed toward sources that come from a certain worldview.

When it comes to abortion, for example, one study found that around 60 percent of the opinions quoted in the "big three" network coverage of abortion were sources who favored abortion.[43] Moreover, abortion rights activists are quoted nearly twice as often as pro-life activists.

Media coverage of debates over gay marriage shows a similar pattern. In one study of nearly 500 articles in 2013, stories slanted in favor of gay marriage outpaced stories slanted against gay marriage by more than 5 to 1. Indeed, nearly half of the stories examined contained at least twice as many statements in support of same-sex marriage as statements opposed.[44] This is in no way a robust, fair-handed comparison of opposing views.

Coverage of debates over evolution and intelligent design in the public square have been equally slanted. Historically, op-ed sections of newspapers have tried to represent the cross-section of views held by the public. That's not the case when it comes to evolution. Even though a large proportion of the American public remains skeptical of unguided Darwinian evolution, their views are largely censored. Out of nearly one thousand opinion essays on evolution and intelligent design published in American newspapers from 2006 to mid 2010, 564 were pro-evolution and only 120 were critical of it.[45] That is almost a 5 to 1 disparity.

Again, the slanted selection of sources shapes your beliefs. When you see the vast majority of people cited expressing anti-biblical views, you are being shaped to think that no one really supports biblical views. You are being demoralized. You are being manipulated. You are being made to feel as if you're standing alone, and if you're alone maybe it's because you're wrong and the vast opposing side is right.

False Reporting

A final way the news and information media shape your view of reality is by presenting false or highly dubious factual claims as if they are true. If a factual claim fits a reporter's worldview, in other words, the reporter is much more likely to promote it uncritically, without qualification, and without making sure it is really true.

One of the most egregious examples of this was actor Jussie Smollett's false claim in 2019 that he had been beaten up by white supporters of Donald Trump.[46] There were all sorts of red flags about his allegations, but the news media ran with Smollett's tale unquestioningly. Some outlets didn't even consistently use qualifying words like "Smollett claims" or "Smollett alleges." CNN, for example, tweeted that "'Empire' actor Jussie Smollett was attacked early Tuesday morning in what Chicago police are calling a possible hate crime. Smollett was attacked by two people 'yelling out racial and homophobic slurs,' according to police."[47] When Smollett's claims turned out to be a hoax, and Smollett himself was tried for disorderly conduct and lying to the police, the media only grudgingly corrected the record, ignoring Smollett's trial and playing down the guilty verdict as much as possible.

I have seen repeated examples of false and inaccurate reporting through my work at Discovery Institute, where since the 1990s I have been involved in public debates over evolution and intelligent design. For example, in 2005 Kansas adopted new science standards for public schools. The media widely reported that the State Board of Education had mandated the teaching of intelligent design in the standards. Here is what the standards actually stated: "We also emphasize that the Science Curriculum Standards do not include Intelligent Design."[48] In other words, the reporting was straight up false.

Similarly, CNN ran a story in 2004 claiming that bills were being considered in multiple states that would fire teachers for not teaching intelligent design. This was false as well, but CNN refused to correct the record even after the error was brought to its attention.[49]

Perhaps the most humorous case I know of regarding an outright falsehood was when President George W. Bush made a statement about intelligent design in 2005. His statement provoked a flurry of media coverage, and my friend and colleague Stephen Meyer was interviewed by the *New York Times*. According to the original article published by the *Times*, Meyer praised Bush for supporting "freedom of inquiry and free speech about the issue of *biblical* origins"[50] (emphasis added). In fact, Meyer had actually said "biological origins." Discovery Institute contacted the reporter, and to her credit, she acknowledged her error. She apparently wrote biological in her notes, but when she typed out the story it came out "biblical."[51] It was telling that her error happened to be one that reinforced the stereotype she likely already believed. And, of course, many people who saw the original article never saw the correction.

The more Christians rely on traditional news media for their information about the world, the more likely they will be reshaped into Stockholm Syndrome Christians.

2. Social Media

The traditional media aren't the only ones shaping your views. Many Americans increasingly get their picture of the world not from traditional media but from social media—Facebook, Twitter/X, YouTube, TikTok, Instagram.

These social media platforms present the illusion of open grass-roots discussion. They are supposed to be bottom-up and not top-down. Social media platforms *can* function this way. But there is a lot more going on. First, much of the content on social media is ultimately derived from news stories and information developed by the traditional news media. So all the slant of the traditional news media feeds into social media.

But it's worse than that. As we now know, social media companies—sometimes at the direction of our government—have been actively censoring, deleting, hiding, and de-emphasizing some messages and promoting, pushing, and repeating other messages.[52] What goes viral and becomes popular isn't always determined just by lots of people being interested in something. Viral news stories—like biological viruses—sometimes are man-made.

When you use social media, your view of the world is being molded, often by people who don't share your views. So if you uncritically imbibe social media, you are opening yourself up to Stockholm Syndrome Christianity.

3. Online Search and Reference

Of course, many people do not think they rely on either social media or traditional news media to set the agenda of what they think about or to select the news stories they will read. They point out that they find their own news stories and information by searching the internet or using online reference sources. But similar problems apply here as well.

Search Engines

Today if someone wants to find information on a topic, they typically search using Google, by far the most dominant search engine. Searches using Google give the illusion of bringing up a cornucopia of different sources from different points of view. Many people probably assume that the sources they retrieve are the most popular or the most recent.

In fact, Google searches are highly manipulated to screen out some sources and emphasize others. They highlight some candidates over others. Especially on polarized topics like abortion or gay rights, Google searches emphasize articles with certain points of view over others. Some sites offering information are blacklisted. Other sites are pushed. You are increasingly seeing a set of options that is curated to push you in a certain direction, but you aren't usually told about the curation.[53]

In 2019, the *Wall Street Journal* did a detailed investigation of how Google increasingly manipulates search results. One part of their investigation looked at organic search results over a period of seventeen days for the term "abortion." Here is what they discovered: 39 percent of all results on the first page had the hostname www.plannedparenthood.org (the site of Planned Parenthood, America's biggest abortion provider). By comparison, only 14 percent of Bing's first page of results came from Planned Parenthood, and only 16 percent of DuckDuckGo's first page of results came from Planned Parenthood.[54]

Or try searching for "crisis pregnancy center" on Google, as I did multiple times over a number of months in 2023. The term "crisis pregnancy center" generally refers to centers dedicated to helping women in a "crisis pregnancy" by providing counseling, resources, and options other than abortion for weathering the challenge. The top three results in my Google searches were websites attacking crisis pregnancy centers. The top search result was especially misleading. It was neutrally labeled "Crisis Pregnancy Center Map and Finder." But it linked to a website that disparages crisis pregnancy centers as places that are "also known as 'fake women's health centers.'"

When it comes to many important topics to Christians, Google searches are far from neutral or unbiased.

Wikipedia

Wikipedia is a crowd-sourced encyclopedia that purports to cover issues neutrally, dispassionately, and accurately. It is used as a resource for facts not just by students and ordinary people, but also by journalists. Because it is free to use, many websites as well as search engines automatically pull from its content. You may not even know sometimes that the content you are reading was basically cut and pasted from Wikipedia.

Wikipedia started out with a vision of being scrupulously neutral in its presentation. But it hasn't been that way for a long time. Larry Sanger, who co-founded Wikipedia and was responsible for its original mission of trying to provide neutral coverage, is now one of Wikipedia's sharpest critics. "Wikipedia can be counted on to cover not just political figures, but political issues as well from a liberal-left point of view," Sanger says, pointing out the slanted coverage in Wikipedia of topics such as abortion, drug legalization, and LGBT adoption.[55]

According to Sanger, the same slant dominates Wikipedia's coverage of religion. He points out that the article on Jesus "simply asserts" as an established truth that progressive scholars' study of the New Testament "has yielded major uncertainty on the historical reliability of the Gospels." It similarly asserts as a fact that "the gospels are not independent nor consistent records of Jesus' life." But these are partisan assertions, not neutral descriptions of what people believe. Sanger notes:

> A great many Christians would take issue with such statements, which means they are not neutral for that reason alone. In other words, the very fact that many Christians, including many deeply educated conservative seminarians, believe in the historical reliability of the Gospels, and that they are wholly consistent, means that the article is biased if it simply asserts, without attribution or qualification, that this is a matter of "major uncertainty."

Christians who depend on Wikipedia are relying on an unreliable source that is likely to lead them down the path to Stockholm Syndrome Christianity.

Artificial Intelligence (AI) Systems

The latest development in online information sources is the creation of AI-driven services like ChatGPT, Google's Bard/Gemini, and Microsoft's Copilot. These services are hyped as all-knowing information systems that continually learn and synthesize huge amounts of data. Ask these services any question you want, and they will respond with seemingly personalized and authoritative answers.

There is no doubt that AI-generated information services are powerful tools, and they will be increasingly influential in the years ahead. But they come with a significant downside. Marketed as if they are omniscient and accurate, in reality they are only as good as the data fed into them and the programming used to process that data. If the data fed into these AI services is skewed, their answers will be no better.

That's bad enough. But the situation is actually far worse. The underlying programming of these systems can lead to the generation and dissemination of *completely fictional statements*. I discovered this firsthand when I experimented with Google's Bard in 2023. I asked it questions about the legality of teaching evidence for intelligent design in public school classrooms.

I had expected Bard to generate the kinds of inaccuracies and bias found in places like Wikipedia. After all, it probably drew on Wikipedia as one of its sources. What I didn't expect was that Bard would invent completely false information, such as claiming (wrongly) that the United States Supreme Court had ruled that teaching intelligent design in public schools is unconstitutional in the case of *Kitzmiller v. Dover*. In reality, *Kitzmiller* was merely a federal district court case, not a Supreme Court case, and its decision only applies to one part of Pennsylvania, not nationwide.

And when I asked it to justify specific claims or to cite its sources, Bard repeatedly invented court rulings *that didn't actually exist*. It generated the names of the purported legal cases and even cited the courts that purportedly issued the rulings. But these court cases and rulings never happened.

Let that sink in. Bard provided fictional sources in support of false claims.

Bard's fanciful answers made Wikipedia's biased entries appear to be paragons of accuracy. I later learned that I had experienced a well-documented flaw of AI systems: They generate all sorts of imaginary facts. In one humorous example, ChatGPT "kept asserting confidently (and incorrectly) that the Russians had sent various numbers of bears into space."[56] ChatGPT even invented names for the imaginary bears (including "Alyosha," "Pushinka," and "Vladimir")! When asked for references, ChatGPT produced fake urls.

If you realize the implications of what I am saying here, you should be frightened. Christians who aren't aware that AI-based information services can be even more biased and inaccurate than other sources are asking for trouble.

4. Entertainment Media

For many Americans, entertainment media shape their view of the world even more powerfully than news and information media. That's because the stories we watch can influence our attitudes and perceptions without us realizing it.

Just like journalists, most creators of entertainment content in America are overwhelmingly secular and overwhelmingly unsympathetic to a biblical worldview.

In 1990, a researcher surveyed thirty-five opinion leaders at the top of the entertainment industry. The results showed a huge gap between the views of Hollywood leaders and the general American population at the time. According to the survey, 40 percent of the American public wanted stricter abortion laws; only 9 percent of Hollywood opinion leaders did. Some 62 percent of the public described themselves as religious persons; only 24 percent of Hollywood opinion leaders did. On gay rights the gap was flipped: Nearly seven in ten Hollywood opinion leaders (68 percent) supported gay rights, but only 12 percent of the public did.[57]

This data is from a few decades ago. Unfortunately, there aren't good surveys from more recent years. But we have some stand-ins to measure the worldview of Hollywood today. One is campaign contributions. In 2018, the *Hollywood Reporter* disclosed the following: "Of the more than $4 million in federal donations made by the top Hollywood executives and entertainers, 99.7 percent went to Democrats and Democratic-leaning political action committees or organizations, according to a *Hollywood Reporter* data review of Federal Election Commission records."[58]

The lopsided partisanship can be seen even in companies that traditionally have produced family entertainment like the Walt Disney

Company. During the 2022 campaign cycle, 89 percent of donations from those who work for Disney went to Democratic candidates in federal elections.[59] Only 10 percent went to Republicans.

Obviously, political donations are not a perfect indicator, and I am not suggesting that supporting more Republicans than Democrats necessarily means one has a more biblical worldview. At the same time, the fact that the vast majority of political donations from Hollywood are directed to socially liberal Democrats is certainly suggestive of how members of Hollywood likely view traditional Christian beliefs in such areas as abortion and sexuality.

Of course, we don't need to rely on political donations to see the disconnect between biblical faith and much of Hollywood. Let's look again at the Walt Disney Company.

In 2022, a video surfaced featuring a Disney employee bragging about how his production wanted to explore "queer stories." He even described putting in place a tracking system to ensure that they were inserting enough "gender nonconforming characters," "canonical trans characters," "canonical asexual characters," and "canonical bisexual characters."[60]

A top Disney executive, meanwhile, declared that "We have many, many, many LGBTQIA in our stories," but pledged she wanted to do even more. The same year Disney launched a new animated series for adults titled *Little Demon*, "which feature[d] a woman who is impregnated by Satan and gives birth to an Antichrist daughter and carries graphic violence and nudity."[61] The character impregnated by Satan is named Laura. The actress who voiced the character said of her role, "I love that we are normalizing paganism. Laura is a pagan. She's a witch. She's jacked."[62]

Apparently one series about sex with Satan wasn't enough. In 2023, Disney announced the development of a new Disney+ series for teens that will "feature a teenage girl becoming pregnant after having a one-night stand with the devil."[63] Remember, these are projects from a company still widely viewed as devoted to "family friendly" productions. The content generated by other Hollywood studios and production companies is even worse.

So how do the entertainment media push Christians toward Stockholm Syndrome Christianity? I'd like to suggest four main ways.

Religion in General Is De-Emphasized

One of the most important things that Hollywood communicates to us is that religion is inconsequential in modern life. Very few stories in films and television show the importance of religion in people's daily lives. People don't go to church; they don't pray; they don't mention God. You are far more likely to see characters having conversations while using urinals than to see characters having conversations as they leave a church building. For the most part, Hollywood airbrushes religion out of human life. This has been true for a long time.

Consider the results of a study of fictional prime time television in the 1990s. Here is the study's summary:

> Findings indicate that the religious side of characters' lives is not typically presented on television. Across 1462 characters, 5.6% had an identifiable religious affiliation. Religious activity was infrequently presented. When it was portrayed, it was rarely a central theme in the storyline and it was most often framed as a personal and private activity. This study concludes that the infrequent presentation of religion and spirituality tends to symbolically convey the message that religion is not very important because it is rarely a factor in the lives of the people on TV or the social setting in which they are portrayed.[64]

It needs to be stressed that this erasure of religion from our culture can be found in "family friendly" content just as much as other productions. A prime example is the Hallmark Channel's annual slate of new "Christmas" movies. These "Christmas" movies have virtually nothing to do with the real meaning of Christmas—the incarnation of Jesus to save us from our sins.

Christians who watch these productions because they think they offer "wholesome" entertainment need to think seriously about how their perspective of Christmas is being secularized by Hallmark. Hallmark's redefinition of Christmas as a secular romantic holiday is arguably worse than simply ignoring Christmas altogether. By redefining Christmas to excise its religious meaning, movie studios are engaging in a destructive act of cultural appropriation in service of secularization.

Biblical Religion Is De-Emphasized Even More

Sometimes the entertainment media do cover religion, but it is often religion that has little to do with the religious views of most Americans. As media scholar Stanley Rothman put it, "In their efforts to entertain large audiences, moviemakers have, since 1965, largely ignored traditional religious themes, dwelling on demonic forces or manifestations of the supernatural that bear little or no relationship to traditional Jewish or Christian stories."[65]

Christianity Is Portrayed Negatively

When Christianity does end up being included in entertainment productions, it is often framed in terms of fanaticism, hypocrisy, and much worse. In the midst of the COVID-19 pandemic in 2020, Netflix premiered *Cursed,* a series whose main villain was a Catholic priest who "leads a group of genocidal 'Christian' monks."[66] As one media critic observed at the time, the series was merely "the latest in a long string of programming by the streaming service that turns everything from Christian prayer to Holy Scripture into a supposed dog whistle for evil."[67] Indeed, "Netflix has been dripping with anti-Christian content for years now, from teen dramadies mocking Christian beliefs to post-apocalyptic movies portraying Christians as diabolical villains."

There are plenty of similar examples.[68] In 2023, an episode of NBC's series *Quantum Leap* featured "a cruel, sadistic psychiatrist who quotes the Bible and has a crucifix on his desk."[69] The same year, HBO's series *The Last of Us* featured a Christian character named David who turns out to be a pedophile and a cannibal. After watching the episode, veteran television actor Rainn Wilson tweeted: "I do think there is an anti-Christian bias in Hollywood. As soon as the David character in *The Last of Us* started reading from the Bible I knew that he was going to be a horrific villain. Could there be a Bible-reading preacher on a show who is actually loving and kind?"[70]

Notably, Wilson is an adherent of the Bahá'í Faith, not Christianity. But even he could see what was going on.

Biblical Sexual Teachings Are Trashed

Biblical moral teachings, especially in the area of sex, are flouted throughout the entertainment media. In 2008, the Parents Television Council released a study of how sex is portrayed on the major broadcast networks. Here is what they concluded: "Across the broadcast networks, verbal references to non-marital sex outnumbered references to sex in the context of marriage by nearly 3 to 1; and scenes depicting or implying sex between non-married partners outnumbered scenes depicting or implying sex between married partners by a ratio of nearly 4 to 1."[71]

In a 2018 study, the Council looked at "family comedies" on network television. The results were no better: "Over 80% (81.5%) of prime-time broadcast network 'family comedies' analyzed for this study contained instances of adults using explicit sexual dialogue in front of children. *ALL* of the 'family comedies' aired on CBS, NBC, and Fox contained instances of sexual dialogue by adults in the presence of children, and 80% of ABC's 'family comedies' did."[72]

These findings relate to broadcast television. Cable television and streaming services like Netflix are far worse. As another Parents Television Council study showed, Netflix is especially egregious. It produces sexually explicit shows about both high school and now middle school students.[73] These shows are obviously intended to target high schoolers and middle schoolers as a key audience. Yet they are rated TV-MA, meaning that they contain so much graphic sex or violence or language that anyone under seventeen isn't supposed to watch. But, of course, Netflix is hoping they do watch. You don't produce series featuring middle schoolers and not expect them to be interested. Netflix is targeting your kids.

It shouldn't be difficult to understand how Christians who uncritically consume mainstream entertainment programming can become Stockholm Syndrome Christians. Spend your time filling yourself with spiritually toxic content, and the toxicity will eventually kill your faith.

5. Scientists

In addition to being shaped by news, information, and entertainment outlets, our view of reality is also influenced by experts. Chief among the expert classes are people claiming to speak in the name of science. In the last several years, science has been increasingly used to justify all sorts of things, including pro-abortion policies, the idea that men are programmed for sexual promiscuity, the claim that homosexuality is genetic, the claim that we must lock down and not attend church for an extended period of time. For the secular world, scientific authority is equivalent to the voice of God. And to question a claim made in the name of science is to commit heresy, no matter how much evidence you have to back up your questioning.

Far too many Americans, including many Christians, accept what I would call the "myth of the scientist in the white lab coat." That is, when they think about scientists, they visualize people in lab coats who have been trained to be impartial, factual, objective. According to one survey pre-COVID, nearly two-thirds of Americans see scientists as neither particularly liberal nor conservative. They think of them as non-partisan and neutral.[74]

The reality is starkly different.

Consider political ideology. According to a 2009 nationwide survey of 2,500+ scientists, 52 percent classified themselves as politically liberal; only 9 percent classified themselves as conservative. That made scientists four times less likely than the general public to identify as conservatives. And it made scientists 2.6 times more likely to identify as liberals as the general public. Or look at party affiliation. A whopping 6 percent of scientists identified as Republicans, whereas 55 percent identified as Democrats—again, completely unrepresentative of the population as a whole.[75]

But scientists are even less representative of the general public when it comes to religion.

While 83 percent of the general public believed in God in 2009, only 33 percent of scientists did.[76] Think about that. Religion impacts our deepest views about the world and what is important. There is a cavernous gulf in this area between most scientists and most of the public. In a 2021 national survey of over 5,000 academic biologists, 89 percent identified as liberal, 85 percent as pro-choice, and 63 percent as non-religious.[77] An earlier national survey from 2007 found that 61 percent of biology professors identified as either atheist or agnostic.[78]

By uncritically accepting claims made by scientists as a class we are going down the path of Stockholm Syndrome Christianity.

6. College and University Professors

Scientists aren't the only experts who shape our beliefs. College and university professors as a whole are also influential through a range of activities, from teaching the next generation of leaders, to advising policymakers, to providing talking heads in the media on a range of issues.

College professors, especially those at the most influential and elite colleges and universities, are overwhelmingly left-wing, secular, and opposed to a biblical worldview. In 1999, researchers surveyed over 1,600 professors at 183 American universities and colleges.[79] Here is what they found:

- 72 percent of those surveyed identified as leftist or liberal.[80]

- 67 percent believed that the "homosexual lifestyle [is] as acceptable as [the] heterosexual" lifestyle.[81]

- 84 percent endorsed a right to abortion.[82]

- 75 percent thought extramarital cohabitation is acceptable.[83]

Researchers also found that certain beliefs were associated with a lack of professional advancement in academia, no matter what your other qualifications: "Being a conservative, a Republican or a practicing Christian confers a disadvantage in professional advancement greater than... other factors" such as "race, gender, ethnicity, and sexual orientation."[84]

According to a 2014 study, colleges and universities across the United States as a whole "had a six to one ratio of liberal to conservative professors. In New England, the figure was 28 to one."[85] Three other studies from 2016–2020 showed that the disparity between registered

Democrats and Republicans among college professors ranged from 8.5 to 1 to 12 to 1, depending on the kind of colleges and universities studied. The more elite institutions had the greater disparities.[86]

In 2007, researchers surveyed nearly 1,500 professors from colleges and universities across America, including community colleges. According to this survey, around 37 percent of professors at elite doctoral universities were atheists or agnostics.[87] Only 1 percent of faculty at such PhD-granting elite universities would describe themselves as "born again" Christians.[88] More than seven in ten professors at these elite universities described the Bible as "an ancient book of fables, legends, history, and moral precepts recorded by men."[89]

There are more religious-identified professors at community colleges and non-doctoral institutions. But that doesn't mean they are sympathetic to orthodox Christianity. Among professors at all colleges and universities, still over half (52 percent) think the Bible is a book of fables and legends.[90] And only about 13 percent of college professors at all types of institutions describe themselves as religious "traditionalists."[91]

7. Celebrities

Experts aren't the only influencers Christians are being shaped by. Our culture worships worldly success, and the Christian subculture is sadly no different. Since at least the 1970s, Christians in America have sought validation from celebrity film stars, musicians, and sports figures who say they have accepted Christ. Some of these celebrities are obviously insincere. The most notorious example was probably Larry Flynt, the flamboyant publisher of the pornographic magazine *Hustler*, who announced to much fanfare in 1977 that he had become a born-again Christian.[92] His subsequent life showed he hadn't.

Many celebrities who identify as Christians may well be sincere. But being sincere doesn't mean the celebrity knows what he or she is talking about or is theologically orthodox or even wise. That is why we have so many Christian celebrities endorsing gay rights or defending abortion. When *Roe v. Wade* was overturned, for example, singer Justin Bieber went on Instagram to proclaim: "For what it's worth,

I think women should have the choice what to do with their own bodies."[93] Of course, a baby inside the womb is a new individual who is distinct from the mother's body. Bieber is fortunate that his own mother, Patricia Mallette, recognized that truth. Mallette refused to abort Justin when she became pregnant with him at age seventeen.[94]

Celebrity pastors and theologians are sometimes no more trustworthy than Christian pop stars. Witness the false or garbled teachings of Andy Stanley or various "prosperity gospel" preachers.

We shouldn't be surprised by this. By definition "celebrity" means being popular. People accustomed to being popular find it very, very hard to hold to biblical teachings that are unpopular or even openly mocked. Some do, of course; and sometimes as a result they fade from view.

Other, less courageous celebrities can quickly become Stockholm Syndrome Christians. And because they're influential, they influence other Christians to likewise accept the world's frame of reference.

Christian celebrities can have a pernicious influence in validating Stockholm Syndrome Christianity.

What Can You Do?

This chapter has presented a lot of information, but the main point is pretty simple: If we listen to the wrong voices, we make it a lot more likely that we or our loved ones will become Stockholm Syndrome Christians. We are more likely to adopt the assumptions and views of those who reject Christianity if we spend most of our time listening to those who reject Christianity.

So what can you do? I'd like to offer two suggestions.

First, choose your information and entertainment sources wisely. You don't have to rely on the secular media for your information about the world. You don't have to be a passive consumer of entertainment. As terrible as things are today, we probably have never had so many good alternatives for our information and even entertainment sources—if we are willing to use them. In the last section of this book ("Resources"), you will find a link to an online list of news, information, and entertainment sources that are more friendly to a Christian worldview.

Second, don't just let your information and entertainment sources shape you. Be discerning and have a healthy skepticism of what you are ingesting. Talk with your Christian friends, your spouse, your parents, or your children about what you're hearing. Help each other evaluate information, rather than simply letting it wash over you.

Acts 17 describes how Paul and Silas brought the gospel to Jews in the Greek city of Berea. Unlike the Jews in some other cities, the Bereans did not give a knee-jerk response. We are told in verse 11: "Now these Jews were more noble than those in Thessalonica; they received the word with all eagerness, examining the Scriptures daily to see if these things were so." The Bereans didn't just accept—or reject—what they were told. Instead, they examined the Scriptures daily to see if the teachings of Paul and Silas were consistent with the Bible. We need to develop that same attitude.

"Do not conform to the pattern of this world, but be transformed by the renewing of your mind," Paul tells us in Romans 12:2. "Then you will be able to test and approve what God's will is—his good, pleasing and perfect will." We aren't supposed to be conformed to the world and its teachings. We are supposed to be *transformed* by Christ and test and approve claims we encounter in our lives and the public square.

8. PLEASING THE
WRONG PEOPLE

IN THE ENDING MONTHS OF WORLD WAR II, C. S. LEWIS DELIVERED a lecture in London. In his talk, he warned about the dangers of pursuing membership in what he called "the inner ring."

The inner ring is the ultimate "in" group. It is the network within an organization or movement where the power ultimately resides. Lewis later turned his lecture into an essay,[1] and he explored the same idea in his supernatural thriller *That Hideous Strength*,[2] where a young academic is drawn into a sinister conspiracy through his pursuit of the inner ring.

In large part, the desire to join the inner ring is a desire for acceptance by those with power or prestige or popularity. At various points as a young man, I felt the pull of this desire.

After my junior year in high school, I participated in a summer school in Washington, DC with high-powered high school students drawn from around America. I started out feeling like an outsider for a variety of reasons, not least of which was that I was a politically conservative Christian, whereas most other participants were secular progressives. As the days progressed, I wanted to fit in. I found myself participating in discussions that I would be ashamed of later, discussions where others were ridiculed and I laughed along with the jokes in order to be accepted.

Later, during both my college and grad school years, I became politically active, and I found myself involved with groups that were unhealthy for me. The groups tended to view themselves as uniquely called to change society, and they adopted an end-justifies-the-means mentality when it came to their agendas. Seeking approval from those in charge was a powerful temptation, and I experienced the reality of what Lewis warned about. Fortunately, in graduate school I became involved in a solid church. Being a part of that church helped temper my desire for the inner ring, and the allure never exerted the same stranglehold again.

Whatever we call it, the desire to please and be approved of by others can exert a powerful influence in our lives. If those we are trying to please are virtuous, this desire may be helpful sometimes. But if we are seeking to please the wrong people, the results can prove disastrous.

I think at the heart of the compromises made by many Stockholm Syndrome Christians is a desire to please and be accepted by the wrong people. I saw this firsthand in my years as a college professor.

The Scandal of the Evangelical Mind

The same year I joined the faculty of Seattle Pacific, historian Mark Noll published his book *The Scandal of the Evangelical Mind* (1994).[3] That book was soon the rage of evangelical college campuses. Everyone seemed to be talking about it. Noll, then a professor of history at Wheaton College, indicted his fellow evangelicals for being anti-intellectual. "The scandal of the evangelical mind is that there is not much of an evangelical mind," he declared.[4] Noll lamented that although American evangelicals had organized "dozens of theological seminaries, scores of colleges, hundreds of radio stations, and thousands of... parachurch agencies," they could not boast "a single research university or a single periodical devoted to in-depth interaction with modern culture."[5]

Noll's appeal to evangelicals to make the life of the mind a priority was admirable. We are called, after all, to love God with all our mind as well as with all our heart, soul, and strength (Matthew 22:37, Mark 12:30, Luke 10:27). Paul encourages Christians to hone their intellectual reasoning skills (2 Corinthians 10:5), and we have many examples of his own gift of philosophical thinking (Acts 17, for one).

Peter, similarly, urges Christians to be prepared to explain their faith to unbelievers (1 Peter 3:15).

But some of the particulars of Noll's indictment were troubling. Take his identification of "biblicism" (which he defined as "reliance on the Bible as ultimate religious authority"[6]) as one of the obstacles to evangelical scholarship.[7] Noll seemed to suggest that the only way "the life of the mind may have a chance" among evangelicals was if they restricted the Bible's authority to "pointing us to the Savior and... orienting our entire existence to the service of God."[8]

That may sound good, but it actually leaves out quite a lot. What about the Bible's accounts of God's actions in history, starting in the Old Testament? What about the Bible's foundational teachings about God's omniscience and omnipotence, His creation of the world and mankind, and the particulars of the moral law? The Bible certainly points us to Jesus, and it definitely orients us to a life of service to God. But it is a precarious endeavor to try to pick and choose what parts of biblical teaching we are to treat as authoritative. As we saw in Chapter 1, that approach does not end well.

Perhaps the biggest problem with Noll's book was that it fed a lust for secular approval among many evangelical intellectuals. Noll himself warned that "the point of Christian scholarship is not recognition by standards established in the wider culture."[9] But that is not how I saw things play out at my university or with scholars at other evangelical educational institutions. Instead, the test for good scholarship increasingly became whether one received approval from secular authorities, or from fellow Christians aligned with secular culture. Time and again, I saw Christian scholars embrace Stockholm Syndrome Christianity as they pursued validation and acceptance from those hostile to orthodox Christianity.

The more a discipline is dominated by secularist scholars, the more powerful the temptation to embrace Stockholm Syndrome Christianity will be. In my experience, Christian biologists face some of the most difficult challenges. Darwin's theory of unguided evolution is so culturally powerful that the pressures to conform can be very hard to resist—and the failure to conform can be painful.

I still remember the day one of my colleagues at Seattle Pacific shared with me something of his own personal journey. He had graduated from SPU during an era when the science faculty were skeptical of Darwin. So when he went to graduate school in biology, he found himself embarrassed and humiliated because he hadn't been taught to embrace evolution. When he eventually returned to SPU as a faculty member, he vowed that what happened to him wasn't going to happen to any of his students. He was going to make sure they fully embraced modern evolutionary theory. They would fit in.

Fitting in seemed to be a strong need for many of my colleagues. They liked to talk about the good relations they had with faculty at the nearby University of Washington, or the secular research grants they had won. Those things were perfectly fine in and of themselves. But they indicated a tendency to base one's self-worth on receiving approval from secular academia. For a Christian scholar, that was unhealthy.

The craving for secular approval on my campus created an uncomfortable atmosphere for the few faculty members on campus who still challenged the secular establishment. Such colleagues were increasingly viewed as compromising SPU's reputation in the secular world. As a result, they were making life harder for the rest of the faculty who were trying their best to achieve secular approval.

I had good relationships with most of my colleagues, at least on the surface. But there was an unpleasant undercurrent that grew over time. I remember a meeting where I was told by a university administrator that I was regarded by some other faculty as a problem. He said they feared I was trying to take SPU back to the bad old days when it was "creationist, fundamentalist, and conservative." They worried I would damage SPU's growing secular respectability. I didn't consider myself either a creationist or a fundamentalist, but that didn't really matter. My colleagues were correct that I was out of step with the secular establishment. And that was the trouble.

Turning on Your Fellow Christians

A lot of the hostility Stockholm Syndrome Christians express towards more orthodox Christians can be explained by their desire to be accepted by secular culture. Christians who are non-compliant with the culture can make it harder for other Christians to gain acceptance. So the traditional Christians are viewed as a threat.

I recall a conversation I had with a prominent Christian scientist who advocates the compatibility of mainstream evolutionary theory and Christianity. At a certain level, we shared significant common ground when it came to science and faith. We both agreed that Christianity and science, properly construed, were compatible. We both agreed that the claim that Christianity was anti-science was destructive as well as false.

Nevertheless, the more we talked, the more it became apparent that our seeming agreement masked a deep difference. For me, believing that Christianity and science were compatible meant exposing the falsity of atheist claims that science refutes the teachings of Christianity. For my discussion partner, however, responding to the claims of scientific atheists didn't seem to be a priority.

Instead, this Christian scientist was more concerned about how Christians were perceived by secular scientists. In this scientist's view, Christians who question Darwin make secular scientists think Christianity is anti-science. That was bad. So Christians should embrace evolution because that would make Christians more acceptable to the secular establishment.

Another Christian scientist I know blames Christians who support intelligent design in biology for making it hard for him to be a Christian scientist at a secular university. Even though this scientist has embraced mainstream evolutionary theory himself, he is upset that other people sometimes assume that he hasn't just because he is a Christian.

The Real Culprits

I am sympathetic with the plight Christian scientists face in academia, especially biologists. The intolerance they encounter can be considerable. But Christian scientists who blame other Christians for the intolerance they face are embracing Stockholm Syndrome Christianity. They are blaming the victim by identifying with the worldview of the aggressor. The real blame for the intolerance they encounter is not Christian scientists who dissent from Darwin. It is secular scientists who are so intolerant they won't allow dissent.

With Friends Like This...

Unfortunately, instead of challenging intolerant secularists, too often Christian academics acquiesce to or even join secularists in their intolerance of other Christians. For example, take Washington University biologist Joshua Swamidass, an evangelical Christian who embraces modern evolutionary theory. Writing for *The Wall Street Journal* in 2021, he called for imposing punitive policies on Christian colleges that teach "creation science."[10]

Swamidass argued that such colleges should retain their accreditation, but only if they agreed to a series of poison pills. Any "deviations from national norms" in their science courses "need to be prominently disclosed, tracked and reported." Any courses teaching "creation science" need to be highlighted on student transcripts, which could easily subject those students to discrimination by employers. "Credit from courses that include creation science should not be used toward science degrees. Nor should they be eligible for transfer to secular institutions," he said. Finally, while these creationist colleges could keep their official statements of faith as is, they would have to agree to not require faculty to adhere to the faith statement provisions on creationism.

Swamidass thinks these recommendations represent a "compromise" that will safeguard the "academic freedom" of Christian institutions who embrace biblical creation. But the fact that he sincerely believes this highlights the problem: Swamidass so identifies with the worldview of his secular colleagues that he has convinced himself that treating Christians who disagree with him as pariahs is treating them fairly.

For my part, I am not a young earth biblical creationist, but I steadfastly support the right of fellow Christians who hold a young earth view to be treated fairly and not as second-class citizens. I identify more with them than with those secularists and Christians who want to silence them.

The journey of Christian academics who embrace Stockholm Syndrome Christianity can be painful to watch. In the early years of the intelligent design movement, I came to know a gifted Christian biologist who did valuable work on ethics. He critiqued Darwinian accounts of ethics for not adequately explaining the reality of altruism, and he had interesting ideas about how our biological capacities reflected nature's underlying intelligent design.

One thing I especially admired about this scholar was his kindness toward others, and how he strove to be fair-minded toward the Darwinian materialists with whom he disagreed. He was insistent that we should be charitable toward our critics and that our rhetoric should be careful and measured. He also was also very measured and precise in what he wrote. He did not want to overstate anything. I respected his absolute integrity as a scholar and as a fellow Christian. I looked up to him as a model to follow.

Then one year this biologist was offered a plum opportunity with a group that advocated theistic evolution. The group also had massive funding to support its efforts. In order to pursue the opportunity, this scholar disassociated himself from his intelligent design connections, although he assured me at the time that he had not changed his views.

Some time later, I learned he was going to speak at my university. I looked forward to seeing him again and hearing his talk. It was a sad experience. He now downplayed the problems with evolutionary accounts of ethics and stressed the value of evolutionary explanations. There was no longer anything about how an intelligent design view might help us better understand the biological underpinnings of morality. In my recollection, the talk wasn't so much wrong as it was completely safe and inoffensive.

A number of years later, this same biologist decided to co-author a public statement denouncing intelligent design as a "science stopper" and "neither sound science nor good theology." Two of his co-authors for the statement were prominent atheist Darwinists.

People can change their views, and this biologist would no doubt say that he changed his views based on his analysis of the evidence. I can respect someone for going where they think the evidence leads, even if I disagree with their conclusions. But one would have to be blind not to see that something more was going on here besides just a change of mind.

For me, his public statement attacking intelligent design was clarifying. The statement itself was filled with inaccuracies and straw-men attacks. I was left to wonder what had become of my friend's previous commitment to accuracy and his emphasis on the need for kindness and charity toward those with whom we disagree. Instead of publicly criticizing my former colleague, I sent him a private letter challenging the accuracy and fairness of what he had written. I never received a response.

What was I left to think? Were my former colleague's prior professions about kindness and fairness insincere? I don't think so. Yet the fact remains that being kind and fair-minded to secularists with cultural power can benefit one's career; being kind and fair-minded to those without cultural power won't. In such cases, it can be hard to disentangle our own true motives. This is true for all of us, including me.

As I reflect on what happened, a Bible verse keeps coming to mind: "Bad company corrupts good morals" (1 Corinthians 15:33 NASB). Sadly, I think that is what happened with my friend. Once we start trying to please the wrong people, it will change us. It may even make us justify double standards we would have previously found unacceptable. The pressure on Christian scholars to embrace Stockholm Syndrome Christianity isn't just motivated by a desire to survive in a hostile academic environment; it also involves the possibility of rewards and affirmation. And it is not limited to the sciences.

The Humanities Aren't Exempt

I knew a Christian scholar in the humanities who in his early years had done significant work defending religious liberty and the right to life. Then one of his books won a particularly prestigious award. I remember speaking with him in the aftermath of all of the publicity. He couldn't stop talking about being interviewed by a certain personality on a major network television news show. It troubled me, because he seemed to be losing his focus on more important things.

Over the years, this scholar has gone on to win more secular acclaim and is now quite distinguished in his discipline. But as near as I can tell from the public record, he has played it safe. The culture-changing promise of some of his early scholarship has been unfulfilled. He is respected by the world. But at what cost?

The desire for acceptance displayed by Christian academics certainly helps explain how widespread Stockholm Syndrome Christianity has become among them. But they are not alone.

Evangelical Elites Want to Be Loved (by the Wrong People)

Thus far in this chapter I have focused on evangelical academics. But the same desire to be liked by the wrong people is pervasive among evangelical elites as a whole, including church and parachurch leaders, journalists, pundits, and public officials. Mark Galli, the former Editor of *Christianity Today*, explains:

> Elite evangelicalism... is too often "a form of cultural accommodation dressed as convictional religion." These evangelicals want to appear respectable to the elite of American culture... I don't know that evangelicals have been sufficiently self-reflective to admit their basic and personal insecurities. It's just no fun being an outsider to mainstream culture. We all just want to be loved, and if not loved, at least liked and respected. Elite evangelicals are not just savvy evangelists but also a people striving for acceptance.[11]

I doubt that Galli would agree with a number of the criticisms contained in this book, but I think his analysis is spot on. In my experience, evangelical leaders of all sorts want to be loved and accepted by the culture. This inevitably feeds into Stockholm Syndrome Christianity. Seeking acceptance, Christians accommodate certain non-biblical cultural norms; then they embrace them; then they despise those who haven't made concessions to secular culture, while themselves identifying more and more with secular culture.

The desire for acceptance by secular culture can be self-perpetuating. A certain Stockholm Syndrome Christian gains acceptance and acclaim in public life. That very acceptance and acclaim attracts other Christian leaders who want to be accepted themselves by secular culture. They then latch onto and promote the Stockholm Syndrome Christian as a model for others to follow. Thus Stockholm Syndrome Christianity expands its circle of influence.

Francis Collins is a good example of what I am talking about. Collins has been celebrated by many evangelical leaders because of his acceptance by the secular establishment. But evangelical leaders might have been wise to reflect on why the secular establishment has been so approving of Collins.

In 2019 the journal *Science* noted that when Collins originally was appointed as NIH Director by President Barack Obama, some worried "that his outspoken Christian faith would influence his leadership."[12] But *Science* went on to assure its readers that the critics need not have worried: "His religion never became an issue—he followed Obama's order to loosen rules for stem cell research, which some Christians oppose, and has defended fetal tissue research despite criticism from antiabortion groups."

A journalist at *Slate* put it even more starkly: "If Collins's faith mollifies even a few political conservatives who would otherwise continue to waste time and money fighting research efforts that violate their specific religious tenets, then the benefits of his faith should outweigh whatever qualms scientists might have."[13]

For more than twelve years, Collins served the secularists' agenda at NIH by providing cover for them to do what they wanted to do anyway. As documented earlier in this book, he championed embryonic stem cell research, the harvesting of baby parts from late term abortions for scientific research, the marginalization of Christian scientists who are skeptical of unguided Darwinian evolution, the embracing of the LGBTQIA+ movement, and most recently, the demonization and persecution of Christians who had conscience issues with the COVID vaccines. The sad reality is that it's precisely because of Collins's abandonment of biblical truth in these areas that he rose to the top of the NIH and then became acting science advisor in the Biden White House. Had Collins not become a Stockholm Syndrome Christian, he wouldn't have been tolerated.

Once Collins became a scion of the establishment, he became attractive to many other evangelical pastors and professors and pundits who themselves wanted approval by the secular culture. And that's what Francis Collins now represented to them. After all, he was on the cover of *TIME*. He was praised by the secular media. If they could somehow associate with him, they would no longer be cultural lepers. As a result, evangelical movers and shakers rushed to promote Collins, acting more like press agents than moral and spiritual leaders.

The result was the invention and propagation of a mythical Collins—Collins as a model for how scientists and others can stand for their faith even at the very top of the scientific establishment. Except, as we saw in Chapter 2, Collins didn't really stand for his faith when it came to public policy.

The growing desire of evangelical elites to be approved of by secular culture can be seen rather painfully in the updated edition of *The Scandal of the Evangelical Mind*, published by Mark Noll in 2022. In his original book, Noll was careful to caution that the test for good Christian scholarship was not secular approval or recognition. In the updated version, that caution seems to have been largely jettisoned. Although Noll glancingly acknowledges that it "is not the only gauge of a culture's intellectual life," he now offers publication by elite university presses as "a shorthand indication" of scholarly excellence.[14] Accordingly, he lists a selection of books by Christian scholars published by presses at Harvard, Yale, Oxford, and Cambridge. He also highlights how fellow Christian historian George Marsden was "awarded the Bancroft Prize, the most distinguished honor bestowed on books in American history."

Whatever Noll may tell himself, today he definitely seems to equate good scholarship with secular approval. Sadly, he also appears to equate having a "mind" with the adoption of a set of partisan policy positions. If you are an evangelical who has the wrong view of Trump or evolution or climate change or COVID-19 policy, Noll makes clear he regards you as an unthinking yahoo.[15]

Noll doesn't even seem to entertain the possibility that a thoughtful Christian might be able to disagree with secular elites on any of these topics. Noll and others lament the lack of an evangelical mind in those with whom they disagree. But it is worth asking whether there is anything distinctly Christian about their own mindset that craves secular approval and is increasingly indistinguishable from the mindset of secular elites.

Shouldn't Christians Be Concerned about Their Reputations?

Most Stockholm Syndrome Christians probably don't think that they are simply craving approval from the powers that be. Instead, they likely justify their actions as a way of rescuing Christianity from misguided or unhelpful Christians.

For example, they may think other Christians are turning people away from the gospel by being so harsh or direct about unpopular beliefs, making Christians seem unloving or unlikeable. Or Stockholm Syndrome Christians may be worried that their fellow Christians too often appear foolish and unwise in the general culture. Or they appear bigoted. Or they appear partisan and wrap themselves in one political party, implying that if you don't support that party you aren't welcome as a Christian.

As a result, say Stockholm Syndrome Christians, many Christians are driving people away from the gospel. According to Stockholm Syndrome Christians, we therefore need to reformulate how we act and how we express ourselves and what we emphasize, in order to win people for the gospel.

The people who express these concerns are usually very concerned about the reputation of Christians in our society. They are embarrassed that evangelical Christians have such a bad reputation in secular culture. They want to change that. They think that in so doing they are removing obstacles to the gospel.

The first thing to say about this line of thinking is: They have a point. Yes, Christians shouldn't be unloving or annoying. Yes, we shouldn't try to join Christianity at the hip with a particular political party. Yes, we should try to offer the most persuasive arguments we can.

Yet there are several problems with focusing too much on our reputation or even on supposed "obstacles" to the gospel.

First, we need to be sure we don't turn our own reputation into an idol. We certainly should strive to be worthy of a good reputation. But in a culture that increasingly thinks good is bad and bad is good, a good reputation may not always be the best indicator of faithful Christianity. In Luke 6:26, Jesus himself warns us, "Woe to you, when all people speak well of you, for so their fathers did to the false prophets." Eric Metaxas rightly advises that "like so many good things, we can make an idol of respectability" and "there may be times when God calls us to do something that doesn't seem 'respectable.'"[16]

Second, we need to make sure we aren't usurping God's role in calling people to Himself (John 6:44). It's not our job to develop a good marketing strategy that waters down the gospel until it's palatable to the world. Indeed, this whole way of thinking is theologically perilous. It amounts to thinking that we ought to protect God from Himself by hiding things from His Word that we worry could turn other people off. But we are not God's press agent, and this human-centered approach effectively denies the role of the Holy Spirit as the only One who softens our hearts to hear God's teaching, including God's teaching about sin. Our role is to faithfully proclaim God's Word, not to add to it or subtract from it in a vain effort to change hearts ourselves.

So, while we definitely don't want to place obstacles of our own making in the way of the gospel being heard, we need to be very careful about what we consider obstacles to the gospel. Are we talking about our own sinful behaviors and shortcomings? Or are we talking about culturally unpopular parts of the gospel that we are embarrassed by and fear will make it hard for many people to become Christians? Bear in mind that Jesus said he himself was an obstacle to people. He's hard to accept. Why? Because he stands for radical obedience to God, not men.[17] So by its very nature, Christianity—following Christ—is an obstacle for many people. We can't remove that obstacle without gutting Christianity.

It seems to me that much of the preoccupation with removing obstacles to the gospel today is focused on downplaying parts of the gospel we think are culturally unpopular. We see it in the messages of Andy Stanley, who makes pretty clear that he thinks biblical teaching itself is an obstacle to the gospel being heard and so that's why we need to downplay it. This same way of thinking, sadly, can be detected in the last years of Tim Keller's ministry. It's also apparent in other recent movements.

My wife Sonja and I were active in a church that eventually embraced what they called the "missional" church. Who could oppose the church being more intentionally focused on its mission? But in our experience, the word "missional" seemed to be used as code word for justifying a de-emphasis on anything that we fear might embarrass us with our secular neighbors. But what kind of gospel are we proclaiming if we do not teach the whole counsel of God when people come inside our doors?

We need to build relationships of trust with our neighbors. We need to meet them where they are, understanding that their backgrounds and experiences are different from ours, and yet still finding common ground with them in our shared humanity (1 Corinthians 9:19–23). But that does not mean watering down God's teachings in the hope that we can reach others more effectively. The full-force gospel is quite capable of reaching people. It does so all the time, including in countries where following Christ means rejection by family, loss of job, and sometimes suffering violence and even death. The gospel reaches people like these not because it's easy, but because it's true.

So we need to ask ourselves hard questions. Are we really trying to stand for the gospel, or are we craving approval from those who reject the gospel? Are we seeking to reach a hostile world with loving truth, or are we becoming Stockholm Syndrome Christians?

9. TOLERATING THE WRONG RULERS

THE SINGLE BIGGEST REASON MANY CHRISTIAN CHURCHES, schools, colleges, and ministries have gone down the path of Stockholm Syndrome Christianity might surprise you. It is not because of the actions of secularists or theological liberals. It is because biblically orthodox Christians in positions of authority have failed to use the authority God has given them. They've been AWOL.

That is what happened at Seattle Pacific University, where—as discussed earlier in this book—the overwhelming majority of faculty now reject the Bible's teachings on sex and other matters. The tragedy of Seattle Pacific is that its collapse as a Christian institution was not inevitable. It was eminently preventable—but those who had the legitimate power to prevent it chose not to do so.

I need to give a personal aside here. I'm not proud to say that in the years since leaving SPU, I have struggled with feelings of bitterness about what happened there. I know the Bible commands us to rid ourselves of bitterness (Ephesians 4:31) and to not let a bitter root grow up inside us (Hebrews 12:15). I thought I had given up most of my hard feelings, but writing this chapter has brought to the surface emotions I thought I had let go. This made me question whether I should even write about what happened at SPU. But I'm convinced that if accounts like this one are never published, we are doomed to repeat the same mistakes time and again. If faithful Christians never learn why their institutions fail, there is little hope for the genuine reformation of those institutions.

So I'm trying to walk a careful line. In this chapter, I will say some pretty direct things about SPU's president during the period in question; but I have chosen not to use his name, because my purpose isn't to hold him up for censure as an individual. It's to reveal the process by which things went wrong, so that other institutions can avoid the same fate in the future. In order to document my claims I do have to mention his name in the endnotes, but I would encourage readers not to focus on him personally. He is long since retired, and I don't want to give him pain, although he likely will find my account painful if he reads it. I think he is a sincere Christian who is personally orthodox. I also think he sincerely thought he was doing the right thing. That makes what happened all the more tragic in my view. I don't think he realized where the path he led SPU down would ultimately lead. Perhaps he does now.

A Squandered Legacy

When I was first hired by Seattle Pacific for a tenure-track position, a member of one of the faculty committees that interviewed me said something I have never forgotten. He warned me that the school had a very theologically conservative board of trustees. In fact, I was told in confidential tones, the board had just recently rejected for tenure a religion professor because the board thought he had unorthodox beliefs. The faculty member telling me this thought he was letting me in on something scandalous.

Little did he know that when I heard his confession, I thought "good for the board members." That's precisely what I believed the board of a Christian institution was called to do: defend the integrity of its mission. SPU was still an evangelical institution when I joined its faculty in the mid-1990s because those in authority had tried their best to keep the university tied to its mission. They hadn't been perfect, and there already were many faculty who weren't biblically orthodox at SPU. But heterodox faculty had to be careful, because they knew there were limits to what would be tolerated.

The board's denial of tenure to a faculty member on grounds of heterodox theology was probably the most powerful message it could have sent to the campus community. Many faculty, especially the theological progressives, didn't like the message, but they understood it. And it certainly chilled their enthusiasm for going even farther afield or for hiring even more unorthodox people. So when I arrived at SPU, it was already divided; but thanks to the actions of its board, it still had a fighting chance as a Christian school.

But soon a new president was hired. To the great delight of some of the faculty, that president gradually convinced board members that they were too involved. They were told they should simply trust him and stay out of the details, especially when it came to tenure and promotion.

As the board became less involved, more and more people were hired who pushed the institution in a new direction. Some of the fruits of those decisions I've already discussed in previous chapters. There is much more I could say, but some of it is beyond the scope of this book. I want to focus here on the watershed moment—the moment of decision on which the future of the institution turned.

SPU's Watershed

Christian thinker Francis Schaeffer once wrote about a snowfield near his home in Switzerland. "The snow was lying there unbroken, a seeming unity," he recalled. "However, that unity was an illusion." In truth, the snow "lay along a great divide." When the snow melted, the runoff on one side of the divide eventually ended up in the North Sea. The snow on the other side flowed into a different valley and ultimately ended up in the Mediterranean.[1]

Schaeffer was making a critical point about the choices we make. At the time of choosing, it might not seem to matter which way we pick. The difference might seem inconsequential. But afterward we may come to see that the two options led in completely opposite directions. That is a watershed moment.

In my view, SPU's watershed moment came in the early 2000s when its president wanted to revamp the university's board of trustees. To convey the significance of what happened, I first need to supply some background.

As of the late 1980s, seventeen of Seattle Pacific's thirty-three trustees were required to be elected by the Free Methodist Church, and two-thirds of board members had to be members of the Free Methodist Church, giving Free Methodists effective control over the school.[2] In addition, all members of the board were supposed to be in agreement with the doctrinal standards of the Free Methodist Church. Because the Free Methodist Church is fairly conservative theologically, these requirements helped ensure that SPU's board would maintain a majority of biblically orthodox members.

But when faculty arrived back on campus in the fall of 2000, we began to hear about a new plan to "strengthen" the school's relationship with its governing church. The president told faculty about the plan at a meeting early in the academic year, but he wouldn't divulge specifics. When I asked him at the meeting if he could share the actual plan with us, he said it wasn't his to share. It was the plan of the bishops of the Free Methodist Church.

The plan remained secret over the next several weeks, despite repeated efforts by various parties to get it released so church members and others could see it. It began to look like the new plan would be approved by the leadership of the Free Methodist Church in private without any open discussion. Only after the plan was adopted would church members and faculty learn what was in it. I grew increasingly alarmed, because from what I was hearing privately, it sounded like the new plan was going to abolish Free Methodist control of the university, not strengthen it. I thought this would place SPU on the path of losing its evangelical identity.

I also worried that SPU's board of trustees had been shut out of the process. It turns out this was not entirely true. According to an article eventually published by the student newspaper, the board had been informed at one of its meetings that a new relationship between the Free Methodist Church and its colleges was under development. But even board members were not given a copy of the actual plan, and they did not spend much time discussing or raising questions about it.

Someone involved in the process did not like the secrecy, and late in the year, he leaked the draft plan to my father-in-law, who had been a longtime professor at SPU but was now retired.

The draft proposal, which the president had said wasn't his, had his name affixed on it as the author.

The proposal declared: "We will form a new Board of Trustees, no longer selected by the denomination or its sponsoring conferences." Free Methodist representatives would be demoted to a new and largely advisory "Board of Governors" whose only real authority was to confirm the Board of Trustees' nomination of the university President.[3]

The president tried to dispel fears that Free Methodist educational institutions would slide from the faith under the new scheme. "Not one of these schools will ever slide toward secularization. Let us have confidence in that fact," he assured church leaders in his draft plan. "Each one of these schools is deeply committed to be Christian and fully evangelical in its purpose and mission."[4]

Again, it's likely that the president believed this statement at the time he made it. But it was foolhardy. "Not one of these schools will *ever* slide toward secularization"? That was not a fact but an assertion—an assertion that conflicted with the history of Christian higher education in America. Later the president pointed out that faithful Christian colleges do exist that aren't governed by sponsoring churches. That's true, but those institutions typically have detailed statements of faith to serve as a substitute for the doctrinal standards of a denomination. SPU did not have such a detailed statement of faith, and the president was not proposing that it adopt one now.

Even a cursory glance back would have provided clear warning of the disastrous implications of implementing the new plan without even the backstop of a rigorous statement of faith. By the time SPU entered into its debate over governance, there had been a great deal of scholarship about how formerly Christian universities had become secularized in America. As I delved into some of this scholarship, it seemed clear that SPU was following the exact same path trod by earlier Christian institutions that failed.

One of the most insightful studies I came across was James Burtchaell's magisterial book, *The Dying of the Light: The Disengagement of Colleges and Universities from Their Christian Churches* (1998).

According to Burtchaell, one signpost along the road of secularization was the end of church control of college governance: "The critical turn, as we have seen, often involved forcing those who spoke for the church out of college governance."[5] Burtchaell further pointed out that the early steps to secularization were not usually recognized as such, and that proponents of separating schools from church governance

> rarely criticized religious sponsorship openly. There was usually no rhetoric of rejection, no breakaway surge, no praise of seculariza- tion... Even when there was a secession from formal oversight by church authorities... the claim and the belief were that the institu- tion would of course remain as Presbyterian, Baptist, or Catholic as ever. Indeed all change was supposed to be gain, without a sense of loss.[6]

Despite the best of intentions, ending church governance often removed a key structural safeguard that helped maintain the religious integrity of colleges and opened the door to secularization in the gen- eration following the change. How? Because trustees have the final say not only over budgets, but over tenure, top administrative positions, and college programs. A change in board structure almost inevitably has long-term consequences for a school's character and mission.

Reading Burtchaell convinced me even more that the future of SPU was at stake, and I spent almost all of my extra time working behind- the-scenes to raise awareness of the proposal. My main initial goal was to get the plan released so it could be openly discussed. There was no way to have an open discussion if the particulars were still hidden.

Once the plan had leaked, I wanted to ensure sure that the board of trustees received a copy so they could become involved before it was too late. So I helped organize a group of alumni to communicate with the board of trustees. Expressing their concerns about the proposal and its secrecy, the alumni sent each board member a copy of the proposal so they could read it for themselves.

After it became public knowledge that the plan had leaked, I finally decided to go public with my concerns. I was interviewed for the student newspaper, where I questioned both the wisdom of the plan and the secrecy of the process. Later I drafted a letter with two colleagues that we sent to the governing board of the Free Methodist Church, urging them not to weaken their role in governance.

The resulting blow-up was not pretty. The president was angry, especially about the charges of secrecy.

"That people thought we were doing anything in secret is beyond me. It is the accusations of secrecy… that are the hardest for me," he told the student newspaper after his draft plan had leaked.[7] Yet even while he denied things were being done in secret, he insisted: "The paper that I wrote was not to be shared, and I wouldn't have shared it had someone asked. It was written as a guiding document for leaders and was confidential. Not secret, confidential."

For me and other critics of the plan, this nuance appeared to be a distinction without any difference at all.

Looking back from the distance of some years, this battle was the turning point of SPU's history as an evangelical Christian university. And the fault in my view lies not only with the president, but with those who met his challenge with a half-hearted response. Upon learning that the president was trying to scrap the current board structure, the board faced a very simple task: They should have replaced him. Instead, they faltered. Yes, the president's plan with regard to SPU was placed on hold. But because a majority of the board did not have the wisdom or courage to discharge the president, it was inevitable that the plan would be resurrected.

Years later I met with a former board member, one of the minority of board members who had tried to stand up for the evangelical identity of the institution at the time. He was a kind, loving, and godly man. He had believed, like me, that revamping the board would undermine SPU's ability to survive as a biblically faithful institution. Even so, it was hard for him to stand up to the president. When he met with me, he recalled the meeting of the board after the president's secret plan had been exposed. This godly board member still felt anguished about the meeting, as if he had done something wrong in standing up to the president.

Think for a moment about how topsy-turvy this situation was: The board of SPU was supposed to be the entity that safeguarded the mission of the institution. SPU's president was supposed to be accountable to the board. Instead, the president was seeking to abolish the current structure of the board (which would include removing many existing board members), and this board member ended up feeling guilty about objecting to the plan. To his credit, he stood up anyway. But others apparently didn't.

There is a critically important point about this history I don't want you to miss: *The SPU board that capitulated—the board that sent SPU down the road of likely no return—was not itself theologically liberal.* It was populated by theologically conservative Christian leaders, many from the world of business. One prominent board member was active in a national Bible study group and missions to China.

And yet in my view, it's some of these theologically conservative board members who bear the most responsibility for the destruction of SPU as a biblically faithful institution. They were personally orthodox. They had the legal and God-given authority to keep their institution on the right track. They chose not to exercise their authority effectively. Though they likely didn't realize it at the time, they had come down on one side of a watershed, and the institution would never be the same.

The residual bitterness I struggle with most about what happened at SPU does not relate to the actions of its president. I disagreed with what he was doing, but he had the courage of his convictions. He fought hard to get his way, which is admirable. My residual bitterness is instead tied to the theologically orthodox board members who should have known better, but who refused to act decisively. I wonder to this day how many of them realize what they actually did.

Once SPU's board showed its failure of nerve, the president waited for things to quiet down. Then he regrouped and began to push the same basic proposal. By 2005, he won. He secured approval for a new proposal that reduced Free Methodist members of the board to only five.[8] That was just one-third of the board. Equally important, these five Free Methodist members were no longer selected directly by the Free Methodist Church. The church nominated people, but the Trusteeship Committee of SPU's board now had to approve them. The board had effectively been neutered, and over time the inevitable consequences occurred.

In the immediate aftermath I was put in the proverbial doghouse by SPU's administration and by many of my fellow faculty members who supported the changes. I was denied a routine pay increase on the pretext that I had been "uncollegial" because I organized events on campus supporting intelligent design. I challenged the denial and prevailed, but the message was clear: Don't dare rock the boat again.

Was it worth it? Would I have spoken out had I known that ultimately both SPU's board and the Free Methodist Church would capitulate? I don't know. Why sacrifice yourself when the appointed guardians of an institution aren't willing to protect it? On the other hand, standing up for what one thinks is the truth surely is a good thing in and of itself.

By the time I left SPU in the summer of 2006, I was out of the doghouse for the most part, and the academic department I chaired was flourishing. So I did not leave because I was forced out. I left largely because I could see the writing on the wall. SPU had been a beacon of truth in the Pacific Northwest, but its light was now flickering and growing ever dimmer. I joined SPU because I really did want to spread Christian truth. It didn't make much sense to stay there when the university was becoming increasingly indistinguishable from the world.

In retrospect, one of my last battles at SPU before departing was telling. I tried to defend a faculty member who was being denied tenure. I will call him "Professor Smith." In my view, Professor Smith was an outstanding colleague and one of the few theologically (and politically) conservative faculty members hired in the last years I was there. He was also one of the few science professors hired who believed in intelligent design and was skeptical of Darwinian evolution.

During his tenure evaluation, Professor Smith was branded as lacking in collegiality. No doubt he had made some enemies on campus because he was plainspoken. For example, he criticized a tenured faculty member for outrageously comparing George W. Bush to Hitler. Although I agreed with Professor Smith's criticism of the other faculty member, it was impolitic for an untenured professor to challenge a senior faculty member in this way. Nevertheless, I had seen Professor Smith's tenure file, including an anonymous survey of his colleagues, and I believed the evidence showed not only that he was an outstanding faculty member, but that he got along fine with the vast majority of his colleagues. Yet in the end, neither the president nor the board was willing to overturn the verdict of the increasingly progressive (and intolerant) faculty.

The case supplied an interesting bookend to my time at SPU. As you will recall, when I began there, the board had denied tenure to a theological liberal. Now, as I was leaving, they were upholding the denial of tenure to a theological and political conservative. Most board members probably didn't know what they were doing—they just trusted the administration and faculty. Still, the result was indicative of where things were headed.

By mid-2012, the president who had initiated the transformation of the board had retired, and the next stage of the makeover of SPU's identity was ready to begin.

In 2014, the new president succeeded in changing the school's Articles of Incorporation. Before that date, the Articles stated that SPU was operated "under the auspices of the Free Methodist Church of North America" and that the board of trustees exercised control "provided that at no time shall action be taken by the Board of Trustees contrary to the regulations, doctrines and standards prescribed in the Book of Discipline of the Free Methodist Church."[9] Both clauses were now dropped. The first one was changed to state merely that SPU is "affiliated with The Free Methodist Church of North America."[10]

There were just enough evangelical board members left on the board to prevent a formal change of the school's statement of faith or its statement on sexuality, because those formal changes required a supermajority. But there were no longer enough biblically solid members to actually control the board or enforce things like hiring only orthodox professors. The previous board of theologically conservative Christians by their inaction had sown the seeds, and now the bitter fruit was being harvested.

Unfortunately, the story of SPU is not an outlier. It is also the story of many other Christian institutions across America.

Recall some of the stories discussed earlier in this book. In 2022, the board of Calvin University authorized the continued employment of faculty members who reject the university's official statements on marriage. Years earlier, the leadership of Gustavus Adolphus College, whose board is selected by a Lutheran denomination, tolerated sociologist Floyd Martinson, who downplayed sex abuse, pedophilia, and incest.

This is how Christian institutions fail. This is why Harvard and Princeton and Yale are no longer Christian institutions. And it's why Seattle Pacific and many other universities are on the same path today. Again: The Stockholm Syndrome Christianity of faculty and administrators isn't the only problem. In many cases their stranglehold on institutions is enabled and unleashed by personally biblically orthodox college presidents and board members who are unwilling or unable to protect the identity of their institutions.

And it's not just the board members of Christian colleges and schools who are culpable.

Failures of Leadership Far and Wide

Church and denominational leaders also routinely provide cover for Stockholm Syndrome Christians, allowing them to continue to exercise authority within the church or claim good standing as faithful Christians even while they are working to subvert Christian teachings.

For example, why is Andy Stanley still the pastor of Northpoint Ministries in Atlanta? His church has a board of elders. Are they all as biblically unfaithful as he is? Maybe. Or maybe they have simply turned a blind eye to his unbiblical teaching and haven't been willing to hold him accountable. In any case, Andy Stanley's continued role as a pastor of that congregation reveals something about the quality of elders at that congregation. You could say the same thing about many other high-profile pastors who abandoned orthodoxy. What are the other leaders in these churches doing? Why aren't they exercising biblical accountability?

And church leaders aren't just failing to hold accountable fellow church leaders. They are also failing to hold accountable political and cultural leaders who are connected to their churches.

As discussed in a previous chapter, one of the key legislators who authorized gay marriage in my home state of Washington was a Republican state senator who was an active leader in her Protestant Christian church. Why wasn't she publicly rebuked by that church?

Nationally, the determining vote on the US Supreme Court for inventing a constitutional right to gay marriage was cast by practicing Catholic Anthony Kennedy. Why wasn't he excommunicated by his church?

In my home state again, one of the biggest persecutors of Christians who don't want to service gay weddings was state Attorney General Bob Ferguson. In the voter's pamphlet, Ferguson boasted about his active membership in a Catholic parish. Why was he not disciplined by the church for persecuting those who were acting in accord with the stated teachings of his own church?

In sum, why are Christian leaders giving cover for so many people in their congregations and denominations who misuse their authority in order to undermine Christian teachings?

The Blessings of Faithfulness

It doesn't have to be this way. In the past, there have been Christian leaders who took their responsibilities for accountability seriously. In the early 1970s, the Lutheran Church—Missouri Synod (LCMS) found itself torn asunder because professors at Concordia, its flagship seminary in St. Louis, embraced the "historical criticism" approach to the Bible discussed in Chapter 1.

LCMS leaders became increasingly concerned that seminary faculty were abandoning biblical orthodoxy. Some professors waffled on the historical accuracy of the Bible.[11] Some questioned whether Old Testament prophesies really pointed to Jesus.[12] One professor suggested that gospel writers may have expanded Jesus's words and attributed "fresh sayings" to him that he did not make during his life on Earth. As a result, "it is impossible to recover without argument the very words of Jesus spoken on a given historical occasion."[13] Another professor openly questioned the virgin birth of Christ and his bodily resurrection.[14] The theological drift of the seminary's professors was consequential because they were responsible for training and shaping the next generation of LCMS clergy.

As church leaders investigated, they heard reports that the seminary's minority of theologically conservative students and professors faced intimidation. A letter from some conservative students at Concordia claimed: "For years we have been harassed and bullied by those who call themselves evangelical."[15] The handful of faculty who didn't accept the modern critical approach to the Bible were publicly marginalized, with the seminary's president declaring that "it is not possible for [a professor] to teach any of his assigned courses at a seminary level of instruction... without using historical-critical methodology."[16]

When LCMS leaders tried to steer the seminary back toward orthodoxy, they provoked a furious response. Faculty and students revolted, staging protests and taking their case to the media. Denominational leaders were denounced as "immoral," "morally bankrupt," "ungodly," "legalist," and under the "judgment of God."[17]

Astonishingly, despite the vilification and protests, LCMS leaders refused to back down.

But the cost of faithfulness was high. In early 1974, after LCMS leaders made clear they wouldn't cave, 90 percent of the seminary's professors departed along with most of their students.[18] An exodus of 250 congregations from the denomination followed.[19] Many observers thought LCMS leaders had killed the seminary and crippled their denomination.

Francis Schaeffer was one of the lonely voices who defended the denomination. In December 1974, while the LCMS was still picking up the pieces, Schaeffer went to speak at Concordia.

"You have done something that is totally unique," he told his audience.[20] By preserving their denomination from theological liberalism, the LCMS's faithful remnant had accomplished something extraordinary:

> I know of no place in the world where this has happened before and certainly there is no place in the United States where this has occurred. It is the only place where those who have held the historic Christian position have been the ones who have held the church,

the historic organization of the church rather than having to leave when the issues are drawn.

Schaeffer emphasized that what had been accomplished "is not the end, it is only the beginning." Those in the LCMS now had "a titanic responsibility... to realize that the question of the infiltration of liberalism never comes to an end.... It is something you must face and continue to face in the years to come." More than that, the biblically orthodox LCMS members "have a responsibility to Christianity as a whole... to show forth that you can hold the church with beauty and with love." Schaeffer ended by imploring them to treat their opponents with "observable love" even while standing for the purity of the church.

Within just a few years, Concordia rebuilt itself and thrived, and so did its denomination. Today the LCMS remains the largest theologically conservative Lutheran denomination in the United States, with 1.8 million baptized members.[21]

Those who left ended up supplying a glimpse of what the LCMS might have become had denominational leaders capitulated. The exiles eventually became part of the Evangelical Lutheran Church in America (ELCA), which, despite its name, is anything but evangelical. According to a 2023 survey of ELCA clergy, 93 percent support same-sex marriage, 84 percent opposed the overturning of *Roe v. Wade*, and 78 percent oppose religious freedom protections for small business owners who may not want to be conscripted to support things like gay weddings.[22]

As might be expected, ELCA clergy are also politically and ideologically skewed. Nearly six in ten identify as Democrats, and nearly seven in ten identify as "liberal."[23] An earlier survey of lay leaders in the ELCA showed that 76 percent agreed that "no Christian group can legitimately claim its beliefs are more true than those held by any other Christian group," and 46 percent agreed that "it is possible for a faithful follower of any religion... to find the truth about God through that religion."[24] Concordia Seminary professors who joined the ELCA helped advance the cause of progressive theology within their new denomination, and by the end of their careers they were among those pushing for the normalization and blessing of gay and lesbian sexuality.[25]

In hindsight, the crisis faced by the LCMS in 1974 was another of Schaeffer's watershed moments. But this time, biblical Christianity was honored. As a result, the faith of millions of Christians was safeguarded, and leaders in at least one other large Protestant denomination (the Southern Baptist Convention) were encouraged to do something similar.[26]

Unfortunately, too few Christian leaders and institutions followed the example of the LCMS in the years to come. We are reaping the results.

The Bottom Line

Here is the bottom line: How can the church be a beacon of truth if its leaders won't stand up for the truth? Before we focus our concerns on what people outside the church are doing, we need to be concerned about what our self-identified Christian politicians, church leaders, writers, and teachers are doing. Board members, pastors, elders, deacons, bishops, and other Christian leaders need to step up to the plate.

We can't control what the secularists do. But within our churches and families and Christian institutions, we do have a great deal of authority under God. And by reforming the church, we might end up reforming the rest of culture. The church has been the most influential institution for good in the history of the world, hands down. If we want to be so again, we need to get our own house in order.

Now how do we do that? That is the focus of the next section of the book, where we move from critique to solutions.

CURES

10. A Call to Wisdom

We've studied the symptoms of Stockholm Syndrome Christianity. We've looked at some of the root causes. Now what should we *do* about Stockholm Syndrome Christianity? That is our focus in our remaining chapters.

We will start with an exploration of the need for wisdom and discernment. The Bible is filled with admonitions for us to get wisdom, be wise, exercise discernment (Proverbs 3:13, 4:7; 2 Chronicles 1:10, Philippians 1:9).

Of course, the Bible teaches that wisdom ultimately derives from the LORD: "For the Lord gives wisdom; from his mouth come knowledge and understanding" (Proverbs 2:6). This should be obvious, but it is still worth saying out loud: If we want true wisdom, we need to immerse ourselves in God's word (Psalm 119:98, 104–105) and continually seek His guidance through prayer (James 1:5–7).

Over the years as I've thought and prayed about the problem of Stockholm Syndrome Christianity and how to respond to it, seven ways to be wise have come to mind that were clarifying for me and, I hope, will be clarifying for you.

1. Beware of a Hollywood View of Evil

In Hollywood stories, evil is often obvious. You can't miss the nefarious characters. They are flamboyantly evil. They are villains on steroids.

Too many Christians expect evil in the real world to look like Hollywood villains. So they are often oblivious to many kinds of actual evil and error.

Some evil is obvious. But evil can also be subtle. It can even *seem* good. This makes sense in a Christian view of evil. Going back to Augustine, many Christian theologians have argued that evil has no substance of its own.[1] That's because Satan can't ultimately create anything. He can only twist the good things that God already created. This means that evil by its very nature is parasitic on good. Evil in fact requires something good to twist. But this means that every evil, every lie, has some truth, some good, it is based on.

Now sometimes the twisting is so complete that the truth and the good may be unrecognizable, as with Hitler. But other times the twisting may be far more subtle, and it requires wisdom and discernment to figure out. Just because something has an element of real truth—for example, that we should love others and be kind—doesn't mean that what is being proposed is good. In fact, in our society, a lot of things are done in the name of love and compassion that aren't truly loving or compassionate at all. But because they are marketed in the name of love, which is something good, even many Christians are misled. These Christians are misguidedly looking for a supervillain, and when they instead hear partial truths, they think that perhaps there is nothing really wrong.

But, again, in a Christian view of evil, every falsehood, every kind of evil, has some truth at its base. *So when approaching the errors of Stockholm Syndrome Christianity, we should expect that they will not always be completely obvious at first glance.*

I love how J. R. R. Tolkien portrayed this truth in his epic trilogy *The Lord of the Rings*. In that saga, Tolkien has a character known as Saruman. Saruman is a great wizard known for his wisdom; he's looked up to by the other wizards. As the story unfolds, the wizard Gandalf is beginning to wonder whether all is right with Saruman. On the surface, Saruman still seems wise and good, but he's doing some things that are raising questions and doubts in Gandalf's mind. In particular, he seems to be ignoring the evil forces that are overtaking Middle Earth.

As the tale progresses, we ultimately learn that Saruman has indeed gone off the true path and is himself doing some very wicked things. But Gandalf—and the readers—only learn this over time, gradually. Gandalf has to piece things together. It doesn't start out being apparent. And even when we begin to learn that Saruman may not be trustworthy, he isn't a stick-figure villain. He says things that sounds like they could be true.

I think Saruman is a great example for Christians be aware of. He shows us that evil, especially in leaders, is not always apparent at first. When someone has always before been worthy of our trust, it's hard to get our minds around the idea that maybe he no longer is. While we shouldn't jump to conclusions, we also shouldn't keep sweeping our nagging concern that something is wrong under the carpet.

Saruman is also a great example of how Hollywood gets evil so wrong. In the film version of *Lord of the Rings*, Tolkien's moral message about discerning whether someone is evil gets completely thrown out when it comes to Saruman. We meet Saruman early in the first film, and right from the start he appears as a maniacal souped-up fiend. It doesn't help that he's played by the great character actor Christopher Lee, who was known for playing all sorts of Hollywood villains, especially Dracula in old-time horror films.

If you get the difference between Tolkien's portrayal of Saruman and Hollywood's portrayal, you will understand what I'm trying to say. If all we are looking for is a Hollywood villain, we are likely going to miss many of the real false teachers promoting Stockholm Syndrome Christianity in the real world.

2. Beware of Syncretism

Syncretism is the tendency of people, even Christians, to mix and match good and bad. For Christians, it means making up our own version of Christianity by mixing it with lots of un-Christian beliefs. As my pastor liked to stress in his sermons on the Old Testament book of Hosea, syncretism was one of the biggest problems Hosea warned people about. The Israelites were mixing their worship of the LORD with pagan rites and beliefs, and calling it the worship of Jehovah.

We have lots of syncretism in our society, and not just in the secular progressive Pacific Northwest where I live. I remember years ago when our family visited New Orleans. I was there to participate in an academic conference, but Sonja and our then-young children came along. Now, Louisiana is part of the Bible Belt, and there are lots of Bible-believing Christians there. But one day we were walking near the Catholic cathedral in New Orleans, and I observed that in the square in front of that Christian cathedral there was a stand selling voodoo dolls. I was struck by the incongruity. You had a culture that had embraced a Christian cathedral, but also embraced voodoo. That's syncretism.

Or let's take an example that might be closer to home. Many Christians have been enthralled over the past decades with the *Star Wars* saga. So maybe it should come as no surprise that *Star Wars* has started to find its way into churches.

In 2015, Zion church in Germany turned its worship service into a *Star Wars* event, featuring the *Star Wars* theme song played on the pipe organ. Around 500 people flocked to the service, "some carrying lightsaber props or wearing Darth Vader masks. It was more than twice as many as usually come to Zion church on a Sunday."[2] The church's pastor, Lucas Ludewig, told a reporter about how happy he was "to see so many people in church."[3] He praised people for trusting the church "to make them part of the church service without making it too Christian or too *Star Wars*, but to find a good compromise."

Not to be outdone, Liquid Church in New Jersey organized a "Cosmic Christmas" series culminating in a *Star Wars*-themed Christmas Eve extravaganza. As a press release put out by the church breathlessly explained:

> On Christmas Eve, Liquid will host New Jersey's only live Star Wars Nativity Scene, with guests invited to line-up for their opportunity to wield a lightsaber and join the Nativity with Leia, Han Solo, Chewy, and R2D2. Children will get the chance to sit on Darth Santa's lap (aka Darth Vader), share their Christmas wish, and take a photo with Lord Vader and his Stormtrooper "elves." Each service includes costumed characters, movie clips, and music designed to wow audiences.[4]

Now I enjoy *Star Wars* (truth be told, mostly the original three films, not the later ones). But we need to be absolutely clear that the theology of *Star Wars* is not the theology of Christianity. Its idea of the "Force" is radically different from the biblical idea of God. Not only is the Force impersonal, but in the *Star Wars* universe, good and evil are both ultimately described as different sides of the same Force.

Syncretism doesn't mean that Christians cannot appreciate truths found among non-Christian writers or artists or philosophers. Early Christians appropriately took much wisdom from ancient Greece and Rome. The early church fathers talked about how the Jews took gold and many other things from Egypt during the Exodus, and they used that as a metaphor for Christians benefiting from the good things found in secular culture.[5] But in taking the gold from Egypt, we need to beware of taking along the golden idols of Egypt as well.

A lot of Stockholm Syndrome Christianity is based on syncretism, trying to meld Christianity with other thought-forms and beliefs that are fundamentally anti-God. That's why we need to be discerning when interacting with Stockholm Syndrome Christians.

3. Beware of the Misuse of Language

Language can be clarifying. But it also can be muddling. And one of the key tools in the toolset of Stockholm Syndrome Christians is redefining terms in a way that obscures what they are really doing.

Sometimes it's the redefinition of good terms to mean something else, to give cover for the abandonment of biblical truth. For example, many evangelical Christian supporters of evolution deny the traditional biblical teaching about Adam and Eve. But they don't want to say that openly. So they claim they do believe in Adam and Eve, but then they redefine Adam and Eve to mean something other than the parents of the entire human race—Adam and Eve existed in history, but they were just one couple among many, and they were not the parents of all humanity. As we saw in Chapter 2, this was the approach adopted early on by the BioLogos Foundation, started by Francis Collins.

Similarly, some evangelical theologians claim they believe the Bible is without error while at the same time claiming that some of its historical accounts are fiction. We saw this with biblical scholar

Mike Licona. These evangelical theologians redefine "inerrancy" to obscure what they are doing. Perhaps they are sincere. Perhaps some of them don't want to lose their jobs. Regardless, they are manipulating language in a way that gives cover to their rejection of the historic Christian understanding of biblical truth.

There are some evangelicals on the left who are now doing something similar with the term "pro-life," upholding certain politicians and movements as pro-life even when those politicians and movements are in fact pro-abortion. These evangelicals are also redefining pro-life to mean policies that fight climate change. So now if you support intrusive policies to fight global warming, you are pro-life.[6] If you don't support those policies, even if you are 100 percent against abortion, you aren't pro-life. This is the manipulation of words to hide what you are really doing. If you want to argue that Christians should be concerned about global warming, fine. But there's nothing admirable or Christ-like about trying to do this surreptitiously by smuggling it in under a term that most people understand as meaning something else.

Sometimes the manipulation of language occurs when Stockholm Syndrome Christians urge Christians to embrace terms like "gay" but redefine those terms in a way that they think makes them okay. In recent years, there has been an ongoing debate among evangelical Christians in the Presbyterian Church in America and elsewhere about whether it is okay for same-sex attracted Christians to affirm themselves as "gay Christians." These Stockholm Syndrome Christians claim that they continue to oppose gay sex as not accepted by the Bible. But they say we need to affirm the gay *identity* as okay.[7]

But when we're talking about male and female (not "happy" or "festive") the term gay inherently includes sex.[8] In the 1890s the word "gay" conveyed promiscuity; a "gay house" was a brothel. Then the word began to be used as a less in-your-face version of homosexual.

Stockholm Syndrome Christians offering their own idiosyncratic redefinition of the term *gay* doesn't change the ordinary meaning of the word. All it does is introduce confusion that provides cover for the abandonment of a biblical view of male and female. And we've actually seen that happen. Some evangelical Christians who started out making this argument have now increasingly morphed into justifying more and more of the gay lifestyle, including gay sex.[9]

The manipulation of language to cover up, confuse, and obscure is one reason it is so important to define your terms when discussing things with Stockholm Syndrome Christians. Make sure you aren't speaking past each other. Pin them down. Stockholm Syndrome Christians don't want to be pinned down.

It's not wrong to seek clarity. Clarity should be your friend.

4. Beware of the Misuse of Relationships

In recent decades, the idea that "Christianity is relational" has become pervasive. There is truth in that claim. Christianity isn't just a set of truths about the world. It is a relationship with the living God, day by day, hour by hour, minute by minute. It is also about our relationships with each other. Christians need to relate to their fellow Christians as brothers and sisters in Christ.

But in my experience, those who most push the "Christianity is relational" banner often do so in the context of diminishing Christianity as truth. They contrast Christianity as truth with Christianity as relational, implying that the relational nature of Christianity should make us willing to de-emphasize the truth, because in their view insisting on truth can break relationships. Yes, unloving adherence to a set of doctrines can work out this way, and that's something we should be concerned about. But it also needs to be said that an over-emphasis on relationships can be just as unhealthy as a brittle adherence to doctrinal truth.

Gangs are relational. So is the mafia. Personal loyalty and connection are everything in those groups. As a result, personal loyalty and relationships justify all manner of evils against people outside of your group. At the very least, it can cause people to abandon their principles in the name of personal relationships.

Don't think this doesn't happen among Christians. Why did Tim Keller host a series of conferences for evangelical leaders to convince them to support theistic evolution? I know some people who asked him about this privately. According to their account, Keller said that he did it because his friend Francis Collins asked him. His relationship with Collins trumped his commitment to the theology of his denomination and the biblical account of the creation of humans as humans.

Similarly, after the full extent of Francis Collins's pro-abortion activities at the NIH became public, there was a noticeable silence from leading evangelicals who might be called the FOFs, friends of Francis. Not only that, there were efforts to shut down those who highlighted the problems with Collins. When I wrote a series of articles criticizing Collins about his public record in 2021, I received a lot of private pushback. Notably, the pushback typically did not identify errors in my articles. It was focused almost entirely on how wrong it was for me to criticize such a wonderful brother in Christ. It was, some thought, not respectful or loving to publicly criticize Collins.

Someone forwarded to me a private exchange with a leader at a notable and theologically conservative Christian organization that I won't name. The leader of that organization condemned one of my pieces on Collins as a "hit piece [that] has no place within the Church." According to him, all it did was "malign the integrity of one of the most important Evangelical Christians and Scholars of this century." He then implied that Collins's record should be excused because he had to act in the way he did to survive in the federal government. My critique was unfair because "it fail[ed] to take into account the political complexity that confronted Collins on a day-to-day basis working with two democratic presidents and a president, who lacked appreciation for science."

This Christian leader also said my article "violat[ed] the spirit of 1 Peter 3:15-16." In that passage, Peter talks about how we should respond with "gentleness and respect" when someone asks us "for a reason for the hope that is in you."

I do take Peter's injunction seriously, but it seems to me that the person criticizing me was wrenching the injunction from its context. Christians should always take care about their rhetoric, but Peter was not talking here about how Christians should address false teaching in the church. He was talking about how we should interact with seekers who want to understand why we believe in Christ. In 2 Peter 2, by contrast, Peter gives an example of how he addresses "false prophets… and false teachers," and there he is anything but gentle. Indeed, his rhetoric is so high-voltage that I normally would not presume to use anything like it.

Peter upbraids the false teachers for being "like irrational animals, creatures of instinct, born to be caught and destroyed, blaspheming about matters of which they are ignorant" (2 Peter 2:12). He says that "for them the gloom of utter darkness has been reserved (2 Peter 2:17). Since Peter was an apostle and writing under the inspiration of the Holy Spirit, I trust he was authorized to use that harsh language. I don't think I am. Nevertheless, neither do I think Christians are forbidden to clearly call out erroneous teachings. If you are trying to follow the full counsel of the Bible, and not just proof-text reasons to avoid challenging Stockholm Syndrome Christians, you will be hard-pressed to show that Christians should never be direct in challenging error.

I am certainly not claiming that my articles about Collins were perfect in tone, and fellow Christians definitely have the right to criticize me when they think I did something wrong. One Christian scientist who was upset over my first article on Collins wrote me directly with his concerns. We had a meaningful exchange, and he convinced me to make a few adjustments to my article where he thought I had been unfair. "Iron sharpens iron" (Proverbs 27:17). We all need accountability.

At the same time, it is difficult for me to take seriously Christians who elevate the importance of relationships but then are selective in how they apply this concern. The Christian leader (mentioned a few paragraphs above) who privately lambasted me never contacted me to express his concerns directly. A scientist with a group that has been closely aligned with Francis Collins called a colleague of mine to complain about one of my articles; but again, the person never communicated with me. For Christians who are concerned about relationships between believers, it was odd to me that these brothers and sisters in Christ didn't feel obliged to follow Matthew 18:15 and raise their concerns with me directly. (For the record, before I published my articles, I repeatedly reached out to Collins's press office at the NIH with my questions and concerns so that he would have a chance to respond. But the inquiries went unanswered.)

The reality is that even the best Christians can be tempted to allow their relationships to compromise their proclamation of the truth. It's a huge temptation, especially if the relationships are with popular or influential people who provide us with validation in some way. For instance, the Rev. Billy Graham was a wonderful and godly man, and he had tremendous integrity. I was fortunate to hear him preach several times in person, and I know he was used powerfully by God. But he also had a soft spot when it came to his relationships with powerful people—a soft spot that led him to do things that sometimes weren't glorifying to God. Late in life, Graham seems to have recognized that his personal friendships with powerful political figures led to regrettable actions.[10]

Here's what happened. Graham was known as the pastor to the presidents. That could be valuable, because certainly our presidents need all the spiritual counsel they can get. But being a friend to presidents was also perilous for Graham, because he had a public platform to influence people, and the presidents knew it. In 1970, Graham invited Republican president Richard Nixon to give a talk at a crusade in Tennessee in the midst of protests over the Vietnam War. The event took on the trappings of a partisan political event.[11] During the same period, Graham held private conversations with Nixon in the White House where he stood by and even added to Nixon's anti-Semitic comments.[12]

Years later, Graham befriended Democratic president Bill Clinton. When Clinton was entangled in the Monica Lewinsky sex scandal, Graham again fell prey to letting his personal relationship with a president cloud his public witness. He went onto NBC's Today Show and seemed to excuse Clinton's behavior by declaring: "He has such a tremendous personality that I think the ladies just go wild over him."[13]

I am not trying to be hard on Graham. I think he was a great man. My point is that if even Billy Graham could let his personal relationships with presidents cloud his witness, then this is something all of us could be tempted to do.

Relationships are important, and we certainly should treat our fellow Christians fairly and according to biblical standards of love. But we shouldn't idolize relationships, especially with public figures. That can lead to excuses for insulating erring leaders and teachers from accountability to the truth. In Christianity, truth and relationships go together. In fact, the best relationships should be founded on truth.

5. Beware of the Misuse of Guilt

A proper sense of guilt is not bad. We are all guilty before God for our sins, and real guilt should drive us into the arms of Christ. He is our only Savior from the consequences of our guilt.

But guilt can also be manipulated by Stockholm Syndrome Christians to avoid accountability. Recall my story in the last chapter about the board member of Seattle Pacific who stood up to the president's plan to re-organize SPU's board. This board member ending up feeling guilty about challenging the president, even though the board member was doing his job by exercising oversight.

We should all respect authority in the church. But the ultimate authority we need to respect is God. If a Christian leader tries to make you feel guilty for raising legitimate questions about whether his teachings are consistent with the Bible or biblical wisdom, then you are being manipulated. It is not godly guilt they are invoking. It is using guilt to avoid oversight and accountability.

During my lifetime, I have seen this tactic employed time and again in order to avoid legitimate oversight. I recall one pastor who was facing serious issues with his elder board. During this period when hard questions were being raised, the pastor gave a sermon in which he went on and on about how the Pharisees challenged and attacked Jesus. Perhaps the sermon had nothing to do with the conflict with the elder board. But the timing definitely seemed to communicate a connection.

In another church, the senior pastor had been repeatedly accused of molesting young men, but the elders had swept the allegations under the rug. So a former elder finally went public in order to force a serious investigation. One of the other pastors went on talk radio and accused this elder of being a "Judas." How is that for heaping guilt on a whistleblower? But the elder turned out to be right. The pastor eventually left in disgrace, and the church finally had to come to terms with what had happened.

I think serious Christians are especially susceptible to false feelings of guilt. If you recognize the reality that you are a sinner, you will always be open to questioning your own motives. That's a good thing. Unfortunately, it's a good thing that manipulators can use to their own advantage. It takes wisdom and discernment to separate false guilt from true guilt.

6. Beware of the Misuse of Secrecy

There are legitimate reasons for secrecy. For example, if your Christian organization has an issue with misconduct of a certain employee, it may need to be treated as confidential for both legal and ethical reasons. I've experienced that reality as an elder at churches, as a department chair at a university, and in my current job.

But secrecy in the operation of churches, denominations, and Christian ministries can be easily abused. Secrecy can be another excuse to avoid accountability for wrongdoing. And secrecy is the friend of Stockholm Syndrome Christians. I saw that at Seattle Pacific, and I've seen it in certain churches. If someone tries to hide what they are doing, don't simply accept their plea for secrecy without a convincing justification.

7. Beware of the Muzzling of Speech

I've seen all too many efforts by evangelical leaders to squelch dissenting voices as a way of pushing forward with Stockholm Syndrome Christianity. Robust discussion in the light of day is the enemy of Stockholm Syndrome Christians. Those whose actions are going against biblical Christianity don't want to be exposed. They don't want to answer questions.

One of the easiest ways to shut down debate is to hide behind concerns about tone—to treat the people raising questions as wrongdoers rather than openly addressing their legitimate concerns. As individuals, we should be concerned that we treat people with respect and that we express ourselves in a way that honors God. Although I believe in free speech as a constitutional right, Christians have additional obligations about how they speak and write. Christians need to be careful that they are not misrepresenting others. Christians shouldn't be needlessly sharp, or judge someone without good evidence. And certainly Christians shouldn't be self-righteous. Christians also should pay proper respect to their leaders both inside and outside of the church. All of this is biblical. All of this is right.

Nevertheless, when Christians use tone as an excuse to shut down legitimate questions, that is a warning sign something is seriously wrong.

Eric Metaxas sagely calls this "the idol of winsomeness."[14] In my experience, one of the most common tactics Stockholm Syndrome Christians use in trying to shut others down is to attack others for not being loving or grace-filled. That was how dissent was often suppressed at my Christian university.

Ironically, some of those who most attack others for not being loving or grace-filled are themselves uncharitable and self-righteous. At SPU, I saw this time and again. Some who raised questions about tone or the need for love were in reality the harshest people on campus when it came to interacting with their own colleagues.

In the national arena, it is the same. Some of the Christian pundits who most talk about civility are themselves anything but civil.

Yet tone is not the only way Stockholm Syndrome Christians try to muzzle speech. They also work to keep people who disagree with their views out of discussions. They make sure their critics aren't represented in meetings or invited to share the platform at events.

Recall how Tim Keller played host for private meetings designed to sell evangelical leaders on theistic evolution. Those meetings specifically excluded Christian scientists and philosophers who disagreed with Darwinism or supported intelligent design. The meetings weren't really discussions, but rather monologues for one viewpoint.

Something similar has happened in debates over the "antiracist" movement and "critical race theory." As mentioned in an earlier chapter, the Southern Baptist Convention has suppressed dissenting voices at their annual meeting, including distinguished African American scholar Carol Swain.

Of course, there are limits to the number of voices that can be heard. But it's suspicious when all the voices that do get heard are saying the same thing.

At Seattle Pacific, one way that dissent was controlled was to convince board members that they should not meet with faculty members on their own to hear their concerns. That meant board members typically only heard from handpicked faculty and staff at board meetings.

If Stockholm Syndrome Christians try to shut you down or keep you out of a discussion, do ask God to show you whether you are doing something wrong. Do make sure your tone is glorifying to God. But don't just assume that those trying to shut you down are right. They may be trying to avoid letting their own actions be exposed to the light of truth.

What's to Be Done?

This chapter has focused on general principles you can use to develop wisdom and discernment when responding to Stockholm Syndrome Christianity. But perhaps you have been wondering about action. In the next chapter, I will supply specific, effective steps you can take in responding to Stockholm Syndrome Christianity. No matter what your stage of life, you have an important role you can play.

11. A Call to Action

I n Matthew 25:14–30, Jesus describes a man leaving on a trip who entrusts his servants with talents (large sums of money) so they might be productive while he is gone. To one servant, he gives five talents. To another, two. To a third servant, he gives one talent. The point is that every servant was given plentiful resources to accomplish something important for his master.

I believe you have been given resources enabling you to challenge Stockholm Syndrome Christianity. In this chapter, I want to discuss what five different groups of people can contribute to the battle: what every Christian can do; what parents and grandparents can do; what young people can do; what pastors and Christian teachers can do; and what Christian leaders with governance responsibility can do. No matter who you are, I am firmly persuaded you have a valuable role you can play.

What Every Christian Can Do

There are three actions every Christian can take to respond to Stockholm Syndrome Christianity.

1. Equip yourself for battle.

For many years, I was part of a Bible study where the person leading it emphasized a point I've never forgotten. He told us we couldn't lead others farther than we have gone ourselves. I think there is a great deal of truth in that statement. So if you want to help push back against Stockholm Syndrome Christianity, you need to look to yourself first.

Have you grounded yourself in God's word? Have you informed yourself about the falsehoods of Stockholm Syndrome Christianity? Are you modelling biblical faithfulness in your own life? If not, you need to do so. Making sure you are equipped and consistent is a prerequisite to making a difference in this area.

2. Do no harm.

There is a key principle in medicine known as "do no harm." The principle is attributed to the ancient Greek physician Hippocrates. Now maybe you think, "I can't do great things. I'm just one person. I don't have a lot of resources or power or influence. I can't change the world myself. Nothing I do will make much difference." I don't agree with those claims. God has given you gifts that you are supposed to steward, and you can make a positive difference by exercising those gifts. However, I'd settle for more Christians just committing to *do no harm.*

Stockholm Syndrome Christianity does not thrive on its own. It takes a lot of support to make it flourish. Let me take just one example: Christian colleges and universities that have turned their backs on biblical Christianity require hundreds of millions of dollars a year to keep doing what they are doing. This money is provided by tuition and by donations. If faithful Christian parents weren't willing to pay the tuition at backsliding Christian schools—if alumni of backsliding Christian schools didn't continue to fork over their donations—these Stockholm Syndrome Christian colleges would either reform or go out of existence. Institutions certainly sit up and take notice if donations fall, especially if they also receive notes explaining why the usual donations aren't forthcoming.

So where do you give your money in the Christian community? I have known many faithful Christians who continue to donate to Christian ministries and colleges well past their pull date, often out of a misplaced sense of sentiment, nostalgia, or guilt. In some cases these Christian donors know full well the slide that's happening at the groups they bankroll, and say they don't like it—but they don't take responsibility for how they themselves are enabling the slide.

It would be far better to give no money at all than to continue to donate to organizations that are undermining biblical Christianity. So at least, do no harm! Even if you think you don't have time to investigate and identify good organizations where you should donate, you can certainly stop giving money to places where the slide has been happening.

But doing no harm isn't just about how we steward our money. It's also about how we steward our time and abilities.

I know of a large church in my region that was historically evangelical, but double-minded. The congregation was a mixture of the biblically orthodox and the not-so-orthodox. Eventually the pastor embraced an affirming view of homosexuality. There were still many members of that congregation who didn't agree with their pastor's new view. But here is the sad thing: A lot of them stayed at the church. They didn't want to leave. Some married couples stayed because one spouse couldn't bring themselves to leave their friends and social relationships. It was too hard.

Where you go to church is one of the most important decisions you can make as a Christian. A Christian who stays at an unbiblical church is not just being neutral. They are actively doing harm. By staying at an unbiblical church, they are facilitating Stockholm Syndrome Christianity.

I'm not saying you should leave a church at the drop of a hat. There are some people who engage in church hopping or who leave the first time they discover that the people at their church are sinners just like they are. That's not good. Nor is it great to leave over disagreements about issues that truly are debatable, issues that aren't explicitly delineated in Scripture or even easily discerned by reading between the lines. But many issues are perfectly clear, and it takes a good bit of fancy footwork to explain away what the Bible says about them. If you are donating your time and abilities to a church like that, where God is not accurately and truthfully proclaimed, you are also doing harm.

I haven't left many churches in my life; I've tended to stay connected with the same church for a long time. But I remember the first time I decided I had to go. The church where I had grown up had installed a new pastor. He was a nice man. But he was far better at articulating his doubts about God and the Bible than he was in proclaiming the truths of the gospel. He even had a hard time explaining the gospel message itself—I mean, at the most basic level, like: We're sinners and merit God's wrath, but by accepting Jesus as Lord and Savior, we are delivered from that wrath through His atoning death on the cross, which pays the penalty for our sins.

Because I had been so active in this congregation since high school, I didn't really want to leave. But at the time, I was a discussion leader in Bible Study Fellowship. A member of my discussion group had just become a Christian and was seeking a church home. One Sunday afternoon when I went out walking and praying, I was suddenly convicted: I couldn't recommend my church to this new Christian, because I didn't think he would get the solid teaching he needed to grow. *But if I couldn't invite someone to my church, what was I doing spending hours each week of my time volunteering for that church?* It made me decide to leave.

When it comes to churches and Christian ministries, how are you stewarding your time and talents as well as your money? We all can at least try to do no harm.

3. Pray.

In seeking to counter Stockholm Christianity, pray for revival in the church and inside yourself. Pray that God will clean out or bring down Christian leaders and Christian groups that have lost their first love and their commitment to the truth. Pray that God will give discernment to his people so that they will not inadvertently help facilitate Stockholm Syndrome Christianity. And pray that the vulnerable will be kept safe from the falsehoods of Stockholm Syndrome Christianity.

We are invited by God to intercede for others and ourselves through prayer. God answers those prayers. He may not answer us on our timetables or in the ways we think best, but he does respond.

In the early years of our marriage, Sonja and I helped lead a Bible study for single professionals. At that time I was still a professor at Seattle Pacific. During that period, SPU decided to invite one of the biggest advocates of open theism to speak on campus. His name was Clark Pinnock. (As a reminder, open theism is the claim that God himself doesn't know exactly how the future will turn out; it's a rejection of historic Christian teaching.) I had no power to stop what was happening. But I decided to ask our fellows leaders in the Bible study to pray as a group that the students on campus would be protected from the falsehoods that they would hear.

Some months later, I talked with the campus dean responsible for the chapel program. He told me that in his view Pinnock's appearance on campus had been a disaster, one of the worst talks they'd ever had. Not because he disagreed with it (I don't think he did), but because according to him, the students couldn't make head or tail of what Pinnock was trying to communicate. They couldn't understand him. It was babble to them.

God had answered our prayer—and how! He had protected the students from falsehood.

I think if we took prayer more seriously, we might be surprised at what God would do on our behalf.

What Parents and Grandparents Can Do

Parents are the primary people responsible for the upbringing and education of their children. I think most Christians would agree with this statement in principle. But much of the world, including many government bureaucrats, college professors, teachers' union officials, Hollywood filmmakers, and journalists do not agree.

Increasingly, they say so out loud. President Biden said this to a group of public school teachers in 2022: "You've heard me say it many times about our children, but it's true: They're all our children... They're not somebody else's children; they're like yours when they're in the classroom."[1]

Several years earlier, MSNBC host Melissa Harris-Perry was even more blunt: "We have to break through our... private idea that kids belong to their parents, or kids belong to their families, and recognize that kids belong to whole communities."[2]

Well, no. Your children do not belong to the government or your neighbors or even their teachers. They belong to God; and God appoints you as their protector and mentor.

Again, I think most Christian parents would agree in principle they are responsible for their children. But in practice, many Christian parents don't act like it. They cede the raising of their kids to the public schools, or to TV or Netflix or YouTube, or to social media, or to Hollywood, or to computer games, or to the music industry. When they do this, all too often by the time their kids reach middle school, let alone high school or certainly college, their worldview may already be unrecognizable.

So if you are a parent, the very first thing to do is to make a commitment to yourself, your spouse, and to God that you will be the primary educators, mentors, and disciplinarians for your own children. You won't farm your kids out to the rest of the culture. Is this hard? Yes. But it's doable, and it's the most worthwhile thing you're ever likely to do.

Maybe your own kids are grown. But perhaps you are a grandparent, or an aunt or uncle. These roles are different from that of a parent, but many of the same principles apply. Even if you're the "fun uncle or aunt," you can help mightily by being someone who isn't swayed by secular culture, and who helps the children in your life learn how to do that too.

So, while much of my advice applies primarily to parents, it applies to family members as well.

Here are six ways you can protect and equip the children in your life:

1. Take control of your children's formal education.

If you send your kids to public schools, you need to intentionally and aggressively supplement what they are learning with books, videos, and experiences you choose.

You also need to engage your kids in discussing—and critiquing—what they are being told in public school. And you need to do this frequently. Ideally, you'd talk with them every evening, helping them reframe their school day's discussions and events from a Christian perspective.

Even if you send your kids to a Christian school, don't simply assume that they are getting a Christian worldview there. Make sure. Review the curriculum for yourself. Ask your kids each day what they are learning. Know who their teachers are and what those teachers really believe. If there are deficiencies anywhere, supplement what your kids are learning in private school in the same way parents should if they send their kids to public schools.

If you homeschool, make sure your curriculum equips your kids to critically evaluate anti-biblical claims being made in culture. Homeschool is not the place to shield your kids from all of the lies of the secular world. Ultimately, you can't shield them from those claims, no matter how much you'd like to. But you can help determine the timetable for when your kids are exposed to certain things, and you can help them see through the lies by exposing them to information and arguments and testimonies that support the truth.

Don't use homeschooling to restrict your kids' education; use it to expand it. Sometimes you may even want to use bad secular textbooks so you can help your kids learn to evaluate their claims. And you can assign additional materials to help your kids do this.

2. Limit your children's access to the internet, social media, and streaming video.

If you don't want your kids to be raised by others, don't give them free access to TikTok or allow them hours of unsupervised time on other social media or YouTube. No, too, to their spending significant time using Google to search the internet, or playing multiplayer video games. This is especially important the younger your kids are. Internet platforms are businesses. They expand their income by manipulating and exploiting users in thousands of ways, and not one of those ways involves teaching strength of character, spiritual development, biblical principles, or the practical application of those principles to daily life. Spending too much time on screens also deprives kids of outdoor time and of in-person interaction with family and friends. These things strengthen children's core sense of real-world identity and increase the likelihood that they will remain believers as adults.

3. Hold a regular family time for Bible study and prayer.

If you want God to be the center of your family, make space each week to study the Bible and pray as a family unit. Do this in addition to going to church. Do this with an attitude of joy and enthusiasm. And have the kids actively participate. Let them say the prayer, read the Scripture, start a song, raise questions, and offer answers.

4. Use your time with your kids to discuss matters of consequence.

Protect the time you spend with your kids. Sometimes really good parents try to overschedule. They spend so much time volunteering for church or the community, or plugging their kids into endless activities to enrich their lives, that their kids don't get to benefit from activities with their own families, including family discussions.

Watch and then discuss videos together that point to the truth of the Bible or God's activities in history or Christianity's positive impact on culture and science.

Make the most of mealtimes, vacation times, and times in the car. Help your kids process and think through things. You can do this while still having fun or getting chores done—in fact, kids are most likely to talk openly to their parents while doing another activity. Raise topics of consequence while walking the dog, raking leaves, washing dishes, playing catch. Throw a question out, and then give your kids time to think and respond.

In general, realize you need to make a concerted effort to keep the lines of communication open. If you've stayed abreast of the news lately, you know that some schools actively encourage kids to talk to their teachers *and not their parents*. If you want your kids to talk to you, and if you want to remain an authority figure in their lives, you'll need to take deliberate steps to make that so. And when topics arise that you find stressful—as they will—do your best to respond calmly. Be a non-anxious presence so your kids know they can safely talk to you about difficult topics.

And let them hear you discuss matters of consequence with your spouse. Kids learn a lot from what they overhear, so don't have every important discussion while locked away in the master bedroom.

5. Emphasize teaching your kids to think critically.

Your kids need to learn to critically examine what they hear from the news media, social media, and Hollywood. You can't be an expert in everything, but pick some key topics where you can point out things being said by politicians, media figures, and advertisers that aren't true.

If a topic arises that you don't know much about, say so—and then demonstrate for your kids how to find trustworthy resources on that topic. Learning how to find sources of information and evaluate them is a valuable skill.

As they get older, occasionally watch age-appropriate popular shows that *don't* present an accurate view of reality, and then ask your kids what problems they saw, and what the real-life consequences of certain views or life choices would most likely be. In other words, don't just lecture—encourage your kids to do the thinking and talking, too.

6. Help prepare your children for college, if that's where they plan to go.

A child's worldview is likely solidified well before college, but college can further solidify that worldview or deconstruct it. As your child reaches high school, you need to be doing things to prepare them not just academically but spiritually for college.

Several years ago, I scripted a documentary for Focus on the Family titled *The Toughest Test in College*. You can find it for free now on YouTube. If your kids are starting to think about college, you should watch it with them, along with the *TrueU* series taught by my friend Steve Meyer, which deals with the historicity of the Bible and how science points to God. (You can find out more information about both resources at the companion website discussed in the "Resources" section at the back of this book.)

You also need to think about what kind of college your kids will go to. Tragically, I saw many parents and their children go into massive debt to come to Seattle Pacific thinking that they were sending their kids to a place where they would be grounded in the faith. Depending on their program of study, that wasn't true, so these parents were basically sacrificing financially to send their kids to a college that could undermine their kids' faith. So if you are considering a particular Christian college, you need to ask its admissions staff some tough questions to make sure it is what you think. (For ideas on questions to pose, check out my article "Ten Questions to Ask When Evaluating a Christian College"[3] at my website.)

It Pays Off

Nothing is perfect. Children grow up and at some point will go their own way. But the more you invest in shaping their upbringing—in equipping them to understand what is true, reject what is false, and ask the right questions—the more likely they will grow up to reject Stockholm Syndrome Christianity, and the more likely that if they stray they will eventually come back.

What Young People Can Do

Maybe you are a young person in your teens or early twenties, and you wonder what you can do. Here are four suggestions.

1. Recognize that preparing yourself to do battle later may be your most important task right now.

Throughout your life, you are going to have lots of things thrown at you by the anti-Christian culture outside the church and by Stockholm Syndrome Christianity within it. That's just the way life is. So get ready. Start thinking through culturally consequential topics. Be proactive in developing a thoroughly Christian worldview. Check out this book's companion website for ideas on where to start. If you are currently enrolled at a Christian school or college where Stockholm Syndrome Christianity is being promoted, doing your own research and preparation is especially critical—even if the time isn't right for you to speak up (see point 4 below). Your most pressing task right now is becoming a well-grounded Christian, not saving others from Stockholm Syndrome Christianity. If you want to rescue other people from drowning, you first need to learn to swim yourself.

2. Prioritize friendships with spiritually mature Christians.

If your friends are primarily non-Christians (or Stockholm Syndrome Christians), you will find yourself pulled increasingly in spiritually unhealthy directions. The same is true if you join a church dominated by those who have embraced Stockholm Syndrome Christianity. The

Apostle Paul wisely warned: "Do not be deceived: 'Bad company ruins good morals'" (1 Corinthians 15:33) and "Do not be unequally yoked with unbelievers" (2 Corinthians 6:14). These warnings are especially important to heed when it comes to the people you date. If you want to stand for God in your future family, you need to seek a godly partner in marriage.

3. Earnestly seek God's particular calling for your life.

One of my favorite verses in the Bible is Ephesians 2:10: "For we are his workmanship, created in Christ Jesus for good works, which God prepared beforehand, that we should walk in them." We are created to do good works "which God prepared *beforehand*" for us to walk into. God already has plans for how you can stand for Him in your home, your church, your work, and your community. Make it a priority to ask God daily how He wants you to make a difference in the years ahead. Trying to make an impact without seeking God's direction is a recipe for failure.

4. Learn when to stay silent.

As a young person, you are not necessarily called to speak out on every issue right now. Instead, you need to follow Jesus's guidance for his followers to "be wise as serpents and innocent as doves" (Matthew 10:16). This can mean strategically keeping silent as you are equipping yourself to stand for truth. For example, you should be discreet when posting about controversial topics on social media. Employers may scour your social media accounts before deciding whether to hire you. Don't make it easy for them to discriminate against you.

In my work, we once encountered a student who initially had been accepted into a graduate program in a scientific field and to a certain professor's lab. But before final acceptance, the student felt compelled to reveal to the professor views rejecting Darwinian evolution. We strongly advised against that, but the student did so anyway. As a result, final admission was denied and the student didn't get into the grad program or lab after all. While I admire the student's desire to be truthful, I don't admire the lack of prudence. You can be truthful without spilling everything or volunteering answers to questions that aren't being asked.

5. Pursue excellence.

If you want to make a difference standing for truth in your chosen fields of endeavor, never forget that it is going to take plenty of hard work. If you want people to listen to you, you will need to demonstrate that you are worth listening to. So commit yourself to pursuing excellence in your vocations at school, work, home, and church. As Paul says in Colossians 3:23, "Whatever you do, work heartily, as for the Lord and not for men."

What Pastors and Teachers Can Do

Maybe you are a pastor or a teacher at a school or homeschool co-op or a group that meets in your home. Here are two things you can do.

1. Set the right agenda.

One of your biggest powers as a pastor or teacher is the same as the media's. Remember, when we talked about the media, I emphasized that the problem isn't just that the media are biased or report untruths. It's that they focus on the wrong things. They shape our view of the world by focusing on some things and ignoring others. That's their agenda-setting function.

By talking about some stories—like the dangerous "right-wing"—but not other stories—like the firebombing and vandalism of churches and pro-life centers—journalists manipulate our view of the world. If you are a pastor or teacher, you can play a key role in offsetting the media in this. You, too, set the agenda of what the people in your charge will think about, what they will consider important. So make sure you set the right agenda. Help draw people's attention to the most important things. You can help people make it a priority to know the truth and stand for it, and to critically evaluate lies, if *you* focus on teaching them about these things.

2. Make sure you address issues where the battle is raging.

If you spend all your time discussing only those biblical truths that everyone agrees with, that aren't controversial, you will have failed.

Francis Schaeffer liked to cite a statement from Martin Luther that I think distills the most important thing a pastor or teacher today needs to know when confronting Stockholm Syndrome Christianity. As it turns out, the statement didn't actually come from Luther. It came from a character in a nineteenth-century novel. But what it expresses is true:

> If I profess with loudest voice and clearest exposition, every portion of the truth of God except precisely that little point which the world and the Devil are at that moment attacking, I am not confessing Christ, however boldly I may be professing Christianity. Where the battle rages the loyalty of the soldier is proved; and to be steady on all the battlefield besides is mere flight and disgrace if he flinches at that one point.[4]

If you are responsible for teaching others—whether children or adults—remember this passage. Don't trim the truth. Don't avoid the hard things that our culture doesn't want to hear. Make sure you teach the whole counsel of God. Even make sure that you are addressing those specific points where culture at the moment is bearing down hard in rejection of biblical truth.

This is one of the biggest failures of Stockholm Syndrome Christians. Consider pundit David French, who took to Twitter to upbraid his fellow Christians for spending so much time raising concerns on issues like transgenderism.[5] Instead, he scolded, why aren't Christians talking more about the sins of gluttony and porn?

Christians should be warned against gluttony, and we certainly should be concerned about pornography. But I don't know many Christians who would argue that either gluttony or porn are good things, or dispute that they are bad. On the other hand, there *are* a growing number of Christians who are befuddled about whether kids should have their breasts or private parts removed or be pumped full of hormones of the opposite sex.

And while you can warn people about gluttony or porn without risking anything, if you oppose gender-destructive medical treatments on defenseless children—*that* will provoke a backlash. Indeed, someone like French might even lose his weekly column at the *New York Times.*

As the nineteenth-century quotation said: You aren't confessing Christ if you aren't confessing the truths from God that are under attack in your society. This particular cultural moment is where you live. It's where the rubber is meeting the road. Helping people know how to apply biblical truths to events happening right now—and happening to many of them personally—is precisely what Christian pastors and teachers are called to do.

What Christian Leaders Involved in Governance Can Do

Maybe you are an elder, a deacon, or a board member. Or maybe you know someone who is a board member or involved in the governance of a church or Christian school or Christian ministry—so even if you aren't one of these leaders, you might be able to influence some of them. Here are five tips for people involved in the governance of Christian organizations—and for those who advise them.

1. Make sure you know what's actually happening in your organization.

Christian organizations don't turn pagan or godless overnight. By the time you see the collapse, the decay has likely been happening for a long time. I'm sure many of the alumni of Seattle Pacific University were shocked when the faculty overwhelmingly voted to reject biblical standards of sexuality. They probably asked: How could such a thing happen out of nowhere?

But, you see, it wasn't out of nowhere. As we've covered in this book, the rot had been spreading for a long time. The public collapse was simply a final manifestation of the inner rot. I think that's generally true with all Christian organizations. For leaders, this means you need to know what's happening at your university or ministry before there is a public collapse.

If you are a board member or involved in governance, one of the first things you need to do is find out what your organization is really doing.

Ask questions of the staff. Dig a little. Ask to see the relevant documents. Don't rely simply on trust. As Ronald Reagan used to say, "trust but verify." Before you try to do anything else, find out what the state of your organization really is. That is what Nehemiah did when he showed up in Jerusalem. He went out at night—secretly—to inspect the walls, to research the sorry state of things (Nehemiah 2:11–18). He needed to know the real state of things before he tried to reform the situation.

2. Find allies in your efforts for reformation and revival.

You won't succeed if you are an army of one. Work to identify other faithful people still in your organization. At a place like a university, that would mean identifying the staff members and faculty who are still faithful.

3. Choose your battles wisely.

In Luke 14:31, Jesus says, "What king, going out to encounter another king in war, will not sit down first and deliberate whether he is able with ten thousand to meet him who comes against him with twenty thousand?" There are some Christians who are afraid to stand up for anything. They always cave. But there are others who are so eager to stand up for the right, they undermine their own efforts. They don't count the cost. They don't think about whether the battle they picked is winnable or whether it is so critical they need to stand up even if they know they will lose. Perhaps they are innocent as doves, but they aren't wise as serpents (Matthew 10:16). They're foolish. Prudence is a virtue, not a vice. It is the practical wisdom of knowing what means are effective to achieving a good end. If you try to fight every battle, you likely won't make progress on any front.

4. Use the power of no.

Most organizations, most boards, most councils, try to govern by consensus. But for this to work, everyone needs to be compliant and go along with the flow. Usually that is what happens. If you are in a lengthy board or council meeting, at a certain point people just want the meeting to end. So the pressure mounts to just go along and finish so you all can go home.

But in most boards or other governing groups, one person or sometimes two can bring this moving train to a screeching halt. They can do this by using the power of no, of deciding *not* to go along without raising questions.

In many board situations, one or two people can pretty much force a discussion of anything. Forcing discussion is death to Stockholm Syndrome Christianity, because a lot of Stockholm Syndrome Christianity depends on getting things done without people noticing. If you notice, and if you do more than that, if you demand that other people notice, you can often derail bad things.

In governance discussions there are usually a number of people who are persuadable if you force a situation where they have to critically examine something that is being proposed.

One way to really muck up the works is to offer an amendment. If you follow *Robert's Rules of Order* and you have at least one person to second your amendment, you can dramatically alter the whole course of the conversation to focus on issues that the Stockholm Syndrome Christians don't want you to address.

Stockholm Syndrome Christians know how to do this for their own causes. Recall again how Critical Race Theory (CRT) was smuggled into the Southern Baptist Convention. Stockholm Syndrome Christians rewrote and amended the original resolution condemning CRT, thereby guaranteeing that the only thing that would be discussed was the watered-down resolution that they wanted to focus on. Biblically faithful Christians in governance positions need to be as wise as those who aren't biblically faithful.

5. Hire—and fire—the right people.

In staffing government there is an important saying: "People are policy." Whether you are running a school or a church or another kind of Christian nonprofit, if you don't hire the right people, you are going to fail.

This may seem elementary. But I can't tell you how many times I have seen a Christian organization begin to fail because its governing board couldn't bring itself to focus enough on personnel. A board may pass great policies and objectives, but if it's not willing to insist that all personnel are committed to the group's mission, those policies and goals will be subverted. This is what happened at my university. The board was convinced to take a hands-off approach in tenure decisions, and orthodoxy rapidly declined. I've seen the same thing happen in other organizations where the staff continually undermine what the board wants.

This is especially true of the appointments to the top of the organization. Yet I've seen cases where boards simply go along with nominations without asking tough questions.

I know of one campus ministry where this occurred. It was a ministry that had a vital role to play on the campus of a major state university, but when the longtime director of the ministry retired, the board hired someone who ended up fundamentally shifting the organization. The board did not intend to do this. But it didn't do the vetting of candidates needed to prevent it.

Sometimes board members or elders are too busy to pay close attention. Sometimes they're trusting souls who want to think the best of people. Giving people the benefit of the doubt generally is a good trait, but it's seriously unhelpful in the hiring process. In a case I learned about through friends, a biblically faithful church inadvertently hired a college minister who strongly "affirmed" homosexuality. This man was very good at not directly answering questions. He evaded. He used some terms in a different way than the hiring committee understood them. Because they were trusting, unsuspicious people, he fooled them—temporarily.

So watch out for slipperiness and non-answers. Insist on crystal-clear responses. In one of the churches where I was an elder, we required candidates for employment to answer specific questions about their view of biblical authority, Jesus as the one way of salvation, and the definition of marriage—in writing. It was an illuminating experience, and it helped winnow the applicant pool.

Once someone had a candidate they wanted hired and they urged us to just let them talk to the candidate verbally about the questions and report back to us. But we insisted that the candidate would have to answer the questions in writing. I don't recall whether the candidate did answer the questions, or simply declined. But insisting on the written answers brought out that they did not in fact agree with the church's statement of faith.

If you want staff who will support your organization, clarity about the beliefs of prospective hires should be non-negotiable.

And again, it's important to *verify*. Don't just listen to applicants' answers. Check their references. And when you do, ask the person providing the reference specific questions, and try hard to pin down specific answers. People providing references can also be evasive. Sometimes there are legal issues limiting what can be said. Sometimes the person giving the reference may want someone else to hire their problematic employee, taking him off their hands. Or the person providing the reference may hold non-biblical positions himself. Any evasiveness or lack of clarity in references should signal a need for further investigation.

And don't forget to check the candidate's social media. Many people reveal their true beliefs online.

Worth the Time and Effort

This chapter has provided twenty-one actions you can take to challenge Stockholm Syndrome Christianity in your own spheres of influence. Of course, there are many more actions that might be taken. But these should give you a good place to start.

Are they a lot of work? Yes, they are. But having the courage of our convictions means doing hard, inconvenient things. And in the long run, our efforts will pay off. I say the same thing to you that Paul said to the church at Corinth: "Therefore, my beloved brothers, be steadfast, immovable, always abounding in the work of the Lord, knowing that in the Lord your labor is not in vain" (1 Corinthians 15:58).

Your work in the Lord is not in vain.

When you feel tired, when you feel daunted, remember Paul's encouraging insight (2 Corinthians 12:9–10 NIV): "God said to me, 'My grace is sufficient for you, for my power is made perfect in weakness.' Therefore I will boast all the more gladly about my weaknesses, so that Christ's power may rest on me. That is why, for Christ's sake, I delight in weaknesses, in insults, in hardships, in persecutions, in difficulties. For when I am weak, then I am strong."

12. A Call to Faithfulness

Sigrun is a wise Christian woman at my church who attended the adult Sunday School class where I first presented many of the ideas of this book. After the class, she sent me her reflections. One of the points she wanted to raise was whether we are ready for persecution. "As this process continues to unfold, anyone who stands up for the Truth will be persecuted with increased hostility," she wrote. "Are we prepared for this?"

This is a difficult question for us to hear in America. We still have more freedom to practice our faith in America than Christians in many other countries, but as we saw earlier, that freedom is eroding. It likely will disintegrate still further in the days to come. Sadly, some of the future persecution may be enabled and even perpetrated by self-identified Christians.

Much of this book has been filled with difficult things about our culture and about fellow Christians who are facilitating its collapse. You may be overwhelmed by what you have read. You may be dispirited.

Please don't be. God is still on His throne. As we seek to serve as Christ's stewards and ambassadors in this fallen world, let me offer four encouragements.

1. We're Called to Be Faithful, Not Successful

In the weeks following the election of 2020, I stumbled across a YouTuber named Chris Yoon. Yoon was attracting hundreds of thousands of views and tens of thousands of comments on his YouTube channel. He was attracting such a following by putting out videos claiming that Donald Trump would stay in the White House for a second term in January 2021 and that Joe Biden would be arrested. (And Chris Yoon wasn't the only one on the internet during this period who made claims that God had showed them that Trump would be installed for a second term in 2021.)

As the days passed and inauguration day approached, I continued to watch Yoon. Frankly, I was morbidly fascinated by his videos. It wasn't that I believed him, but he seemed so earnest and sincere. He didn't act the part of a schlocky false prophet. He didn't have a wild hairdo or a snake-oil salesman demeanor. He didn't shout or scream. He was clean-cut, quiet-spoken, and serious.

And unlike many so-called prophets that were clearly charlatans, Chris Yoon made predictions tied to a pretty short and definite time-table. He put his reputation on the line. Everyone would know in just a few weeks whether he really knew what he was talking about. It was engrossing to read the comments posted by all the people who were following him. Clearly, many Christians who had voted for Trump wanted to believe in a message that Trump would miraculously be returned to office.

Of course, Chris Yoon and his compatriots turned out to be wrong. They were false prophets. If they had lived in Old Testament Israel, they would have been in a precarious predicament—then, even one false prophesy got you the death penalty (Deuteronomy 18:20). You didn't get a second chance.

In Chris Yoon's case, it was amazing how after events disproved his predictions, he didn't really repent of his falsehoods.[1] In fact, you can still find him on YouTube offering new messages he claims come from God.

For me, the proliferation of all of these false prophets telling people what they wanted to hear in the name of God was disturbingly revealing. It showed just how desperate many Christians are for *this*-world success—despite the fact that Jesus said time and time again that his kingdom was not of this world (John 18:36).

And it's not just when it comes to elections. There are the mega-church pastors who preach that God will grant you financial prosperity or miraculous cures if only you have enough faith—or if only you are faithful enough to donate to their ministry.[2] For many Christians, earthly success is a clear sign of God's approval and God's power, and so they become obsessed with seeking it. This most decidedly is not a scriptural perspective.[3]

This craving for worldly success can lead us to idolize Christians who achieve it, or to follow those Christians who promise we can achieve it by following them.

But just because a pastor has a megachurch doesn't necessarily mean he is a success according to God's standards. Witness the sad case of Andy Stanley, whom we've discussed multiple times throughout this book.

I've also seen the idolization of success infect the Christian nonprofit world, where donors are increasingly being encouraged to judge the worth of nonprofits by evaluating them according to the same quantitative standards they'd apply to a commercial business. Thus, the more funds you raise, the more worthwhile you must be and the more successful you are at your mission. I recall some donors to the nonprofit where I work being concerned as to why we weren't as financially successful as a certain other ministry, which had a much larger budget. That other ministry raised their budget by building themselves around a single charismatic leader who was used to inspire support. Fundraising consultants told us we needed to be more like that ministry.

We're not told that anymore—because the group we were told to emulate, Ravi Zacharias Ministries, doesn't exist anymore. Its charismatic leader ended up being ensnared in a variety of sex scandals, and everything collapsed after his death when the whole thing exploded into the public arena. The outward measures that had made Ravi Zacharias's ministry look like a success had been misleading. They didn't reveal anything about the group's inward problems, or its success according to God's standards.

Don't get me wrong: Results are important, and, yes, so is fundraising. But the obsession of many evangelicals with worldly success above all is not biblical, and it can easily drag Christians down by making them anxious and burdened anytime they don't think they are meeting the world's standards for success. Sometimes the most important results aren't visible or measurable, at least not immediately. Raising children is like that—you pour years of effort and time into them, and then finally when they're adults, the fruit of your labors becomes visible. Or consider mission work in areas hostile to Christianity. The gospel spreads, but it spreads quietly, underground—until finally it explodes into the light, and the results of decades, or even centuries, of quiet faithfulness become visible.

The good news when fighting Stockholm Syndrome Christianity is that we are primarily called to be faithful, not successful, at least the way the world judges success. We should be far more concerned about the faithfulness of our behavior, the faithfulness of our teaching, and the faithfulness of our hearts, than we are about the size of our churches, the size of our pocketbooks, or the amount of praise the culture heaps on us. If we are faithful in stewarding our resources, no matter how limited they may be, we will be rewarded (Matthew 25:23). God blesses those who are faithful, not those who hurry to be rich, which can be understood broadly as a desire for worldly success (Proverbs 28:20).

So don't be discouraged when fighting Stockholm Syndrome Christianity if you don't think you are being successful. Be discouraged if you aren't being faithful. Be encouraged if you are trying to be faithful.

2. It *Doesn't* Depend All on Us

If you are the type of person who is so laid back that you rarely feel a burden of responsibility for getting things done, or always have a ready excuse for not standing up for what's right—then perhaps you should skip over what I'm going to be saying in the paragraphs to follow. You need to take responsibility, and you should stop assuming that it's no big deal if you don't do your part.

But if you are one of the many faithful Christians who sincerely tries to do the right thing, who takes responsibility for your family and for your actions, but feels guilty because you think you still aren't doing enough, then this encouragement is for you.

Ronald Reagan in his first inaugural address told the affecting story of Martin Treptow, a barber from Iowa, who enlisted in the army in 1917 and fought in the trenches in World War I. Martin died there, and later they found in his diary a New Year's resolution titled "My Pledge," where he wrote: "America must win this war. Therefore I will work, I will save, I will sacrifice, I will endure, I will fight cheerfully and do my utmost, as if the issue of the whole struggle depended on me alone."[4]

It's a wonderful story, and in many ways the sentiment expressed is admirable.

But in a very real sense, Martin Treptow—and those of us who are tempted to think like him—are quite wrong. The whole struggle of the world most assuredly does *not* depend on us, even less does it depend on us alone. We are not Atlas, carrying the heavenly sphere on our shoulders.

That's God's role. Ultimately everything depends on God, and that includes the outcomes of wars, the rise and fall of nations, who is elected president or governor, and how our own society will turn out (Psalm 3:8, Psalm 22:28, Proverbs 21:31, 1 Samuel 2:9, Daniel 4:17). This is our Father's domain. The world is His, and all that is in it (Psalm 50:12). Although He allows men and women to work alongside Him, He is the one in charge. Although He currently allows Satan a great deal of leeway, and allows us to suffer many of the consequences of our own and other people's sinful choices, He is still in control. Not even a sparrow falls apart from His will (Matthew 10:29). And ultimately, "Thanks be to God! He gives us the victory through our Lord Jesus Christ" (1 Corinthians 15:57).

So as long as we are faithful, we shouldn't try to carry the weight of the world on our shoulders. Because we can't. And we aren't asked to. God is God, and we are not. We need to remember that truth every day, every hour, every minute.

And that leads me to my next point. Once we realize history doesn't ultimately depend on us, but depends on God, we also need to accept that God can surprise us.

3. The Mysterious and Surprising Sovereignty of God

Nothing in this life is a sure thing. And no success in this life is so overwhelming as to be permanent. Think of the declarations around the fall of the old Soviet Union that we were entering a "new world order" where nations could live in harmony with each other. How long did that last?

At the same time, it is also true that no situation is so bleak as to be hopeless. Indeed, in a Christian view of reality, hopelessness is hopelessly out of kilter with reality. The great author Dorothy Sayers once wrote perceptively:

> Short of damnation… there can be no Christian tragedy. Indeed, if a man is going to write a tragedy of the classic type, he must be careful to keep Christianity out of it… where Christ is, cheerfulness will keep breaking in… The disciples of Jesus, plunged into cowardice and despondency by the human tragedy of the Crucifixion, needed only to be convinced by the Resurrection that that which had suffered and died was in actual historical fact the true Being of all things, to recover their courage and spirits in a manner quite unparalleled, and to proclaim the Divine Comedy loudly and cheerfully, with the utmost disregard for their own safety.[5]

The Bible makes clear that God is sovereign over history, and He will eventually heal all hurts and usher in a new heaven and a new earth. But God's sovereignty isn't just for the distant future. It exists now. That means that no matter how winding and circuitous the route may seem to that new heaven and earth, God will be in control every step of the way. This belief has given comfort and inspiration to Christians for the past two thousand years.

Consider the testimony of William Cowper, a poet and hymn writer in England in the 1700s. He was a friend and collaborator of John Newton, the former slave-trader who repented, turned to Christ, and then wrote the hymn "Amazing Grace." Cowper struggled with deep depression throughout his life, at one point attempting suicide.[6] But through the depression, he clung to the reality that God is in charge. In his most famous hymn, he wrote:

> God moves in a mysterious way, His wonders to perform;
> He plants his footsteps in the sea, and rides upon the storm…

Ye fearful saints, fresh courage take; the clouds ye so much dread
are big with mercy, and shall break in blessings on your head.[7]

In another hymn, Cowper wrote:

Sometimes a light surprises the Christian while he sings;
it is the Lord who rises with healing in His wings;
when comforts are declining, He grants the soul again
a season of clear shining, to cheer it after rain.[8]

God's mysterious and surprising ways are something for us to
cling to when everything seems to be going wrong. We should also
remember God's surprises throughout history. That's one of the main
themes of the Old Testament—remember the wonders God has done
on behalf of his people, not merely because those acts are of historical
interest, but because He's the same God today, "who acts on behalf of
those who wait for him" (Isaiah 64:4; see also Psalm 103).

If you and I were Christians in the early decades after the resurrection, we might have thought all was lost after the waves of persecution that washed over Christians in the Roman empire. Think about
the terrible Emperor Nero turning Christians into human torches
and having them torn by animals in front of spectators.[9] But God
surprises. God takes the worst the world can inflict—death by crucifixion, for instance—and turns it around to produce astonishing good.
What did he do with the persecution inflicted by the Romans? Just a
few hundred years later, Christianity had spread far and wide because
Christians fled from areas of persecution into other regions—and at
the same time, Christianity had become the official religion of the
entire Roman empire. (We can debate whether that was a completely
good thing, especially the official part—I don't think it was.[10] But if
you had lived through the efforts to annihilate Christians, you likely
would have been encouraged.)

Move ahead in time. You now have a Christian empire. But it
degenerates and is increasingly attacked by the Goths, the Vandals
and Northern tribes. Rome itself is even sacked. As you saw this
play out, if you were a good *Roman* Christian, you could be forgiven
for thinking that this was the end of the world. Christianity itself
was on the ropes. But God's sovereign will surprised everyone again:

The new conquerors themselves began to embrace Christianity (if imperfectly). In part, this happened because the captives the conquerors brought from their battles were Christians, who ended up sharing their Christianity with their captors. Rome may have fallen, but Christianity didn't.

Or think about another part of the world. Imagine you were one of the Christians in China in the 1940s. When the communists took over, you probably thought it was the end of Christianity in your country, especially after foreign missionaries were expelled in the 1950s. But God wasn't done. According to a recent article, "Over the past four decades, Christianity has grown faster in China than anywhere else in the world. Daryl Ireland, a Boston University School of Theology research assistant professor of mission, estimates that the Christian community there has grown from 1 million to 100 million."[11]

Or let's take American history. Sometimes we pine for a past when America was supposed to be founded as a Christian nation. The Puritans and Pilgrims were certainly Christians, and many people at the time of the Revolution were Christians of some sort. The culture definitely operated on assumptions derived in large part from a biblical worldview.

At the same time, a number of America's most prominent founders were not biblical Christians. Thomas Jefferson and John Adams both rejected Christ as God. Even George Washington's Christianity was ambiguous. He attended church, although not weekly, but as an adult he refrained from participating in Communion, and his own private writings indicate very little about his beliefs about Jesus.[12]

At a societal level, by the early years of the new republic, Unitarians were taking over the old Puritan churches throughout New England. The state-supported religion in New England became Unitarianism, not Christianity. (Among other problems, Unitarianism denies the Trinity, claiming Jesus was inspired by God but was not God.) Leaders of Congress, meanwhile, invited noted anti-Christian activist Fanny Wright to give a special public address to Congress. She was a "reformer" who had proposed a "Declaration of Mental Independence" that denounced private property, traditional religion, and marriage as "a TRINITY of the most monstrous evils that could be combined to inflict mental and physical evil upon [the] whole race" of man.[13]

Many evangelical Christians were distraught. They thought the end had come for Christianity in America.

But again, sometimes God surprises. As a result of the ferment of what historians call the Second Great Awakening, there was a huge revival of belief in orthodox Christianity. New churches and colleges and parachurch ministries transformed the landscape. The Second Great Awakening had some issues, but because of it, much of America was arguably far more Christian at its centennial than it had been at its founding.

What's true for our nation as a whole is also true for the individual institutions within it. Throughout this book, I have shared the tragic story of how Seattle Pacific University departed from its Christian moorings. But in the latter part of writing this book, some surprising things began to happen at the university. The president resigned, and so did key board members. It now appears that the remaining board members are trying to change the institution's course back to the school's original Christian mission.

Will they succeed? I don't know. I am skeptical that the board members understand the fundamental changes that will be required to transform what happens in the classroom and in campus life. Cosmetic reforms are not going to cut it. As if confirming my continued skepticism, the university in 2024 allowed its gymnasium to be used for a festival celebrating and promoting the LGTBQ movement. The student newspaper gushed that the gym "was teeming with queer joy and affirmation."[14] One of the bands playing at the event even advertised that there would be a "Drag Performance," although I've learned that the university did put its foot down about that.[15] As I said, it's not clear that the new administrators and board members understand what needs to be done to rebuild SPU.

Even so, I am no longer writing off the possibility of restoration.

I don't pretend to know what God has in store for Seattle Pacific University, and I don't pretend to know what God has in store for the United States. We may be at the end of our nation as currently constituted. Throughout history, major powers rise and fall, and they tend to degenerate. We may have reached that point; then again, we may not have.

Whatever happens, God is still on his throne. He still reigns. As long as we worship and obey Him, we can set aside our anxiety over our ultimate fate. And God really does move in mysterious—and surprising—ways. So don't think all is lost, even in this life. God may yet surprise you, as he has past generations of Christians.

4. Outposts of the Kingdom

In 2022, my wife and I visited Turin, Italy—a city probably best known as the location of the famous Shroud of Turin, which many Christians believe is the burial cloth of Christ. I was there to speak at a conference. On Sunday, we went to worship at the English-speaking International Church of Torino.

It was a hot summer Sunday morning. The church was a fairly long way from our hotel, so we took a cab. The church met in an upper room, and that room was packed with people from Italy, the rest of Europe and the UK, Africa, South America, and the United States. The church was a beautiful expression of different peoples from different places gathering together in unity because they were brothers and sisters in Christ.

It was an inspiring morning. Afterward, one of the pastors and his wife asked us to go to lunch with them, and they shared something about their church. Years before it had broken away from a mainline Protestant English-speaking church that had gone down the path of Stockholm Syndrome Christianity.

God had blessed the new church's faithfulness. Now it was the largest English-speaking Protestant church in the city, and it was a solid, Bible-based church. Though they were currently renting a room to meet in, they had just raised money to purchase their own building. They had plans to offer Bible and theology classes to train Christian leaders in their city and region. They were reaching people who originated from every part of the globe who lived in Turin.

They were making a difference. They were an outpost for the kingdom of God in their city and beyond.

There are many outposts of the kingdom, far more than we might think.

One of the things I enjoy when traveling is finding a new place to worship on Sundays. It's not because I don't love my home church. I certainly do. It's because finding a Bible-believing church in a place far away from where I live helps bring home the reality that we're not alone. If you are a Christian, you have millions of brothers and sisters all around the world—right now.

So wherever you may go, whatever city you may find yourself in, you likely have family there—Christian brothers and sisters who can encourage you, who can worship with you, who can help you in your time of need.

Remember the prophet Elijah, who once in discouragement felt like he was the only faithful person left. But God told him, "I have reserved seven thousand for myself who have not bowed the knee to Baal" (I Kings 19, repeated by Paul in Romans 11:3–6).

Make no mistake: God is at work in this world, and his outposts are far and wide. Just because the search algorithms of Google or the reporters of the *New York Times* or the anchors of CNN don't want you to know what God is doing, doesn't mean He isn't doing it. Just because they don't want you to know about the pockets of His kingdom throughout our land doesn't mean they don't exist.

So take heart! Whatever happens to our culture, whatever happens to churches and institutions that abandon the gospel, the kingdom of God is moving forward. It's moving forward around the world. It's moving forward right where you are. And you and I have the privilege of being part of that advancing kingdom.

RESOURCES FOR ACTION

GUIDE TO THE COMPANION WEBSITE

Ready to take action? The companion website for this book contains many additional free resources to help you stand for truth in your family, your church, and your community:

- An online assessment will help you diagnose whether you, your church, or your family and friends exhibit symptoms of Stockholm Syndrome Christianity.

- Discussion/study questions suitable for small groups and adult education classes will help you apply what you have learned.

- A curated list of resources (books, articles, websites, videos, and key organizations) will enable you to equip yourself to deal with the challenges of Stockholm Syndrome Christianity before they become acute in your circles of influence.

www.StockholmSyndromeChristianity.com

ENDNOTES

INTRODUCTION: STOCKHOLM SYNDROME CHRISTIANITY

1. *Merriam-Webster*, s.v. "Stockholm Syndrome," accessed September 4, 2023, https://www.merriam-webster.com/dictionary/Stockholm_syndrome.

2. Theodore Dalrymple, "What the New Atheists Don't See," *City Journal* (Autumn 2007), reprinted at *Catholic Education Resource Center*, https://www.catholiceducation.org/en/controversy/persecution/what-the-new-atheists-dont-see.html. Richard Dawkins has more than once touted the virtues of a Christian society while rejecting Christian theology. See John Stonestreet and Shane Morris, "Richard Dawkins, a 'Cultural Christian,'" *Breakpoint*, April 9, 2024, https://www.breakpoint.org/richard-dawkins-a-cultural-christian/. See also Tom Holland's *Dominion: The Making of the Western Mind*, helpfully reviewed by Gerald Hiestand, "Tom Holland and the Liberating Power of Christianity," *Theopolis Institute*, January 25, 2022, https://theopolisinstitute.com/tom-holland-and-the-liberating-power-of-christianity/; and Daniel Strand, "Are We All Christians Now?," *Providence*, June 17, 2020, https://providencemag.com/2020/06/book-review-tom-holland-dominion-christian-revolution-remade-world/. It should go without saying that none of these authors, or myself, argue that Christian principles guarantee improved behavior. Plenty of people pay lip service to these principles while behaving abominably.

3. Christopher Klein, "Stockholm Syndrome: The True Story of Hostages Loyal to Their Captor," *History*, last modified August 23, 2023, https://www.history.com/news/stockholm-syndrome.

4. Quoted in Klein, "Stockholm Syndrome."

5. "Bible School," *1929 Cascade* (Seattle: Associated Students of Seattle Pacific College, 1929), 28.

6. See photo and description in Seattle Pacific University–Alumni, "#ThrowbackThursday to McKinley Hall, Home to SPU's Music and Theatre Departments," *Facebook*, October 4, 2018, https://www.facebook.com/seattle.pacific.university.alumni/photos/a.258618594184123/1971234532922512.

7. "SPU Alumnus Jacob DeShazer," *Seattle Pacific University*, November 10, 2011, https://spu.edu/about-spu/news/articles/2011/nov/deshazer-people-of-hope.aspx; also see "U.S. Air Force Oral History Interview: Rev. Jacob D. DeShazer," *Seattle*

Pacific Library Digital Commons @ SPU, October 10, 1989, https://digitalcommons. spu.edu/jfdeshazer_overview/7/; and "My Enemy, My Friend," *Seattle Pacific University Response*, Spring 2004, https://spu.edu/depts/uc/response/spring2k4 /friend.html.

8. The "Valiant for the Truth" motto can be seen on the last page of "Evening Classes, Winter Quarter Jan. 4th to March 18 1965," *Seattle Pacific Library Digital Commons @ SPU*, https://digitalcommons.spu.edu/archives_publications_spc/14.

9. Arthur W. Lindsley, "Profiles in Faith: Francis Schaeffer," *C. S. Lewis Institute*, September 4, 2001, https://www.cslewisinstitute.org/resources/profiles-in-faith -francis-schaeffer/.

10. The C. S. Lewis Institute on campus was different from the national organization now called by the same name. SPU's Institute was directed for many years by English professor Michael Macdonald; in later years, I co-directed it with Dr. Macdonald and the Institute became a joint project with Discovery Institute, where I work.

11. "SPU Facts," *Seattle Pacific University*, last modified October 19, 2022, https://spu.edu/about-spu/spu-facts.

12. "This We Believe: A Statement of Faith," *Seattle Pacific University*, accessed September 4, 2023, https://spu.edu/about-spu/statement-of-faith.

13. "Christian College Consortium Member Institutions," *Christian College Consortium*, accessed September 4, 2023, https://www.ccconsortium.org/member -institutions/.

14. "Faith at SPU," *Seattle Pacific University*, accessed September 4, 2023, https://spu.edu/undergraduate-admissions/why-spu/christian-life.

15. Elise Takahama, "Seattle Pacific University Faculty Votes 'No Confidence' in Leadership after Board Upholds Discriminatory Hiring Policy," *Seattle Times*, April 21, 2021, https://www.seattletimes.com/education-lab/seattle-pacific -university-faculty-votes-no-confidence-in-school-leadership-after-board -upholds-discriminatory-hiring-policy/.

16. Statement on Human Sexuality," *Seattle Pacific University*, November 14, 2005, https://spu.edu/about-spu/spu-facts/statement-on-human-sexuality.

17. Carlene Brown, Chair, Faculty Senate, quoted in Carlos Snellenberg-Fraser, "Faculty Sends Swift Rebuke to Board of Trustees," *Falcon*, April 14, 2021, https://thefalcon.seapacmedia.com/10290/news/faculty-sends-swift-rebuke -to-board-of-trustees/.

18. Sara Koenig, Professor of Biblical Studies, quoted in Snellenberg-Fraser, "Faculty Sends Swift Rebuke."

19. Matthew Bellinger, Assistant Professor of Communication, quoted in Snellenberg-Fraser, "Faculty Sends Swift Rebuke."

20. "Tries to Serve Two Masters, but Fails," *Glassdoor*, August 3, 2013, https://www.glassdoor.com/Reviews/Employee-Review-Seattle-Pacific -University-RVW2893443.htm.

21. Unless otherwise noted, all quotations of scripture use the English Standard Version translation of the Bible

1. MERELY HUMAN

1. "Welcome," *Northpoint Ministries*, accessed September 4, 2023, https://northpointministries.org/.

2. Paul J. Pastor, "Andy Stanley: The Agile Apologetic—Part 1," *Outreach Magazine*, February 5, 2017, https://outreachmagazine.com/interviews/21383-andy -stanley-2.html.

3. Home page, *AndyStanley*, accessed September 4, 2023, https://andystanley.com/.

4. Interview with Ed Stetzer, "Andy Stanley on Communication (Part 2)," *ChristianityToday.com*, March 5, 2009, https://web.archive.org/web /20150215150002/http://www.christianitytoday.com/edstetzer/2009/march /andy-stanley-on-communication-part-2.html.

5. Michael Gryboski, "Andy Stanley Apologizes for Saying People Who Go to Small Churches 'Are So Stinkin' Selfish,'" *Christian Post*, March 4, 2016, https://www.christianpost.com/news/andy-stanley-apologizes-for-saying-people -who-go-to-small-churches-are-so-stinkin-selfish.html.

6. Michael Gryboski, "Christians Must 'Unhitch' Old Testament from Their Faith, Says Andy Stanley," *Christian Post*, May 9, 2018, https://www.christianpost.com /news/christians-must-unhitch-old-testament-from-their-faith-says-andy-stanley .html.

7. Andy Stanley, *Irresistible: Reclaiming the New that Jesus Unleashed for the World* (Grand Rapids: Zondervan, 2018), 140.

8. Stanley, *Irresistible*, 166.

9. Stanley, *Irresistible*, 136.

10. Stanley, *Irresistible*, 278.

11. Stanley, *Irresistible*, 154.

12. Stanley, *Irresistible*, 140.

13. Stanley, *Irresistible*, 198.

14. Stanley, *Irresistible*, 156.

15. Stanley, *Irresistible*, 158.

16. Stanley, *Irresistible*, 95.

17. Stanley, *Irresistible*, 280.

18. Stanley, *Irresistible*, 157.

19. Stanley, *Irresistible*, 304. In reality, there is strong evidence for both the Exodus and the Bible's account of the conquest of Jericho. See Stephen Meyer and Titus Kennedy, "What Archaeology Reveals about the Historicity of the Exodus," *YouTube*, January 12, 2024, https://youtu.be/P2r2xXGzx4U?si=m2dK5CP -QaUsg9Mx; "Jericho Unearthed: The Archaeology of Jericho Explained," *YouTube*, August 12, 2022, https://youtu.be/C27CmsSGx5Y?si=CVKDK wQnpvF-Afvp. Although I don't quote it, Stanley also includes "a worldwide flood" in his list of historical events reported by the Bible but denied by secular scholars. That example is more complicated, because there is some debate among faithful Bible scholars about whether the biblical text necessarily requires a geographically worldwide flood. For a summary of the different views, see James M.

Rochford, "The Genesis Flood: Global or Local?," *Evidence Unseen*, accessed May 27, 2024, https://www.evidenceunseen.com/articles/science-and-scripture/the-genesis-flood-global-or-local/. Regardless, there is good evidence that people groups around the globe have a cultural memory of a great flood. See Eric Lyons and Kyle Butt, "Legends of the Flood," *Apologetics Press*, November 1, 2003, https://apologeticspress.org/legends-of-the-flood-64/.

20. Stanley, *Irresistible*, 314.

21. Stanley, *Irresistible*, 304.

22. Stanley, *Irresistible*, 306.

23. Stanley, *Irresistible*, 280.

24. Stanley, *Irresistible*, 284. Placing Luke first in the New Testament is far from a perfect fix for Stanley, since Luke, although a gentile writer and focused more on a gentile audience, nevertheless quotes frequently from the Old Testament. See Wayne Jackson, "Luke and the Old Testament," *The Christian Courier*, accessed May 22, 2024, https://christiancourier.com/articles/luke-and-the-old-testament.

25. Kevin DeYoung, "Marcion and Getting Unhitched from the Old Testament," *Gospel Coalition*, May 11, 2018, https://www.thegospelcoalition.org/blogs/kevin-deyoung/marcion-getting-unhitched-old-testament/; "What is Marcionism?" *Got Questions?*, accessed September 4, 2023, https://www.gotquestions.org/marcionism.html; Samuel Loncar, "Christianity's Shadow Founder: Marcion, Anti-Judaism, and the Birth of Liberal Protestantism," *Marginalia*, November 19, 2021, https://themarginaliareview.com/christianitys-shadow-founder-marcion-anti-judaism-and-the-birth-of-liberal-protestantism/.

26. Thomas Jefferson, "The Life and Morals of Jesus of Nazareth" [1820], accessed May 2024, *Smithsonian's National Museum of American History*, https://americanhistory.si.edu/JeffersonBible/the-book/#1.

27. Thomas Jefferson to William Short, August 4, 1820, *Founders Online*, United States National Archives, https://founders.archives.gov/documents/Jefferson/03-16-02-0132.

28. Thomas Jefferson, "Doctrines of Jesus Compared with Others," April 21, 1803, *United States National Archives: Founders Online*, accessed May 2024, https://founders.archives.gov/documents/Jefferson/01-40-02-0178-0002.

29. John Connelly, "Hitler's Gospel," *Commonweal*, February 22, 2010, https://www.commonwealmagazine.org/hitler%E2%80%99s-gospel; also see "Jewish References Erased in Newly Found Nazi Bible," *Daily Mail*, last modified August 7, 2006, https://www.dailymail.co.uk/news/article-399470/Jewish-references-erased-newly-Nazi-Bible.html.

30. Stanley, *Irresistible*, 20.

31. Stanley, *Irresistible*, 76.

32. See Aquinas's discussion of law in the *Summa Theologiae*, First Part of the Second Part, questions 90–108, *New Advent*, 2017, https://www.newadvent.org/summa/2.htm; and Calvin's discussion of government and its relationship to the Mosaic law, John Calvin, *Institutes of the Christian Religion*, trans. Henry Beveridge (Grand Rapids, MI: Eerdmans, 1989), Book 4, chap. 20.

33. Michael Rydelnik and Edwin Blum, eds., *The Moody Handbook of Messianic Prophecy: Studies and Expositions of the Messiah in the Old Testament* (Chicago: Moody Publishers, 2019).

34. See Calvin, *Institutes*, Book 2, Chapter 8, 317; Martin Luther, "How Christians Should Regard Moses," in Timothy F. Lull, editor, *Martin Luther's Basic Theological Writings* (Minneapolis: Fortress Press, 1989), 142. I would argue that the spiritual commands in the Ten Commandments against idolatry, taking God's name in vain, and keeping the sabbath also apply to Christians today, although Christians have differed about whether the "sabbath" kept should be the "Christian sabbath" (i.e., Sunday) or the original Jewish sabbath.

35. Stanley, *Irresistible*, 314.

36. See Geoffrey W. Bromiley, *Theological Dictionary of the New Testament, Abridged in One Volume* (Grand Rapids, MI: William B. Eerdmans Publishing Co., 1985), 128–129; also see Hebrews 1, where the author attributes various Old Testament texts to God Himself.

37. On the question of why the Bible has historically been viewed as an authoritative collection (a canon), see Michael J. Kruger, "The Biblical Canon," *Gospel Coalition,* accessed May 2024, https://www.thegospelcoalition.org/essay/the-biblical-canon/. See also Kruger's scholarly works on the topic, *The Question of Canon* (Downers Grover, IL: IVP Academic, 2013) and *Canon Revisited* (Wheaton, IL: Crossway, 2012). Also see F. F. Bruce, *The Canon of Scripture* (Downers Grover, IL: IVP Academic, 1988) and Andrew Steinmann, *The Oracles of God: The Old Testament Canon* (St. Louis, MO: Concordia, 1999). These writers also discuss the handful of debated texts (the Apocrypha) and whether they should or not should not be part of the canon.

38. Flavius Josephus, *Against Apion*, in John M. G. Barclay, *Flavius Josephus: Translation and Commentary*, ed. Steve Mason, trans. John M. G. Barclay (Boston: Brill, 2007), vol. 10, 31–32.

39. Clement of Rome, "First Epistle to the Corinthians," chap. XLV, *Christian Classics Ethereal Library,* accessed May 2024, https://ccel.org/ccel/clement_rome/first_epistle_to_the_corinthians/anf01.ii.ii.xlv.html.

40. Irenaeus, *Against Heresies,* vol. II, chap. XXVIII.2, *Christian Classics Ethereal Library,* accessed May 2024, https://ccel.org/ccel/irenaeus/against_heresies_ii/anf01.ix.iii.xxix.html.

41. Augustine to Jerome [AD 405], *Letters of St. Augustine,* Letter 82, chap. 1, par. 3, *New Advent,* accessed May 2024, https://www.newadvent.org/fathers/1102.htm.

42. Thomas Aquinas, *Summa Theologiae,* Second Part of the Second Part, Question 110, Article 3, Reply to Objection 1, *New Advent,* accessed May 2024, https://www.newadvent.org/summa/3110.htm.

43. Selections 240 and 269 in Ewald M. Plass, ed., *What Luther Says: A Practical In-Home Anthology for the Active Christian* (St. Louis: Concordia Publishing House, 1959), 79, 88.

44. "The Westminster Confession of Faith" [1646], Chapter I, Article V, *The Westminster Standard,* accessed May 2024, https://thewestminsterstandard.org/the-westminster-confession/.

45. "Belgic Confession" [1561], Article 5: The Authority of Scripture, *Christian Reformed Church*, accessed May 2024, https://www.crcna.org/welcome/beliefs /confessions/belgic-confession.

46. "Belgic Confession," Article 7: The Sufficiency of Scripture.

47. Joseph M. Holden and Don Stewart, "Were the New Testament Manuscripts Copied Accurately?," *Defending Inerrancy*, August 5, 2019, https:// defendinginerrancy.com/were-nt-mss-copied-accurately/; Norman L. Geisler, "A Note on the Percent of Accuracy of the New Testament Text," *Norman Geisler* accessed May 2024, https://normangeisler.com/a-note-on-the-percent-of -accuracy-of-the-new-testament-text/; Paul D. Wenger, "The Reliability of the Old Testament Manuscripts," in Wayne Grudem, C. John Collins, and Thomas R. Schreiner, *Understanding Scripture: An Overview of the Bible's Origin, Reliability, and Meaning* (Wheaton, IL: Crossway, 2012), 101–109; Daniel B. Wallace, "The Reliability of the New Testament Manuscripts," in Grudem, *Understanding Scripture*, 111–117; Craig L. Blomberg, *Can We Still Believe the Bible?: An Evangelical Engagement with Contemporary Questions* (Grand Rapids, MI: Brazos Press, 2014), Kindle edition, chap. 1.

48. Rudolf Bultmann, "The Mythological Element in the Message of the New Testament and the Problem of Its Re-interpretation, Part 1," in Bultmann et al., *Kerygma and Myth* (London: SPCK, 1953), https://www.religion-online.org /book-chapter/the-mythological-element-in-the-message-of-the-new-testament -and-the-problem-of-its-re-interpretation-part-i/. Emphasis in original.

49. John Snyder, "Did Bultmann Change His Mind About the Resurrection?," *Theology/Mix*, March 18, 2016, https://theologymix.com/apologetics/did -bultmann-change-his-mind-about-the-resurrection/.

50. Michael Gleghorn, "Historical Criticism and the Bible," *Probe*, May 9, 2021, https://probe.org/historical-criticism-and-the-bible/.

51. John S. Feinberg, "The Authority of Scripture," *Crossway*, April 17, 2018, https://www.crossway.org/articles/the-authority-of-scripture/.

52. Richard Dawkins, *The God Delusion* (New York: Mariner Books Edition, 2008).

53. Dawkins, *The God Delusion*, 268.

54. Dawkins, *The God Delusion*, 51.

55. Phillip Stitter, "ISU Professor Hector Avalos, Renowned in Latino/a/x, Atheist/Agnostic Communities, Dies at 62," *Ames Tribune*, April 22, 2021, https://www.amestrib.com/story/news/education/2021/04/22/iowa-state -university-professor-hector-avalos-leaves-legacy-multiple-communities -atheism/7292678002/.

56. Hector Avalos, *Fighting Words: The Origins of Religious Violence* (Amherst, NY: Prometheus Books, 2005), 369.

57. Avalos, *Fighting Words*, 371.

58. Avalos, *Fighting Words*, 370.

59. Avalos, *Fighting Words*, 318–319. Of course, Avalos also blamed early Christians for what happened: "The Nazi Holocaust represents the synthesis of attitudes found in both the New Testament and the Hebrew scriptures" (Avalos, 318).

60. J. Gresham Machen, *Christianity and Liberalism* (New York: Macmillan, 1923), https://archive.org/details/christianitylibe00mach_0.

61. Robert H. Gundry, *Matthew: A Commentary on His Literary and Theological Art* (Grand Rapids: Eerdmans Publishing Company, 1982), 27.

62. Gundry, *Matthew*, 27.

63. Gundry, *Matthew*, 34–35.

64. Gundry, *Matthew*, 630.

65. "ETS Constitution (Prior to 2021 Incorporation)," *The Evangelical Theological Society*, https://www.etsjets.org/about/constitution.

66. Leslie R. Keylock, "Evangelical Scholars Remove Gundry for His Views on Matthew," *Christianity Today*, February 3, 1984, https://www.christianitytoday.com/ct/1984/february-3/evangelical-scholars-remove-gundry-for-his-views-on-matthew.html; Norman Geisler, "Editorial Comments on ETS Gundry Decision in 1983," *Norman Geisler*, February 1, 2014, https://normangeisler.com/the-ets-vote-on-robert-gundry-at-their-annual-meeting-in-december-1983/.

67. "A Seat of Honor," *Westmont Magazine*, Fall 1999, https://www.westmont.edu/seat-honor.

68. "Retiring Faculty," *Westmont Magazine*, Spring 2000, https://www.westmont.edu/retiring-faculty.

69. "Articles of Religion," Free Methodist Church USA, accessed May 2024, https://fmcusa.org/articlesofreligion.

70. Philip Ryken, "Inerrancy and the Patron Saint of Evangelicalism: C. S. Lewis on Holy Scripture," *Desiring God*, September 28, 2013, https://www.desiringgod.org/messages/inerrancy-and-the-patron-saint-of-evangelicalism-c-s-lewis-on-holy-scripture.

71. Jesse La Tour, "Faith Undercut by Liberal Interpretation," *Falcon*, April 24, 2002.

72. Bruce Ware, *God's Lesser Glory: The Diminished God of Open Theism* (Wheaton, IL: Crossway, 2000), 31–42; John Wesley, "Sermon 58: On Predestination," *Sermons on Several Occasions*, Christian Classics Ethereal Library, accessed May 2024, https://www.ccel.org/ccel/wesley/sermons.vi.v.html.

73. Quoted in Ware, *God's Lesser Glory*, 33.

74. The quotations come from an email "Mary" sent me after I asked her to document for me her experience. I was hoping to share her experiences with someone in authority who might be able to change the direction of the school.

75. Lincoln John Keller, *The Creed of Compromised Christianity: Scripture & Sexuality at Seattle Pacific University* (Seattle: Amazon Digital Services, 2021), loc. 108, Kindle.

76. Keller, *The Creed of Compromised Christianity*, loc. 75.

77. Russell D. Moore, "Evangelical Theological Society Rejects 'Open Theism,' Affirms God's Foreknowledge," *Baptist Press*, November 20, 2001, https://www.baptistpress.com/resource-library/news/evangelical-theological-society-rejects-open-theism-affirms-gods-foreknowledge/.

78. Jeff Robinson, "Theological Society Retains Open Theists Pinnock, Sanders," *Southern Baptist Theological Seminary: News & Features*, November 20, 2003, https://news.sbts.edu/2003/11/20/theological-society-retains-open-theists-pinnock-sanders/.

79. For Licona's views on this topic, see Michael R. Licona, *Why Are There Differences in the Gospels? What We Can Learn from Ancient Biography* (New York: Oxford University Press, 2017) and Michael R. Licona, *Jesus, Contradicted? Why the Gospels Tell the Same Story Differently* (Grand Rapids, MI: Zondervan Academic, 2024).

80. Licona, *Jesus, Contradicted?*, 66, 228–230.

81. Licona, *Jesus, Contradicted?*, 75, 73–75. Of course, if Matthew was in fact trying to draw such a parallel in his gospel, it could have been because he truly believed Jesus did give his sermon on a mountain. There is no good reason to jump to the speculative conclusion that Matthew would have invented a false location to make his theological point.

82. Michael Licona, *The Resurrection of Jesus: A New Historiographical Approach* (Downers Grove, IL: IVP Academic, 2010), 185, Kindle.

83. Licona, *The Resurrection of Jesus*, 552.

84. For examples, see Norman Geisler, "An Open Letter to Mike Licona on His View of the Resurrected Saints in Matthew 27:52–53," *Defending Inerrancy*, 2011, https://normangeisler.com/an-open-letter-to-mike-licona-on-his-view-of-the -resurrected-saints-in-matthew-27/; Norman Geisler, "The Early Fathers and the Resurrection of the Saints in Matthew 27:51–54," *Defending Inerrancy*, June 14, 2014, https://defendinginerrancy.com/early-fathers-resurrection-saints/; Christopher Travis Haun, "Did Roman Christians Detect the Influence of Roman Historiography in Matthew 27:45–54?," *Defending Inerrancy*, April 30, 2014, https://defendinginerrancy.com/historical-testing-for-the-genre-theories/.

85. "At present I am just as inclined to understand the narrative of the raised saints in Matthew 27 as a report of a factual (i.e., literal) event as I am to view it as an apocalyptic symbol." Statement from Michael Licona published in "Michael Licona on the Resurrection of the Saints in Matthew 27," *Wintery Knight*, September 9, 2011, https://winteryknight.com/2011/09/09/michael-licona-on-the-resurrection -of-the-saints-in-matthew-27/.

86. Licona, *Why Are There Differences in the Gospels?*, 166.

87. Lydia McGrew, *The Mirror or the Mask: Liberating the Gospels from Literary Devices* (Tampa, FL: DeWard Publishing Company, 2019), 359; also see Lydia McGrew, "Review of Michael Licona's *Why Are There Difference in the Gospels?*," *Global Journal of Classic Theology*, February 1, 2019, 13, available at http://www .globaljournalct.com/wp-content/uploads/2019/02/Global-Journal-15.3-Lydia -McGrew-Review-of-Why-Are-There-Differences-in-the-Gospels.pdf.

88. Licona, *Why Are There Differences in the Gospels?*, 165–166.

89. Licona, *Why Are There Differences in the Gospels?*, 181.

90. Licona, *Jesus, Contradicted?*, 42–46.

91. Licona, *Jesus, Contradicted?*, 42.

92. McGrew, *The Mirror or the Mask*.

93. McGrew, *The Mirror or the Mask*, 254.

94. Licona, *Jesus, Contradicted?*, 193–222.

95. Michael Licona, "ETS 2023: CSBI Needs a Facelift," *Risen Jesus*, May 1, 2024, https://www.risenjesus.com/wp-content/uploads/ets-2023.pdf, 6-10, 12.

96. Results for "Statement 16," *The State of Theology*, 2022, https://thestateoftheology.com/.

97. Results for "Statement 7," *The State of Theology*.

98. "American Worldview Inventory 2023, Release #3: How the Faith of Americans Has Shifted Since the Start of the Pandemic," *Arizona Christian University: Cultural Research Center*, April 20, 2023, https://www.arizonachristian.edu/wp-content/uploads/2023/04/CRC_AWVI2023_Release_03.pdf.

99. Alvin J. Schmidt, *How Christianity Changed the World* (Grand Rapids, MI: Zondervan, 2004), 151–169.

100. Schmidt, *How Christianity Changed the World*, 272–291.

101. Schmidt, *How Christianity Changed the World*, 97–124.

102. "What is FGM, Where Does It Happen and Why?," *BBC News*, February 6, 2019, https://www.bbc.com/news/world-47131052.

103. "Saudi Arabia's Ban on Women Driving Officially Ends," *BBC News*, June 24, 2018, https://www.bbc.com/news/world-middle-east-44576795.

104. Schmidt, *How Christianity Changed the World*, 170–193, 218–247, 292–373.

2. SECULARIST SCIENCE

1. "International Human Genome Sequencing Consortium Announces 'Working Draft' of Human Genome," *National Human Genome Research Institute*, June 2000, https://www.genome.gov/10001457/2000-release-working-draft-of-human-genome-sequence.

2. Francis Collins, *The Language of God: A Scientist Presents Evidence for Belief* (New York: Free Press, 2006).

3. "A Farewell to Dr. Francis Collins," *National Institutes of Health*, December 16, 2021, https://www.nih.gov/farewell-dr-francis-collins; "Collins Named Acting Science Advisor to President Biden," *NIH Record*, March 18, 2022, https://nihrecord.nih.gov/2022/03/18/collins-named-acting-science-advisor-president-biden.

4. David French (@DavidAFrench), "Francis Collins is a national treasure," *Twitter*, October 5, 2021, https://x.com/DavidAFrench/status/1445400222780301321.

5. Russell Moore (@drmoore), "I admire greatly the wisdom, expertise, and, most of all, the Christian humility and grace of Francis Collins," *Twitter*, October 5, 2021, https://twitter.com/drmoore/status/1445363320089944064.

6. See Alvin J. Schmidt, *How Christianity Changed the World* (Grand Rapids, MI: Zondervan, 2004), 48–60; Michael J. Gorman, *Abortion & the Early Church: Christian, Jewish & Pagan Attitudes in the Greco-Roman World* (Eugene, Oregon: Wipf and Stock, 1998).

7. David Klinghoffer, "Francis Collins on Abortion: Obama's Pick for NIH and His 'Devout' Views on Terminating Down Syndrome Children," *Beliefnet*, July 2009, https://www.beliefnet.com/columnists/kingdomofpriests/2009/07/francis-collins-on-abortion.html.

8. Collins, *Language of God*, 256.

9. Peter J. Boyer, "The Covenant," *New Yorker*, August 30, 2010, https://www.newyorker.com/magazine/2010/09/06/the-covenant.

10. Chris Wilson, "Jesus Goes to Bethesda: Just How Religious Is Obama's Nominee for Director of NIH?," *Slate*, July 9, 2009, https://slate.com/technology/2009/07/just-how-religious-is-francis-collins-obama-s-nominee-for-director-of-the-nih.html.

11. Francis Collins, "'God is Not Threatened by Our Scientific Adventures': A Genome Researcher Explains How He Reconciles Science with His Deep Christian Faith," interviewed by Laura Sheahen, *Beliefnet*, August 2006, https://web.archive.org/web/20081117130443/http:/www.beliefnet.com/News/Science-Religion/2006/08/God-Is-Not-Threatened-By-Our-Scientific-Adventures.aspx?p=3.

12. David Prentice, "Backgrounder: We Need a New NIH Director," *Charlotte Lozier Institute*, April 25, 2017, https://lozierinstitute.org/backgrounder-we-need-a-new-nih-director/.

13. Mary Margaret Olohan, "Biden Team Reverses Trump's Ban on Using Aborted Fetal Tissue for Taxpayer-Funded Research," *Daily Signal*, April 19, 2021, https://www.dailysignal.com/2021/04/19/biden-admin-reverses-trumps-ban-on-using-aborted-fetal-tissue-for-taxpayer-funded-research/.

14. Madeline Osburn, "University of Pittsburgh Uses Taxpayer-Funded Aborted Babies For Medical Research," *Federalist*, May 7, 2021, https://thefederalist.com/2021/05/07/university-of-pittsburgh-uses-taxpayer-funded-aborted-babies-for-medical-research/.

15. Yash Agarwal, Cole Beatty, Sara Ho, et al., "Development of Humanized Mouse and Rat Models with Full-Thickness Human Skin and Autologous Immune Cells," *Scientific Reports* 10, no. 14598 (2020), https://doi.org/10.1038/s41598-020-71548-z.

16. Katrina Furth, "Fetal EEGs: Signals from the Dawn of Life," *Charlotte Lozier Institute*, November 27, 2018, https://lozierinstitute.org/fetal-eegs-signals-from-the-dawn-of-life/.

17. "Fetal Development: The 1st Trimester," *Mayo Clinic*, June 3, 2022, https://www.mayoclinic.org/healthy-lifestyle/pregnancy-week-by-week/in-depth/prenatal-care/art-20045302.

18. "Fetal Development: The 2nd Trimester," *Mayo Clinic*, June 3, 2022, https://www.mayoclinic.org/healthy-lifestyle/pregnancy-week-by-week/in-depth/fetal-development/art-20046151.

19. "Judicial Watch: New HHS Documents Reveal Millions in Federal Funding for University of Pittsburgh Human Fetal Organ Harvesting Project Including Viable and Full-Term Babies," *Judicial Watch*, August 3, 2021, https://www.judicialwatch.org/hhs-documents-organ-harvesting/.

20. "Aborted Infants' Continued Blood Flow Advertised in Racist University of Pittsburgh Grant Application to NIH," *The Center for Medical Progress*, August 3, 2021, https://www.centerformedicalprogress.org/2021/08/aborted-infants-continued-blood-flow-advertised-in-racist-university-of-pittsburgh-grant-application-to-nih/.

21. "BREAKING: University of Pittsburgh ADMITS Hearts Beating While Harvesting Aborted Infants' Kidneys," *The Center for Medical Progress*, August 4, 2021,

https://www.centerformedicalprogress.org/2021/08/breaking-university-of
-pittsburgh-admits-hearts-beating-while-harvesting-aborted-infants-kidneys/.

22. Francis Collins, "From the NIH Director: NIH 2021 Pride Month," *National Institutes of Health*, June 4, 2021, https://www.edi.nih.gov/blog/news/nih-director-nih-2021-pride-month.

23. Megan Basham, "How the Federal Government Used Evangelical Leaders To Spread COVID Propaganda To Churches," *The Daily Wire*, February 2, 2022, https://www.dailywire.com/news/how-the-federal-government-used-evangelical-leaders-to-spread-covid-propaganda-to-churches. Also see Megan Basham, *Shepherds for Sale: How Evangelical Leaders Traded the Truth for a Leftist Agenda* (New York: Broadside Books, 2024), Chapter 5.

24. Karl Giberson, *Saving Darwin: How to Be a Christian and Believe in Evolution* (New York: HarperOne, 2008), 10, emphasis in the original.

25. Irenaeus, *Against Heresies*, Book II, chap. 1, in *The Ante-Nicene Fathers, Vol. 1: The Apostolic Fathers, Justin Martyr, Irenaeus,* eds. Arthur Cleveland Coxe, Alexander Roberts, and James Donaldson (New York: Christian Literature Publishing, 1885), http://www.ccel.org/ccel/schaff/anf01.ix.iii.ii.html.

26. Philip Schaff, *History of the Christian Church* (Grand Rapids, MI: Eerdmans Publishing, 1980), vol. 3, 668.

27. See discussion in Schaff, *History of the Christian Church,* vol. 2, 538–541; also see the comparative table of creedal statements on 536–537.

28. *History of the Christian Church,* 540.

29. See discussion in John G. West, *Darwin Day in America: How Our Politics and Culture Have Been Dehumanized in the Name of Science* (Wilmington, DE: ISI Books, 2007), 5–10.

30. Theophilus, *Theophilus to Autolycus,* Book 1, chap. 5, available in *Design in the Bible and the Early Church Fathers* (Seattle: Discovery Institute, 2009), http://www.discovery.org/scripts/viewDB/filesDB-download.php?command=download&id=4431, 11.

31. Theophilus, *Theophilus to Autolycus,* 11.

32. Dionysius, *The Books on Nature,* Part II, II in *Design in the Bible and the Early Church Fathers,* 13.

33. Dionysius in *Design in the Bible and the Early Church Fathers,* 14.

34. Lactantius, *The Divine Institutes,* Book 1, chap. 9, in *Design in the Bible and the Early Church Fathers,* 19.

35. For further examples, see *Design in the Bible and the Early Church Fathers,* 11–22; also see *The Patristic Understanding of Creation: An Anthology of Writings from the Church Fathers on Creation and Design,* eds. William A. Dembski, Wayne J. Downs, and Father Justin B. A. Frederick (Riesel, TX: Erasmus Press, 2008).

36. Hippolytus, *The Refutation of All Heresies,* Book VI, chap. XXVIII, in *The Ante-Nicene Fathers, Vol. 5: Hippolytus, Cyprian, Caius, Novatian, Appendix,* eds. Alexander Roberts and James Donaldson, http://www.ccel.org/ccel/schaff/anf05.iii.iii.iv.xxix.html.

37. Irenaeus, *Against Heresies*, Book I, chap. XXVI, in *The Ante-Nicene Fathers, Vol. 1: The Apostolic Fathers, Justin Martyr, Irenaeus*, http://www.ccel.org/ccel/schaff /anf01.ix.ii.xxvii.html.

38. Thomas Aquinas, *Summa Theologiae*, First Part, Question 2, Article 3, *New Advent*, accessed May 2024, https://www.newadvent.org/summa/1002.htm.

39. John Calvin, *Institutes of the Christian Religion*, trans. Henry Beveridge (Grand Rapids, MI: Eerdmans, 1989), Book I, Chapter V.2.

40. John Calvin, *Institutes of the Christian Religion*.

41. C. S. Lewis, *Miracles: A Preliminary Study*, 1960 ed. (New York: Macmillan, 1978), 106.

42. Rodney Stark, *For the Glory of God: How Monotheism Led to Reformations, Science, Witch-Hunts, and the End of Slavery* (Princeton: Princeton University Press, 2003), 123.

43. Stark, *For the Glory of God*, 123.

44. Peter Harrison, "The Bible and the Emergence of Modern Science," *Science and Christian Belief* 18, no. 2 (2006): 115.

45. Hugh Elliot, *Modern Science and Materialism* (London: Longmans, Green, and Co., 1927), 138.

46. Charles Darwin, *The Autobiography of Charles Darwin and Selected Letters*, ed. F. Darwin (New York: Dover Publication, 1958 reprint of 1892 ed.), 63.

47. Karl Marx to Ferdinand Lassalle, January 16, 1861, *Karl Marx and Friedrich Engels: Collected Works* (New York: International Publishers, 1975–2005), 41:247.

48. For an example of one of the best scientific critiques of Darwinian natural selection during Darwin's lifetime, see George Mivart, *On the Genesis of Species*, 2nd ed. (New York: Macmillan, 1871).

49. Peter Bowler, *Darwinism* (New York: Twayne Publishers, 1993), 6.

50. Michael A. Flannery and Alfred Russel Wallace, *Intelligent Evolution: How Alfred Russel Wallace's World of Life Challenged Darwinism* (Nashville, TN: Erasmus Press, 2020); Michael A. Flannery, *Alfred Russel Wallace: A Rediscovered Life* (Seattle, WA: Discovery Institute Press, 2011).

51. See Richard Dawkins, *The God Delusion* (New York: Mariner Books, 2008); Sam Harris, *Letter to a Christian Nation* (New York: Alfred Knopf, 2006); and Daniel Dennett, *Darwin's Dangerous Idea: Evolution and the Meanings of Life* (New York: Touchstone, 1996).

52. Richard Dawkins, *River Out of Eden: A Darwinian View of Life* (New York: Basic Books, 1995), 133.

53. Daniel Dennett, *Darwin's Dangerous Idea: Evolution and the Meanings of Life* (New York: Touchstone, 1995), 18.

54. George V. Coyne, "The Dance of the Fertile Universe," 7, accessed May 2024, https://web.archive.org/web/20051104052227/http://www.aei.org/docLib /20051027_HandoutCoyne.pdf.

55. John Polkinghorne, *Quarks, Chaos, and Christianity* (New York: Crossroad Publishing Company, 2005), 113.

56. Kenneth R. Miller, *Finding Darwin's God: A Scientist's Search for Common Ground between God and Evolution* (New York: HarperCollins, 1999), 272; see also 244.

57. Kenneth Miller, comments during "Evolution and Intelligent Design: An Exchange," March 24, 2007, at the "Shifting Ground: Religion and Civic Life in America Conference," Bedford, NH, sponsored by the New Hampshire Humanities Council.

58. Giberson, *Saving Darwin: How to Be a Christian and Believe in Evolution*, 12.

59. Ronald Numbers, quoted in Gwen Evans, "Reason or Faith? Darwin Expert Reflects," *University of Wisconsin-Madison*, February 3, 2009, https://news.wisc.edu/reason-or-faith-darwin-expert-reflects/.

60. Collins, *Language of God*, 205.

61. Collins, *Language of God*, 136.

62. Casey Luskin, "Francis Collins' Junk DNA Arguments Pushed into Increasingly Small Gaps in Scientific Knowledge," *Evolution News and Science Today*, May 2, 2011, https://evolutionnews.org/2011/05/francis_collins_junk_dna_argum/.

63. Casey Luskin, "The ENCODE Embroilment: Research on 'Junk DNA' Verifies Key Predictions of Intelligent Design," *Discovery Institute*, October 16, 2021, https://www.discovery.org/a/67180/.

64. Casey Luskin, "Junk No More: ENCODE Project Nature Paper Finds 'Biochemical Functions for 80% of the Genome,'" *Evolution News and Science Today*, September 5, 2012, https://evolutionnews.org/2012/09/junk_no_more_en_1/.

65. Casey Luskin, "Noncoding 'Junk' DNA Is Important for Limb Formation," *Evolution News and Science Today*, May 21, 2021, https://evolutionnews.org/2021/05/noncoding-junk-dna-is-important-for-limb-formation/.

66. Casey Luskin, "Craig Venter in Seattle: 'Life Is a DNA Software System,'" *Evolution News and Science Today*, October 24, 2013, https://evolutionnews.org/2013/10/craig_venter_in/.

67. Maria Stitz et al., "Satellite-Like W-Elements: Repetitive, Transcribed, and Putative Mobile Genetic Factors with Potential Roles for Biology and Evolution of *Schistosoma mansoni*," *Genome Biology and Evolution* 13, no. 10 (October 2021). See also Casey Luskin, "Scientific Paper on Repetitive Elements Slams 'Junk DNA,'" *Evolution News and Science Today*, October 7, 2021, https://evolutionnews.org/2021/10/scientific-paper-on-repetitive-elements-slams-junk-dna/.

68. David Klinghoffer, "On Junk DNA Claim, Francis Collins Walks It Back, Admitting 'Hubris,'" *Evolution News and Science Today*, July 19, 2016, https://evolutionnews.org/2016/07/on_junk_dna_fra/.

69. For more information about Behe, see his website, https://michaelbehe.com/.

70. Collins, *Language of God*, 192.

71. Casey Luskin, "Study Challenges Evolutionary Relationship Between Flagellum and Type III Secretory System," *Evolution News and Science Today*, May 14, 2021, https://evolutionnews.org/2021/05/study-challenges-evolutionary-relationship-between-flagellum-and-type-iii-secretory-system/.

72. "Irreducible Complexity, Bacterial Flagellum and the Type III Secretory System," *YouTube*, June 2, 2020, video, 12:30, https://youtu.be/G581HlqXSFg?si=wSXWp320vWxSXtHB.

73. Casey Luskin, "Loss of Function in Stickleback Fish = Loss of Another Argument for 'Macroevolution' for Francis Collins," *Evolution News and Science Today*, January 12, 2009, https://evolutionnews.org/2009/01/loss_of_function_in_sticklebac/.

74. See Michael Behe, *Darwin Devolves* (New York: HarperOne, 2019); and Casey Luskin, "Vindicated but Not Cited: Paper in *Nature Heredity* Supports Michael Behe's Devolution Hypothesis," *Evolution News and Science Today*, February 16, 2021, https://evolutionnews.org/2021/02/vindicated-but-not-cited-paper-in-nature-heredity-supports-michael-behes-devolution-hypothesis/.

75. Peter Wehner, "NIH Director: 'We're on an Exponential Curve,'" *Atlantic*, March 17, 2020, https://www.theatlantic.com/ideas/archive/2020/03/interview-francis-collins-nih/608221/.

76. Collins, "Foreword" to Giberson, *Saving Darwin*, v, vii.

77. Collins, back cover blurb for Kenneth Miller, *Only a Theory: Evolution and the Battle for America's Soul* (New York: Penguin Books, 2009).

78. "The 'Evidence for Belief': An Interview with Francis Collins," *Pew Research Center*, April 17, 2008, https://www.pewresearch.org/religion/2008/04/17/the-evidence-for-belief-an-interview-with-francis-collins-2/.

79. The BioLogos Foundation, https://biologos.org/.

80. Jay Richards, ed., *God and Evolution: Protestants, Catholics, and Jews Explore Darwin's Challenge to Faith* (Seattle: Discovery Institute Press, 2010), n. 25, 334.

81. "About the BioLogos Foundation," *BioLogos*, archived September 29, 2010, https://web.archive.org/web/20100929185000/http://biologos.org/about/.

82. Francis Collins, *Faith and Reason*, PBS, date unknown, transcript accessed May 2024, http://www.pbs.org/faithandreason/transcript/coll-body.html.

83. "Report of the Creation Study Committee," *Presbyterian Church in America*, 2000, https://www.weswhite.net/wp-content/uploads/2011/05/Creation-report.pdf.

84. "Critical Breakthroughs in Christian Higher Education," *CCCU Advance*, Spring 2010, https://issuu.com/cccu/docs/cccu_advance_spring2010/28.

85. For more background about the impact of this book see the *Darwin on Trial* website, https://darwinontrial.com/.

86. William Dembski, *The Design Revolution: Answering the Toughest Questions about Intelligent Design* (Downers Grove, IL: InterVarsity Press, 2004).

87. John G. West, *Darwin Day in America: How Our Politics and Culture Have Been Dehumanized in the Name of Science* (Wilmington, DE: ISI Books, 2007), 123–162.

88. See "Why the Royal Society Meeting Mattered," *Evolution News and Science Today*, January 1, 2017, https://evolutionnews.org/2017/01/1_happy_new_yea/.

89. See, for example, Michael Denton, *Evolution: A Theory in Crisis* (Chevy Chase, MD: Adler and Adler, 1986); Michael Behe, *Darwin's Black Box: The Biochemical Challenge to Evolution* (New York: Free Press, 1996); Michael Behe, *Darwin Devolves: The New Science About DNA That Challenges Evolution* (New York: HarperOne, 2019); William Dembski, *No Free Lunch: Why Specified Complexity Cannot Be Purchased without Intelligence* (Lanham, MD: Rowman and Littlefield, 2002);

John Angus Campbell and Stephen C. Meyer, eds., *Darwinism, Design, and Public Education* (East Lansing, MI: Michigan State University Press, 2003); William A. Dembski and Michael Ruse, eds., *Debating Design: From Darwin to DNA* (New York: Cambridge University Press, 2004); Stephen Meyer, *Signature in the Cell: DNA and the Evidence for Intelligent Design* (New York: HarperOne, 2010); Stephen Meyer, *Darwin's Doubt: The Explosive Origin of Animal Life and the Case for Intelligent Design* (New York: HarperOne, 2013).

90. John West, "Scientist Says His Peer-Reviewed Research in the *Journal of Molecular Biology* 'Adds to the Case for Intelligent Design,'" *Evolution News and Views*, January 10, 2007, http://www.evolutionnews.org/2007/01/journal_of_molecular _biology_a.html. Also see Douglas D. Axe, "Estimating the Prevalence of Protein Sequences Adopting Functional Enzyme Folds," *Journal of Molecular Biology* 341, no. 5 (August 27, 2004): 1295–1315.

91. "Response from Ralph Seelke to David Hillis Regarding Testimony on Bacterial Evolution before Texas State Board of Education, January 21, 2009," *Discovery Institute*, March 23, 2009, http://www.discovery.org/a/9951; see also A. K. Gauger, S. Ebnet, P. F. Fahey, and R. Seelke, "Reductive Evolution Can Prevent Populations from Taking Simple Adaptive Paths to High Fitness," *BIO-Complexity* 2 (2010): 1–9, https://bio-complexity.org/ojs/index.php/main/article/viewFile /BIO-C.2010.2/BIO-C.2010.2.

92. The complete list of signers of the statement can be viewed at http://www.dissentfromdarwin.org.

93. Philip Skell, "Open Letter to the South Carolina Education Oversight Committee," *Discovery Institute*, January 23, 2006, http://www.discovery.org/a/3174.

94. Marcos Eberlin, *Foresight: How the Chemistry of Life Reveals Planning and Purpose* (Seattle: Discovery Institute Press, 2019).

95. David Klinghoffer, "Physicist and Nobel Laureate Brian Josephson—Intelligent Design Is 'Valid Science,'" *Evolution News and Science Today*, March 16, 2021, https://evolutionnews.org/2021/03/physicist-and-nobel-laureate-brian -josephson-intelligent-design-is-valid-science/.

96. Darrel Falk, "BioLogos and the June 2011 'Christianity Today' Editorial," *Biologos*, June 6, 2011, archived January 3, 2012, https://web.archive.org/web /20120103053148/http://biologos.org/blog/biologos-and-the-june-2011 -christianity-today-editorial.

97. Richard N. Ostling, "The Search for the Historical Adam," *Christianity Today*, June 3, 2011, https://www.christianitytoday.com/ct/2011/june/historicaladam.html.

98. For an account of how this claim was refuted, and what the science actually shows, read Casey Luskin, "Lessons from the Evangelical Debate about Adam and Eve," *Evolution News and Science Today*, November 15, 2021, https://evolutionnews.org /2021/11/lessons-from-the-evangelical-debate-about-adam-and-eve/.

99. Some background on how I am using these terms: Intelligent design is the idea that biology and the rest of nature show evidence that they were the product of a mind, not an undirected process. It starts with the data from nature and sees what inferences can be drawn from that data. Intelligent design may have religious implications, but it is not based on religious premises, and by itself will not tell you who the designer is. Creationism, on the other hand, typically starts with what the

Bible says, and then sees how the findings of science can be harmonized with the Bible's account. In America, the dominant form of creationism is "young earth creationism," which holds that the Earth was created thousands of years ago. Another variety of creationism, "old earth creationism," holds that the Earth and universe were created billions of years ago. Both forms of creationism place significant emphasis on how to interpret Genesis 1, whereas intelligent design limits its focus to what can be understood from the data of nature alone. Intelligent design falls into what historically has been known as "general revelation," the things God has revealed to all human beings through his creation and through the moral laws He has written on all people's hearts. See Romans 1:19–20 and 2:14–15.

100. See Angus J. Menuge, Brian R. Krause, and Robert J. Marks, eds., *Minding the Brain* (Seattle: Discovery Institute Press, 2023) for an in-depth discussion of why it's clear the mind is a separate entity from the brain.

3. Sexual Suicide

1. "Moral Issues," *Gallup*, accessed November 6, 2023, https://news.gallup.com /poll/1681/moral-issues.aspx.

2. Jeff Diamant, "Half of U. S. Christians Say Casual Sex between Consenting Adults Is Sometimes or Always Acceptable," *Pew Research Center*, August 31, 2020, https://www.pewresearch.org/short-reads/2020/08/31/half-of-u-s -christians-say-casual-sex-between-consenting-adults-is-sometimes-or-always -acceptable/.

3. Jess Cohen, "Bachelorette's Luke Parker Sounds Off on Controversial Hannah Brown Sex Argument," *E! News*, October 17, 2019, https://www.eonline.com /news/1083546/bachelorette-s-luke-parker-sounds-off-on-controversial-hannah -brown-sex-argument; Jodi Guglielmi, "Luke Parker Claims Bachelorette Hannah Brown Told Him She Wanted to Wait for Sex until Marriage," *People*, October 17, 2019, https://people.com/tv/the-bachelorette-luke-parker -addresses-hannah-brown-exit/.

4. Jessica Sager, "'The Bachelorette' Hannah B. Had Sex with Pete W. in Windmill Four Times, Says Elimination Was 'Really Hard,'" *Fox News*, July 30, 2019, https://www.foxnews.com/entertainment/the-bachelorette-hannah-b-pete -windmill-sex-elimination.

5. Jessica Napoli, "'Bachelorette' Star Hannah Brown Confesses She Had Sex 'in a Windmill,'" *Fox News*, July 2, 2019, https://www.foxnews.com/entertainment /hannah-brown-bachelorette-sex-windmill.

6. Napoli, "'Bachelorette' Star."

7. Dana Rose Falcone, "Bachelorette Hannah Finally Sends Luke Home after Argument about Sex: 'I Don't Owe You Anything,'" *People*, July 15, 2019, https://people.com/tv/hannah-brown-bachelorette-fantasy-suites-recap/.

8. "'Bachelorette' Hannah Brown Opens Up about the Sex Talk That Changes Everything (Exclusive)," *Entertainment Tonight* on *YouTube*, June 18, 2019, video, 2:04, https://www.youtube.com/watch?v=3KRuXwVlP30&t=89s.

9. David J. Ayers, *After the Revolution: Sex and the Single Evangelical* (Bellingham, WA: Lexham Press, 2022), 116.

10. Ayers, *After the Revolution*, 110.

11. Ayers, *After the Revolution*, 79.

12. Justin McCarthy, "Same-Sex Marriage Support Inches Up to New High of 71%," *Gallup*, June 1, 2022, https://news.gallup.com/poll/393197/same-sex-marriage -support-inches-new-high.aspx.united.

13. McCarthy, "Same-Sex Marriage Support."

14. "United Church of Christ Endorses Gay Marriage," *NBC News*, July 4, 2005, https://www.nbcnews.com/id/wbna8463741.

15. "ELCA Assembly Opens Ministry to Partnered Gay and Lesbian Lutherans," *Evangelical Lutheran Church in America*, August 21, 2009, https://www.elca.org /News-and-Events/6587.

16. Helen Regan, "Presbyterian Church Votes to Recognize Same Sex Marriage," *TIME*, March 18, 2015, https://time.com/3748485/ same-sex-marriage-presbyterian-church-vote-redefine-protestant/.

17. "United Methodist Church of the Resurrection," *Wikipedia*, accessed September 6, 2023, https://en.wikipedia.org/wiki/United_Methodist_Church_of _the_Resurrection.

18. Michael Gryboski, "Megachurch Pastor Adam Hamilton Says Christians Can Support Gay Marriage and Not Be Heretical," *The Christian Post*, July 27, 2018, https://www.christianpost.com/news/megachurch-pastor-adam-hamilton-says -christians-can-support-gay-marriage-and-not-be-heretical.html.

19. Jonathan Merritt, "Mega-Church Pastor Adam Hamilton's Scandalous Take on Scripture," *Religion News Service*, May 1, 2014, https://religionnews.com /2014/05/01/adam-hamilton-offers-scandalous-take-on-scripture/.

20. Elizabeth Dias, "How Evangelicals Are Changing Their Minds on Gay Marriage," *TIME*, January 15, 2015, https://time.com/3669024/evangelicals -gay-marriage/.

21. *The Reformation Project*, https://reformationproject.org/. For more information about the resources and money that have been devoted to changing evangelical views on homosexuality, see Chapter 8 in *Megan Basham, Shepherds for Sale: How Evangelical Leaders Traded the Truth for a Leftist Agenda* (New York: Broadside Books, 2024).

22. Alex Murashko, "'Evangelicals for Marriage Equality' Launch Draws Harsh Criticism: No Coherent Argument Made That Supports Same-Sex Marriage," *The Christian Post*, September 12, 2014, https://www.christianpost.com/news /evangelicals-for-marriage-equality-launch-draws-harsh-criticism-no-coherent -argument-made-that-supports-same-sex-marriage-126224/.

23. Albert Mohler, "Is the Megachurch the New Liberalism?," *Albert Mohler*, May 1, 2012, https://albertmohler.com/2012/05/01/is-the-megachurch-the -new-liberalism.

24. Sarah Eekhoff Zylstra, "Andy Stanley Sermon Illustration on Homosexuality Prompts Backlash," *Christianity Today*, May 3, 2012, https://www.christianity today.com/ct/2012/mayweb-only/andy-stanley-homosexuality.html.

25. Michael Gryboski, "Andy Stanley: Churches Should Be 'Safest Place on the Planet' for Gay Youth," *The Christian Post*, April 18, 2015, https://www.christianpost.

com/news/andy-stanley-churches-should-be-safest-place-on-the-planet-for-gay
-youth.html.

26. "Manhattan Declaration," November 20, 2009, https://www.manhattandeclaration
.org/.

27. David and Tim Bayly, "Tim Keller on Preaching about Homosexuality," *Bayly Blog*, April 6, 2010, http://www.baylyblog.com/blog/2010/04/tim-keller
-preaching-about-homosexuality-ummmm-it%E2%80%99s-just-it
%E2%80%99s-just-think-about-you-know. The audio of the exchange can be found here: http://www.baylyblog.com/sites/baylyblog.com/files/baylyblog
/keller-on-homosexuality.mp3. It should be noted that Keller did briefly review two books about same-sex relationships for his church newsletter in 2013. Tim Keller, "Christianity and Homosexuality: A Review of Books," *Redeemer Report*, October 2013, https://www.redeemer.com/redeemer-report/article/christianity
_and_homosexuality_a_review_of_books. He also published a short commentary on Romans 1–7 in 2014 that affirmed the view that "homosexuality is... *a* sin." (Emphasis by Keller.) But Keller in the same commentary seemed to downplay its seriousness and caricature those who held to the traditional view. Describing those who are unloving and self-righteous toward homosexuals, he stated: "We might characterize this as a 'conservative' approach." Timothy Keller, *Romans 1–7 For You* (Charlotte, NC: The Good Book Company, 2014), Kindle, 35.

28. Robert A. J. Gagnon, "Rev. Tim Keller's Disappointing Comments on Homosexuality (with Postscript)," *Robert Gagnon*, September 14, 2012, http://www.robgagnon.net/TimKellerHomosexuality.htm.

29. Jon Ward, "Evangelicals Face Growing Tension Between Political and Personal Views of Gay Marriage," *HuffPost*, last modified March 27, 2013, https://www
.huffpost.com/entry/evangelicals-gay-marriage_n_2956917. A later printed tran-
script provided slightly different wording of Keller's statement ("you *could* believe homosexuality is a sin..."), but Keller himself accepted as accurate the quote the way it was initially published. For the later transcript, see "Dr. Timothy Keller at the March 2013 Faith Angle Forum," *Ethics & Public Policy Center*, April 18, 2013, https://eppc.org/publication/dr-timothy-keller-at-the-march-2013-faith
-angle-forum/.

30. Ward, "Evangelicals Face Growing Tension."

31. Tim Keller, "Keller Clarifies Position on Same-Sex Marriage," *Gospel Coalition*, March 29, 2013, https://www.thegospelcoalition.org/article/keller-clarifies
-position-on-same-sex-marriage/.

32. "President Jimmy Carter Authors New Bible Book, Answers Hard Biblical Questions," *HuffPost*, March 19, 2012, https://www.huffpost.com/entry/president
-jimmy-carter-bible-book_n_1349570.

33. Emily Birnbaum, "Jimmy Carter: 'I Believe That Jesus Would Approve of Gay Marriage,'" *The Hill*, July 9, 2018, https://thehill.com/homenews/
news/396058-jimmy-carter-i-believe-that-jesus-would-approve-of-gay-marriage/.

34. Mark 10: 4–9 and Matthew 19: 4–6. Jesus said this in the context of a conversa-
tion about divorce. The "one flesh" point refers to male and female biology, making the point that God created our bodies to function a certain way sexually. As one commentator further notes, "In Mark 7:21–23, Jesus says, 'For it is from within,

out of a person's heart, that evil thoughts come—sexual immorality, theft, murder, adultery... all these evils come from inside and defile a person.' The Greek word translated 'sexual immorality' is *porneia*, which is a term that includes many sexual sins, including homosexuality. First century Jews who heard that word would think of the sexual sins listed in the Mosaic Law, which includes homosexual sex." Alan Shlemon, "Jesus Didn't Say Anything about Homosexuality," *Stand to Reason*, March 5, 2013, https://www.str.org/w/jesus-didn-t-say-anything -about-homosexuality.

35. Daniel James Devine, "The Kids Are Not All Right," *WORLD*, March 21, 2015, https://wng.org/articles/the-kids-are-not-all-right-1617327222. For studies, see Daniel James Devine, "Study: Same-Sex Parents Just Aren't the Same," *WORLD*, February 17, 2015, https://wng.org/sift/study-same-sex-parents-just-arent-the -same-1617408989; and Daniel James Devine, "Depression and Same-Sex Parenting," *WORLD*, July 5, 2016, https://wng.org/sift/depression-and-same-sex -parenting-1617407758.

36. Andrew Garber, "Historic Senate Vote Clears Way for Gay Marriage in State," *Seattle Times*, updated February 2, 2012, https://www.seattletimes.com/seattle -news/historic-senate-vote-clears-way-for-gay-marriage-in-state/; Nicole Nerou- lias, "Washington State Senate Passes Gay Marriage Bill," *Reuters*, February 1, 2012, https://www.reuters.com/article/us-gay-marriage-washington -idUSTRE81109E20120202.

37. Cheryl Pflug, "Curriculum Vitae," *Senator Cheryl Pflug*, archived October 29, 2013, https://web.archive.org/web/20131029121933/http://pflug.com /curriculum-vitae/.

38. Mark Joseph Stern, "There Have Been No Direct Threats, I'm Delighted to Say," *Slate*, May 30, 2014, https://slate.com/news-and-politics/2014/05/meet-judge -john-jones-who-brought-marriage-equality-to-pennsylvania.html; "Judge Jones Interviewed by *The Lutheran*," *National Center for Science Education*, October 11, 2006, https://ncse.ngo/judge-jones-interviewed-lutheran; Mark A. Staples, "'Not Science': Judge John E. Jones," *Lutheran*, October 2006, 19–21.

39. Justice Antonin Scalia, dissenting opinion, *Obergefell v. Hodges* (2015), https://supreme.justia.com/cases/federal/us/576/14-556/.

40. Danielle Burton, "10 Things You Didn't Know About Anthony Kennedy," *U. S. News & World Report*, October 1, 2007, https://www.usnews.com/news/national /articles/2007/10/01/10-things-you-didnt-know-about-anthony-kennedy.

41. Jeffrey Toobin, *The Nine: Inside the Secret World of the Supreme Court* (New York: Anchor Books, 2008), 62–63.

42. Tim Keller, "The Bible and Same Sex Relationships: A Review Article," *Redeemer Report*, June 2015, 1, 4–8.

43. Brianna Herlihy, "Respect for Marriage Act Passes the House, Heads to Biden's Desk," *Fox News*, December 8, 2022, https://www.foxnews.com/politics/respect -marriage-act-passes-house-heads-bidens-desk.

44. Carl Esbeck, "Everything You Need to Know About the Respect for Marriage Act," *Christianity Today*, November 17, 2022, https://www.christianitytoday.com /ct/2022/november-web-only/same-sex-marriage-religious-liberty-respect -marriage-act.html.

45. Timothy Dalrymple, "Is It Time for Evangelicals to Stop Opposing Gay Marriage?" *Patheos*, November 26, 2012, https://www.patheos.com/blogs /philosophicalfragments/2012/11/26/is-it-time-for-evangelicals-to-stop -opposing-gay-marriage/.

46. Megan Basham, "When Christian Leaders Capitulate on Marriage, Innocent Children Suffer," *Federalist*, November 28, 2022, https://thefederalist.com /2022/11/28/when-christian-leaders-capitulate-on-marriage-innocent -children-suffer/. You can read Dalrymple's explanation for why he attended a same-sex wedding in Gabriel Hughes, "What Does *Christianity Today* Believe the Bible Says about LGBTQ," *Pastor Gabe*, February 13, 2023, https://themajestysmen.com/pastorgabe/whatdoeschristianitytodaybelieve/.

47. David French, "An Open Letter to Those Who Think I've Lost My Christian Faith," *Dispatch*, November 23, 2022, https://thedispatch.com/newsletter /frenchpress/an-open-letter-to-those-who-think-ive-lost-my-christian-faith/.

48. David French, "Why I Changed My Mind About Law and Marriage, Again," *Dispatch*, November 20, 2022, https://thedispatch.com/newsletter/frenchpress /why-i-changed-my-mind-about-law-and-marriage-again/.

49. Alistair Begg and Bob Lepine, "'The Christian Manifesto' Interview," *Truth for Life*, September 1, 2023, https://www.truthforlife.org/resources/sermon/christian -manifesto-interview/.

50. Alistair Begg, "Compassion vs. Condemnation," *YouTube*, January 29, 2024, video, 46:58, https://www.youtube.com/watch?v=t2bmFuA40T4&t=1s.

51. David Clyde Jones, "The Westminster Confession on Divorce and Remarriage," *Covenant Seminary Review* 16 (Spring 1990): 31.

52. Barton Gingerich, "The Millennial Generation's Acceptable Sin," *Gospel Coalition*, January 7, 2013, https://www.thegospelcoalition.org/article/ the-millennial-generations-acceptable-sin/.

53. Charles Darwin, *The Descent of Man, and Selection in Relation to Sex* (Princeton: Princeton University Press, 1981; reprint of the original first edition in 1871), vol. 2:362. Also see discussion in West, *Darwin's Conservatives: The Misguided Quest* (Seattle: Discovery Institute Press, 2006), 19–32; and West, *Darwin Day in America: How Our Politics and Culture Have Been Dehumanized in the Name of Science* (Wilmington, DE: ISI Books, 2007), 23–42.

54. John G. West, *Darwin's Corrosive Idea: The Impact of Evolution on Attitudes about Faith, Ethics, and Human Uniqueness* (Seattle: Discovery Institute, 2016), 10.

55. Darwin, *The Descent of Man*, 2:358–359.

56. Alfred C. Kinsey, Wardell B. Pomeroy, and Clyde E. Martin, *Sexual Behavior in the Human Male* (Philadelphia: W. B. Saunders Co., 1948).

57. James Jones, *Alfred C. Kinsey: A Public/Private Life* (New York: W.W. Norton, 1997), 534–600.

58. Kinsey, *Sexual Behavior in the Human Male*, 667.

59. Kinsey, *Sexual Behavior in the Human Male*, 669.

60. Kinsey, *Sexual Behavior in the Human Male*, 589.

61. Kinsey, *Sexual Behavior in the Human Male*, 222.

62. Alfred C. Kinsey, Wardell B. Pomeroy, Clyde E. Martin, and Paul H. Gebhard, *Sexual Behavior in the Human Female* (Philadelphia: W.B. Saunders Co., 1953), 121.

63. Kinsey, *Sexual Behavior in the Human Male*, 592.

64. Kinsey, *Sexual Behavior in the Human Male*, 589.

65. West, *Darwin Day in America*, 276.

66. Kinsey, *Sexual Behavior in the Human Male*, 263.

67. Kinsey, *Sexual Behavior in the Human Female*, 10.

68. Kinsey, *Sexual Behavior in the Human Female*, 8.

69. See discussion of Kinsey's influence on public policy in West, *Darwin Day in America*, 277–278, 288–310.

70. West, *Darwin Day in America*, 280–281.

71. West, *Darwin Day in America*, 281–282.

72. West, *Darwin Day in America*, 282–283.

73. West, *Darwin Day in America*, 291–321.

74. Herb Seal, "Cross Cultural Sexual Practices," in Kirkendall and Whitehurst, *The New Sexual Revolution*, 21.

75. Albert Ellis, "A Rational Sexual Morality," in Kirkendall and Whitehurst, *The New Sexual Revolution*, 53.

76. Rustum and Della Roy, "Is Monogamy Outdated?," in Kirkendall and Whitehurst, *The New Sexual Revolution*,142–143.

77. Lorna Brown, ed., *Sex Education in the Eighties: The Challenge of Healthy Sexual Evolution* (New York: Plenum Press, 1981).

78. Floyd Martinson, "The Sex Education of Young Children," in Brown, *Sex Education in the Eighties*, 63–71.

79. Martinson, "The Sex Education of Young Children," 67.

80. Martinson, "The Sex Education of Young Children," 69.

81. Martinson, "The Sex Education of Young Children," 70.

82. Steve Waldhauser, "'Songs of Thy Triumph': A Short History of Gustavus Adolphus College," *Gustavus Adolphus College*, https://gustavus.edu/about /campushistory.pdf, 14.

83. Ira L. Reiss, "In Memory of Floyd Martinson," *The Journal of Sex Research* 37, no. 4 (2000): 391, https://www.tandfonline.com/doi/abs/10.1080/00224490009552063.

84. Floyd M. Martinson, "Pioneer Research in Childhood Sexuality," in *How I Got Into Sex*, eds. Bonnie Bullough et al. (Amherst, NY: Prometheus, 1997), https://www.ipce.info/booksreborn/martinson/articles/1997_pioneer.html.

85. West, *Darwin Day in America*, 310–312.

86. "True Love Waits," *Lifeway*, accessed May 2024, https://www.lifeway.com/en /product-family/true-love-waits; "True Love Waits—History," *Lifeway*, accessed May 2024, https://www.lifeway.com/en/product-family/true-love-waits/history.

87. West, *Darwin Day in America*, 312–321.

88. Joe Carter, "The FAQs: What You Should Know About Purity Culture," *Gospel Coalition*, July 24, 2019, https://www.thegospelcoalition.org/article/faqs-know -purity-culture/.

89. Brandon Robertson, "It's Time to Embrace a Sex-Positive Christianity," *Nomad Notes*, December 28, 2022, https://nomadnotes.substack.com/p/its-time-to-embrace-a-sex-positive.

90. Aili Nahas, "Bachelorette Hannah Brown: People Questioned My Faith After I Revealed I Had Sex on the Show," *People*, August 1, 2019, https://people.com/tv/bachelorette-hannah-brown-on-sex-intimacy-faith/.

91. Patrick S. Cheng, *From Sin to Amazing Grace: Discovering the Queer Christ* (New York: Seabury Books, 2012).

92. "Supporting Transgender and Gender Non-Binary Students" with Samantha King (event on January 20, 2022), email announcement sent by Seattle Pacific University School of Education, December 17, 2021.

93. Aubrey Rhoadarmer, "Letter of Exhortation Asked Board to Maintain Debated Hiring Policy," *Falcon*, April 29, 2021, https://thefalcon.seapacmedia.com/10497/news/letter-of-exhortation-asked-board-to-maintain-debated-hiring-policy/.

94. Casey Kuhn, "Grand Canyon University to Provide Same-Sex Marriage Benefits," *Fronteras*, November 13, 2015, https://fronterasdesk.org/content/219905/grand-canyon-university-provide-same-sex-marriage-benefits; "Grand Canyon University Statement on Same-Sex Marriage Employee Benefits," *GCU News*, November 24, 2015, https://news.gcu.edu/gcu-news/same-sex-marriage-employee-benefits-2/.

95. Morgan Lee, "Azusa Pacific Drops Ban on Same-Sex Student Relationships, Again," *Christianity Today*, March 19, 2019, https://www.christianitytoday.com/news/2019/march/azusa-pacific-university-apu-reversal-gay-relationships.html; Emily Jones, "Christian University, Azusa Pacific, Lifts Ban on LGBTQ Relationships—Again," CBN, March 21, 2019, https://www2.cbn.com/news/us/christian-university-azusa-pacific-lifts-ban-lgbtq-relationships-again; Morgan Lee, "Azusa Pacific Okays Gay Romance (But Not Sex and Marriage), *Christianity Today*, September 25, 2018, https://www.christianitytoday.com/2018/09/azusa-pacific-university-lgbt-sexuality-statement-apu/.

96. Deepa Bharath, "California Evangelical Seminary Ponders Changes That Would Make It More Welcoming to LGBTQ Students," Associated Press, May 27, 2024, https://apnews.com/article/evangelical-seminary-lgbtq-samesex-marriage-10f734487e3097055ae3052d75618f06; Christopher B. Hays and Richard B. Hays, *The Widening of God's Mercy: Sexuality within the Biblical Story* (New Haven: Yale University Press, 2024), 2, 7–8. For a critical review of the book by Hays and Hays, see Thomas Schreiner, "A Review of 'The Widening of God's Mercy: Sexuality within the Biblical Story' by Christopher B. Hays and Richard B. Hays," CBMW.org, August 28, 2024, https://cbmw.org/2024/08/28/a-review-of-the-widening-of-gods-mercy-sexuality-within-the-biblical-story-by-christopher-b-hays-and-richard-b-hays/.

97. Yonat Shimron, "Calvin University Board Votes to Keep Faculty Who Disagree with Stand on Sex," *Religion News Service*, November 2, 2022, https://religionnews.com/2022/11/02/calvin-university-board-votes-to-keep-faculty-who-disagree-with-stand-on-sex/.

98. Jack Hobbs, "We Met Working at Walmart and Cheated on Our Spouses—You Should Follow Your Heart," *New York Post*, updated January 5, 2023,

https://nypost.com/2023/01/03/we-met-working-at-walmart-and-cheated
-on-our-spouses-you-should-follow-your-heart/.

99. Of course, there are many ways to show love to a gay couple without celebrating
something we know to be wrong. As Christian writer Bethel McGrew points out,
"We can be available when they're in need, give them gifts for other occasions, and
celebrate other milestones or worthy achievements that aren't bound up with their
sin." See Bethel McGrew, "Matching Actions and Words," *WORLD*, January 26,
2024, https://wng.org/opinions/matching-actions-and-words-1706229116.

100. Advocates for Youth, "How High Is the Risk for STDs? Answer Key," undated pdf.

101. Andrew Solomon, "How Polyamorists and Polygamists Are Challenging Family
Norms," *New Yorker*, March 15, 2021, https://www.newyorker.com/magazine
/2021/03/22/how-polyamorists-and-polygamists-are-challenging-family-norms.

102. Nicole Russell, "The Left's Appalling Efforts to 'Normalize' Pedophilia," *Daily
Signal*, November 18, 2021, https://www.dailysignal.com/2021/11/18/the-lefts
-appalling-efforts-to-normalize-pedophilia/.

103. Robert Knight, "'Drag Queen Story Hour' Shows What's Gone Wrong in America," *Washington Times,* October 11, 2019, https://www.washingtontimes.com/
news/2019/oct/11/drag-queen-story-hour-shows-whats-gone-wrong-in-am/; John
Stonestreet, "The Trans Sexualization of Our Children Has Begun," *Christian
Post*, December 30, 2019, https://www.christianpost.com/votice/the-trans
-sexualization-of-our-children-has-begun.html.

104. Jen Christensen, "Gender-Affirming Surgeries in US Nearly Tripled From 2016
to 2019, Study Finds," *CNN*, August 23, 2023, https://www.cnn.com
/2023/08/23/health/gender-affirming-surgery-study/index.html; Tyler O'Neil,
"THOUSANDS of Minors Went Under the Knife to 'Affirm' a Trans Identity,
Study Shows," *Daily Signal,* September 1, 2023, https://www.dailysignal.com
/2023/09/01/exposed-more-3500-minors-underwent-transgender-surgeries
-5-years-study-says/.

105. Jeffrey M. Jones, "LGBT Identification in U. S. Ticks Up to 7.1%," *Gallup*,
February 17, 2022, https://news.gallup.com/poll/389792/lgbt-identification
-ticks-up.aspx.

106. Margaret Peppiatt, "Almost 40 Percent of Students Identify as LGBTQ at
Liberal Arts Colleges: Survey," *College Fix*, December 16, 2022, https://www
.thecollegefix.com/almost-40-percent-of-students-identify-as-lgbtq-at-liberal-arts
-colleges-survey/.

107. Jones, "LGBT Identification."

108. Jones, "LGBT Identification."

109. "Francis Collins Won't Say CDC's Pro-Trans 'Pregnant People' Language Is Untrue Or Unscientific," *YouTube*, September 20, 2021, video, 3:46, https://youtu.be
/sI0ymYgkNS8?si=dmqb6Xu38Q3KdRdN.

110. "Pregnant and Recently Pregnant People," *Centers for Disease Control and Preven-
tion*, updated October 25, 2022, https://www.cdc.gov/coronavirus/2019-ncov
/need-extra-precautions/pregnant-people.html.

111. Here is a longer quote with more context: "the fact that a person can get a room in
a library and hold a Drag Queen Story Hour and get people to come? That's one of

the blessings of liberty." David French, quoted in Benjamin Wallace-Wells, "David French, Sohrab Ahmari, and the Battle for the Future of Conservatism," *New Yorker*, September 12, 2019, https://web.archive.org/web/20230630143820 /https://www.newyorker.com/news/the-political-scene/david-french-sohrab -ahmari-and-the-battle-for-the-future-of-conservatism.

112. David French, "Viewpoint Neutrality Protects Both Drag Queens and Millions of American Christians," *National Review*, September 9, 2012, https://www .nationalreview.com/corner/viewpoint-neutrality-protects-drag-queens-and -millions-american-christians/.

113. Glenn T. Stanton, "The Health Benefits of Marriage," *Focus on the Family*, October 8, 2012, https://www.focusonthefamily.com/marriage/the-health-benefits-of -marriage/; Linda J. Waite and Maggie Gallagher, *The Case for Marriage: Why Married People Are Happier, Healthier, and Better Off Financially* (New York: Doubleday, 2000); Robert Lerman, "Effects of Marriage on Family Economic Well-Being," US Department of Health and Human Services: Office of the Assistant Secretary for Planning and Evaluation, June 30, 2002, https://aspe.hhs.gov /reports/effects-marriage-family-economic-well-being.

114. "Sexual Activity," *Sex & Unexpected Pregnancies: What Evangelical Millennials Think & Practice*, National Association of Evangelicals/Grey Matter Research, May 2012, https://www.nae.org/wp-content/uploads/2015/05/Data-Sheet-1 _Sexual-Activity.pdf.

115. "Religious Engagement & Sexual Activity," *Sex & Unexpected Pregnancies: What Evangelical Millennials Think & Practice*, National Association of Evangelicals /Grey Matter Research, May 2012, https://www.nae.org/wp-content/uploads /2015/05/Data-Sheet-3_Religious-Engagement-and-Sexual-Activity.pdf.

116. Ayers, Figure 5-1, *After the Revolution*, 131.

117. Ayers, Figure 5-1, *After the Revolution*, 131.

118. Ayers, Figure 6-3, *After the Revolution*, 175.

119. Ayers, *After the Revolution*, 184.

120. Ritch C. Savin-Williams and Kara Joyner, "The Dubious Assessment of Gay, Lesbian, and Bisexual Adolescents of Add Health," *Archives of Sexual Behavior* 43, no. 3 (April 2014): 416.

121. Savin-Williams and Joyner, "The Dubious Assessment." For a critique, see Gu Li, Sabra Katz-Wise, and Jerel Calzo, "The Unjustified Doubt of Add Health Studies on the Health Disparities of Non-Heterosexual Adolescents: Comment on Savin-Williams and Joyner (2014)," *Archives of Sexual Behavior* 43, no. 6 (August 1, 2014): 1023–26.

122. See discussion in "Can Sexual Orientation Change?," chapter 12 in Neil Whitehead and Briar Whitehead, *My Genes Made Me Do It! Homosexuality and the Scientific Evidence*, 3rd ed. (Whitehead Associates, October 2013), archived at https://web.archive.org/web/20161220102909/http://www.mygenes.co.nz/PDFs /Ch12.pdf.

123. "Lisa Diamond on Sexual Fluidity of Men and Women," *YouTube*, December 6, 2013, video, 44:26, youtu.be/m2rTHDOuUBw. The comment quoted is at 43:15.

124. Pien Rawee, Judith G. M. Rosmalen, Luuk Kalverdijk, and Sarah M. Burke, "Development of Gender Non-Contentedness During Adolescence and Early

Adulthood," *Archives of Sexual Behavior* (February 27, 2024), https://doi.org /10.1007/s10508-024-02817-5.

125. "Treatment: Gender Dysphoria," *National Health Service* (United Kingdom), accessed September 6, 2023, https://www.nhs.uk/conditions/gender-dysphoria /treatment/.

126. Jon Brown, "Multiple States Crack Down on Transgender Treatments for Minors Amid Growing Legal Debate," *Fox News*, December 8, 2022, https://www .foxnews.com/us/multiple-states-crack-down-transgender-treatments-minors -growing-legal-debate; "Doubts Are Growing about Therapy for Gender-Dysphoric Children," *The Economist*, May 13, 2021, https://www.economist.com /science-and-technology/2021/05/13/doubts-are-growing-about-therapy-for -gender-dysphoric-children; Jamie Reed, "I Thought I Was Saving Kids. Now I'm Blowing the Whistle," *The Free Press*, February 9, 2023, https://www.thefp.com /p/i-thought-i-was-saving-trans-kids.

4. Rebuilding the Walls of Hostility

1. "George Floyd Death: Last Two Ex-Officers Sentenced to Prison," *BBC*, July 27, 2022, https://www.bbc.com/news/world-us-canada-62321191.

2. Jack Cashill, "Chauvin Did Not Murder George Floyd: And Prosecutors Knew It," *American Spectator*, October 22, 2023, https://spectator.org/chauvin-did-not -murder-george-floyd/. For a contrary view, see Saranac Hale Spencer, "No Change in George Floyd's Cause of Death, Despite Viral False Claims," *FactCheck*, November 6, 2023, https://www.factcheck.org/2023/11/no-change -in-george-floyds-cause-of-death-despite-viral-false-claims/.

3. Maya Rao, "Riots, Arson Leave Minnesota Communities of Color Devastated," *Minneapolis Star-Tribune*, June 2, 2020, https://www.startribune.com/riots -arson-leave-minnesota-communities-of-color-devastated/570921492/.

4. Robin DiAngelo, *White Fragility: Why It's So Hard for White People to Talk about Racism* (Boston: Beacon Press, 2018); Latasha Morrison, *Be the Bridge: Pursuing God's Heart for Racial Reconciliation* (Colorado Springs: Waterbrook, 2019); Jemar Tisby, *The Color of Compromise: The Truth about the American Church's Complicity in Racism*, ePub edition (Grand Rapids: Zondervan, 2018).

5. DiAngelo, *White Fragility*, 142–143.

6. DiAngelo, *White Fragility*, 127.

7. DiAngelo, *White Fragility*, 50.

8. "Ibram Kendi: "Antiracists Fundamentally Reject 'Savior Theology' and Embrace Liberation Theology," *YouTube*, March 23, 2021, video, 3:01, https://www.youtube .com/watch?v=azJh4N69Q5k.

9. James H. Cone, *A Black Theology of Liberation: Fiftieth Anniversary Edition* (Maryknoll, NY: Orbis Books, 2020), 26.

10. James H. Cone, *God of the Oppressed*, rev. ed. (Maryknoll, NY: Orbis Books, 2019), xi.

11. Cone, *Black Theology of Liberation*, 33.

12. Cone, *God of the Oppressed*, xi.

13. Cone, *God of the Oppressed*, xii.

14. Cone, *God of the Oppressed*, xv.

15. Sean Moran, "Raphael Warnock Mentored by Radical Theologian James Cone, Who Railed Against "Satanic Whiteness," *Breitbart*, November 13, 2020, https://www.breitbart.com/faith/2020/11/13/raphael-warnock-mentored-by -radical-theologian-james-cone-who-railed-against-satanic-whiteness/.

16. Aidan McLaughlin, "Sen. Raphael Warnock Deletes Easter Tweet After Being Accused of 'Heresy,'" *Mediate*, April 4, 2021, https://www.mediaite.com/politics /sen-raphael-warnock-deletes-easter-tweet-after-being-accused-of-heresy/.

17. DiAngelo, *White Fragility*, 143.

18. DiAngelo, *White Fragility*, 149.

19. DiAngelo, *White Fragility*, 150.

20. "Whiteness 101: Foundational Principles Every White Bridge Builder Needs to Understand," *Be the Bridge*, 2017, https://static1.squarespace.com/ static/558850fde4b0892e071e7960/t/5a7b4ea9e2c483ccb42b 9a73/1518030506168/BetheBridge.pdf, 17–18.

21. *Human Zoos: America's Forgotten History of Scientific Racism* (Seattle: Discovery Institute, 2018), available at https://humanzoos.org/.

22. Nate Dimeo, "Olympic-Sized Racism," *Slate*, August 21, 2008, https://slate.com /culture/2008/08/remembering-the-anthropology-days-at-the-1904-olympics.html.

23. "Pygmies May Be the Missing Link," *St. Louis Republic*, July 10, 1904, https://tile.loc.gov/storage-services/service/ndnp/mohi/batch_mohi_ingalls _ver01/data/sn84020274/00294559747/1904071001/0188.pdf.

24. "Pygmy in the Monkey House," *HumanZoos*, accessed May 2024, https://humanzoos.org/category/explore/pygmy-in-the-monkey-house/.

25. "Man and Monkey Show Disapproved by Clergy," *New York Times*, September 10, 1906, https://humanzoos.org/wp-content/uploads/sites/18/2018/01 /manandmonknyt091006.pdf.

26. "Negro Clergy Protest," *New-York Daily Tribune*, September 11, 1906, https://tile.loc.gov/storage-services/service/ndnp/dlc/batch_dlc_liberia _ver01/data/sn83030214/00175041473/1906091101/0251.pdf.

27. "Topics of the Times: Send Him Back to the Woods," *New York Times*, September 11, 1906, https://humanzoos.org/wp-content/uploads/sites/18/2018/01 /sendhimnyt091106.pdf.

28. "Topics of the Times: The Pygmy Is Not the Point," *New York Times*, September 12, 1906, https://humanzoos.org/wp-content/uploads/sites/18/2018/01 /pigmynotpointnyt091206.pdf.

29. Charles Darwin, *The Descent of Man, and Selection in Relation to Sex* (London: John Murray, 1871), vol. 1, 201, available online, http://darwin-online.org.uk/content /frameset?keywords=the%20or%20and%20between%20negro%20australian%20 gorilla&pageseq=214&itemID=F937.1&viewtype=text.

30. Darwin, *The Descent of Man*, 110, http://darwin-online.org.uk/content/frameset? keywords=of%20distinct%20men%20races&pageseq=123&itemID=F937.1&vie wtype=text.

31. Olufemi Oluniyi, *Darwin Comes to Africa: Social Darwinism and British Imperial-ism in Northern* Nigeria (Seattle: Discovery Institute Press, 2023), 24.

32. Stephen Jay Gould, *Ontogeny and Phylogeny* (Cambridge, MA: Belknap Press/ Harvard University Press, 1977), 127.

33. Haley A. Branch, Amanda N. Klingler, et al., "Discussions of the 'Not So Fit': How Ableism Limits Diverse Thought and Investigative Potential in Evolutionary Biology," *The American Naturalist* 200, no. 1 (July 2022), https://doi. org/10.1086/720003, 101.

34. "Most Horrible: Details of the Burning at the Stake of the Holberts," *Vicksburg Evening Post*, February 13, 1904, https://www.newspapers.com/image /194307712, 4; also see "Mob Vengeance in the Delta: Negro Man and Woman Burned at the Stake," *The Leader* (Brookhaven, MS), February 10, 1904, https://www.newspapers.com/image/854365958, 2.

35. Justin Taylor, "Is Segregation Scriptural? A Radio Address from Bob Jones on Easter of 1960," *The Gospel Coalition*, July 26, 2016, https://www.thegospel coalition.org/blogs/evangelical-history/is-segregation-scriptural-a-radio-address -from-bob-jones-on-easter-of-1960/.

36. Sylvester Jacobs with Linette Martin, *Born Black* (London: Hodder and Stough-ton, 1977), 66–67.

37. Jacobs, *Born Black*, 69.

38. Jacobs, *Born Black*, 70.

39. Jacobs, *Born Black*, 68–69.

40. Jacobs, *Born Black*, 70.

41. Jacobs, *Born Black*, 69.

42. "Madison Grant and the American Nation," *Radix Journal*, October 8, 2016, https://radixjournal.altright. com/2016/10/2016-10-6-madison-grant-and-the-american-nation/.

43. Brian Resnick, "Psychologists Surveyed Hundreds of Alt-Right Supporters. The Results Are Unsettling," *Vox*, August 12, 2018, https://www.vox.com/science -and-health/2017/8/15/16144070/psychology-alt-right-unite-the-right.

44. Quoted in David Klinghoffer, "James von Brunn, Evolutionist," *Kingdom of Priests*, June 2009, https://www.beliefnet.com/columnists/kingdomofpriests/2009/06 /james-von-brunn-evolutionist.html.

45. Quoted in John G. West, "How Science Fueled the White Supremacist Mass Murderer in Buffalo, NY," *Evolution News and Science Today*, May 16, 2022, https://evolutionnews.org/2022/05/ how-science-fueled-the-white-supremacist-mass-murderer-in-buffalo-ny/.

46. Thomas Achord and Darrell Dow, eds., *Who Is My Neighbor? An Anthology in Natural Relations*, ebook (Thomas Achord, 2021).

47. Rod Dreher, "Thomas Achord Confesses," *American Conservative*, November 28, 2022, https://www.theamericanconservative.com/thomas-achord-confesses/.

48. @TuliusAadland, *Twitter*, March 11, 2020, reprinted in Alastair Roberts, "On Thomas Achord," *Alastair's Adversaria*, November 27, 2022, https://alastairadversaria.com/2022/11/27/the-case-against-thomas-achord/.

49. @TuliusAadland, *Twitter*, June 7, 2020, reprinted in Roberts, "On Thomas Achord."

50. Tisby, *Color of Compromise*, 42.

51. "The Northwest Ordinance (1787)," *National Constitution Center*, https://constitutioncenter.org/the-constitution/historic-document-library /detail/the-northwest-ordinance.

52. Anson Phelps Stokes, *Church and State in the United States* (New York: Harper and Brothers, 1950), 2:121.

53. Stokes, *Church and State*, 2:123–124

54. Stokes, *Church and State*, 2:123.

55. Stokes, *Church and State*, 2:133–156.

56. Samuel Stanhope Smith, *The Lectures, Corrected and Improved, Which Have Been Delivered for a Series of Years, in the College of New Jersey; on the Subjects of Moral and Political Philosophy* (Trenton, NJ: Daniel Fenton, 1812), 2: 171–176.

57. John G. West, Jr., *The Politics of Revelation and Reason: Religion and Civic Life in the New Nation* (Lawrence, KS: University Press of Kansas, 1996), 112n64, 252–253.

58. Bertram Wyatt-Brown, *Lewis Tappan and the Evangelical War Against Slavery* (Cleveland: Press of Case Western Reserve University, 1969).

59. Tisby, *The Color of Compromise*, 71.

60. Thomas Livermore, *Numbers and Losses in the Civil War in America, 1861–65* (Boston: Houghton, Mifflin and Co., 1900), 9, 47–48.

61. Stokes, *Church and State*, 2:158–174.

62. "Income in the United States: 2022," *US Census Bureau*, September 21, 2023, Table A-1, "Income Summary Measures by Selected Characteristics: 2021 and 2022," https://www.census.gov/library/publications/2023/demo/p60-279.html.

63. "Selected Population Profile in the United States, American Community Survey, ACS 1-Year Estimates Selected Population Profiles," *US Census Bureau*, accessed August 16, 2024, Table S0201, 2022.

64. "Selected Population Profile in the United States," Table S0201, comparing "White alone" and "Nigerian," https://data.census.gov/table?q=S0201%20 nigerian&t=002:Income%20(Households,%20Families,%20Individuals)&y=2022.

65. Jordan Boyd, "Smithsonian Pushes Racist Material Claiming 'White Culture' Is 'Nuclear Family,' 'Self-Reliance,' Being 'Polite,'" *Federalist*, July 15, 2020, https://thefederalist.com/2020/07/15/smithsonian-pushes-racist-material -claiming-white-culture-is-nuclear-family-self-reliance-being-polite/.

66. Glenn Loury, Ian Rowe, and Robert Woodson, "Not Buying It: Glenn Loury, Ian Rowe, and Robert Woodson Debunk Myths about the Black Experience in America," interview by Peter Robinson at the Old Parkland Conference, Dallas, TX, May 13, 2022, posted on *YouTube*, July 25, 2022, video, 58:51, https://www .youtube.com/watch?v=hIiyIEyUxu8&t=13s.

67. Historical Statistics of the United States: Colonial Times to 1970, part 1 (Washington, DC: US Bureau of the Census, 1975), 382.

68. Thomas Sowell, "A Legacy of Liberalism," *Creators*, November 18, 2014, https://www.creators.com/read/thomas-sowell/11/14/a-legacy-of-liberalism.

69. "1921 Tulsa Massacre," *Tulsa History*, accessed May 8, 2024, https://www
    .tulsahistory.org/exhibit/1921-tulsa-race-massacre/.

70. Carlos Moreno, "Decades After the Tulsa Race Massacre, Urban 'Renewal'
    Sparked Black Wall Street's Second Destruction," *Smithsonian Magazine*, June 2,
    2021, https://www.smithsonianmag.com/history/
    black-wall-streets-second-destruction-180977871/.

71. Jemar Tisby, "An Open Letter to the Board of Trustees at Grove City College,"
    Footnotes by Jemar Tisby, May 18, 2022, https://jemartisby.substack.com/p/an
    -open-letter-to-the-board-of-trustees#details.

72. "What We Believe," *Black Lives Matter*, April 12, 2020, https://web.archive.org
    /web/20200412161536/https://blacklivesmatter.com/what-we-believe/;
    "#DefundThePolice," *Black Lives Matter*, May 30, 2020, https://blacklivesmatter
    .com/defundthepolice/; Mike Gonzalez, "Marxism Underpins Black Lives Matter
    Agenda," *Heritage Foundation*, September 8, 2021, https://www.heritage.org
    /progressivism/commentary/marxism-underpins-black-lives-matter-agenda.

73. Jemar Tisby, "Now We Call It White Christian Nationalism. It Used to Just Be
    Called the KKK," *Footnotes by Jemar Tisby*, April 21, 2023, https://jemartisby
    .substack.com/p/now-we-call-it-white-christian-nationalism.

74. Jemar Tisby, "Congratulations, America. You Have a White Christian
    Nationalist for Speaker of the House," Oct. 29, 2023, *Footnotes by Jemar Tisby*,
    https://jemartisby.substack.com/p/congratulations-america-you-have.

75. Jemar Tisby, "A Virtual Roundtable on the Threat of Christian Nationalism, Part
    2 of 4 by Jemar Tisby," *Footnotes by Jemar Tisby*, February 12, 2023, https://
    jemartisby.substack.com/p/a-virtual-roundtable-on-the-threat.

76. A 2022 video on "White Christian Nationalism" narrated by Tisby features foot-
    age of Texas Governor Greg Abbott as an example. See "The New Crusades:
    White Christian Nationalism and the Threat to Democracy," *YouTube*, November
    6, 2022, video, 4:23, https://www.youtube.com/watch?v=TRhGdXUJ3uw, at
    1:15 minutes.

77. Jemar Tisby, "It Can Happen Here: The Links Between White Christian Nation-
    alism and Fascism," *Footnotes by Jemar Tisby*, April 27, 2023, https://jemartisby
    .substack.com/p/heres-how-white-christian-nationalism?r=dfab0.

78. Tisby, "A Virtual Roundtable."

79. Tisby, "A Virtual Roundtable."

80. Justin McCarthy, "Americans Remain Steadfast on Policing Reform Needs in
    2022," *Gallup*, May 27, 2022, https://news.gallup.com/poll/393119/americans
    -remain-steadfast-policing-reform-needs-2022.aspx.

81. M. C. Brown, "Black Americans Less Confident, Satisfied with Local Police,"
    Gallup, September 18, 2023, https://news.gallup.com/poll/511064/black
    -americans-less-confident-satisfied-local-police.aspx.

82. Frank Newport, "Most in U. S. Oppose Colleges Considering Race in Admis-
    sions," *Gallup*, July 8, 2016, https://news.gallup.com/poll/193508/oppose-colleges
    -considering-race-admissions.aspx.

83. "In 2019, Relatively Small Shares Said Employers Should Consider Applicants'
    Race and Ethnicity," *Pew Research Center*, June 16, 2023, https://www

.pewresearch.org/short-reads/2023/06/16/americans-and-affirmative-action
-how-the-public-sees-the-consideration-of-race-in-college-admissions-hiring
/sr_2023-06-16_affirmative-action_3/.

84. Justin McCarthy, "Age Plays Key Role in Black Views of Affirmative Action
Case," Gallup, January 16, 2024, https://news.gallup.com/poll/578645/age-plays
-key-role-black-views-affirmative-action-case.aspx.

85. Susannah Cullinane, "Retired St. Louis Police Captain Killed after Responding
to a Pawnshop Alarm During Looting," *CNN*, https://www.cnn.
com/2020/06/03/us/david-dorn-st-louis-police-shot-trnd/index.html.

86. "About Ryan Bomberger," *Radiance Foundation*, accessed May 2024,
https://radiancefoundation.org/ryan/.

87. Voddie Baucham, Jr., *Fault Lines: The Social Justice Movement and Evangelicalism's
Looming Catastrophe* (Washington DC: Salem Books, 2021).

88. Darrell Harrison and Virgil Walker, *Just Thinking: About Ethnicity*, Kindle edition
(Cape Coral, FL: Founders Press, 2024).

89. Carol Swain and Christopher Schorr, *Black Eye for America: How Critical Race
Theory Is Burning Down the House* (Nashville: Be the People Books, 2021).

90. "Delano Squires," *Heritage Foundation*, https://www.heritage.org/staff/delano
-squires; Samuel Sey, *Slow to Write*, https://slowtowrite.com/.

91. "Eric M. Wallace Biography," *Freedom's Journal Institute*, https://freedoms
journalinstitute.org/eric-m-wallace-bio; "Jennifer L. Wallace Biography," *Freedom's Journal Institute*, https://freedomsjournalinstitute.org/jennifer-wallace-bio.

92. "Thomas Sowell," *Hoover Institution*, https://www.hoover.org/profiles/thomas
-sowell.

93. "John H. McWhorter," *Columbia University Center for American Studies*,
https://americanstudies.columbia.edu/people/john-h-mcwhorter.

94. Coleman Hughes, *The End of Race Politics: Arguments for a Colorblind America*
(New York: Thesis, 2024).

95. Rachel Ferguson, "The Sowell of Black America," *Religion & Liberty Online*,
accessed May 2024, https://web.archive.org/web/20230719004740/https://rlo
.acton.org/archives/123381-the-sowell-of-black-america.html; "John McWhorter," *Freedom from Religion Foundation*, accessed May 2024, https://ffrf.org/ftod-cr
/item/40813-john-mcwhorter; "A Christian and an Atheist in Conversation: Race
and Religion with Coleman Hughes," *Sean McDowell*, December 17, 2021,
https://seanmcdowell.org/blog/a-christian-and-an-atheist-in-conversation
-race-and-religion-with-coleman-hughes.

96. John McWhorter, *Woke Racism: How a New Religion Has Betrayed Black America*
(New York: Portfolio, 2021).

97. James Doubek, Steve Inskeep, Barry Gordemer, and Reena Advani, "'Woke
Racism': John McWhorter Argues against What He Calls a Religion of
Anti-Racism," *NPR*, November 6, 2021, https://www.npr.org/2021/11
/05/1052650979/mcwhorters-new-book-woke-racism-attacks-leading
-thinkers-on-race.

98. Baucham, *Fault Lines*, 138–149.

99. Tom Ascol, "Resolution 9 and the Southern Baptist Convention 2019," *Founders Ministries*, https://founders.org/articles/resolution-9-and-the-southern -baptist-convention-2019/.

100. Baucham, *Fault Lines*, 245–251.

101. "About," *CarolMSwain*, accessed May 2024, https://carolmswain.com/about/.

102. Julie Carr, "All Star Panelist Carol Swain Shut Down on Critical Race Theory at Southern Baptist Convention," *The Tennessee Star*, June 17, 2021, https://tennesseestar.com/news/all-star-panelist-carol-swain-shuts-down -on-critical-race-theory-at-southern-bapstist-convention/jcarr/2021/06/17/.

103. Richard Land, "When Southern Baptists Officially Apologized to All African-Americans," *The Christian Post*, June 20, 2020, https://www.christianpost.com /voices/when-southern-baptists-officially-apologized-to-all-african-americans .html.

104. Baucham, *Fault Lines*, 138.

105. Vincent Lloyd, "A Black Professor Trapped in Anti-Racist Hell," *Compact*, February 10, 2023, https://compactmag.com/article/a-black-professor -trapped-in-anti-racist-hell.

106. Stanley, *Irresistible*, 148.

107. Stanley, *Irresistible*, 150.

108. "The Laws of Manu," trans. George Bühler, *Internet Sacred Texts Archive*, accessed May 2024, https://sacred-texts.com/hin/manu/manu01.htm, chapter 1.

109. For a good discussion of Africans in the Bible, see H. C. Felder, *The African American Guide to the Bible*, second Kindle edition (Meadville, PA: Christian Faith Publishing, 2018), chap. 13–14.

110. "A Journey in Chains," *Library of Congress*, https://www.loc.gov/classroom -materials/immigration/african/journey-in-chains/.

111. Leonard Rutgers, "Roman Policy Towards the Jews," *Printed Matter*, October 3, 2017, https://primolevicenter.org/printed-matter/roman-policy-towards-the-jews -expulsions-from-the-city-of-rome-during-the-first-century-c-e/. For an in-depth discussion of Jewish slaves under Roman rule, and of the ways Jews (even those who were slaves) could become Roman citizens, see Martin Goodman, *Rome and Jerusalem* (New York: Vintage Books, 2007), 155–157.

112. Alvin Schmidt, *How Christianity Changed the World* (Grand Rapids, MI: Zondervan 2004), 274.

113. Schmidt, *How Christianity Changed the World*, 274–285.

114. Jacobs, *Born Black*, 120.

115. Samuel Sey, "The Forgotten White People," *Slow to Write*, October 7, 2023, https://slowtowrite.com/the-forgotten-white-people/.

116. Tanya de Sousa et al., "The 2023 Annual Homelessness Assessment Report (AHAR) to Congress," US Department of Housing and Urban Development, December 2023, 13.

117. Emily A. Shrider and John Creamer, "Poverty in the United States: 2022," *US Census Bureau*, September 2023), https://www.census.gov/content/dam/Census /library/publications/2023/demo/p60-280.pdf, 5.

118. Police Shootings Database, *Washington Post*, accessed May 2024, https://www.washingtonpost.com/graphics/investigations/police-shootings-database/.

119. Eric C. Miller, "The American Church's Complicity in Racism: A Conversation with Jemar Tisby," *Religion & Politics Fit for Polite Company*, April 2, 2019, https://religionandpolitics.org/2019/04/02/the-american-churchs-complicity-in-racism-a-conversation-with-jemar-tisby/.

120. Rachel Sheffield and Robert Rector, "The War on Poverty After 50 Years," *Heritage Foundation*, September 15, 2014, https://www.heritage.org/poverty-and-inequality/report/the-war-poverty-after-50-years.

121. "Historical Poverty Tables: People and Families—1959 to 2022," *US Census Bureau*, Table 4, "Poverty Status of People by Type of Family, Presence of Related Children, Race, and Hispanic Origin," https://www.census.gov/data/tables/time-series/demo/income-poverty/historical-poverty-people.html.

122. Rafael A. Mangual, Brad Wilcox, Seth Cannon, and Joseph E. Price, "Stronger Families, Safer Streets: Exploring Links Between Family Structure and Crime," *Institute for Family Studies*, December 12, 2023, 3.

123. "Births: Final Data for 2021," *National Vital Statistics Report* 72, no. 1 (January 31, 2023): 5, https://www.cdc.gov/nchs/data/nvsr/nvsr72/nvsr72-01.pdf?ftag=MSF0951a18; "Table H3. Households, by Race and Hispanic Origin of Household Reference Person and Detailed Type: 2022," *US Census Bureau*, https://www.census.gov/data/tables/2022/demo/families/cps-2022.html.

124. "Births: Final Data for 2021"; Table H3.

125. Timothy Keller, *Generous Justice: How God's Grace Makes Us Just* (New York: Viking, 2010).

126. Walter E. Williams, *Race & Economics: How much can be blamed on discrimination?* (Stanford, CA: Hoover Institution Press, 2011), 8.

127. Loury, Rowe, and Woodson, "Not Buying It."

128. *How Congress Can Reform Government's Misguided Homelessness Policies* (Seattle: Discovery Institute Center on Wealth & Poverty, October 2022), 15–16.

129. *How Congress Can Reform*, 13–20.

130. Loury, Rowe, and Woodson, "Not Buying It."

131. Table 236.55, "Total and Current Expenditures per Pupil in Public Elementary and Secondary Schools: Selected School Years, 1919–20 through 2020–21," *National Center for Education Statistics*, https://nces.ed.gov/programs/digest/d23/tables/dt23_236.55.asp. Also see Andrew J. Coulson, "State Education Trends: Academic Performance and Spending over the Past 40 Years," *Policy Analysis* 746, March 18, 2014, https://www.cato.org/sites/cato.org/files/pubs/pdf/pa746.pdf; Ben DeGrow and Ed Hoang, "School Spending and Student Achievement in Michigan: What's the Relationship?," *Mackinac Center for Public Policy*, 2016, https://www.mackinac.org/archives/2016/s2016-02.pdf.

132. Vertex Partnership Academies, accessed May 2024, https://www.vertexacademies.org/.

133. "Guiding Principles," Vertex Partnership Academies, accessed May 2024, https://www.vertexacademies.org/about-us/guiding-principles.

134. "New York City Charter School Center Test Score Analysis 2022–23," *New York Charter School Center*, December 14, 2023, https://public.tableau.com/app/profile /richard.bellis/viz/NewYorkCityCharterSchoolCenterTestScoreAnalysis2022-23 /Story1.

135. "New Poll: School Choice Support Soars from 2020," *American Federation for Children*, July 11, 2023, https://www.federationforchildren.org/new-poll -school-choice-support-soars-from-2020/.

5. We Must Obey Men Rather than God

1. "Targeted for Believing in Jesus, Russell Vought Barely Confirmed as Pence Casts Tie-Breaker," *CBN News*, March 2, 2018, https://www2.cbn.com/news/politics /targeted-believing-jesus-russell-vought-barely-confirmed-pence-casts-tie -breaker; Joe Carter, "Two U. S. Senators Apply an Anti-Christian Religious Test for Government Officials," *The Gospel Coalition*, June 8, 2017, https://www .thegospelcoalition.org/article/two-u-s-senators-apply-an-anti-christian -religious-test-for-government-officials/.

2. Greg Lukianoff, "FAU College Student Who Didn't Want to Stomp on 'Jesus' Runs Afoul of Speech Code," *Forbes*, March 26, 2013, https://www.forbes.com /sites/realspin/2013/03/26/fau-college-student-who-didnt-want-to-stomp-on -jesus-runs-afoul-of-speech-code/?sh=7e73572d24ae; Myra Adams, "'Jesus Stomping' Professor/FAU Story Continues with Non-Apology, Then Apology, and Now Charges Filed Against Student Who Complained," *PJ Media*, March 25, 2013, https://pjmedia.com/tatler/2013/03/25/jesus-stomping-professor -fau-story-continues-with-non-apology-then-apology-and-now-charges-filed -against-student-who-complained-n177429; Robert Shibley, Florida Atlantic 'Jesus Stomp' Case: A Screwup from Start to Finish," *FIRE*, April 1, 2013, https://www.thefire.org/news/florida-atlantic-jesus-stomp-case-screwup -start-finish.

3. Michael F. Haverluck, "Md. College Denies Applicant: 'Not the Place for Religion,'" *One News Now*, April 25, 2014, https://web.archive.org /web20140428132750/http://www.onenewsnow.com/education/2014/04/25 /md-college-denies-applicant-not-the-place-for-religion#.U15XZ7nP1qZ; Carrie Wells, "Community College Applicant Alleges He Was Rejected Because of Religious Beliefs," *The Baltimore Sun*, April 23, 2014, https://www.baltimoresun.com /education/bs-xpm-2014-04-23-bs-md-ccbc-lawsuit-20140423-story.html

4. Heather Clark, "Maryland College Leveled with Second Suit for Rejecting Student Because of Faith," *Christian News*, September 10, 2014, https://christiannews .net/2014/09/10/maryland-college-leveled-with-second-suit-for-rejecting-student -because-of-faith/.

5. Joe Carter, "U. S. Civil Rights Commission: 'Religious Freedom' Is Code Word for Racism, Homophobia, and 'Christian Supremacy,'" *Gospel Coalition*, September 13, 2016, https://www.thegospelcoalition.org/article/u-s-civil-rights -commission-religious-freedom-is-code-word-for-racism-homophobia-and -christian-supremacy/.

6. "Attacks on Catholic Churches Since May 2020," accessed August 14, 2024, https://docs.google.com/spreadsheets/d/1F4Nb9bs96onlFv6WPKs4 _V1gfJ1u94LFzEt4_P96ZLw/edit#gid=0; "Tracking Attacks on Pregnancy Centers & Pro-Life Groups," *Catholic Vote*, updated August 9, 2024, https://catholicvote.org/pregnancy-center-attack-tracker/.

7. Stephanie Nichols, "The MED Act: Why We Must Preserve Rights of Conscience for Medical Professionals," *Alliance Defending Freedom*, June 16, 2023, https:// adflegal.org/article/med-act-why-we-must-preserve-rights-conscience-medical -professionals; Wesley J. Smith, "Anti-Conscience Mandates Force Doctors to Violate Their Religious Beliefs," *Epoch Times*, October 21, 2021, https://www .theepochtimes.com/opinion/anti-conscience-mandates-force-doctors-to -violate-their-religious-beliefs-4062156; M. Casey Mattox and Matthew S. Bow- man, "Your Conscience, Your Right: A History of Efforts to Violate Pro-Life Medical Conscience, and the Laws that Stand in the Way," *Linacre Quarterly* 77, no. 2, https://doi.org/10.1179/002436310803888754; Anne Marie Williams, "Pro-Life Healthcare Professionals Face Conscience Protection Issues… Even at Catholic Hospitals," *Live Action News*, August 2, 2020, https://www.liveaction .org/news/pro-life-healthcare-professionals-conscience-catholic-hospitals/.

8. Andrea Peyser, "Persecuting Christians Who Refuse to Do Work for Same-Sex Weddings Is Nothing Less Than Bigotry," *New York Post*, September 30, 2022, https://nypost.com/2022/09/30/persecuting-christians-who-refuse-to-do-work- for-same-sex-weddings-is-nothing-less-than-bigotry/; Stephen Beale, "Gay Perse- cution of Christians: The Latest Evidence," *Crisis*, October 10, 2013, https:// crisismagazine.com/opinion/gay-persecution-of-christians-the-latest-evidence.

9. "Alaska Airlines: At Alaska Airlines, If You're Not Woke, You're Not Welcome," *First Liberty Institute*, accessed July 2024, https://firstliberty.org/cases/alaska -airlines/#simple1.

10. Audrey Conklin, "Southwest Flight Attendant Awarded $5M after Firing over Abortion Stance," *Fox Business*, July 15, 2022, https://www.foxbusiness.com /politics/southwest-flight-attendant-awarded-5m-after-firing-over-abortion -stance.

11. Mary Margaret Olohan, "Virginia Restaurant Kicks Out Family Foundation Over Abortion, Traditional Marriage," *Daily Signal*, December 6, 2022, https://www.dailysignal.com/2022/12/06/ virginia-restaurant-kicks-pro-family-organization-family-foundation/.

12. Douglas Ernst, "Christian Activists Booted from Seattle Shop: 'I'm Gay. You Have to Leave,'" *Washington Times*, October 6, 2017, https://www .washingtontimes.com/news/2017/oct/6/christian-activists-booted -from-seattle-coffee-sho/.

13. National Committee for Religious Freedom, https://thencrf.org/.

14. Jerry Bowyer, "Leading Religious Liberty Advocate Gets De-Banked," *The Chris- tian Post*, November 14, 2022, https://www.christianpost.com/news/leading -religious-liberty-advocate-gets-de-banked.html; Matthew McDonald, "Pro- Religious Freedom Political Action Committee Says Big Bank 'Chase-d' It Away," *National Catholic Register*, October 27, 2022, https://www.ncregister.com /news/pro-religious-freedom-political-action-committee-says-big-bank-chase -d-it-away.

15. Douglas Laycock, "Sex, Atheism, and the Free Exercise of Religion," *University of Detroit Mercy Law Review* 88 (2011), https://heinonline.org/HOL/Landing Page?handle=hein.journals/udetmr88&div=22&id=&page=, 407.

16. Todd Starnes, "Federal Court Rules New York City Can Ban Schools from Churches," *Fox News*, June 3, 2011, https://www.foxnews.com/us/federal-court -rules-new-york-city-can-ban-schools-from-churches; Nicola Menzie, "NYC Churches Shut Out of Public Schools Starting Sunday," *Christian Post*, February 11, 2012, https://www.christianpost.com/news/nyc-churches-shut-out-of-public -schools-starting-sunday.html; Chuck Colson, "Empty Buildings: NYC Kicks Churches Out of Schools," *Christian Post*, February 17, 2012, https://www .christianpost.com/news/empty-buildings-nyc-kicks-churches-out-of-schools .html.

17. Brittany Smith, "NYC Megachurches Mostly Silent on Church Ban Issue," *Christian Post*, February 6, 2012, https://www.christianpost.com/news/nyc -megachurches-mostly-silent-on-church-ban-issue.html.

18. Smith, "NYC Megachurches."

19. Smith, "NYC Megachurches."

20. Smith, "NYC Megachurches."

21. Smith, "NYC Megachurches."

22. Timothy Keller, "Op-ed: Tim Keller on 'NYC School's Decision to Ban Church-es," *A Journey Through NYC Religions*, February 7, 2012, https://nycreligion.info /oped-tim-keller-nyc-schools-decision-ban-churches/.

23. "Bronx Church's 20-Year Legal Battle Led to Freedom for New Yorkers of All Faiths," *Alliance Defending Freedom*, August 1, 2023, https://adflegal.org/article /bronx-churchs-20-year-legal-battle-led-freedom-new-yorkers-all-faiths.

24. Gregory S. Baylor, "What You Should Know About the Respect for Marriage Act," *Alliance Defending Freedom*, December 14, 2022, https://adflegal.org/article /what-you-should-know-about-respect-marriage-act; Roger Severino, "Fact-Checking 7 Claims by Defenders of Democrats' Same-Sex Marriage Bill," *Daily Signal*, November 17, 2022; Letter and Legal Analysis Submitted to US Congress, US Conference of Catholic Bishops, November 23, 2022, https://www.usccb.org /resources/Dolan_Barron_Letter_to_Congress_RMA_11-23-22.pdf.

25. Cameron Gerber, "Senator Roy Blunt: A Timeline of His Career," *Missouri Times*, March 8, 2021, https://themissouritimes.com/ us-senator-roy-blunt-a-timeline-of-his-career/

26. "Multifaith Statement of Support for Respect for Marriage Act," *Interfaith Alli-ance*, November 28, 2022, https://interfaithalliance.org/wp-content/uploads /2022/11/Multifaith-Statement-of-Support-RfMA-Bipartisan-Amend-11-28-22 .docx.pdf.

27. "Religious Liberty Provisions in Respect for Marriage Act," *National Association of Evangelicals*, December 9, 2022, https://www.nae.org/religious-liberty -provisions-in-respect-for-marriage-act/.

28. Carl Esbeck, "Everything You Need to Know About the Respect for Marriage Act," *Christianity Today*, November 17, 2022, https://www.christianitytoday.com /ct/2022/november-web-only/same-sex-marriage-religious-liberty-respect -marriage-act.html.

29. "Sweet Cakes by Melissa Case," *First Liberty Institute*, accessed May 2024, https://firstliberty.org/cases/kleins/; Kelsey Bolar, "Oregon Official Who Shut Down Sweet Cakes Loses Election Bid to a Republican," *The Daily Signal*, November 15, 2016, https://www.dailysignal.com/2016/11/15/oregon-official-who-shut-down-sweet-cakes-loses-election-bid-to-a-republican/; "When Government Condemns Religious Beliefs, Society Soon Follows," First Liberty Institute on *YouTube*, March 1, 2018, video, 3:10, https://youtu.be/OKZdmJ2M59k?feature=shared.

30. Barronelle Stutzman, "In Her Own Words: Barronelle's Legal Journey Comes to an End," *Alliance Defending Freedom*, November 17, 2021; revised August 24, 2023, https://adflegal.org/article/her-own-words-barronelles-legal-journey-comes-end.

31. Stutzman, "In Her Own Words: Barronelle's Legal Journey."

32. Stutzman, "In Her Own Words: Barronelle's Legal Journey."

33. "Bob Ferguson," *Voters' Pamphlet, Washington State Elections 2020*, Washington State Secretary of State's Office, https://www.sos.wa.gov/sites/default/files/2023-05/--ed07king-south%2Cse.pdf?uid=652b2f61ba8c8, 48; "Bob Ferguson," *Voter's Guide, 2016 General Election*, Washington State Secretary of State's Office, https://eledataweb.votewa.gov/OVG/onlinevotersguide?language=en&electionId=63&countyCode=xx&Group=Statewide; "Bob Ferguson," *Voter's Guide, 2012 General Election*, Washington State Secretary of State's Office, https://eledataweb.votewa.gov/OVG/onlinevotersguide?language=en&electionId=46&countyCode=xx&Group=Statewide.

34. See the *amicus* brief filed in the *Masterpiece Cakeshop v. Colorado Civil Rights Commission* case on September 17, 2017 by the United States Conference of Catholic Bishops, the Colorado Catholic Conference, the Catholic Bar Association, the Catholic Medical Association, the National Association of Catholic Nurses—U.S.A., and the National Catholic Bioethics Center, https://www.cathmed.org/wp-content/uploads/2018/03/Masterpiece-Cake-Amicus-2017-USCCB.pdf.

35. Kirsten Powers, "Jim Crow Laws for Gays and Lesbians?," *USA Today*, February 18, 2014, https://www.usatoday.com/story/opinion/2014/02/18/gays-lesbians-kansas-bill-religious-freedom-christians-column/5588643/.

36. Powers, "Jim Crow Laws for Gays and Lesbians?"

37. Lucinda Borkett-Jones, "John Kasich Christian Faith: How Governor Was Drawn to God—'My Faith Is Part of Me,'" *Christian Today*, August 7, 2015, https://www.christiantoday.com/article/john.kasich.christian.faith.how.governor.of.ohio.was.drawn.to.god/61269.htm.

38. Samuel Smith, "John Kasich Tells Christian Bakers Who Refuse Gay Wedding to 'Move On,' 'Make Them a Cupcake,'" *Christian Post*, February 24, 2016, https://www.christianpost.com/news/john-kasich-christian-bakers-gay-wedding-move-on-make-them-a-cupcake.html.

39. Cassie Spodak and Eric Bradner, "Kasich's Wish for More Attention Proves to Be Blessing and a Curse," *CNN*, February 22, 2016, https://www.cnn.com/2016/02/22/politics/john-kasich-increased-media-attention/index.html.

40. "Here It Is: The Text of Indiana's Religious Freedom Law," *Indianapolis Star*, April 2, 2015, https://www.indystar.com/story/news/politics/2015/03/27/text-indianas-religious-freedom-law/70539772/.

41. Mark Hemingway, "For Social Conservatives and Fans of Religious Liberty, Pence Pick Will Sting," *The Weekly Standard*, July 14, 2016, https://web.archive .org/web/20160818031526/http://www.weeklystandard.com/for-social -conservatives-and-fans-of-religious-liberty-pence-pick-will-sting/article /2003296.

42. *303 Creative LLC v. Elenis*, US Supreme Court, June 30, 2023, https://www.law.cornell.edu/supremecourt/text/21-476.

43. "Masterpiece Cakeshop v. Scardina," *Alliance Defending Freedom*, https://adflegal .org/case/masterpiece-cakeshop-v-scardina#case-documents. Majority Opinion, *Masterpiece Cakeshop, Inc. v. Scardina*, Advance Sheet, Colorado Supreme Court Case No. 23SC116, October 8, 2024, 29, https://dm1l19z832j5m.cloudfront.net /2024-10/Scardina-v-Masterpiece-Cakeshop-2024-10-08-Colorado-Supreme -Court-Decision.pdf.

44. See statement of facts in dissent by Justice Samuel Alito, *Calvary Chapel Dayton Valley v. Steve Sisolak, Governor of Nevada*, US Supreme Court, July 24, 2020, https://www.supremecourt.gov/opinions/19pdf/19a1070_0811.pdf.

45. Michelle Rindels and Jackie Valley, "Democrat Sisolak, Longtime Clark County Politician, Praises Dandoval as He Enters Race for Governor," *The Nevada Independent*, June 22, 2017, https://thenevadaindependent.com/article/sisolak -longtime-clark-county-politician-set-to-announce-bid-for-governor.

46. "John Roberts' Catholic Connections," *Beliefnet*, August 2005, https://www .beliefnet.com/news/2005/08/john-roberts-catholic-connections.aspx.

47. "Town Hall on Evangelicals and the COVID-19 Vaccine," *Wheaton College: Humanitarian Disaster Institute*, April 27, 2021, https://vimeo.com/542269714.

48. *All In with Chris Hayes*, MSNBC, September 9, 2021, transcript, https://www .msnbc.com/transcripts/transcript-all-chris-hayes-9-9-21-n1278904.

49. Francis Collins, interview with Selena Simmons-Duffin, NPR's *All Things Considered*, December 7, 2021, https://www.npr.org/sections/health-shots /2021/12/07/1061940326/the-nih-director-on-why-americans-arent-getting -healthier-despite-medical-advanc.

50. Vinay Prasad, "At a Time When the US Needed Covid-19 Dialogue between Scientists, Francis Collins Moved to Shut It Down," *STAT*, December 23, 2021, https://www.statnews.com/2021/12/23/at-a-time-when-the-u-s-needed-covid-19 -dialogue-between-scientists-francis-collins-moved-to-shut-it-down/.

51. "Many Leaders against Religious Exemptions for Vaccine," *Journal Gazette*, February 13, 2022, https://www.journalgazette.net/news/many-leaders-against -religious-exemptions-for-vaccine/article_8960bbc1-5064-50e2-a9f5 -6fc291698007.html.

52. Bishop Athanasius Schneider, "Resisting Abortion-Tainted Vaccines and the Culture of Death," *Crisis*, April 1, 2021, https://crisismagazine.com/opinion/re- sisting-abortion-tainted-vaccines-and-the-culture-of-death; David Prentice and Tara Sander Lee, "What You Need to Know about the COVID-19 Vaccines," *Charlotte Lozier Institute*, December 8, 2020, https://lozierinstitute.org/what -you-need-to-know-about-the-covid-19-vaccine/.

53. Peter Smith, "Many Faith Leaders Say No to Endorsing Vaccine Exemptions," *Associated Press*, September 17, 2021, https://apnews.com/article/health -religion-united-states-coronavirus-pandemic-coronavirus-vaccine -9c947acecd6ba26b4c78827b7b87c185.

54. Paul Casey, "Debunking the Lie That All Medicines Were Tested on Fetal Cells," *Lifesite News*, December 10, 2021, https://www.lifesitenews.com/opinion /debunking-the-lie-that-all-medicines-were-tested-on-fetal-cells/; Horatio G. Mihet, "What about Tylenol and Other Drugs?," *Liberty Counsel*, October 26, 2021, https://lc.org/full-article/1026what-about-tylenol-and-other-drugs.

55. Of course, even if the claim made by Jeffress had been true, that doesn't mean people might not have had valid (non-contradictory) reasons to refrain from tak-ing the COVID-19 vaccine while still taking other drugs similarly developed. For example, someone who had already recovered from COVID-19 might have de-cided that the vaccine would provide little or no benefit to them. It's one thing to use a drug developed illicitly when there is a very clear benefit; it is quite another thing to use a drug one thinks was developed illicitly for no clear benefit. In the latter case, the moral calculus is different.

56. Raymond Wolfe, "Hospital System Makes Workers Vow to Give Up Antibiotics, Tylenol to Get COVID Vaccine Exemptions," *Lifesite News*, September 17, 2021, https://www.lifesitenews.com/news/hospital-system-makes-employees-swear -off-tylenol-antibiotics-to-get-covid-vaccine-exemptions/.

57. David French, "It's Time to Stop Rationalizing and Enabling Evangelical Vaccine Rejection," *Dispatch*, August 29, 2021, https://thedispatch.com/newsletter /frenchpress/its-time-to-stop-rationalizing-christian/.

58. Matthew E. Oster et al., "Myocarditis Cases Reported after mRNA-Based COVI-19 Vaccination in the US From December 2020 to August 2021," *Journal of the American Medical Association* 327, no. 4 (January 25, 2022): 331–340, doi:10.1001/jama.2021.24110.

59. See documentation in John G. West, "The Rise of Totalitarian Science, 2022 Edi-tion," *Evolution News and Science Today*, January 31, 2022, https://evolutionnews .org/2022/01/the-rise-of-totalitarian-science-2022-edition/.

60. "Tim Keller: Christians Will Be Purged From Govt + Schools, And 'We Brought It On Ourselves," Woke Preacher Clips on *YouTube*, March 10, 2021, video, 4:12, https://www.youtube.com/watch?v=QULvu16tBiU&t=1s. The original podcast with Keller's full remarks in context can be heard here: Jason Daye, "Timothy Keller: How to Know If You Are a Christian Nationalist," *Church Leaders*, March 10, 2021, https://churchleaders.com/podcast/391233-timothy-keller-christian -nationalist.html.

61. "Bournemouth Abortion Clinic Protesters Lose Prayer Campaign Case," *BBC*, December 15, 2023, https://www.bbc.com/news/uk-england-dorset-67731454; Gabriel Hays, "UK Woman Arrested for Silently Praying across from Abortion Clinic: 'Terrifying,'" *New York Post*, December 15, 2022, https://nypost.com /2022/12/22/uk-woman-arrested-for-praying-across-from-abortion-clinic/; Emma Camp, "In Britain, You Can Be Arrested for Silently Praying Outside an Abortion Clinic," *Reason*, February 10, 2023, https://reason.com/2023/02/10 /in-britain-you-can-be-arrested-for-silently-praying-outside-an-abortion-clinic/;

Kevin J. Jones, "Woman Arrested for Silent Prayer at UK Abortion Clinics Gets Police Apology," *National Catholic Register*, September 22, 2023, https://www .ncregister.com/cna/woman-arrested-for-silent-prayer-at-uk-abortion-clinics -gets-police-apology.

62. Jon Brown, Christian Politician Facing Third Trial for Bible Tweet Submits Defense to Finland's Supreme Court," *The Christian Post*, May 23, 2024, https://www.christianpost.com/news/christian-politician-submits-defense-to -finlands-top-court.html.

63. Timothy H. J. Nerozzi, "Finnish Lawmaker Wins Second 'Hate Speech' Case over Quoting the Bible, *Fox News*, November 15, 2023, https://www.foxnews.com /world/finnish-lawmaker-wins-second-hate-speech-case-quoting-bible; Caleb Parke, "Finnish Politician under 'Hate Crime Investigation' for Sharing Bible Verse on Facebook," *Fox News*, September 5, 2019, https://www.foxnews.com /world/bible-verse-lgbt-hate-crime-investigation.

64. Michael Donnelly, "HSLDA Files Asylum Application for German Homeschool Family," *Home School Legal Defense Association*, November 17, 2008, https://hslda .org/post/hslda-files-asylum-application-for-german-homeschool-family; Andrea Grunau and Elizabeth Schumacher, "European Court Rules against German Homeschooling Family," *Deutsche Welle*, January 10, 2019, https://www.dw.com /en/european-court-rules-against-german-homeschooling-family/a-47021333.

65. "Romeike Case: History and Timeline," *Home School Legal Defense Association*, September 18, 2023, https://hslda.org/post/romeike-fact-sheet; "Romeike Family Facing Deportation After 15 Years," *Home School Legal Defense Association*, September 18, 2023, https://hslda.org/post/romeike.

66. There is some ambiguity about precisely when homeschooling was banned in Germany. There was a compulsory schooling law enacted in 1919, but it may not have prevented homeschooling. In 1938 (under the Nazis) criminal penalties were imposed. Christian Poole, "The Nazi Origins of Germany's Ban on Homeschooling," *ThinkingWest*, June 22, 2020, https://thinkingwest.com/2020/06/22/nazi -ban-homeschooling/; Rodger Williams, "Yes, The Nazis Did Outlaw Homeschooling In Germany," *Homeschooling Backgrounder*, August 17, 2023, https:// homeschoolingbackgrounder.com/yes-the-nazis-did-outlaw-homeschooling-in -germany/; Thomas Spiegler, "Home Education in Germany: An Overview of the Contemporary Situation," *Evaluation and Research in Education* 17, no. 2 and 3 (2003), 180.

67. Udo Middelman, "Thoughts from Udo," *Francis A. Schaeffer Foundation*, March 18, 2013, https://www.theschaefferfoundation.com/notes-from-udo.php.

68. Katie Gilbert, "How Homeschooling Evolved from Subversive to Mainstream," *JSTOR Daily*, September 8, 2021, https://daily.jstor.org/how-homeschooling -evolved-from-subversive-to-mainstream/.

69. Spiegler, "Home Education," 181.

70. See, for example, Brian D. Ray and Carlos Valentine, "The Academic and Social Benefits of Homeschooling," *The James G. Martin Center for Academic Renewal*, May 13, 2020, https://www.jamesgmartin.center/2020/05/the-academic-and -social-benefits-of-homeschooling/; Brian D. Ray, "Homeschool Progress Report 2009," *HSDLA*, accessed May 2024, https://eric.ed.gov/?id=ED535134; and

Michael F. Cogan, "Exploring Academic Outcomes of Homeschooled Students," *Journal of College Admission* (Summer 2010), https://files.eric.ed.gov/fulltext/EJ893891.pdf.

71. Todd M. Johnson and Peter F. Crossing, "Religions by Continent," *Journal of Religion and Demography* 9, no. 1–2 (October 14, 2022), https://doi.org/10.1163/2589742x-bja10013, 91-110.

72. Oscar Amaechina, "Why Christians Should Speak Out When Fellow Brethren Are Victimized," *Christian Post*, December 6, 2023, https://www.christianpost.com/voices/why-christians-should-speak-out-when-christians-are-victimized.html.

6. SOME SLOPES REALLY ARE SLIPPERY

1. Ryan T. Meeks, "Who I Am," *Ryan T. Meeks*, archived August 23, 2021, https://www.ryantmeeks.com/who-i-am.

2. "Who We Are," *EastLake Community Church*, accessed September 6, 2023, https://www.eastlakecc.com/who-we-are.

3. Ironically, they weren't following the actual example of Fred Rogers. Rogers continued to identity as a Christian throughout his life and attended church weekly, prayed daily, and viewed his television career as a ministry. See Adelle M. Banks, "'He Acted His Faith'—Fred Rogers' Widow Talks about His Commitment to Prayer, Church, Children," *Salt Lake Tribune*, November 16, 2019, https://www.sltrib.com/religion/2019/11/16/he-acted-his-faith-fred/.

4. Ryan and Michelle Meeks, "Who We Are," *Nautilus Integration*, accessed May 13, 2024, https://nautilusintegration.com/whoweare.

5. Francis A. Schaeffer, *The Great Evangelical Disaster* (Westchester, IL: Crossway Books, 1984), 146.

6. Queerty, "Megachurch Pastor Puts Homophobic Christians on Blast in Viral Video Sermon," *MSN*, January 30, 2023, https://www.msn.com/en-us/news/us/megachurch-pastor-puts-homophobic-christians-on-blast-in-viral-video-sermon/ar-AA16UeHQ.

7. Ryan Visconti (@ryanvisconti), "Here's another text I sent," *Twitter*, January 28, 2023, https://twitter.com/ryanvisconti/status/1619382519312568320?s=20.

8. Brian Kruckenberg (@briankruck), "This is 100 what we all felt," *Twitter*, January 27, 2023, https://twitter.com/ryanvisconti/status/1619207302338461697?s=20; Luke Simmons (@lukesimmon), "I was there and corroborate Ryan's recounting of the story," *Twitter*, January 26, 2023, https://twitter.com/ryanvisconti/status/1618752779253862400?s=20.

9. "The 25 Most Influential Evangelicals in America: Brian McLaren," *TIME*, February 7, 2005, archived August 14, 2013, https://web.archive.org/web/20130814192626/http://www.time.com/time/specials/packages/article/0,28804,1993235_1993243_1993300,00.html.

10. Tim Challies, "The False Teachers: Brian McLaren," *@Challies*, May 1, 2014, https://www.challies.com/articles/the-false-teachers-brian-mclaren/.

11. Brian D. McLaren, *A New Kind of Christianity: Ten Questions That Are Transforming the Faith* (New York, HarperCollins e-books, 2010), 103, Kindle edition.

12. Challies, "The False Teachers: Brian McLaren."

13. Howard Van Till, "SOBIG: A Symposium on Belief in God," *Theology and Science* 14, no. 1 (2016): 7–8, https://www.tandfonline.com/doi/full/10.1080/14746700 .2015.1122323.

14. Giberson, *Saving Darwin: How to Be a Christian and Believe in Evolution* (New York: HarperOne, 2008), 155.

15. Giberson, *Saving Darwin*, 155–156.

16. Karl W. Giberson, *Saving the Original Sinner: How Christians Have Used the Bible's First Man to Oppress, Inspire, and Make Sense of the World* (Boston: Beacon Press, 2015), 39.

17. Matthew 28:28–20, Mark 16: 14–18, Luke 24:44–49, Acts 1:4–8. Old Testament passages about God's intention to call all nations include Isaiah 42:6–7, Isaiah 49:6, and Psalm 22:27.

18. Giberson, *Saving the Original Sinner*, 29.

19. See "Did Jesus Say He Is God?," *Got Questions*, accessed May 13, 2024, https://www.gotquestions.org/did-Jesus-say-He-is-God.html.

20. Giberson, *Saving the Original Sinner*, 176.

21. Giberson, *Saving the Original Sinner*, 176.

22. Warren Cole Smith, "Growing up Schaeffer," *WORLD*, October 13, 2007, https://wng.org/articles/growing-up-schaeffer-1617336069. For critical reviews of Frank Schaeffer's accounts of his parents and his own theological evolution, see Douglas Groothuis, "Franky Plays Schaeffer Card, Again," *The Pearcey Report*, December 2007, https://www.pearceyreport.com/archives/2007/12/franky_plays _sc_1.php; Os Guinness, "Fathers and Sons," Books and Culture, March/April 2008, https://www.booksandculture.com/articles/2008/marapr/1.32.html; Douglas Groothuis, "Frank Schaeffer: Still the *Enfant Terrible*," *Christian Research Journal* 38, no. 3 (2015), https://www.equip.org/PDF/JAF8383.pdf.

23. Rod Dreher, "Frank Schaeffer: Go to Hell, Pro-Lifers," *The American Conservative*, November 30, 2012, https://www.theamericanconservative.com/frank -schaeffer-go-to-hell-pro-lifers/.

24. Frank Schaeffer, *Why I Am an Atheist Who Believes in God* (Create Space, 2014).

25. Frank Schaeffer, "Why I Am an Atheist Who Believes in GOD," *YouTube*, August 18, 2015, video, 54:51, https://www.youtube.com/watch?v=-33BUmx91BE.

26. Micah Danney, "Religious Right Defector Frank Schaeffer Takes on Pro-Trump Evangelicals and Abortion Alike," *Newsweek*, February 24, 2020, https://www .newsweek.com/religious-right-defector-frank-schaeffer-takes-pro-trump -evangelicals-abortion-alike-1488650.

27. Frank Schaeffer, *Fall in Love, Have Children, Stay Put, Save the Planet, Be Happy* (Boca Raton, FL: Health Communications, 2021), 12.

28. Frank Schaeffer (@Frank_Schaeffer), "Roe now, gay rights next," *Twitter*, May 3, 2022, https://twitter.com/Frank_Schaeffer/status/1521390368188731393?s=20.

29. Frank Schaeffer, "The Left Has *Minutes* to Get Its Act Together," *YouTube*, June 24, 2022, video, 9:24, https://youtu.be/CLgKkFYDrz0?si= _0HJxZlTMyT1pMom.

30. Günter Bechly, "A Long Surrender: A Scientist's Arduous Path from Hard Atheism to Faith," *Salvo* 62 (Fall 2022), https://salvomag.com/article/salvo62/a-long-surrender.

31. Part of this story is told in the documentary *Revolutionary: Michael Behe and the Mystery of Molecular Machines* (Seattle: Discovery Institute, 2006), https://revolutionarybehe.com/.

32. Robert W. Yarbrough, "Eta Linnemann: Friend or Foe of Scholarship?," *The Master's Seminary Journal* 8, no. 2 (Fall 1997), 163–189.

33. "Eta Linnemann Testimony," Grace Valley Christian Center, November 7, 2001, https://gracevalley.org/teaching/eta-linnemann-testimony/.

34. With regard to "prophesies," I realize there is a lot of debate among Christians about whether the prophetic gifts mentioned in the New Testament are still available today, and, if so, under what circumstances and limitations. But entering into that debate is well beyond the scope of this book. With regard to miracles, there are many books that may be consulted for a Christian perspective, including Eric Metaxas, *Miracles: What They Are, Why They Happen, and How They Can Change Your Life* (New York: Viking, 2014); C. S. Lewis, *Miracles: A Preliminary Study*, revised edition (New York: HarperOne, 2015); Craig S. Keener, *Miracles* (Grand Rapids, MI: Baker Academic, 2011); and Craig S. Keener, *Miracles Today* (Grand Rapids, MI: Baker Academic, 2021).

7. Listening to the Wrong Voices

1. Naomi Forman-Katz and Mark Jurkowitz, "U.S. Journalists Differ from the Public in Their Views of 'Bothsidesism' In Journalism," *Pew Research Center*, July 13, 2022, https://www.pewresearch.org/short-reads/2022/07/13/u-s-journalists-differ-from-the-public-in-their-views-of-bothsidesism-in-journalism/.

2. "2022 Pew Research Center Journalist Survey, Topline, February 16–March 17, 2022," *Pew Research Center*, https://www.pewresearch.org/journalism/wp-content/uploads/sites/8/2023/04/PJ_2023.04.04_Journalist-Survey_TOPLINE.pdf, 17.

3. "2022 Pew Research Center Journalist Survey," 18.

4. "Survey of Journalists, Final Topline, November 20-1998-February 11, 1999," *Pew Research Center*, https://www.pewresearch.org/wp-content/uploads/sites/4/legacy-questionnaires/67.pdf, 9.

5. "2007 Survey of Journalists, Final Topline, September 17-December 3, 2007," *Pew Research Center*, https://assets.pewresearch.org/wp-content/uploads/sites/5/legacy-questionnaires/403.pdf, 55.

6. "Religious Landscape Study: Attendance at Religious Services," *Pew Research Center*, 2007, https://www.pewresearch.org/religion/religious-landscape-study/attendance-at-religious-services/.

7. "2007 Survey of Journalists," 55.

8. Lydia Saad, "U. S. Political Ideology Stable with Conservatives Leading," *Gallup*, August 1, 2011, https://news.gallup.com/poll/148745/political-ideology-stable-conservatives-leading.aspx.

9. Hans J. G. Hassell, John B. Holbein, Matthew R. Miles, "There Is No Liberal Media Bias in Which News Stories Political Journalists Choose to Cover," *Science Advances*, April 1, 2020, https://www.science.org/doi/10.1126/sciadv.aay9344, 2.

10. "Supplementary Materials for 'There Is No Liberal Media Bias in Which News Stories Political Journalists Choose to Cover,'" *Science Advances*, April 1, 2020, https://www.science.org/doi/suppl/10.1126/sciadv.aay9344/suppl_file/aay9344 _sm.pdf, Figure S3.

11. Jeffrey M. Jones, "U. S. Party Preferences Evenly Split in 2022 after Shift to GOP," *Gallup*, January 12, 2023, https://news.gallup.com/poll/467897/party -preferences-evenly-split-2022-shift-gop.aspx.

12. Lars Willnat, David H. Weaver, and Cleve Wilhoit, "The American Journalist Under Attack: Media, Trust & Democracy, Key Findings 2022," Syracuse University: S.I. Newhouse School of Public Communications, 2022, https://www.theamericanjournalist.org/_files/ugd/46a507 _4fe1c4d6ec6d4c229895282965258a7a.pdf, 11.

13. For a useful summary of some of the data, see Rich Noyes, "The Liberal Media," *Media Research Center,* June 30, 2004, https://web.archive.org/web /20150910083017/https://archive.mrc.org/specialreports/2004/pdf/liberal _media.pdf, 9-12.

14. Jeffrey M. Jones, "As Industry Grows, Percentage of U.S. Sports Fans Steady," *Gallup*, June 17, 2015, https://news.gallup.com/poll/183689/industry-grows -percentage-sports-fans-steady.aspx.

15. "Religion," *Gallup*, accessed May 29, 2024, https://news.gallup.com/poll/1690 /religion.aspx.

16. "How a Nation Engages with Art: Highlights from the 2012 Survey of Public Participation in the Arts," *NEA Research Report* 57 (September 2013, revised October 2015), https://www.arts.gov/sites/default/files/highlights-from-2012 -sppa-revised-oct-2015.pdf, 10.

17. "A Decade of Arts Engagement: Findings from the Survey of Public Participation in the Arts, 2002–2012," *NEA Research Report* 58 (January 2015): 95.

18. "How a Nation Engages with Art," 10.

19. "How a Nation Engages with Art," 9.

20. In 2018–19 the figure was 65 percent. See "In U.S., Decline of Christianity Continues at Rapid Pace," *Pew Research Center,* October 2019, https://www .pewresearch.org/religion/2019/10/17/in-u-s-decline-of-christianity -continues-at-rapid-pace/.

21. General Social Survey results for 2022, available through the GSS Data Explorer, https://gssdataexplorer.norc.org/trends?category=Religion%20%26%20Spirituality &measure=attend.

22. Paul Best, "Nashville School Shooter Audrey Hale: Who is 28-Year-Old Trans-gender Former Student Who Opened Fire at School," *Fox News Channel*, March 27, 2023, https://www.foxnews.com/us/nashville-shooter-audrey-hale -transgender-woman-opened-fire-covenant-school.rans.

23. Aleks Phillips, "'Trans Day of Vengeance' Date, Details as Activists Say 'We Choose to Fight,'" *Newsweek*, March 30, 2023.

24. See, for example, Andrew Demillo "Trans People Face Rhetoric, Disinformation after Shooting," *Associated Press*, April 2, 2023, https://apnews.com/article /nashville-school-shooting-transgender-lgbtq-disinformation-6cef2f5909c68993 caae9d3123608ec7; Fenit Nirappil, "The Right Exploits Nashville Shooting to Escalate Anti-Trans Rhetoric," *Washington Post*, March 30, 2023, https://www .washingtonpost.com/health/2023/03/30/nashville-shooting-transgender-shooter/.

25. "Why the Royal Society Meeting Mattered," *Evolution News and Science Today*, January 1, 2017, https://evolutionnews.org/2017/01/1_happy_new_yea/.

26. "A Scientific Dissent from Darwinism," https://dissentfromdarwin.org/.

27. Kenneth Chang, "Few Biologists but Many Evangelicals Sign Anti-Evolution Petition," *New York Times*, February 21, 2006, https://www.nytimes.com/2006 /02/21/science/sciencespecial2/few-biologists-but-many-evangelicals-sign.html.

28. John G. West, "Did the *New York Times* Suppress the Results of Its Own Investigation into Darwin's Scientific Critics in Order to Promote a Stereotype?," *Evolution News and Science Today*, March 3, 2006, https://evolutionnews.org/2006 /03/did_the_new_york_times_suppres/.

29. Erin R. Brown, "Holy Week: Media Worship Earth Day, Attack Easter," *Newsbusters*, April 20, 2011, https://newsbusters.org/blogs/nb/erin-r-brown /2011/04/20/holy-week-media-worship-earth-day-attack-easter.

30. Brown, "Holy Week."

31. Tim Graham, "The Trashing of the Christ: Contrasts in Media Treatment of *The DaVinci Code* and *The Passion*," *Media Research Center*, May 23, 2006, https://web .archive.org/web/20150922123036/http://archive.mrc.org/SpecialReports/2006 /pdf/Trashing-of-the-Christ.pdf, i.

32. Graham, "The Trashing of the Christ," i.

33. Graham, "The Trashing of the Christ," i.

34. Graham, "The Trashing of the Christ," ii.

35. George Yancey and Alicia L. Brunson, *Prejudice in the Press? Investigating Bias in Coverage of Race, Gender, Sexuality and Religion* (Jefferson, NC: McFarland & Company, 2019).

36. Yancey and Brunson, *Prejudice in the Press?*, 90.

37. Yancey and Brunson, *Prejudice in the Press?*, 13.

38. Yancey and Brunson, *Prejudice in the Press?*, 94.

39. Yancey and Brunson, *Prejudice in the Press?*, 95.

40. Research by the author.

41. John Carmody, "The TV Column," *The Washington Post*, October 30, 1989, https://www.washingtonpost.com/archive/lifestyle/1989/10/30/the-tv-column /e363c5c7-4d8e-4608-a1fb-8ba963e49023/.

42. Tim Graham and Clay Waters, "Roe Warriors: The Media's Pro-Abortion Bias," *Media Research Center*, July 22, 1998, esp. section 1.

43. Carmody, "The TV Column."

44. "News Coverage Conveys Strong Momentum for Same-Sex Marriage," *Pew Research Center*, June 17, 2013, https://www.pewresearch.org/wp-content/uploads /sites/8/legacy/EMBARGOED_Same-SexMarriageandNews.pdf.

45. Research by author.

46. Christina Maxouris, "Jussie Smollett Convicted in Hate Crime Hoax. Here's How We Got Here," *CNN*, December 9, 2021, https://www.cnn.com/2021/11/29 /us/jussie-smollett-how-we-got-here/index.html; Tim Murtaugh, "In 2021 Media Did More to Erode Trust Than to Repair It," *The Daily Signal*, December 30, 2021, https://www.dailysignal.com/2021/12/30/in-2021-media-did-more-to -erode-trust-than-to-repair-it/.

47. @CNN, January 29, 2019, https://twitter.com/CNN/status /1090308638638567431?s=20.

48. John West, *Darwin Day in America: How Our Politics and Culture Have Been Dehumanized in the Name of Science* (Wilmington, DE: ISI Books, 2007), 258.

49. West, *Darwin Day in America*, 257–258.

50. Elisabeth Bumiller, "Bush Remarks Roil Debate on Teaching of Evolution," *New York Times*, August 3, 2005, https://www.nytimes.com/2005/08/03/politics /bush-remarks-roil-debateon-teaching-of-evolution.html.

51. Robert Crowther, "A Mistake Made in Haste," *Evolution News and Science Today*, August 3, 2005, https://evolutionnews.org/2005/08/a_mistake_made_in_haste/; John G. West, "Freudian Slip at The *New York Times*? The Paper of Record Mangles Quote from DI's Spokesman, Substituting 'Biblical' for 'Biological,'" *Evolution News and Science Today*, August 3, 2005, https://evolutionnews.org /2005/08/freudian_slip_at_the_new_york_times_the/.

52. The documentation of social media censorship and manipulation is voluminous and growing. See, for example, the 800-page report generated by the House Select Subcommittee on the Weaponization of the Federal Government, "The Censor-ship-Industrial Complex: How Top Biden White House Officials Coerced Big Tech to Censor Americans, True Information, and Critics of the Biden Adminis-tration," May 2024, https://judiciary.house.gov/sites/evo-subsites/republicans -judiciary.house.gov/files/evo-media-document/Censorship-Industrial-Complex -WH-Report_Appendix.pdf. See also Memorandum Ruling, *Missouri v. Biden*, US District Court, Western District of Louisiana, Monroe Division, July 4, 2023, https://ago.mo.gov/wp-content/uploads/missouri-v-biden-ruling.pdf; Gabriel Nicholas, "Shadowbanning Is Big Tech's Big Problem," *Atlantic*, April 28, 2022, https://www.theatlantic.com/technology/archive/2022/04/social-media -shadowbans-tiktok-twitter/629702/. Matt Taibbi, "The Twitter Files," *Twitter Files Substack*, April 12, 2023, https://twitterfiles.substack.com/p/1-thread-the -twitter-files; Allum Bokhari, *#Deleted: Big Tech's Battle to Erase a Movement and Subvert Democracy* (New York: Center Street, 2020).

53. For examples, see Mike Wacker, "Google's Manual Interventions in Search Re-sults," *Medium*, July 2, 2019, https://medium.com/@mikewacker/googles-manual -interventions-in-search-results-a3b0cfd3e26c; Eric Lieberman, "Google's New Fact-Check Feature Almost Exclusively Targets Conservatives Sites," *Daily Caller*, January 9, 2018, https://dailycaller.com/2018/01/09/googles-new-fact-check -feature-almost-exclusively-targets-conservative-sites/; Matthew Boyle, "'Silent Donation': Corporate Emails Reveal Google Executives' Efforts to Turn Out Latino Voters Who They Thought Would Vote for Clinton," *Breitbart*, September 10, 2018, https://www.breitbart.com/politics/2018/09/10/silent-donation

-corporate-emails-reveal-google-executives-efforts-to-swing-election-to
-hillary-clinton-with-latino-outreach-campaign/; Robert Epstein and Ronald E.
Robertson, "The Search Engine Manipulation Effect (SEME) and Its Possible
Impact on the Outcome of Elections," *Proceedings of the National Academy of Sciences*, August 4, 2015, https://www.pnas.org/doi/full/10.1073/pnas.1419828112;
Robert Epstein, "Why Google Poses a Serious Threat to Democracy, and How to
End that Threat," Testimony by Robert Epstein before the US Senate Judiciary
Subcommittee on the Constitution, July 16, 2019, https://www.judiciary.senate
.gov/imo/media/doc/Epstein%20Testimony.pdf.

54. Kirsten Grind, Sam Schechner, Robert McMillan, and John West [no relation to
author], "How Google Interferes with Its Search Algorithms and Changes Your
Results," *Wall Street Journal*, November 15, 2019, https://www.wsj.com/articles
/how-google-interferes-with-its-search-algorithms-and-changes-your
-results-11573823753.

55. Larry Sanger, "Wikipedia Is Badly Biased," *LarrySanger*, May 14, 2020,
https://larrysanger.org/2020/05/wikipedia-is-badly-biased/.

56. Gary Smith, "Internet Pollution—If You Tell a Lie Long Enough," *Mind Matters*,
January 15, 2024, https://mindmatters.ai/2024/01/
internet-pollution-if-you-tell-a-lie-long-enough/.

57. Table 3, "Social Liberalism, American Public and Hollywood Opinion Leaders,
1990," in David F. Princlde, and James W. Endersby, "Hollywood Liberalism,"
Social Science Quarterly 74, no. 1, March 1993, 145.

58. Jeremy Barr, "Top Hollywood Execs Give Overwhelmingly to Democrats for
Midterms," *Hollywood Reporter*, October 12, 2918, https://www.hollywood
reporter.com/news/general-news/top-hollywood-execs-give-99-percent-political
-donations-democrats-midterms-1151392/.

59. Congressional candidate donations from Walt Disney Co. employees, 2022 election cycle, *Open Secrets*, accessed October 20, 2023, https://www.opensecrets.org
/orgs/walt-disney-co/recipients?id=d000000128.

60. Christopher F. Rufo (@realchrisrufo), "SCOOP: Disney production coordinator
Allen March says his team is committed to 'exploring queer stories," *Twitter*,
March 29, 2022, https://twitter.com/realchrisrufo/status/1508934581092765700
?s=20. Also see Andrew Mark Miller, "Disney Exposed: Leaked Videos Show
Officials Pushing LGBT Agenda, Saying DeSantis Wants to 'Erase' Gay Kids,"
Fox Business, March 29, 2022, https://www.foxbusiness.com/politics/disney
-officials-leaked-videos-pushing-lgbt-agenda-saying-desantis-erase-gay-kids.

61. Anugrah Kumar, "One Million Moms Issues 'Urgent Warning' to Parents in Response to Disney's FX Series 'Little Demon,'" *Christian Post*, September 5, 2022,
https://www.christianpost.com/news/disneys-fx-series-little-demon-is-extremely
-dangerous.html.

62. Jordan Liles, "Is 'Little Demon' a Disney Show about Satan and the Antichrist?,"
Snopes, September 6, 2022, https://www.snopes.com/fact-check/little-demon
-disney-show/.

63. Izz Scott LaMagdeleine, "Did Disney+ Order a Show about a Teenager Impregnated by Devil?," *Snopes*, May 31, 2023, https://www.snopes.com/fact-check
/disney-show-teenage-girl-pregnant-devil/.

64. Thomas Skill, James D. Robinson, John S. Lyons, and David Larson, "The Portrayal of Religion and Spirituality on Fictional Network Television," *Review of Religious Research* 35, no. 3 (March 1994), https://www.jstor.org/stable/3511892, 251.

65. Stanley Rothman, "Is God Really Dead in Beverly Hills? Religion and the Movies," *American Scholar* 65, no. 2 (Spring 1996), https://www.jstor.org/stable/41212479, 272.

66. Elise Ehrhard, "Cursed: Netflix's Latest Anti-Christian Drama," *Newsbusters*, July 20, 2020, https://www.newsbusters.org/blogs/culture/elise-ehrhard/2020/07/20/cursed-netflixs-latest-anti-christian-drama.

67. Ehrhard, "Cursed."

68. Paul Hair, "Entertainment Industry Ramps Up Its Hatred of Christianity in Lead Up to Easter," *Bounding Into Comics*, April 6, 2023, https://boundingintocomics.com/2023/04/06/entertainment-industry-ramps-up-its-hatred-of-christians-in-lead-up-to-easter/.

69. Elise Ehrhard, "NBC's 'Quantum Leap' is Latest Show with Caricatured 'Christian' Villain," *Newsbusters*, March 21, 2023, https://www.newsbusters.org/blogs/culture/elise-ehrhard/2023/03/21/nbcs-quantum-leap-latest-show-caricatured-christian-villain.

70. Tierin-Rose Mandelburg, "DUH! 'The Office' Star Rainn Wilson Calls Out Hollywood's 'Anti-Christian' Bias," *Newsbusters*, March 13, 2023, https://www.newsbusters.org/blogs/culture/tierin-rose-mandelburg/2023/03/13/duh-office-star-rainn-wilson-calls-out-hollywoods.

71. "Happily Never After: How Hollywood Favors Adultery and Promiscuity over Marital Intimacy on Prime Time Broadcast Television," *Parents Television Council*, August 5, 2008, https://www.parentstv.org/resources/Marriagestudy-PDF-4_200224_173834.pdf.

72. "Lewd by Example: Adults Talking about Sex in Front of Kids on Prime-Time Broadcast Network 'Family Comedies,'" *Parents Television Council*, September 2018, https://web.archive.org/web/20210423023516/https://go.parentstv.org/lewd-by-example/documents/Lewd-By-Example.pdf, 11.

73. "Teen-Targeted Broadcast TV Can Be Vulgar... But Stranger Things Are Happening at Netflix," *Parents Television Council*, April 23, 2020, https://www.parentstv.org/resources/Teen-Report.pdf.

74. Brian Kennedy and Cary Funk, "Majority of Americans Say Scientists Don't Have an Ideological Slant," *Pew Research Center*, November 9, 2015, https://www.pewresearch.org/short-reads/2015/11/09/majority-of-americans-say-scientists-dont-have-an-ideological-slant/.

75. "Public Praises Science; Scientists Fault Public, Media," *Pew Research Center*, July 9, 2009, https://www.pewresearch.org/wp-content/uploads/sites/4/legacy-pdf/528.pdf, 7.

76. "Public Praises Science," 36.

77. Steven Andrew Jacobs, "Biologists' Consensus on 'When Life Begins,'" *SSRN*, July 25, 2018, https://papers.ssrn.com/sol3/papers.cfm?abstract_id=3211703, 11.

78. Neil Gross and Solon Simmons, "How Religious are America's College and University Professors?," *SSRC*, February 6, 2007, http://religion.ssrc.org/reforum/Gross_Simmons.pdf, 5.

79. Stanley Rothman, S. Robert Lichter, and Neil Nevitte, "Politics and Professional Advancement Among College Faculty," *Forum* 3, no. 1 (2005).

80. Rothman, Lichter, and Nevitte, "Politics and Professional Advancement," 4.

81. Rothman, Lichter, and Nevitte, "Politics and Professional Advancement," 7.

82. Rothman, Lichter, and Nevitte, "Politics and Professional Advancement," 7.

83. Rothman, Lichter, and Nevitte, "Politics and Professional Advancement," 7.

84. Rothman, Lichter, and Nevitte, "Politics and Professional Advancement," 12.

85. Scott Jaschik, "Professors, Politics and New England," *Inside Higher Education*, July 4, 2016, https://www.insidehighered.com/news/2016/07/05/new-analysis-new-england-colleges-responsible-left-leaning-professoriate.

86. Mitchell Langbert and Sean Stevens, "Partisan Registration and Contributions of Faculty in Flagship Colleges," *National Association of Scholars*, January 17, 2020, https://www.nas.org/blogs/article/partisan-registration-and-contributions-of-faculty-in-flagship-colleges.

87. Gross and Simmons, "How Religious Are America's College and University Professors?," 4.

88. Gross and Simmons, "How Religious Are America's College and University Professors?," 5.

89. Gross and Simmons, "How Religious Are America's College and University Professors?," 6.

90. Gross and Simmons, "How Religious Are America's College and University Professors?," 6.

91. Gross and Simmons, "How Religious Are America's College and University Professors?," 6.

92. Daniel Silliman, "Religious Conversion Is Incredibly Personal. But It Also Invites Public Scrutiny," *Christianity Today*, January 31, 2022, https://www.christianitytoday.com/ct/2022/january-web-only/public-confessions-rebecca-davis-religious-conversion.html.

93. Justin Bieber News (@jbtraacker), Twitter, June 25, 2022, https://twitter.com/jbtraacker/status/1540706576604045312.

94. Courtney Hazlett, "Justin Bieber's Mom Tells Why She Chose Not to Abort at 17," *Today*, September 14, 2012, https://www.today.com/news/justin-biebers-mom-tells-why-she-chose-not-abort-17-999256.

8. PLEASING THE WRONG PEOPLE

1. C. S. Lewis, "The Inner Ring," in C. S. Lewis, *The Weight of Glory and Other Essays*, revised and expanded edition (New York: Macmillan, 1980), 93–105.

2. C. S. Lewis, *That Hideous Strength: A Modern Fairy-Tale for Grown-Ups* (New York: Macmillan, 1965).

3. Mark Noll, *The Scandal of the Evangelical Mind* (Grand Rapids: Eerdmans Publishing Co., 1994).

4. Noll, *The Scandal of the Evangelical Mind*, 3.

5. Noll, *The Scandal of the Evangelical Mind*, 3–4.

6. Noll, *The Scandal of the Evangelical Mind*, 8.

7. Noll, *The Scandal of the Evangelical Mind*, 230.

8. Noll, *The Scandal of the Evangelical Mind*, 244.

9. Noll, *The Scandal of the Evangelical Mind*, 248.

10. S. Joshua Swamidass, "A Compromise on Creationism," *Wall Street Journal*, March 4, 2021, https://www.wsj.com/articles/a-compromise-on-creationism -11614901537.

11. Mark Galli, "The Galli Report 10.08.21," *Galli Report*, October 8, 2021, https://web.archive.org/web/20220129135229/https://markgalli.substack.com /p/the-galli-report-100821.

12. Jocelyn Kaiser, "For a Decade, Francis Collins Has Shielded NIH—While Making Waves of His Own," *Science*, August 15, 2019, https://www.science.org /content/article/ decade-francis-collins-has-shielded-nih-while-making-waves-his-own.

13. Chris Wilson, "Jesus Goes to Bethesda," *Slate*, July 09, 2009, https://slate.com /technology/2009/07/just-how-religious-is-francis-collins-obama-s-nominee -for-director-of-the-nih.html.

14. "Afterword (2022)" in Mark Noll, *The Scandal of the Evangelical Mind* (Grand Rapids: Eerdmans Publishing Company, 2022), Kindle edition.

15. "Preface (2022)" in Noll, *The Scandal of the Evangelical Mind*. Noll specifically mentions each of these disparagingly.

16. Eric Metaxas, *Religionless Christianity: God's Answer to Evil* (New York: Regnery Faith, 2024), Kindle edition, 85–86.

17. Matthew 21. See also Isaiah 8:13–15, 1 Peter 2:8, Romans 9:33. For one discussion of the Christ as a stumbling stone, see "How Is Jesus a Rock of Offense?," *Compelling Truth*, accessed May 15, 2024, https://www.compellingtruth.org /rock-of-offense.html.

9. TOLERATING THE WRONG RULERS

1. Francis A. Schaeffer, *The Great Evangelical Disaster* (Westchester, IL: Crossway Books, 1984), 43.

2. "Articles of Amendment" to Seattle Pacific University's Articles of Incorporation, September 22, 1987, 1.

3. Philip W. Eaton, "A New Covenant: AFMEI and the FM Church, A Position Paper on Renewal," August 8, 2000.

4. Eaton, "A New Covenant."

5. James Tunstead Burtchaell, *The Dying of the Light: The Disengagement of Colleges and Universities from their Christian Churches* (Grand Rapids, MI: Eerdmans, 1998), 834.

6. Burtchaell, *The Dying of the Light*, 827.

7. Philip Eaton, quoted in Lisa Reitmeier and Yvonne Schindler, "New Relationship with Church?," *The Falcon*, January 24, 2001, 4.

8. "Restated Articles of Incorporation of Seattle Pacific University," June 30, 2005, 2.

9. "Restated Articles of Incorporation of Seattle Pacific University," 2.

10. "Restated Articles of Incorporation of Seattle Pacific University," June 5, 2014, 1.

11. J. A. O. Preus, *Report of the Synodical President to The Lutheran Church—Missouri Synod* (September 1, 1972), 65–70, http://www.ctsfw.net/media/pdfs/PreusJAOReportoftheSynodicalPresident1971.pdf.

12. Preus, *Report of the Synodical President*, 22–23, 77–78.

13. Frederick W. Danker, *Jesus and the New Age According to St. Luke, a Commentary on the Third Gospel* (St. Louis: Clayton Publishing House, 1972), xviii.

14. One professor stated at a pastoral conference in 1972: "I have problems with the virgin birth, real presence, bodily resurrection…. I can't bear the burden of Scriptural infallibility." Quoted in Board of Control, Concordia Seminary, *Exodus from Concordia: A Report on the 1974 Walkout* (St. Louis: Concordia Seminary, 1977), 56, https://archive.org/details/ConcordiaSemBdOfControlWalkoutOf1974/page/n65/mode/2up.

15. Quoted in Board of Control, *Exodus from Concordia*, 109.

16. Quoted in Board of Control, *Exodus from Concordia*, 32.

17. Board of Control, *Exodus from Concordia*, 135–136.

18. Board of Control, *Exodus from Concordia*, 129.

19. Matthew C. Harrison, "Historical Introduction" in *Rediscovering the Issues Surrounding the 1974 Concordia Seminary Walkout*, ed. Ken Schaub (St. Louis: Concordia Publishing House, 2023), Kindle edition, 32.

20. Francis Schaeffer, "Current Problems in the Lutheran Church-Missouri Synod" (lecture, Concordia Seminary, St. Louis, December 12, 1974), https://scholar.csl.edu/context/synodhistory/article/1076/type/native/viewcontent.

21. *2021 Annual Report, Lutheran Church—Missouri Synod* (Lutheran Church Missouri Synod, 2022), https://files.lcms.org/file/preview/DDCFD8B0-7812-4213-93D2-022A50CC2B94, 33.

22. *Clergy and Congregations in a Time of Transformation: Findings from the 2022–2023 Mainline Protestant Clergy Survey* (Washington, DC: Public Religion Research Institute, [2023]), 12, 13, https://www.prri.org/research/clergy-and-congregations-in-a-time-of-transformation-findings-from-the-2022-2023-mainline-protestant-clergy-survey/.

23. *Clergy and Congregations*, 7.

24. Kenneth W. Inskeep, *Lutherans Say, No. 6: The Religious Beliefs and Practices of Lutheran Lay Leaders in the ELCA* (Evangelical Lutheran Church in America, February 3, 2009), 36, https://download.elca.org/ELCA%20Resource%20epository/Lutherans_Say_6.pdf.

25. John T. Pless, "After the Walkout: Publications by the Faculty of Seminex," in *Rediscovering the Issues*, 434–435, 439, 442.

26. Paige Patterson, "Consequences of Revolution: The Conservative Resurgence in the SBC," *YouTube*, August 11, 2015, video, 1:06:12, at 00:13:15, https://youtu.be/EBWeK0oBAYs?si=ECS1ceuixh8GtuYs&t=796; Michael Foust, "25 Years Ago, Conservative Resurgence Got Its Start," Baptist Press, June 15, 2004, https://www.baptistpress.com/resource-library/news/25-years-ago-conservative-resurgence-got-its-start/.

10. A CALL TO WISDOM

1. Augustine, *The Confessions*, Book VII, chap. 12 and 16, *New Advent*, https://www.newadvent.org/fathers/110107.htm.

2. "German Church Celebrates Star Wars with Sci-Fi Sunday Service," *Guardian*, December 20, 2015, https://www.theguardian.com/world/2015/dec/20 /german-church-celebrates-star-wars-with-sci-fi-sunday-service.

3. "German Church Celebrates Star Wars with Sci-Fi Sunday Service."

4. "'The Force Awakens' at Liquid Church, with Over-the-Top Star Wars Themed 'Cosmic Christmas' Services Announced," *PR Newswire*, December 9, 2015, https://www.prnewswire.com/news-releases/the-force-awakens-at-liquid-church -with-over-the-top-star-wars-themed-cosmic-christmas-services-announced -300190241.html.

5. Augustine, *The Confessions*, Book VII, chap. 9, sec. 15, *New Advent*, https:// www.newadvent.org/fathers/110107.htm VII.ix.15; Augustine, *On Christian Doctrine*, Book II, chap. 40, *New Advent*, https://www.newadvent.org/fathers /12022.htm.

6. Hayden Ludwig, "'Creation Care': Redefining Pro-Life," *Capital Research Center*, December 7, 2020, https://capitalresearch.org/article/creation-care-part-4/.

7. Mary Jackson and Todd Vician, "Identity Crisis," *WORLD*, October 21, 2022, https://wng.org/articles/identity-crisis-1666367393.

8. "Gay," *The Online Etymology Dictionary*, accessed May 15, 2024, https://www .etymonline.com/word/gay. Also, "Homosexuality is considered to be same-sex attraction and behavior and 'gay' is a synonym of homosexuality," Natasha Tracy, "What Does It Mean to Be Gay?," *Healthy Place*, accessed May 15, 2024, https:// www.healthyplace.com/gender/gay/what-is-gay-definition-and-meaning-of-gay.

9. Bethel McGrew, "How the Side B Project Failed," *First Things*, March 14, 2023, https://www.firstthings.com/web-exclusives/2023/03/how-the-side-b-project -failed; Carl R. Trueman, "Into the anthropological chaos: The moral turn of Revoice," *WORLD*, October 24, 2022, https://wng.org/opinions/into-the -anthropological-chaos-1666613075.

10. Jeff Greenfield, "When Richard Nixon Used Billy Graham," *Politico*, February 21, 2018, https://www.politico.com/magazine/story/2018/02/21/billy-graham -death-richard-nixon-217039/.

11. Bill Halton, "The Crusade: When Billy Graham Brought Richard Nixon to Knoxville," *Tennessean*, June 2, 2020, https://www.tennessean.com/story /opinion/2020/06/02/when-billy-graham-brought-richard-nixon-knoxville /5312372002/.bill.

12. "Graham Apologizes for Anti-Semitic Conversation with Nixon 30 Years Ago," *Fox News*, March 1, 2002, https://www.foxnews.com/story/graham-apologizes -for-anti-semitic-comments-in-conversation-with-nixon-30-years-ago.

13. Cal Thomas, "Go and Sin Some More," *WORLD*, March 21, 1998, https://wng.org/articles/go-and-sin-some-more-1617302184.

14. Metaxas, *Religionless Christianity*, 84.

11. A CALL TO ACTION

1. "Remarks by President Biden at the 2022 National and State Teachers of the Year Event," *White House*, April 27, 2022, https://www.whitehouse.gov/briefing-room /speeches-remarks/2022/04/27/remarks-by-president-biden-at-the-2022-national -and-state-teachers-of-the-year-event/. Also see Javier Manjarres, "Florida School District Official Says Parents 'Don't Know What's Best for Their Child,'" *Floridian*, June 23, 2021, https://floridianpress.com/2021/06/florida-school-district -official-says-parents-dont-know-whats-best-for-their-child/; John Stonestreet, "Journal of Medical Ethics Says Parents Should Lose Rights over Children," *Breakpoint*, July 26, 2021, https://www.breakpoint.org/journal-of-medical -ethics-says-parents-dont-have-rights-over-children/.

2. Hollie McKay, "Critics Slam MSNBC Host's Claim That Kids Belong to Community, Not Parents," *Fox News*, April 9, 2013, https://www.foxnews.com /entertainment/critics-slam-msnbc-hosts-claim-that-kids-belong-to-community -not-parents; Peter Weber, "Do Kids Belong to Their Parents, Or Their Community?," *The Week*, January 10, 2015, https://theweek.com/articles/465627/kids -belong-parents-community.

3. John G. West, "Ten Questions to Ask When Evaluating a Christian College," *JohnGWest.com*, January 22, 2024, https://johngwest.com/2024/ten-questions -to-ask-when-evaluating-a-christian-college/.

4. Elizabeth Rundle Charles, *Chronicles of the Schönberg-Cotta Family* (New York: Dodd, Mead & Company, 1871), chap. 19, https://www.gutenberg.org/files /36433/36433-h/36433-h.htm.

5. French's discussion took place over several posts on Twitter on April 27, 2023. Here are three of the most relevant: https://twitter.com/DavidAFrench /status/1651679236732645413; https://twitter.com/DavidAFrench/status /1651679243116376083; https://twitter.com/DavidAFrench/status /1651679244559216653.

12. A CALL TO FAITHFULNESS

1. For some of the many critiques of Yoon's predictions, see "Chris Yoon's Prophesies," *ChrisYoonFalseProphet*, https://web.archive.org/web/20211226231343 /https://www.chrisyoonfalseprophet.com/; "Chris Yoon Exposed," YouTube, January 22, 2021, https://www.youtube.com/watch?v=Rz0J5dHdLhs.

2. Gary Gilley, "Joel Osteen and the Prosperity Gospel," *Narrow Path*, May 17, 2014, https://thenarrowingpath.com/2014/05/17/joel-osteen-and-the -prosperity-gospel/.

3. See, for instance, the teachings of Jesus in Luke 12:13–34, Luke 13:1–5, John 9:1–3, and Matthew 10:16–39. Jesus made it crystal-clear that prosperity doesn't mean people are good in God's eyes, and that misfortune doesn't mean they're more sinful than other people.

4. "The Story of Martin Treptow," *1776 History*, July 26, 2014, https://1776history .com/2014/07/26/the-story-of-martin-treptow/.

5. Dorothy Sayers, *The Man Born to Be King* (London: Victor Gollancz Ltd., 1969), 27–28.

6. "William Cowper," *Hymnary*, accessed October 21, 2023, https://hymnary.org/person/Cowper_W.

7. William Cowper, "God Moves in a Mysterious Way," *Hymnary*, https://hymnary.org/text/god_moves_in_a_mysterious_way.

8. William Cowper, "Sometimes a Light Surprises," *Hymnary*, https://hymnary.org/text/sometimes_a_light_surprises.

9. "Tacitus on the Persecution of Christians under Nero," *Early Church Texts*, https://www.earlychurchtexts.com/public/tacitus_persecution_under_nero.htm.

10. For the record, I think using government power to promote Christianity is a very bad idea. See the section "A Rejection of Theocracy" in my essay, "Eric Metaxas, Francis Schaeffer, and the Great Evangelical Disaster," *JohnGWest.com*, May 10, 2024, https://johngwest.com/2024/eric-metaxas-francis-schaeffer-the-great-evangelical-disaster/.

11. Marc Chalufour, "What's behind Boom of Christianity in China?," *Brink*, February 2, 2023, https://www.bu.edu/articles/2023/why-is-christianity-growing-in-china/.

12. See documentation in John G. West, *The Politics of Revelation and Reason* (Lawrence, KS: University Press of Kansas, 1996), 36–40, 49–53, 56–67.

13. For documentation, see John G. West, "Nineteenth-Century America," in *Building a Healthy Culture: Strategies for an American Renaissance*, ed. Don Eberly (Grand Rapids, MI: Eerdmans Publishing Company, 2001), 181–189.

14. Alysia Meyer, "Queer Joy at SPU's [Redacted] Fest," *The Falcon*, May 29, 2024, https://thefalcon.seapacmedia.com/17459/featured-stories/queer-joy-at-spus-redacted-fest/.

15. "Redacted Fest," image posted on Instagram, accessed June 8, 2024, https://www.instagram.com/cloverbandd/.

ACKNOWLEDGMENTS

I began working on this book in earnest in early 2021. Within weeks, I learned that faculty at my old educational institution, Seattle Pacific University, had voted overwhelmingly in opposition to the biblical teaching that marriage should be reserved for a man and a woman. The vote crystallized for me the pressing need for this book. Christian leaders and institutions in America are failing and flailing. We need strategies for reforming faithless institutions and for preserving faithful ones. As someone who has observed institutional failures from the inside, I thought I might be able to contribute something.

A big thank you to my pastor, Rich Hamlin of Evangelical Reformed Church of Tacoma, WA, for asking me to teach an adult Sunday school class on the topic of this book during the first half of 2023. Without that class, this book might still be unfinished. The class nudged me to complete drafts of many of the chapters. A thank you as well to the more than one hundred adults who regularly attended the class. Their suggestions and questions helped me further refine my ideas.

I am grateful too for all who read advanced drafts and gave me input, including those whose disagreements strengthened the final product. Usually I would list advance readers. But I realize this book may prove controversial, and some readers might face pushback if they were recognized here. So I have chosen not to list them publicly.

At Discovery Institute, I would like to thank president Steve Buri for his support and encouragement; Jonathan and Amanda Witt of Discovery Institute Press for their meticulous editing and editorial suggestions; and Nate Jacobson for the provocative cover design (and for his own reflections on the manuscript). As always, Sandra Jurca did a wonderful job on the typesetting.

If you have questions or comments, feel free to contact me through the book's website, StockholmSyndromeChristianity.com. As time and schedule allows, I will do my best to respond.

ABOUT THE COVER

The Bible says a lot about sheep and wolves. Perhaps most famously, God's people are compared to sheep, and they are warned against "false prophets, who come to you in sheep's clothing but inwardly are ravenous wolves" (Matthew 7:15). In thinking about how to visualize Stockholm Syndrome Christianity, I was struck by an image involving sheep and a wolf. Imagine a flock of sheep where right in the midst of the flock you see a wolf. Not a wolf in sheep's clothing, but an out-of-the-closet, in-your-face, ravenous wolf. Then imagine that rather than being afraid of this wolf, or trying to flee him, some of the sheep gather around the wolf as if he is their leader and friend. These sheep convince themselves that the wolf is the good guy and they are the problem. When the wolf starts devouring some of their fellow sheep, these sheep are grateful and think the wolf is doing something good. They even start helping the wolf choose his next victims. They argue that they are being loving and kind by doing this. That is an image of Stockholm Syndrome Christianity. The wolf represents anti-Christian secular culture, and the sheep represent Christians who have embraced the assumptions of that culture—either wittingly or unwittingly.

INDEX

Printed in the USA
CPSIA information can be obtained
at www.ICGtesting.com
CBHW021156201124
17504CB00008B/4